"Catharine Theimer Nepomnyashchy was an inspiring intellectual force of nature. She made an indelible mark in two fields—Slavic studies and comparative literature—and distinguished herself as a caring teacher, a visionary academic leader, and an adventurous scholar whose thirst for interdisciplinary knowledge and understanding was contagious. This volume gathers her most important writing on poetry, dance, fiction, and television and organizes it with a view to her abiding concern for the specter of empire in Russian culture and society. Her characteristic curiosity and insight jump from every page."

—*Rory Finnin*, University of Cambridge

"An inspirational figure for generations of students, Catharine Theimer Nepomnyashchy was a tirelessly inventive scholar of Russian culture with a rare talent for forging connections and opening up new angles of inquiry. This valuable collection showcases her extraordinary range of intellectual interests across the span of modern Russian cultural history, from innovative studies of classic authors (Pushkin, Nabokov) to authoritative accounts of temporality in late Soviet literature (Pasternak, Solzhenitsyn, Sinyavsky), from the gender politics of ballet to pathbreaking analyses of Soviet and post-Soviet popular culture. Throughout, we are in the presence of a scholar whose penetrating interpretative gaze and acute feel for the social life of culture nurtured a commitment to understanding Russian culture within a global context and in resistance to state-centric narratives. She is much missed, and this collection is a fitting testament to her legacy in Slavic Studies and beyond."

—*Edward Tyerman*, University of California, Berkeley

From Pushkin to Popular Culture
Essays by Catharine Theimer Nepomnyashchy

Catharine Theimer Nepomnyashchy. 2000s.
Courtesy of the Harriman Institute, Columbia University.

Ars Rossica

Series Editor
David Bethea (University of Wisconsin, Madison)

Other Titles in this Series

The Imperial Script of Catherine the Great: Governing with the Literary Pen
Vera Proskurina

Essays on Anton P. Chekhov: Close Readings
Robert Louis Jackson,
Edited by Cathy Popkin; with an introduction by Robin Feuer Miller

The Irony of the Ideal: Paradoxes of Russian Literature
Mikhail Epstein

Postmodern Crises: From Lolita to Pussy Riot
Mark Lipovetsky

Dostoevsky beyond Dostoevsky: Science, Religion, Philosophy
Edited by Svetlana Evdokimova & Vladimir Golstein

Before They Were Titans: Essays on the Early Works of Dostoevsky and Tolstoy
Edited by Elizabeth Cheresh Allen, with an afterword by Caryl Emerson

By Fables Alone: Literature and State Ideology
    in Late Eighteenth- and Early Nineteenth-Century Russia
Andrei Zorin
Translated by Marcus C. Levitt

The Englishman from Lebedian': A Life of Evgeny Zamiatin
J.A. E. Curtis

FROM PUSHKIN TO POPULAR CULTURE

Essays by
Catharine Theimer Nepomnyashchy

Edited by Emily D. Johnson, Irina Reyfman, and Carol R. Ueland

BOSTON
2024

Library of Congress Cataloging-in-Publication Data

Names: Nepomnyashchy, Catharine Theimer, author. | Johnson, Emily D., 1966-editor. | Reyfman, Irina, editor. | Ueland, Carol, editor.
Title: From Pushkin to popular culture / essays by Catharine Theimer Nepomnyashchy; edited by Emily D. Johnson, Irina Reyfman, and Carol R. Ueland.
Other titles: Ars Rossica.
Description: Boston : Academic Studies Press, 2024. | Series: Ars Rossica | Includes bibliographical references and index.
Identifiers: LCCN 2023045278 (print) | LCCN 2023045279 (ebook) | ISBN 9798887194233 (hardback) | ISBN 9798887194240 (paperback) | ISBN 9798887194257 (adobe pdf) | ISBN 9798887194264 (epub)
Subjects: LCSH: Pushkin, Aleksandr Sergeevich, 1799-1837—Criticism and interpretation. | Russian literature—19th century—History and criticism. | Russian literature—20th century—History and criticism. | Popular culture—Soviet Union. | Popular culture—Russia (Federation)
Classification: LCC PG3011 .N445 2024 (print) | LCC PG3011 (ebook) | DDC 891.71/3—dc23/eng/20231115
LC record available at https://lccn.loc.gov/2023045278
LC ebook record available at https://lccn.loc.gov/2023045279

Copyright © 2024, Academic Studies Press
ISBN 9798887194233 (hardback)
ISBN 9798887194240 (paperback)
ISBN 9798887194257 (adobe pdf)
ISBN 9798887194264 (epub)

Book design by Tatiana Vernikov
Cover design by Ivan Grave

Published by Academic Studies Press
1577 Beacon Street
Brookline, MA 02446 USA
press@academicstudiespress.com
www.academicstudiespress.com

Contents

Introduction: Catharine Theimer Nepomnyashchy   VII
   as a Scholar of Russian Culture
   Emily D. Johnson, Irina Reyfman, and Carol R. Ueland

Part I. Pushkin, Pushkin, Pushkin, and Katkov

  1. The Poet, History, and the Supernatural: 2
     A Note on Pushkin's "The Poet" and *The Bronze Horseman*

  2. Pushkin's *The Bronze Horseman* and Irving's   16
     "The Legend of Sleepy Hollow":
     A Curious Case of Cultural Cross-Fertilization?

  3. A Note on Curiosity in Pushkin's *The Blackamoor of Peter the Great*   38

  4. Katkov and the Emergence of the *Russian Messenger*   54

Part II. Russia and the West

  5. Jane Austen in Russia: Hidden Presence and Belated Boom   77

  6. King, Queen, Sui-Mate: Nabokov's Defense   101
     against Freud's "Uncanny"

  7. "Imperially, My Dear Watson":   123
     Sherlock Holmes and the Decline of the Soviet Empire

Part III. The Soviet/Post-Soviet Experience

  8. Pasternak's *Doctor Zhivago*: The Resurrection of the Living Past   144

  9. *One Day in the Life of Ivan Denisovich* and Its Intertexts: 176
     Aksakov's "Stepan Mikhailovich's Good Day"
     and Kataev's *Time Forward!*

  10. *Koshkin Dom*: Following the Golden Shoelace   205

  11. Tatiana Tolstaia: The Text of Family   221
     and the Family in the Text—Genealogy,
     Gender, and the Rhetoric of Lineage

Part IV. Russian Culture, High and Low

12. Dance as Metaphor: 240
    The Russian Ballerina and the Imperial Imagination
13. The Blockbuster Miniseries on Soviet TV: 261
    Isaev-Shtirlits, the Ambiguous Hero of *Seventeen Moments in Spring*
14. Markets, Mirrors, and Mayhem: 281
    Aleksandra Marinina and the Rise of the New Russian *Detektiv*

Selected Publications by Catharine Theimer Nepomnyashchy 313
Index 317

Figures

FRONTISPIECE. Catharine Theimer Nepomnyashchy. 2000s. I
 Courtesy of the Harriman Institute, Columbia University.
FIGURE 1. *Education of a Serf Dancer*. By an unknown artist. 241
 Late eighteenth century. From the collection of the Bakhrushin Museum.
FIGURE 2. *Rubinstein as Cleopatra*, by Leon Bakst. 251
 From the collection of Nina and Nikita D. Lobanov-Rostovsky.
FIGURE 3. Tamara Karsavina, 1911. In the role of the Firebird. 252
 E. O. Hoppé Estate Collection/Curatorial Inc.
FIGURE 4. Liubov Tchernicheva as Cleopatra in *Cleopatra*, 1918. 253
 E. O. Hoppé Estate Collection/Curatorial Inc.

Introduction

Catharine Theimer Nepomnyashchy as a Scholar of Russian Culture

Emily D. Johnson, Irina Reyfman, and Carol R. Ueland

Catharine Theimer Nepomnyashchy (1951–2015) achieved extraordinary success during her almost four-decade-long career in Slavic studies. She published *Abram Tertz and the Poetics of Crime* (Yale University Press, 1995), the first English-language monograph on the writer, and, along with her close friend Slava Yastremski, completed a translation of Terts's *Strolls with Pushkin* (Yale University Press, 1993) that won the translation award from the American Association of Teachers of Slavic and East European Languages. She co-edited a landmark volume titled *"Under the Sky of My Africa": Pushkin and Blackness* with Nicole Svobodny and Ludmilla Trigos (Northwestern University Press, 2006) and a volume honoring Marina Ledkovsky with Hilde Hoogenboom and Irina Reyfman.[1] She was the first female director of Columbia University's influential Harriman Institute for Russian, Eurasian, and East European Studies (2001–2009) and a member of the board of ASEEES (2003–2006). She served as the president of AATSEEL (2005–2007) and received the association's award for Outstanding Contribution to the Profession in 2011. She was a lifetime member of the Council on Foreign Relations, gave more than eighty papers at conferences, and organized symposia, panels, and events on everything from "Narratives of Jewish-Slavic Encounters" to analytical approaches to understanding Russian politics after the presidential election of 2008. She also mentored generations of students and junior faculty

---

1   Marina Ledkovsky also published under the name Marina Astman.

members in her role as a faculty member at Barnard College and Columbia University as well as through her work with the Harriman Institute.

Yet, at the end of her life Nepomnyashchy had so much more that she wanted to do. Even in her last days, she continued to work on a book on post-Stalinist Russian literature titled *The Politics of Tradition: Rerooting Russian Literature after Stalin*. She also was hard at work on developing her ideas for a book that would have focused on Nabokov's relationship to the "opponents" that he reacted against over the course of his career: Freud, Pasternak, and the detective novel as a genre.[2]

This volume brings together some of Nepomnyashchy's most important published and unpublished work. We hope that it will highlight her extraordinary scholarly contributions to the field of Slavic studies and, for that matter, to the discipline of comparative literature. In selecting articles for it, we have tried to capture the general trajectory of Nepomnyashchy's evolution as a writer and researcher as well as the breadth of her scholarly interests. We have included work from every decade of Nepomnyashchy's scholarly career (1970s–2010s) and on many of the topics that most preoccupied her, including favorite writers (Pushkin, Nabokov, Pasternak, Tertz, Tolstaia), the detective novels that constituted her preferred leisure reading material, the world of ballet that she adored, and the television serials that entertained and fascinated her. Because Nepomnyashchy's book-length publications are well-known and readily accessible, we have chosen not to take excerpts from them. The previously published work included in this volume consists almost exclusively of articles and chapters drawn from volumes edited by other scholars.[3] Some of the scholarly pieces that are gathered here appeared originally in comparative literature venues and, as a result, may not be well-known to many Slavists. The two previously unpublished chapters are both taken from the incomplete

---

[2] For more on this project, see: Ronald Meyer, "Catharine Theimer Nepomnyashchy: Nabokov and the Detective Novel," introduction to Catharine Theimer Nepomnyashchy, "Revising Nabokov Revising the Detective Novel: Vladimir, Agatha, and the Terms of Engagement," *Harriman Magazine* (Fall 2015): 48–49, accessed May 30, 2023, http://www.columbia.edu/cu/creative/epub/harriman/2015/fall/harriman_winter_2015.pdf.

[3] The one exception is Nepomnyashchy's chapter from the volume honoring Marina Ledkovsky: "Dance as Metaphor: The Russian Ballerina and the Imperial Imagination," in *Mapping the Feminine: Russian Women and Cultural Difference*, ed. Hilde Hoogenboom, Catharine Theimer Nepomnyashchy, and Irina Reyfman (Bloomington: Slavica, 2008), 185–208. It was selected as the best example of Nepomnyashchy's work on ballet.

manuscript for *The Politics of Tradition*, which Nepomnyashchy was working on at the time of her death.

We hope that the mix of materials that we have chosen highlights the impact of Nepomnyashchy's scholarly work and also brings back happy memories for her friends. Many of the articles published here originated as conference papers that Nepomnyashchy delivered on the challenging and joyful panels she helped organize at ASEEES, AATSEEL, and MLA year after year. They were shaped by the research travel that she undertook over the years, time spent in archives and libraries and with the writers and artists whose works she studied. Because the articles included in this volume date to such different periods, they reflect changing scholarly and publishing norms. In exploring this sampling of work, readers will gain perspective on how our field has evolved over time as well as on the shifting interests and unique perspective of a colleague and scholar who was one of the most important figures in Slavic studies of her generation.

Nepomnyashchy's untimely death meant that she saw only the beginning of Putin's aggressive efforts to expand the Russian Federation's influence and territory, which culminated in the terrible war in Ukraine. Both the 2014 invasion of Ukraine and Russia's 2008 imperialist attack on Georgia horrified and frightened Nepomnyashchy: she was frustrated that, in the wake of these events, more attention was not being paid to the region. Speaking to the *New York Times* right after the 2008 Russian invasion of Georgia, Nepomnyashchy noted "This is a world event of the first order," and then added, "I say that because I am scared."[4] Although the scholarly work that appears in this volume does not directly address the current war in Ukraine or the monumental changes that have taken place in Russian, East European, and Eurasian Studies since February 24, 2022, many of the chapters that we have included speak to issues that are of obvious relevance to our field now such as the imperialist impulses and rhetoric that infused both nineteenth- and twentieth-century Russian culture; the surprising resiliency and post-Soviet afterlife of Stalinist mythic and cultic formulas; and problems connected with dissent, censorship, and displacement. Nepomnyashchy was very aware of the darker aspects of

---

4   Nicholas Phillips, "For Often Unsung Scholars, a War Means Center Stage," *New York Times*, August 24, 2008, accessed June 24, 2023, https://www.nytimes.com/2008/08/24/nyregion/thecity/24russ.html.

Russian history and culture and worked in her scholarly writing to elucidate these larger issues.

The Life and Career of Catharine Theimer Nepomnyashchy

Catharine Theimer was born in East Orange, New Jersey, in 1951. Her father Ernst Theimer (1911–1994) was a fragrance chemist and also, as Nepomnyashchy recalled, invented an early form of sunscreen. In his spare time, he wrote crossword puzzles for the *New York Times*, played chess well enough to win several regional tournaments, and, in later life, took up bridge, writing extensively on it. He was an avid fan of detective novels and Sherlock Holmes, something that perhaps helped shape Nepomnyashchy's own later interests. Nepomnyashchy's mother Jo-Anne Wright Theimer (1918–2016) grew up in the East Orange area and attended Mount Holyoke for a time before transferring to Washburn University where she graduated with a BA in 1939. During World War II she worked in radio communications at RCA in New York City. Later in life, she was active in the organization Monmouth Arts and the First Presbyterian Church of Rumson. In addition to Catharine, Ernst and Jo-Anne also had a son, James, who was born in 1958. The family was close-knit and enjoyed vacations every year at Silver Bay on Lake George as well as at a house on St. Martin.

Nepomnyashchy attended college at Brown University, where she graduated in 1973 with BAs in French and Russian as well as an MA in French. Nancy Condee, who was a graduate student at Brown at the time, recalls that Nepomnyashchy was allowed to take graduate seminars in Russian literature while still an advanced undergraduate and "held her own in the seminar environment," showing real "grit" and determination. In summer 1970, following her freshman year at Brown, Nepomnyashchy took the first of many trips to the Soviet Union and, on a beach in Sochi, met and fell in love with Viacheslav (Slava) Nepomnyashchy (1947–2011). She travelled back to the Soviet Union to see him in summer 1971 and winter 1971–1972; during the latter trip, the couple got engaged. At the time, relationships between Soviet citizens and foreigners were viewed with hostility by the Soviet state. Viacheslav was denied exit visas for five years and sent to a punitive construction brigade in Siberia for two years (1972–1974) after he continued to press for permission to leave. Nepomnyashchy was not allowed to travel to the USSR to marry him during this period—although she did manage a short trip in 1975 during which she and Viacheslav preregistered for a wedding at a Russian registration office. Throughout their separation Nepomnyashchy tirelessly petitioned the US State Department and her senators for help. Slava was finally allowed to emigrate, and the couple married in Rumson, New Jersey in 1977. In this same year, Nepomnyashchy and Slava testified on the cruelty of their treatment by Soviet authorities before the Commission on Security and Cooperation in Europe at hearings on the implementation of the Helsinki Accords.[5]

By this time, Nepomnyashchy was already working on her PhD in Russian Literature at Columbia University, the institution where she would spend her entire forty-year scholarly career. At the time, the Columbia-Barnard Slavic Department was home to Rufus W. Mathewson, Jr., Richard Gustafson, William Harkins, Robert A. Maguire, Robert Belknap, and Marina Ledkovsky (Astman). Nepomnyashchy took seminars on everything from Old Church Slavonic to the literature of the NEP period. All the while, she and Slava were living with their beloved dachshund Aleks (short for Aleksandr Pushkin) on the upper Westside in a cramped studio with a loft bed. Early on, Nepomnyashchy decided that she would write her dissertation on "The Poetics of Motivation: Time, Narrative, and History in the Works of Pasternak, Sinyavsky, and Solzhenitsyn." While working on this topic, she had the chance to meet Solzhenitsyn and developed a friendship with Siniavskii and his wife, gaining insights from these contacts that helped supplement more traditional library research. Nepomnyashchy's broad interests, however, also led her, even early in her career, to take on topics outside of her primary area of specialization. In addition to working on the post-Stalin period, she wrote on nineteenth-century literary figures such as Mikhail Katkov and Aleksandr Pushkin.

In connection with her fellowship at Columbia, Nepomnyashchy taught sections of Russian-language courses and also, from 1984 to 1987, Literature Humanities, the year-long survey of the Western canon that all Columbia College freshmen take as part of the Columbia College core. The experience of teaching the Columbia College core, as Nepomnyashchy acknowledged repeatedly later in her career, instilled in her the intellectual courage and

---

[5] "Basket Three: Implementation of the Helsinki Accords," Hearings before the Council on Security and Cooperation in Europe, Ninety-Fifth Congress, First Session on the Implementation of the Helsinki Accords, vol. 1, Wednesday, February 23–24, 1977, 108–114, accessed October 15, 2022, https://www.csce.gov/sites/helsinkicommission.house.gov/files/Official%20Transcript%20-%20Implementation%20of%20the%20Helsinki%20Accords%20Vol.%20I.pdf.

flexibility of mind that would later allow her to take on challenging interdisciplinary projects in both teaching and research. With the aim of earning extra income and building on her skills as a teacher, Nepomnyashchy also accepted additional teaching work as a graduate student. She taught in Columbia's summer language program, the Summer Practicum, serving as its director in summer 1986. Outside of Columbia, Nepomnyashchy taught Russian and Russian history to students in grades 7–12 at the Columbia Grammar and Preparatory School (1980–1982) and served as an instructor at the State University of New York at Stony Brook. This last position, in particular, gave her an important opportunity to establish herself as an independent force in Russian studies and to apply the skills she had learned in graduate school in a radically different context. While at SUNY Stony Brook, Nepomnyashchy organized a conference on the relationship between émigré and Soviet literatures, a project that laid the seeds for her later involvement in and support of émigré publishing ventures, including collaborations with the *New Journal* (Novyi zhurnal), the influential journal founded in 1942 by Mark Aldanov and Mikhail Tsetlin with the assistance of Ivan Bunin.

Along with other Columbia graduate students, Nepomnyashchy worked to launch *Ulbandus Review*, a peer-reviewed journal, edited and published entirely by graduate students. Its first two issues appeared in 1977 and the third, in 1979. Nepomnyashchy served as the editor for the first and the third issues, contributing articles to both. Run on a shoestring and funded initially by bake sales, *Ulbandus* taught generations of Columbia University graduate students how to edit, finance, and distribute a scholarly publication, not to mention how to write for one. Although the journal was dormant in the 1990s, it was revived in 2002 on Nepomnyashchy's initiative. Currently, it is still going strong: its latest issue, "(Re)writing History," appeared in 2022. The journal was one of Nepomnyashchy's greatest gifts to the department and its graduate students.

As Nepomnyashchy was finishing her dissertation, "The Poetics of Motivation" (defended in October of 1987 with Robert Maguire as her advisor), she was hired by Barnard College and joined its faculty as an assistant professor. At the time of Nepomnyashchy's appointment to the Barnard faculty, both the Soviet visa and censorship regimes were at last liberalizing. Nepomnyashchy travelled through the United States, giving lectures on the changes that were taking place as a result of glasnost and, in summer 1989, returned to the Soviet Union for the first time since 1975. She had been barred from the Soviet Union for years as a result of her relationship with Slava, and then, when travel became feasible again in the mid-1980s, was initially reluctant to go: why would she want to visit a place that had treated her and Slava so abysmally? After Slava returned to the Soviet Union for his father's funeral and other friends also traveled without incident, Nepomnyashchy rethought her position: she wanted to see the changes that were taking place in the Soviet Union for herself. On the trip in summer 1989, she got to know Slava's relatives and had the opportunity to meet with leading contemporary authors such as Venedikt Erofeev, members of the Pasternak family, including Evgenii Borisovich Pasternak, and the journalists Iurii Shchekochikhin and Nadezhda Azhgikhina. On a follow-up trip in winter 1989–1990, Nepomnyashchy met the critic Galina Belaia, Andrei Voznesenskii, Zoia Boguslavskaia, Fazil Iskander, Anatolii Rybakov, and many other notable writers and cultural figures. The new openness of the glasnost era gave American scholars of Russian literature like Nepomnyashchy the chance to meet major writers in person both in Russia and the United States and to build deep friendships with them. The lasting connections that Nepomnyashchy made on her first two trips back to the Soviet Union in 1989–1990 helped pave the way for many of the projects that she undertook later in her career.

The trip that Nepomnyashchy made to the USSR in August 1991 in connection with the Congress of Compatriots (Kongress sootechestvennikov) was no less significant. The Congress attracted 700 international participants drawn from twenty different countries, most of whom arrived on August 17 and 18 and were housed in the Hotel Rossiia, just off Red Square.[6] On August 19, the morning when the congress was scheduled to begin, tanks rolled into central Moscow and the group calling itself the State Committee on the State of Emergency appeared on the main Soviet television station to announce that it had seized control of the Soviet government. Nepomnyashchy and the other foreign delegates quickly realized that they had a front-row seat to history. Along with her friends Jamey Gambrell and Nadezhda Azhgikhina, Nepomnyashchy spent the next few days in the thick of the protests that quickly formed on the streets of Moscow, an experience that she and Nadezhda later memorialized in their 2014 book *Three Days in August* (Tri dnia v avguste). The trips that Nepomnyashchy made to Russia following the dissolution of the Soviet Union also helped grow her network of friends and professional

---

6   On the Congress, see: M. N. Tolstoi, "Pervyi Kongress sootechestvennikov," *Peterburgskii istoricheskii zhurnal* 3 (2014): 71–87.

connections. She met Gorbachev in the early 1990s at a reception that she attended with Iurii Shchekochikhin and later made the acquaintance of many other political figures whom she would in future years invite to give talks at Columbia University's Harriman Institute.

Even amidst these exciting events, Nepomnyashchy managed to make steady progress on publications, releasing a stream of articles, the translation of Terts's *Strolls with Pushkin*, and her monograph on Tertz/Siniavski by 1995. She successfully earned tenure and promotion to associate professor in 1997. After tenure, Nepomnyashchy's career trajectory only accelerated. In 1999 she assumed the post of associate director of the Harriman Institute. She was promoted to full professor in 2000 and also simultaneously stepped in as chair of the Barnard Slavic Department.

A significant portion of Nepomnyashchy's professional life was connected with the Harriman Institute at Columbia, the first academic center in the United States for the study of Russia and the Soviet Union. Founded in 1946 as the Russian Institute, it became the W. Averell Harriman Institute for the Advanced Study of the Soviet Union in 1982. After the fall of the Soviet Union, the institute expanded its mission to include, in addition to Russia and the former Soviet states, Eurasia, and Eastern Europe. Nepomnyashchy's affiliation with the institute began early in her graduate career. In 1976, she received her Russian Institute Certificate, joining scores of Columbia graduate students who broadened their professional horizons by studying for the certificate, which requires completing coursework in a range of different disciplines. Nepomnyashchy was passionate about the institute's role in encouraging interdisciplinary engagement with the region and in bringing together scholars with different interests and diverse qualifications. This belief in the importance of the Harriman Institute's mission led Nepomnyashchy to devote so much of her career to its administration.

In 2001, Nepomnyashchy became the Harriman Institute's first female director. She remained in this position for two terms, until 2009. Devoted to interdisciplinary studies of a vast region—spreading from the Balkans to the Far East Pacific shore—the institute was an ideal fit for Nepomnyashchy's expansive interests. When Masha Udensiva-Brenner interviewed her for *Harriman Magazine*, Nepomnyashchy shared her vision of an ideal scholar—not simply "broadly educated," but always open to new knowledge, new subjects of inquiry, striving for "intellectual independence that would allow you to follow your instincts and take your attention away from the immediate goal" to the broader issues.[7] As the Harriman Institute's director, Nepomnyashchy followed her instincts. The years of her directorship were an exciting time to be affiliated with the institute.

To begin with, as the Harriman Institute's director, Nepomnyashchy significantly extended its scope both geographically and in terms of areas of study. She encouraged the institute to organize programming on Transcaucasia and Central Asia, effectively claiming Eurasian studies as part of its purview. She also brought a sharper focus on culture, literature, and arts in contrast to the institute's traditional emphasis on the social sciences. The speakers Nepomnyashchy invited to give presentations as part of the Annual W. Averell Harriman Lectures included not only politicians, such as Mikhail Gorbachev and Vojislav Kostunica, then president of the Federal Republic of Yugoslavia; but also writers, such as Imre Kertesz, recipient of the 2002 Nobel prize in Literature, and Ismail Kadare, Albania's best-known poet and novelist. In addition, Nepomnyashchy's passion for ballet influenced the institute's programming. In 2003, the series of events that marked the tercentennial of the founding of St. Petersburg included several devoted to this form of classical dance. They were curated by Lynn Garafola, then professor of dance at Barnard College, who several years later also organized a celebration of the 100th anniversary of the Ballets Russes.

Nepomnyashchy transformed the institute physically to match her vision of it as the space for interdisciplinary exchange. Early in her second term, she spearheaded the redesign of the institute's offices, opening up a largely unused central room and creating an atrium, which is now used for art exhibits and institute functions. Nepomnyashchy's devotion to the institute's mission and her contributions to its growth and expansion were recognized in 2013, when she became the Harriman Institute Alumna of the Year.

As a teacher at both Columbia and Barnard, Nepomnyashchy was extraordinary. Because the Columbia and Barnard Slavic Departments for many years functioned as one instructional program, her teaching schedule always included, in addition to dedicated Barnard classes such as freshman seminars, courses for Columbia graduate students and advanced undergraduate classes in Russian literature and culture for mixed groups of Columbia and Barnard

---

7   Masha Udensiva-Brenner, "Catharine Theimer Nepomnyashchy in Profile," *Harriman Magazine* (Summer 2015): 26, accessed October 4, 2022, http://www.columbia.edu/cu/creative/epub/harriman/june13/harriman_mag_june13.pdf.

students. By the early 2000s she also often co-taught interdisciplinary classes with colleagues in history and political sciences for the Harriman Institute's curriculum. "Legacies of the Russian Empire and the Soviet Union," a colloquium that Nepomnyashchy designed with Mark von Hagen and often taught with him or Alexander Motyl represents one important example. Some of Nepomnyashchy's most popular courses included Sex and Revolution; Russian Ballet: Snapshots from Petersburg, Paris, and New York; Cities and Civilizations: An Introduction to Eurasian Studies; and Kino-Eyes: The Culture and Practice of Russian and Soviet Film.

The way Nepomnyashchy spent the last summer of her life illustrates the kind of teacher she was. That summer, not knowing that a dire diagnosis awaited her in August, she, together with a colleague from the History Department at Columbia, took a group of fourteen students on a train journey from Berlin to Moscow, and on to Beijing. The trip was part of a Columbia Global Scholars Program Summer Workshop. Nepomnyashchy designed it as a month-long lesson on socialist and post-socialist cities, and drew the students' attention to what the train passed on its way from Berlin to Beijing. This was the kind of teaching and mentoring that most appealed to Nepomnyashchy. She left a mark on countless students who went on to have careers connected with Russia, Eastern Europe, and Eurasia.[8]

From her first years at Barnard, Nepomnyashchy served as undergraduate advisor for Barnard College students interested in Slavic studies. She was known as a devoted mentor, continuing to advise many of these students as they turned their college interest in Russia and Eastern Europe into careers. Similarly, Nepomnyashchy was unsurpassed as a graduate adviser at Columbia, guiding her advisees through all stages of the dissertation writing process as well as revisions for publication. Nepomnyashchy was particularly good at nudging students through the final stages of the dissertation process. She spent hours every week meeting one-on-one and in small groups with graduate students, always offering encouragement and sharing her enthusiasm for academic work. Ludmilla Trigos notes that, "as an advisor," Nepomnyashchy "was always generous with her time and her resources, giving scholarly tips as well as pointers for life." Often she offered graduate students their first opportunity to TA a literature class, a first "real" job, or a first publishing opportunity,

---

8 For a report on the Moscow—Beijing part of the journey, see Robyn Miller Jensen, "Moscow—Beijing: A Journey across Eurasia," *Harriman Magazine* (Winter 2015): 8–11.

thereby "giving them entrée into the world of academic scholarship." She also helped her advisees with the job search, writing countless letters of recommendation and giving invaluable advice. Many scholars in the Slavic field are Nepomnyashchy's students. They continue, each in their own way, Nepomnyashchy's legacy.

One of the greatest joys of Nepomnyashchy's life was motherhood. She and Slava adopted their beloved daughter Olga from Russia in 2001. All through Nepomnyashchy's tenure as the director of the Harriman Institute, Olga was at her side, often attending Harriman receptions and national and international conferences along with her mother. As Olga got older, Nepomnyashchy and Slava delighted in taking her to choir practices in Brooklyn and ballet classes at Lincoln Center. They vacationed every summer as a family at Silver Bay on Lake George just as Nepomnyashchy's family had. Slava's untimely death in 2011 brought Nepomnyashchy and Olga even closer: Olga accompanied Nepomnyashchy on most of her international travels over the next few years, visiting Central Asia, Australia, New Zealand, Japan, and many other regions of the globe. Their last trips together took place in summer 2014, just before Nepomnyashchy was diagnosed with cancer.

Nepomnyashchy's diagnosis in late summer 2014 was a terrible blow to her friends, colleagues, and former students, many of whom responded by delivering meals to Nepomnyashchy and Olga, taking Nepomnyashchy and Olga to appointments, and sitting with Nepomnyashchy at night during her last weeks. Some of those close to Nepomnyashchy traveled very long distances multiple times in this period to spend time with her and help with her care. Nepomnyashchy's death in 2015 remains a raw wound for all those who loved her. We remember her as a loving mother who adored her daughter Olga, as a dedicated teacher and academic leader, a generous friend, and as an innovative researcher. We hope that this volume will help highlight Nepomnyashchy's contributions and also preserve her memory.

Chapter Overview

This volume is structured thematically. Its first section includes many of the best pieces that Nepomnyashchy wrote on nineteenth-century topics and focuses on her contributions to Pushkin scholarship. Two of the articles included reflect Nepomnyashchy's lasting interest in Pushkin's narrative poems; a third grew out of her work on the groundbreaking co-edited book *Under the Sky of My Africa: Alexander Pushkin and Blackness*. The last article in this section is the very first Nepomnyashchy ever published while still a relatively junior graduate student at Columbia. It appeared in the first issue of *Ulbandus*. Even now, after several book-length studies of Mikhail Katkov have appeared in Russian and English, Nepomnyashchy's pioneering article remains an indispensable source for anyone working on this important and understudied figure.

The second section reflects Nepomnyashchy's broad knowledge of world literature, which gave her keen insight into the relationship between Russian and Western literatures. One article represents the product of Nepomnyashchy's efforts to prove that Jane Austen was known in Russia earlier than it is commonly believed and might have influenced the writers of Pushkin's generation. Others investigate Nabokov's disagreement with Freud, as evident in his novel *The Defense*, and Soviet television adaptations of Sherlock Holmes novels.

The third section contains a mixture of published and unpublished work by Nepomnyashchy. It opens with two essays extracted from her unfinished book manuscript *The Politics of Tradition*, a monograph on which Nepomnyashchy worked in the years before her death. The first section of the manuscript that we have chosen to publish here examines the structure of Pasternak's *Doctor Zhivago*; the second interprets Solzhenitsyn's *One Day in the Life of Ivan Denisovich* as a response to Valentin Kataev's *Time, Forward!* and as a refutation of socialist-realist values. In terms of previously published work, this section includes a little-known article that focuses on Andrei Siniavskii's posthumously published novel, *The Cat's House* (Koshkin dom) as well as an article on Tatiana Tolstaia's references to her own genealogy in her fiction and in interviews.

The last section of our volume showcases Nepomnyashchy's interest in non-verbal arts. She was a passionate fan of classical dance and knew the history of Russian ballet better than many specialists. The article on the image of the Russian ballerina that opens this section demonstrates her expertise in this area. This last section also includes articles on late twentieth and early twenty-first century popular culture as represented by detective novels and television serials. Nepomnyashchy not only followed the new developments in post-Soviet culture, enjoying new films and TV shows and reading trendy detective novels, but also took a scholarly view of this cultural production, looking for innovation and change in these genres. Her article on Aleksandra Marinina, which we include in this section, demonstrates this very well: Nepomnyashchy was among the very first scholars to pay attention to the swift changes in post-Soviet literary institutions, in this case, the transformation of literature from high art into marketable goods.

Editorial Approach

Beyond reconciling the formatting and transliteration systems and correcting typos and other minor errors, we have made minimal changes to the previously published work that appears here. In some cases we have lightly edited Nepomnyashchy's texts to remove time references that seemed dated or to smooth out a passage that struck us as potentially unclear. We have also trimmed down some of Nepomnyashchy's discursive notes to adhere to contemporary editing standards. In the case of the previously unpublished chapters, we edited out references to Nepomnyashchy's larger book project and some associated framing so that each could read as a free-standing article. We also checked references and passages, often working from queries that Nepomnyashchy herself had left in the text. In all cases, we used the author's editorial sensibilities as a guide.

Nepomnyashchy often quoted her material in the original Russian. In all these cases we have provided translations, which are our own unless otherwise indicated. In general, when citations are provided in both English and Russian, we have placed English first in the interest of readability. However, in the case of poetry we have placed the Russian first.

We rely on a modified Library of Congress transliteration system throughout this volume except for in the case of well-known cultural figures such as Tolstoy and Herzen.

Acknowledgments

Financial support for this volume was provided by Columbia University's Harriman Institute for Russian, Eurasian, and East European Studies as well as the provost, the vice-president for Research, the College of Arts and Sciences, and the Department of Modern Languages, Literatures, and Linguistics of the University of Oklahoma. We are particularly grateful to the publishing venues that have allowed us to republish work by Nepomnyashchy and to Nepomnyashchy's daughter Olga Nepomnyashchy for her support of this project and for permission to publish the unpublished material as well as those published pieces for which the copyright remained with the author. We thank James E. Falen for allowing us to cite from his translation of Pushkin's *Eugene Onegin*. Anna Oborina, Nadezhda Azhgikhina, James Theimer, Nancy Condee, and Milla Trigos shared memories of Nepomnyashchy that helped us flesh out the account of her life that we have provided here We also thank Alla Rachkov, Ronald John Meyer, and Robert H. Davis, Jr. for their help throughout the project.

Part I

Pushkin, Pushkin, Pushkin, and Katkov

1

The Poet, History, and the Supernatural: A Note on Pushkin's "The Poet" and *The Bronze Horseman*

The question of the poet's responsibility to history or, in a more global sense, the question of the poet's *a priori* responsibility to any principles of valuation beyond the logic of his own artistic universe is one of the most persistently recurring motifs in Pushkin's narrative poetry. Thus, in the *Gavriiliada* the snake, that spellbinding manipulator of words whose linguistic prowess allows him to usurp the rights of the Divine Ruler, militantly declares that he is not a "court historian": "No ia, pover,—istorik ne pridvornyi, / Ne nuzhen mne proroka vazhnyi chin" (But I, believe me, am not a court historian, / I do not need the weighty rank of prophet).[1]

By the same token, Pushkin's *Poltava*, a poem which because of its duality has been accused of lacking unity, is constructed on a thematic and stylistic opposition between the personal and the historical, between the love of Mariia and Mazepa cast in the mode of the Romantic ballad and the story of Peter the Great and the battle of Poltava couched in the language and form

---

Originally published in *The Supernatural in Slavic and Baltic Literature: Essays in Honor of Victor Terras*, ed. Amy Mandelker and Roberta Reeder (Columbus: Slavica Publishers, 1988), 34–46. Reproduced by permission of Slavica Publishers and Olga Nepomnyashchy—eds.

1   A. S. Pushkin, *Polnoe sobranie sochinenii v shestnadtsati tomakh* (Moscow: Izdatel'stvo AN SSSR, 1937–1959), 4:127. Henceforth volume and page references will appear in parentheses in the text.

of the Classical ode.² Far from being an indication that the poem has slipped from the poet's control, that the diverse elements of its structure have not been integrated, this duality is rather the very point of the long poem (*poema*), as indicated by the epilogue. Thus, "proshlo sto let" (a hundred years went by) and Peter, the victor at Poltava, has been enshrined by history, while the ill-fated Mariia has been forgotten . . . but not completely.³ Her story lives on in the songs of the blind Ukrainian bard, and this is a telling detail (5:63–64). It is the poet's declaration that the matter of history is not necessarily the matter of art, that he will not be a court historian confined to chronicling the deeds of history's conquerors.

Yet, if the poet is not to run with courtiers and kings (or, should we say, tsars), if he is not dutifully to sing the praises of history's victors, who is he to be and what is he to write about? In the two long poems (*poemy*) adduced above, Satan (the snake), the archetypal social outcast, and the blind singer of tales, perhaps the lowliest habitant of the Ukrainian social hierarchy, taken as poet figures, would seem to suggest that, by society's standards, the poet is at

---

2   While himself arguing for the unity of *Poltava*'s plot, A. I. Sokolov writes about two plot lines in *Poltava* and points out Belinskii's role in perpetuating this point of view. A. I. Sokolov, "'Poltava' Pushkina i 'Petriady,'" *Pushkin. Vremennik pushkinskoi komissii* 4–5 (1939): 61. On the stylistic duality of *Poltava* see also A. I. Sokolov, "'Poltava' Pushkina i zhanr romanticheskoi poemy," *Pushkin. Issledovaniia i materialy* 4 (1962): 154–72; and B. I. Koplan, "'Poltavskii boi' Pushkina i ody Lomonosova," *Pushkin i ego sovremenniki* 38–39 (1930): 113–21. Koplan's article contains an observation of substantial importance to the central argument of my "note": "The stylistic device of returning to Classicism (if not of the epoch of Lomonosov, then of Derzhavin, or even to the latest epoch of the young Zhukovskii) can be noted in other works of Pushkin as well, precisely in those cases in which the poet remembers historical events and historical heroes." Koplan, "'Poltavskii boi' Pushkina," 116n2.

3   The same line—"Proshlo sto let" (A hundred years went by)—appears also in the introduction to *The Bronze Horseman* (5:135; 151). A number of critics have noted the identity between these lines and have commented on it. See, for example, Wacław Lednicki, *Pushkin's Bronze Horseman: The Story of a Masterpiece* (Berkeley: University of California Press, 1955), 18–19. I have made a point of drawing attention to these identical lines here in order to underscore the fact once again—as I shall throughout this article—that the appearance of the same or similar line(s) in two different Pushkin poems suggests a thematic kinship between the two works. (All translations of *The Bronze Horseman* are by Catharine T. Nepomnyashchy, in *The Ardis Anthology of Russian Romanticism*, ed. Christine Rydel [Ann Arbor: Ardis Publishers, 1984], 151–55. Henceforth page references to this translation will appear in parentheses in the text, separately or after volume and page numbers of the original—eds.)

best a dweller on the fringe, a nonentity. This "hint" is developed in Pushkin's 1827 lyric "The Poet" (Poet):

> Пока не требует поэта
> К священной жертве Аполлон,
> В заботах суетного света
> Он малодушно погружен;
> Молчит его святая лира;
> Душа вкушает хладный сон,
> И меж детей ничтожных мира,
> Быть может, всех ничтожней он.
>
> Но лишь божественный глагол
> До слуха чуткого коснется,
> Душа поэта встрепенется,
> Как пробудившийся орел.
> Тоскует он в забавах мира,
> Людской чуждается молвы,
> К ногам народного кумира
> Не клонит гордой головы;
> Бежит он, дикий и суровый,
> И звуков, и смятенья полн,
> На берега пустынных волн,
> В широкошумные дубровы. (3:65)

> Until Apollo summons the poet
> To perform the sacred sacrifice
> In the cares of the vain world
> He, faint-hearted, is immersed.
> His sacred lyre is silent;
> His soul partakes of cold sleep,
> And among the world's insignificant children
> He, perhaps, is most insignificant of all.
>
> But as soon as the divine word
> Reaches his keen hearing,
> The poet's soul quivers
> Like an awakened eagle.
> He is bored by society's amusements,
> Avoids people's chatter,
> He doesn't bow his proud head
> To the feet of the people's idol;

> He runs wild and stern,
> Full of sounds and tumult,
> To the bank of barren waves,
> To the broadly murmuring groves.

Here a distinct opposition is posited between the rules of society and the rules of poetry. Not only is the poet a social nobody, but—and more to the point for our further discussion,—he is licensed to a higher, supra-civic, or even supernatural authority. To pursue the implications of this opposition further, let us turn to a consideration of the notable linguistic and structural correspondences between "The Poet" and Pushkin's greatest long poem, *The Bronze Horseman* (Mednyi vsadnik, 1833).

Even at first glance these correspondences are striking, especially the almost complete identity of the first line of *The Bronze Horseman* ("Na beregu pustynnykh voln"; On the shores by barren waves) with the penultimate line of "The Poet" ("Na berega pustynnykh voln"; To the shores by barren waves). Yet these linguistic similarities would be no more than literary trivia if they did not reflect a deeper thematic parallelism between the two works. Leaving aside for the time being the "Introduction" (Predislovie) to *The Bronze Horseman*, we find that the two poems follow essentially the same trajectory: a man, first immersed in the petty concerns of the world, is transformed, becomes indifferent to the everyday affairs of the masses, refuses to bow down before an idol (*kumir*), and ends up "On the bank by deserted waves." Seen in this light, Evgenii's story in *The Bronze Horseman* appears as a literal working out of the archetype of the poet outlined in the earlier lyric, and *The Bronze Horseman* becomes a literary manifesto of sorts, in which Pushkin adroitly manipulates poetic subtexts and the conventions of the rival literary "schools" of his day in order to expand the boundaries of poetry.

At the center of the argument stands Pushkin's semi-anonymous plebeian hero, and there is ample evidence within the text of *The Bronze Horseman* to suggest that Evgenii is meant to evoke the figure of the poet. He is twice associated with poets, once in the first part of the poem and once in the second. In the first instance, which occurs shortly after Evgenii's first appearance in the work, Pushkin employs a direct simile: "Evgenii tut vzdokhnul serdechno / I razmechtalsia, kak poet" (At that Evgeny deeply sighed / And, like a poet, set to musing; 5:139; 152). The second example comes after the flood; when the now deranged Evgenii abandons his room, it is let to a poet:

> Прошла неделя, месяц—он
> К себе домой не возвращался.
> Его пустынный уголок
> Отдал в наймы, как вышел срок,
> Хозяин бедному поэту. (5:146)
>
> A week, a month had passed, but he
> Did not return to his home.
> And when the period was up,
> The landlord let the empty chamber
> To a poor poet. (154)

This apparently gratuitous detail takes on new meaning when we look at Evgenii as himself in some sense a poet. On the one hand, this image suggests a relatively superficial similarity between the material circumstances of the "poor poet" and those of "poor Evgenii" when we first meet him in the poem. On the other hand, this replacement of Evgenii by a poet, who, significantly, takes over not only the poor clerk's home but apparently also all of his worldly belongings ("Evgenii za svoim dobrom / Ne prikhodil"; Evgeny / Did not go back to fetch his things; 5:146; 154), especially at this crucial moment when Evgenii, crazed by grief, appears to have entered a state of madness akin to poetic inspiration, suggests that the symbolic identity between these two figures may be deeper.

Yet, it is the earlier comparison between Evgenii and the poet which is the richer of the two, for it contains a triple irony constructed on the contrast between the semantically loaded "deeply sighed" and "like a poet" and the prosaic, even petty desires that follow, beginning with the line "Zhenit'sia? Nu ... zachem zhe net?" (Get married? Well ... Why should not I?; 5:139; 152). The first and most obvious irony is, of course, based on the disjunction between the traditional, exalted vision of the poet and the pettiness of Evgenii's hopes along with the conversational tone of the language in which they are couched. The second irony lies in the fact that this opposition assumes the function of an autocommentary on *The Bronze Horseman* itself as a work of art defining its own boundaries. Thus, simply by the act of having chosen a petty clerk as the hero of his poem and, moreover, a petty clerk whose appearances in the work are marked by a particularized stylistic stratum characterized by a conversational lexicon and, the frequent use of enjambement, the poet lays claim to this material as appropriate to the long poem and, therefore, to the meditations of the poet.⁴ Finally, the third irony appears only in relation to the vision of poetic creation espoused in "The Poet." For if, when not in a state of poetic inspiration, the poet is indeed "iz detei nichtozhnykh mira, / Byt' mozhet, vsekh nichtozhnei on" (among the world's insignificant children / He, perhaps, is most insignificant of all; 3:65), then, logically, this "insignificance" should be reflected in his thoughts and dreams as well as, as in Evgenii's case, in his social position. Certainly it is no accident that in his analysis of *The Bronze Horseman*, Valerii Briusov, perhaps inspired by his intuition as a fellow poet, repeatedly refers to Evgenii as "insignificant" (*nichtozhnyi*) and even as "the most insignificant of the insignificant" (*nichtozhneishii iz nichtozhnykh*).⁵ Yet, even aside from these lines directly associating Evgenii with the figure of a poet, the profession of clerk contains inherent resonances with the profession of the poet, leaving us free to view the clerk as in some sense a bastardized poet. After all, the clerk, like the poet, writes for a living, although this writing is not original creation but the uninspired copying of official documents. That Pushkin was aware of the implications of the clerk as a pseudopoet is indicated in a passage from one of the early drafts of "Ezerskii."⁶ In this early variant he writes:

Порой сей поздней и печальной
(В том доме, где стоял и я)

---

4   For a comprehensive discussion of the stylistic devices which Pushkin employs in the characterization of Evgenii in *The Bronze Horseman* (specifically as contrasted with the poet's use of the stanzaic structure and lexicon of the eighteenth-century ode in passages devoted to Peter), see L. Timofeev, "'Mednyi vsadnik' (iz nabliudenii nad stikhom poemy)," in *Pushkin. Sbornik statei*, ed. A. Egolin (Moscow: Gosudarstvennoe izdatel'stvo khudozhestvennoi literatury, 1941), 214–42.

5   Valerii Briusov, "Mednyi vsadnik," in his *Moi Pushkin* (Moscow: Gosudarstvennoe izdatel'stvo, 1929), 72.

6   For a discussion of the relationship between "Ezerskii" and *The Bronze Horseman*, see O. S. Solov'eva, "'Ezerskii' i 'Mednyi vsadnik'. Istoriia teksta," *Pushkin. Issledovaniia i materialy* 3 (1960): 268–344. For the purposes of this article, it is unnecessary to review the long-standing controversy over this question. Whether or not "Ezerskii" is in fact an early variant of *The Bronze Horseman*, the associative links between the figures of Ezerskii and Evgenii are well enough documented to validate our introduction of evidence from the earlier fragment in this context. In other words, whether the two texts represent separate works or merely variants on the same conception, the striking linguistic and thematic similarities between them adequately demonstrate the fact that they represent a unified semantic cluster in Pushkin's poetic universe.

Один [при] свете свечки сальной
В конурке пятого жилья
Писал чиновник—скоро смело
Перо привычное скрипело
Как видно малый был делец—
Работу кончив наконец
Он стал тихонь<ко> раздеваться
Задул огарок—лег в постель
Под заслуженную шинель—
И стал мечтать....[7]

At this late and sad time
(In the same house where I'd also lived)
Alone, by the light of a tallow candle,
In a hovel on the fifth floor
The clerk was writing—his accustomed pen
Scraped quickly, boldly
Evidently the fellow was a smart operator—
Having finally finished his work,
He slowly began to undress,
Snuffed out the candle's end—got into bed
Under his long-serving overcoat—
And began to muse…

Thus, when we first meet the hero of the poem as envisioned in the above-quoted draft, he is writing, "finishing his work." Moreover, Briusov points out that "at one time Pushkin even thought of making of him [Ezerskii] if not a poet, then at least a person in some way interested in literature," and cites the following variant lines to support his contention:

Мой чиновник
Был сочинитель и любовник.
Как все, он вел себя не строго,
Как мы, писал стихами много.[8]

---

[7] A. S. Pushkin, "'Ezerskii' variant," in *Mednyi vsadnik*, ed. N. V. Izmailov (Leningrad: Nauka, 1978), 93–94.

[8] Valerii Briusov, "Mednyi vsadnik," 73. The quoted passage is on this page.

> My clerk
> Was a poet and a lover.
> Like others, his behavior wasn't always strict,
> Like us, he wrote lots of poems.

The "like us" in the last line here leads to the final argument to be adduced in favor of viewing Evgenii as a poet figure, that is, the autobiographical references which, as a number of critics have pointed out, Pushkin embedded in the portrayal of his hero.[9] We need not review these autobiographical ties in detail. It is sufficient to our purpose to draw attention to the similarity between Pushkin's and Evgenii's social positions as members of impoverished noble families. What Pushkin says about Evgenii's family name applies equally to his own: "Khotia v minuvshi vremena / Ono, byt' mozhet, i blistalo, / I pod perom Karamzina / V rodnykh predan'iakh prozvuchalo" (Although in days gone by / It perhaps shone, / And beneath Karamzin's pen / Sounded in native lore; 5:138). Furthermore, both the poet and his character initially look forward to imminent happiness in marriage; a dream, which, as Jakobson has pointed out, is threatened in Pushkin's case and destroyed in Evgenii's by the intervention of a statue.[10] Thus, through these associations, Evgenii is likened not just to any poet, but to Pushkin himself.

Having postulated Evgenii's function as a poet figure in *The Bronze Horseman*, we may now go on to reconsider his role. Just as in the lyric the poet is called from the world of the petty and everyday by "the divine word" (*bozhestvennyi glagol*) into the realm of poetic inspiration, so Evgenii is jarred from "insignificance" by the flood and the tragedy it precipitates, and, significantly, the flood is also of divine origin. This is indicated by the line "Narod / Zrit Bozhii gnev i kazni zhdet" (The people see the wrath of God, / And they await their punishment) as well as by the words which Pushkin puts in Alexander I's mouth: "S Bozhiei stikhiei / Tsariam ne sovladet'" (Not even tsars can overcome / The anger of God's elements; 5:141; 153). Once touched by divine intervention both the poet and Evgenii become estranged from the world of society and everyday life, as can be seen from a comparison of the lines

---

9   See, for example, Lednicki, *Pushkin's Bronze Horseman*, especially the chapter entitled "Petersburg, Peter the Great, The Emperor," 42–84.

10 Roman Jakobson, "The Statue in Puškin's Poetic Mythology," in his *Puškin and His Sculptural Myth*, trans. and ed. John Burbank (The Hague: Mouton, 1975), 1–44.

"Liudskoi chuzhdaetsia molvy" (Avoids the people's chatter; 3:65) from "The Poet" and "On skoro svetu / Stal chuzhd" (Soon / He became alien from the world; 5:146) from *The Bronze Horseman*. The theme of Evgenii's estrangement from the crowd is elaborated in *The Bronze Horseman* in the contrast between Evgenii's tragic fate and the insensitive mercantilism of the Petersburg populace after the flood, thematically echoing yet another poem from Pushkin's poet cycle, the 1828 lyric "The Poet and the Crowd" (Poet i tolpa), in which the poet again declares his freedom from any sort of moral or educational responsibility to the masses, chiding the crowd: "Poidite proch'—kakoe delo / Poetu mirnomu do vas!" (Go away—what does / The peaceful poet have to do with you?; 3: 142).

In our reading of *The Bronze Horseman*, then, Evgenii's madness is equated with the state of poetic inspiration. This is supported, on the one hand, by linguistic parallelisms between "The Poet" and *The Bronze Horseman* and, on the other, by the motif of the identification of madness and poetry, which appears in other works by Pushkin dating from the early 1830s. Unbalanced by Parasha's death, the roar of the storm-tossed Neva reverberates in Evgenii's ears, blocking out all else:

> Но бедный, бедный мой Евгений....
> Увы! его смятенный ум
> Против ужасных потрясений
> Не устоял. Мятежный шум
> Невы и ветров раздавался
> В его ушах. (5:145)

> Alas, my poor, grief-torn Evgenii....
> Bewildered by the dreadful shocks,
> His rattled mind could not hold up.
> The roar of the rebellious Neva
> And the winds rang in the ears. (154)

And later: "On oglushen / Byl shumom vnutrennei trevogi" (The noise of his inner unease / Drowned out all other sounds around him; 5:146; 154). These lines appear as a paraphrase and elaboration of the line "I zvukov i smiaten'ia poln" (Full of sounds and tumult) from "The Poet." Moreover, the thematic equation of madness and poetry is suggested in stanza XXXIX of the eighth chapter of *Evgenii Onegin* in the lines describing Onegin's suffering over his infatuation with Tat'iana: "I on ne sdelalsia poetom, / Ne umer, ne soshel s uma"

(He didn't die, or lose his reason, / Or turn a poet in despair).[11] However, the motif of the poet as madman is most fully developed in and, in fact, serves as the basis for "God Let Me Not Go Out of My Mind" (Ne dai mne Bog soiti s uma). This lyric, written in 1833, the same year as *The Bronze Horseman*, likens the persecution of the poet to the imprisonment of a madman and, as a corollary, the free ravings of a lunatic to the free creativity of the poetic imagination.

Thus, the flood becomes Evgenii's muse, the "divine word" which calls him into the realm of madness and poetry, and, in this context, it is irrelevant to our reading that a year elapses between the time of the flood and that of Evgenii's confrontation with the statue. The most obvious reason for this temporal displacement was Pushkin's desire to associate Evgenii's mad revolt against the statue with the "mad" revolt of the Decembrists in 1825. In any case, the two times, that of the flood (1824) and that of Evgenii's remembrance of it, spurred by the recurrence of foul November weather a year later, merge in the madman's confused mind and become one. Just as the poet called by the "divine word" "quivers" (*vstrepenetsia*), so Evgenii "shuddered" (*vzdrognul*; 5:147). He suddenly recognizes Peter as the author of his suffering and confronts the statue, circling to the front of the monument so that the statue no longer has its back turned to him, and the two meet one another for the first time face to face. Thus, just as the poet of the 1827 "K nogam narodnogo kumira / Ne klonit gordoi golovy" (He doesn't bow down his proud head, / To the feet of the people's idol), so Evgenii now stands up to his own "idol." Significantly, the word "idol" (*kumir*) is used four times in *The Bronze Horseman* to describe the statue of Peter, and it is one of the words to which the censor objected, thereby blocking publication of the tale during the poet's lifetime.[12] Pushkin makes it clear that the man and the statue are now meeting on equal terms not only through the change in the location of the two figures relative to one another, but also through a corresponding change in the lexicon used to describe Evgenii. Peter and his statue are described consistently throughout in the elevated language of the solemn ode in marked contrast to the

---

11 Pushkin, *Evgenii Onegin*, 6:184; Alexander Pushkin, *Eugene Onegin: A Novel in Verse*, trans. James E. Falen (Carbondale: Southern Illinois University Press, 1990), 216.

12 G. P. Makogonenko, *Tvorchestvo A. S. Pushkina v 1830-e gody* (Leningrad: Izdatel'stvo "Khudozhestvennaia literatura," 1974), 315–16; Lednicki, *Pushkin's Bronze Horseman*, 81–82.

conversational style of the passages devoted to Evgenii. At this moment, however, the language used to describe Evgenii is also elevated, notably by the inclusion of Church Slavonicisms, and the man and the statue therefore meet on equal terms in a linguistic sense as well.[13]

Transformed by the inspiration of madness, Evgenii brings the previously imperturbable statue to life in his imagination, thus forcing the bronze tsar to recognize him as an equal, at least in his own realm. The victory is short-lived, however, for after a night pursued by his grotesque fantasy, Evgenii returns to the world of the insignificant and everyday only to be found dead shortly thereafter on the ruins of Parasha's house. Figuratively, if not literally, Evgenii, like the poet, ends up "on the bank by deserted waves," for, as Dmitrii Blagoi has demonstrated by tracing the linguistic parallels between the introduction and the ending, the poem's closing lines have the function of closing the "ring" structure, of returning the poem to its beginning.[14]

Thus, from the ending we are brought back, at last, to the introductory section of the poem and, inevitably, to Peter, who after all is the figure first seen "on the bank by deserted waves." And this is only just, for Peter is a creator in his own right, and it is his Petersburg, "Petra tvoren'e" (Peter's creation; 5:136; 151), which provides the setting and even the catalyst for the action of the poem. Seen in this light, the confrontation between the man and the statue, Peter's incarnation in the body of the poem, becomes a confrontation between two creators, but creators in radically different modes. Peter's creation is tangible, a city which still stands, which still determines the fates of its inhabitants after "Proshlo sto let" (A hundred years went by; 5:135; 151) and which presumably will continue to stand for many years to come. Moreover, the city is preeminently a creation in and of history, just as Peter himself is an actor in history and an embodiment of historical forces. This is reflected in the linguistic substratum of the poem in Pushkin's consistent use of the language and stanzaic structure of the classical ode in his depictions of Peter, the city, and the statue, for, as in *Poltava*, in *The Bronze Horseman* the odic genre is equated with the court poet and, through him, with the history he dutifully depicts. Moreover, both the city and the statue are classical images *par excellence*, manifestations of what Pumpianskii terms "the architectural fixation of classical

---

13 Timofeev, "'Mednyi vsadnik,'" 239.

14 D. D. Blagoi, "Kompozitsiia 'Mednogo vsadnika' Pushkina," *Izvestiia Akademii Nauk SSSR, Otdelenie literatury i iazyka* 14, no. 5 (1955): 433.

poetry."¹⁵ In contrast, Evgenii's creation is intangible, is denied even the validity of the historical artifact. In other words, poetry does not reside in the physical incarnation of the poetic text, but rather in the actual moment of poetic creation. This gives new meaning to the transformation which Evgenii works on the bronze horseman in his crazed and inspired fantasy. The immobile statue, that quintessential image of the classical tradition, is metamorphosed into a Romantic grotesque in the manner of Hoffmann or, perhaps more to the point here, Washington Irving.¹⁶ The image of pursuit which follows the initial transformation is particularly significant, for it neatly summarizes the dilemma of the duality between the two creators. Evgenii here triumphs, at least in the realm of poetic imagination; by making the statue recognize him as a threat he thereby lures him down from his pedestal and into pursuit. Yet, the statue remains the pursuer, and retains the superiority of physical force. In other words, the poet remains a victim in the historical realm.

Anna Akhmatova has been credited with the observation that, "the artistic resolution of the struggle in the poem is indisputable: the struggle is resolved in favor of history." In fact, as I have tried to demonstrate in this paper, the solution is not so simple. The answer to the question "who wins," Evgenii or Peter, repeated *ad nauseam* by critics of *The Bronze Horseman* is—neither. Each retains supremacy in his own mode, the historical activist in history and the poet in poetry. Thus, at the poem's end after Evgenii's death, Peter's city continues to stand, a durable monument to its creator. Yet, in a symbolic sense

---

15 L. V. Pumpianskii, "'Mednyi vsadnik' i poeticheskaia traditsiia XVIII veka," in his *Klassicheskaia traditsiia: sobranie trudov po istorii russkoi literatury* (Moscow: Iazyki russkoi literatury, 2000), 180.

16 Anna Akhmatova originally focused attention on Irving's "Legend of the Arabian Astrologer" as a source for Pushkin's *The Golden Cockerel*. A. A. Akhmatova, "Posledniaia skazka Pushkina," *Zvezda* 1 (1933): 161–76. Jakobson in "The Statue in Puškin's Poetic Mythology," 10, made the explicit connection between the "bronze horseman" of Irving's tale and his "namesake" in Pushkin. However, in referring to the American writer here, I have in mind an episode from another Irving story—a confrontation between a "petty official" and a fantastic horseman—which perhaps deserves further study in relation to *The Bronze Horseman*. I am speaking, of course, of the midnight encounter between the schoolteacher Ichabod Crane and the Headless Horseman in Irving's "The Legend of Sleepy Hollow." For a survey of Soviet scholarship on Pushkin and Irving, see John C. Fiske, "The Soviet Controversy over Pushkin and Washington Irving," *Comparative Literature* 7, no. 1 (Winter 1955): 25–31. The comparison is developed in my article on Pushkin's *The Bronze Horseman* and Irving's "The Legend of Sleepy Hollow" (reprinted in this collection, 16–37—eds.).

the epilogue to *The Bronze Horseman* negates Peter's creation by returning to the site of the city's prehistory. Thus, while the revolt of the individual against the state remains madness in a historical sense, the poet still, through the only means available to him, poetry, rejects the role of court poet and reclaims his freedom to create and the autonomy of his poetic universe.

But, to conclude, let us return to the poetic vision itself, to the bronze statue brought to life, an image that inherently equates madness and the supernatural. Poetry is sanctioned not only to disdain the socially acceptable, but to defy natural law as well, if only in one brief moment of fantastic delusion. So *The Bronze Horseman*—and "The Poet," which it follows—may be seen as a paradigm for all of the downtrodden clerks and social nonentities in Russian literature who, at the end of their humble and humiliated careers, are vouchsafed a transcendent vision into a world beyond the oppressive reality of everyday life. Apart from Pushkin's own Germann in "The Queen of Spades," we may cite Gogol's Chichikov with his flying troika, the mad "King of Spain" from "Diary of a Madman," and, of course, Akakii Akak'evich Bashmachkin as only the most famous of Evgenii's "brothers." Each finds a certain rude justice, even vindication, when called from the realm of the ordinary. Poetry, then, as an alternate, "supranatural" world becomes the province and sole refuge of society's victims, or, to paraphrase Pushkin in more colloquial terms, if politics is the "art of the possible," then poetry is the "art of the impossible."

Works Cited

Akhmatova, A. A. "Posledniaia skazka Pushkina." *Zvezda* 1 (1933): 161–76.

Blagoi, D. D. "Kompozitsiia 'Mednogo vsadnika' Pushkina." *Izvestiia Akademii Nauk SSSR, Otdelenie literatury i iazyka* 14, no. 5 (1955): 420–35.

Briusov, Valerii. "Mednyi vsadnik." In his *Moi Pushkin*, 63–94. Moscow: Gosudarstvennoe izdatel'stvo, 1929.

Fiske, John C. "The Soviet Controversy over Pushkin and Washington Irving." *Comparative Literature* 7, no. 1 (Winter 1955): 25–31.

Jakobson, Roman. "The Statue in Puškin's Poetic Mythology." In his *Puškin and His Sculptural Myth*, translated and edited by John Burbank, 1–44. The Hague: Mouton, 1975.

Koplan, B. I. "'Poltavskii boi' Pushkina i ody Lomonosova." *Pushkin i ego sovremenniki* 28–29 (1930): 113–21.

Lednicki, Wacław. *Pushkin's Bronze Horseman: The Story of a Masterpiece*. Berkeley: University of California Press, 1955.

Makogonenko, G. P. *Tvorchestvo A.S. Pushkina v 1830-e gody*. Leningrad: Izdatel'stvo "Khudozhestvennaia literatura," 1974.

Pumpianskii, L. V. "'Mednyi vsadnik' i poeticheskaia traditsiia XVIII veka." In his *Klassicheskaia traditsiia: sobranie trudov po istorii russkoi literatury*, 158–96. Moscow: Iazyki russkoi literatury, 2000.

Pushkin, A. S. *The Bronze Horseman*. Translated by Catharine T. Nepomnyashchy. In *The Ardis Anthology of Russian Romanticism*, edited by Christine Rydel, 151–55. Ann Arbor: Ardis Publishers, 1984.

———. *Mednyi vsadnik*. Edited by N. V. Izmailov. Leningrad: Nauka, 1978.

———. *Polnoe sobranie sochinenii v shestnadtsati tomakh*. Moscow: Izdatel'stvo AN SSSR, 1937–1959.

——— [Alexander Pushkin]. *Eugene Onegin: A Novel in Verse*. Translated by James E. Falen. Carbondale: Southern University Press, 1990.

Sokolov, A. I. "'Poltava' Pushkina i 'Petriady.'" *Pushkin. Vremennik pushkinskoi komissii* 4–5 (1939): 57–90.

———. "'Poltava' Pushkina i zhanr romanticheskoi poemy." *Pushkin. Issledovaniia i materialy* 4 (1962): 154–72.

Solov'eva, O. S. "'Ezerskii' i 'Mednyi vsadnik.' Istoriia teksta." *Pushkin. Issledovaniia i materialy* 3 (1960): 268–344.

Timofeev, L. "'Mednyi vsadnik' (iz nabliudenii nad stikhom poemy)." In *Pushkin. Sbornik statei*, edited by A. Egolin, 214–42. Moscow: Gosudarstvennoe izdatel'stvo khudozhestvennoi literatury, 1941.

2

Pushkin's *The Bronze Horseman* and Irving's "The Legend of Sleepy Hollow": A Curious Case of Cultural Cross-Fertilization?

> *Yankee* [. . .] A nickname given to Americans; its meaning is unknown to us.
>
> —A. S. Pushkin, *John Tenner* (Dzhon Tenner)

As is well known, "influence" studies have fallen into disrepute in recent decades in western literary criticism. Linda Hutcheon rightly points out that this development constitutes an inevitable corollary to Roland Barthes's announcement of the "death of the author" in 1968, shifting the site of meaning away from the flesh-and-blood author onto the interaction between text and reader, placing at issue "the *locus* of textual appropriation. On the one hand, we are dealing with *authorial* intent and with the historical issue of sources and influences; on the other, it is a question of *reader* interpretation whereby visible sources become signs of plagiarism, and influences yield to 'intertextual'z

---

Epigraph: A. S. Pushkin, "Dzhon Tenner," in his *Polnoe sobranie sochinenii v shestnadtsati tomakh* (Moscow: Izdatel'stvo Akademii nauk SSSR, 1937–1959), 12:132 (hereafter *PSS*). Pushkin's article was originally published in *Sovremennik* 3 (1836): 205–56, signed "The Reviewer." I have combined the word *yankee* Pushkin uses in English in the concluding sentence of the article with the "editor's" footnote accompanying the word—C. T. N. This article initially appeared in *Slavic Review* 58, no. 2 (Summer 1999): 337–51. Reproduced with the permission of Cambridge University Press through PLSclear—eds.

2. Pushkin's *The Bronze Horseman* and Irving's "The Legend of Sleepy Hollow"

echoes."[1] Hardly surprisingly, this Franco-American trend has made relatively few inroads in Russian criticism, for, after decades of Soviet privileging of the conceit of the writer as the source and arbiter of the meaning of his (or her) works, the author remains very much alive in Russian culture and criticism. While an exploration of the fascinating cultural implications of this divergence lies beyond the scope of this study, I would simply argue against dismissing this "aberration" as an instance of the, sadly, all too frequently invoked Russian "backwardness." Rather we should regard it as a healthy corrective to the universalist claims of western literary theory. We know, after all, that a real historical person "makes" the literary work, even if, as Wolfgang Iser maintains, it is "the convergence of text and reader [that] brings the literary work into existence."[2] Writers are, after all, readers as well, and they react to what they read, as we all do, incorporating it into their own writing, in the process transforming it, arguing with it, making it their own. Moreover, while an examination of the process of crafting a literary work certainly has value in its own right, the juxtaposition of "genetically" related literary artifacts enriches the critic's—and reader's—experience of both texts. Taking these premises as my starting point, I will suggest that Pushkin's writing of his masterwork *The Bronze Horseman* (Mednyi vsadnik) was informed by his reading of Washington Irving's "The Legend of Sleepy Hollow."

Irving's story was published as the concluding piece in *The Sketchbook of Geoffrey Crayon, Gent.* (1819–1820), the first work that Irving, who originally took up writing as "the gentlemanly exercise of the pen," unabashedly published to ameliorate his tenuous financial position and establish himself as a professional writer.[3] The first American writer to achieve an international reputation, Irving is nonetheless credited with possessing but a limited literary

---

1 Linda Hutcheon, "Literary Borrowing . . . and Stealing: Plagiarism, Sources, Influences, and Intertexts," *English Studies in Canada* 12, no. 2 (1986): 230 (emphasis in the original—C. T. N.). For Roland Barthes's "The Death of the Author," see his *Image-Music-Text*, trans. Stephen Heath (New York: Fontana Press, 1977), 142–48.

2 Wolfgang Iser, "The Reading Process: A Phenomenological Approach," in *Reader-Response Criticism: From Formalism to Post-Structuralism*, ed. Jane P. Tompkins (Baltimore: John Hopkins University Press, 1980), 50.

3 Henry A. Pochmann, "Washington Irving: Amateur or Professional?," in *Essays on American Literature in Honor of Jay B. Hubbell*, ed. Clarence Gohdes (Durham: Duke University Press, 1967), 66.

talent.⁴ Yet along with the other "stand-out" piece in this traveler's compendium, "Rip Van Winkle," "The Legend of Sleepy Hollow" continues to exercise the American imagination to this day.⁵

At first glance, Irving's comic tale and Pushkin's somber *poema* would seem to have little in common. "The Legend of Sleepy Hollow" focuses on an itinerant Connecticut Yankee named Ichabod Crane who has taken up the post of schoolmaster in the New York community of Sleepy Hollow, a prosperous Dutch settlement in a valley by the Hudson River. A voracious consumer of the local plenty, despite the awkward lankiness betokened by his surname, and a credulous enthusiast of supernatural tales and legends whose favorite book is Cotton Mather's *History of New England Witchcraft*, Ichabod occupies a cozy, if nomadic, niche in the community:

> When the school hours were over, he was even the companion and playmate of the larger boys; and on holyday afternoons would convoy some of the smaller ones home, who happened to have pretty sisters, or good housewives for mothers, noted for the comforts of the cupboard. Indeed, it behooved him to keep on good terms with his pupils. The revenue arising from his school was small, and would have been scarcely sufficient to furnish him with daily bread, for he was a huge feeder, and though lank, had the dilating powers of an Anaconda; but to help out his maintenance, he was, according to country custom in those parts, boarded and lodged at the houses of the farmers, whose children he instructed. With these he lived successively a week at a time, thus going the rounds of the neighborhood, with all his worldly effects tied up in a cotton handkerchief.⁶

Ichabod, however, reserves his amorous attentions for one Katrina Van Tassel, the daughter of a flourishing Dutch farmer, enticed by her father's abundant

---

4   See, for example, Pochmann, "Washington Irving," 75; and John Clendenning, "Irving and the Gothic Tradition," in *A Century of Commentary on the Works of Washington Irving (1860–1974)*, ed. Andrew B. Myers (Tarrytown: Sleepy Hollow Restorations, 1976), 387.

5   The 1949 Disney animated version of "The Legend of Sleepy Hollow" (narrated by Bing Crosby) not only kept the work alive in the American cultural consciousness but also stands as testimony to the enduring appeal of Irving's tale.

6   Washington Irving, *The Sketchbook of Geoffrey Crayon, Gent.*, in *The Complete Works of Washington Irving*, ed. Haskell Springer, gen. ed. Richard Dilworth Rust (Boston: Twayne Publishers, 1978), 275.

2. Pushkin's *The Bronze Horseman* and Irving's "The Legend of Sleepy Hollow" | 19

possessions and the bounteous fertility of his lands. He finds he has a formidable rival for Katrina's affections in the local bully, Brom Van Brunt (nicknamed Brom Bones), who prowls the neighborhood with his gang of Sleepy Hollow boys, playing pranks and generally raising hell. One fateful evening, Ichabod goes to a party at the Van Tassel farm and finds his suit rejected. On his way home on a decrepit borrowed nag, he encounters the *genius loci* of Sleepy Hollow, the Headless Horseman, purportedly the ghost of a Hessian soldier decapitated by a cannon ball during a battle in the Revolutionary War who haunts the precincts of Sleepy Hollow seeking his lost head. The specter pursues Ichabod through the night, and the next day there is no trace of the hapless schoolmaster in Sleepy Hollow, leaving Brom Van Brunt free to wed the farmer's daughter. The narrative leaves us with two versions of Ichabod's fate: either he has indeed been spirited away by the supernatural rider or, scared out of his wits by Brom Van Brunt dressed up as the Headless Hessian and humiliated by Katrina's rejection, "he had changed his quarters to a distant part of the country; had kept school and studied law at the same time, had been admitted to the bar, turned politician, electioneered, written for the newspapers, and finally had been made a Justice of the Ten Pound Court."[7] Either way Ichabod survives in the old wives' tales of Sleepy Hollow lore.

As a point of departure for my discussion of the striking, if not immediately obvious, convergences between Irving's work and Pushkin's, I would like to invoke Roman Jakobson's account of what he terms the myth of the destructive statue in Pushkin's works—specifically *The Stone Guest* (Kamennyi gost'), *The Bronze Horseman*, and "The Tale of the Golden Cockerel" (Skazka o zolotom petushke)—in his "The Statue in Pushkin's Poetic Mythology." Jakobson offers us a paradigm and typology for Pushkin's appropriations of other works, and, moreover, a paradigm that emerges from the intersection of the poet's personal experiences, poetic structure and image, and, at least implicitly, social and political context. Jakobson relates the significant structural parallels respecting a statue in the three Pushkin works he surveys, all dating to the early 1830s, to the biographical facts of Pushkin's life during the period of their composition, specifically to the problems that attended the poet's marriage and his wife's ambiguous relationship with the tsar. For the sake of brevity, I shall merely cite Jakobson's topic sentences, which isolate the most significant points of similarity he identifies among the plots of the three

---

7   Irving, *Sketchbook*, 295–96.

Pushkin works and, more importantly, establish a structural model for Pushkin's literary appropriations:

1. *A man is weary, he settles down, he longs for rest, and this motif is intertwined with desire for a woman.*

2. *The statue, more precisely the being which is inseparably connected with the statue, has a supernatural, unfathomable power over this desired woman.*

3. *After a vain resistance the man perishes through the intervention of the statue, which has miraculously set itself into motion, and the woman vanishes.*[8]

Also pertinent is Jakobson's comment defending his thesis against the possible objection that Pushkin's works are borrowed from foreign sources:

> Someone may object that we are not dealing with completely independent *themes*—*The Golden Cockerel* is actually an elaboration of Irving's "Legend of the Arabian Astrologer"; *The Stone Guest* is a variation on a traditional legend and borrows diverse details from Moliere's *Festin de pierre* and the libretto of Mozart's *Don Juan*. In fact, however, a comparison of Puškin's poems with their foreign models clearly demonstrates the *originality* of his myth. From his models he selects only elements consistent with his own conception, and he transforms in his own way whatever contradicts it.[9]

I am concerned with this particular passage from Jakobson's argument for two reasons. First of all, Jakobson here gives an efficient statement describing *how* Pushkin employs his sources: he reshapes the source material to conform to his own personal "myth." Second, we should note the significant absence in Jakobson's list of a foreign source for Pushkin's masterwork. Irving's "The Legend of Sleepy Hollow" seems to fill this gap.[10]

---

8   Roman Jakobson, *Puškin and His Sculptural Myth*, trans. and ed. John Burbank (The Hague: Mouton, 1975), 4, 5, 6 (emphasis in the original—C. T. N.).

9   Jakobson, *Puškin and His Sculptural Myth*, 9–10.

10 No dearth of sources have been put forward for Pushkin's *Bronze Horseman*. Pushkin himself, in his foreword and notes to the poem, mentions the historian Vasilii Nikolaevich Berkh, the Italian journalist Francesco Algarotti, and the poets Petr Andreevich Viazemskii, Adam Mickiewicz, and Vasilii Grigor'evich Ruban as having inspired lines or sections of the poem. Critics and poets have added to this list, including Valerii Briusov, who remarked that "the image of the statue come alive might have been suggested to Pushkin by M. Iu. Viel'gorskii's story about a certain marvelous dream." Valerii Briusov, "Mednyi

2. Pushkin's *The Bronze Horseman* and Irving's "The Legend of Sleepy Hollow"

Both "The Legend of Sleepy Hollow" and *The Bronze Horseman* are constructed around the following pattern (which, while deviating somewhat from Jakobson's paradigm, adheres to the basic principle of structural borrowing it exemplifies): the central character, a petty official, constructs dreams of future happiness dependent on marriage with a desired woman. In the course of the story, these dreams are shattered. The stories both culminate in a scene in which the "hero" confronts his "rival," the figure responsible for bringing to an end the desired relationship, in the guise of a supernatural horseman, brought to life either from death (the Headless Horseman) or out of a state of inanimateness (the statue of Peter the Great).[11] The protagonists, Ichabod and Evgenii, flee their apparently fantastic pursuers through the night. In the aftermath of this adventure, both, in the end, disappear from the scene, exiled from the precincts over which the horsemen reign. Despite evident differences in tonality and treatment that mask their similarity, then, the tales follow isomorphous plot lines. There are also some striking coincidences in detail between the two tales, a comparison of which suggests how Pushkin may have adapted the material provided by Irving, not only to his own personal associations (as Jakobson proposes), but also to the historical and social realities of his cultural context.

Both Irving and Pushkin begin by locating the action in relation to a historically important river, thus setting the stage for the clash between historical forces played out in each work at the moment of confrontation between protagonist and horseman. As *The Bronze Horseman* opens, Peter stands

---

vsadnik," in his *Moi Pushkin* (Moscow: Gosudarstvennoe izdatel'stvo, 1929), 86–87. Wacław Lednicki has gone so far as to speak of the "mosaic character of the poem" in relation to its sources. Wacław Lednicki, *Pushkin's Bronze Horseman: The Story of a Masterpiece* (Berkeley: University of California Press, 1955), 19. To date, however, no one has proposed a source that might account for the plot structure of the poem as a whole. For a recent overview of possible sources that have been suggested for the poem, see Andrew Kahn, *Pushkin's* The Bronze Horseman (London: Bristol Classical Press, 1998), 98–108.

11   In this context, Lednicki makes the following observation in his discussion of *The Bronze Horseman*: "This motif of the animation of a statue or a portrait was especially popular among the romantics, since it served to illustrate their idea of the irrational magic of art. Hoffmann, Maturin, *Washington Irving*, Gogol, Odoevsky, Lermontov, and many others exploited this old motif." Lednicki, *Pushkin's Bronze Horseman*, 17 (emphasis mine— C. T. N.).

"Na beregu pustynnykh voln" (Upon the bank by barren waves), looking out over the Neva.¹² "The Legend of Sleepy Hollow" opens with the sentence:

> In the bosom of one of those spacious coves which indent the eastern shore of the Hudson, at that broad expansion of the river denominated by the ancient Dutch navigators the Tappan Zee, and where they always prudently shortened sail, and implored the protection of St. Nicholas when they crossed, there lies a small market town or rural port, which by some is called Greensburgh, but which is more generally and properly known by the name of Tarry Town.¹³

We first note Pushkin's economy and Irving's loquaciousness, a contrast that may go a long way toward explaining why the similarities between the two tales have previously been overlooked. More important, the references to the Neva and the Hudson define a basic semiotic framework within which the conflict in each work unfolds. The river serves not only as a point of entry for Europe to what had hitherto been wilderness but as a permeable boundary as well, marking the limit of the privileged space that serves as the locus of each tale and also allowing the ingress of potentially disruptive outsiders. Irving emphasizes the centrality of spatial locus by identifying his tale in the title by the geographical locale in which it takes place: "The Legend of *Sleepy Hollow*." Pushkin, in like fashion, subtitles his work "A Petersburg tale" (Peterburgskaia povest'). Moreover, arguably the statue of the Bronze Horseman itself, from which the *poema* draws its title, functions as a metonym of place.¹⁴

Both Evgenii and Ichabod, in the parallel passages in which they elaborate their visions of future marital bliss, reveal their powers of imagination. While Evgenii's musings ("Zhenit'sia? Nu . . . za chem zhe net?"; Get married? Well . . . Why shouldn't I?), in which he envisions the course of his life to the grave,

---

12 A. S. Pushkin, *Mednyi vsadnik*, in *PSS*, 5:135; A. S. Pushkin, "The Bronze Horseman," trans. Catharine T. Nepomnyashchy, in *The Ardis Anthology of Russian Romanticism*, ed. Christine Rydel (Ann Arbor: Ardis Publishers, 1984), 151.

13 Irving, *Sketchbook*, 272.

14 Interestingly, one translation appeared under the title "Bezgolovyi mertvets" (The headless dead man) thus focusing attention—as does the title *The Bronze Horseman*—on the supernatural character as the central figure in the work. On the significance of titles in Pushkin's works, see Jakobson, *Puškin and His Sculptural Myth*, 3–4. For an overview of readings of *The Bronze Horseman* that have focused on the image of Petersburg in the poem, see Kahn, *Pushkin's* The Bronze Horseman, 89–97.

2. Pushkin's *The Bronze Horseman* and Irving's "The Legend of Sleepy Hollow" 23

are pointedly prosaic, this passage is prefaced by the remark, "i razmechtalsia kak poet" (and, like a poet, set to musing), cautioning us not to dismiss his ability to dream too lightly.[15] In the corresponding passage from "The Legend of Sleepy Hollow," Ichabod reveals himself as a restless Yankee, his heart set more on the bounty Katrina represents than on the young woman herself. He confuses Katrina with the property owned by her father and dreams of the liquidation of these holdings, the transformation of the place into movable assets, disclosing an imagination as fertile as the land he covets:

> As the enraptured Ichabod fancied all this, and as he rolled his great green eyes over the fat meadow lands, the rich fields of wheat, of rye, of buckwheat, and Indian corn, and the orchards burthened with ruddy fruit, which surrounded the warm tenement of Van Tassel, his heart yearned after the damsel who was to inherit these domains, and his imagination expanded with the idea, how they might be readily turned into cash, and the money invested in immense tracts of wild land, and shingle palaces in the wilderness. Nay, his busy fancy already realized his hopes, and presented to him the blooming Katrina, with a whole family of children, mounted on the top of a waggon loaded with household trumpery, with pots and kettles dangling beneath; and he beheld himself bestriding a pacing mare, with a colt at her heels, setting out for Kentucky, Tennessee, or the Lord knows where.[16]

Both Evgenii's and Ichabod's dreams, of course, come to naught, defeated by the competing visions of their more powerful rivals.

In this context I would finally point to what to my mind is the most significant convergence between the Pushkin and Irving works: the nature and function of the "supernatural" horsemen. In both cases, the figure represents an incursion of the past into the present. Moreover, the Headless Hessian, like the Falconet statue of Peter the Great, embodies a historical moment of revolutionary social upheaval, the effects of which shape contemporary life just as the Petrine "revolution" has created not only the physical setting but the social context that determines the sad course of Evgenii's life and demise. The confrontations between Ichabod and the Headless Horseman, on the one hand, and between Evgenii and Peter, on the other, thus represent a clash of

---

15 *PSS*, 5:139; Pushkin, "The Bronze Horseman," 152.

16 Irving, *Sketchbook*, 279–80.

historical forces that, despite appearances, leaves the "victor" and his "victory" in an ethically and even ontologically and aesthetically ambiguous position. Before exploring this contention further, however, let me first lay out the evidence that Pushkin in fact read "The Legend of Sleepy Hollow."

Recognition of the indebtedness of other of Pushkin's works to Irving dates back to the poet's lifetime.[17] The American writer enjoyed a tremendous vogue in Russia in the 1820s and 1830s, and there were those among the original reviewers of Pushkin's *The Tales of Belkin* (Povesti Belkina) who were quick to note the similarities in prose technique between the two authors.[18] In the twentieth century, scholars have established more specific instances of influence. In a 1926 article, the Soviet comparatist M. P. Alekseev traced the conception of Pushkin's unfinished prose fragment "The History of the Village of Goriukhino" (Istoriia sela Goriukhina) to Irving's *A History of New York,* and in more recent years scholars have postulated sources for Pushkin's *Tales of Belkin* in Irving's *The Sketchbook of Geoffrey Crayon, Gent.* (in which, of course, "The Legend of Sleepy Hollow" also appears).[19] While other commentators have been concerned, in this context, exclusively with Pushkin's prose, Anna Akhmatova, in a well-known article originally published in 1933, extended the issue into Pushkin's poetry, identifying Irving's "The Legend of the Arabian Astrologer" as the source for Pushkin's "The Tale of the Golden Cockerel."[20]

---

17   Pushkin mentions Irving only once in passing in his critical works, in "Dzhon Tenner." (For articles concerning Pushkin's citation of Irving in "John Tanner," see the last note in this article.) For a possible second reference to Irving by Pushkin, see A. N. Nikoliukin, *Literaturnye sviazi Rossii i SShA: Stanovlenie literaturnykh kontaktov* (Moscow: Nauka, 1981), 238.

18   For a detailed discussion of Irving's reception in Russia, see Nikoliukin, *Literaturnye sviazi Rossii i SShA*, especially the chapters "Vashington Irving i rannie perevody amerikanskikh pisatelei" (180–223) and "Pushkin i amerikanskaia literatura" (224–55).

19   For an overview of this debate, see John C. Fiske, "The Soviet Controversy over Pushkin and Washington Irving," *Comparative Literature* 8, no. 1 (1955): 25–31.

20   Most notably, the Soviet scholar N. Ia. Berkovskii in 1962 identified Irving's story "The Spectre Bridegroom," also from the *Sketchbook*, as a source for Pushkin's "Metel'" (The snowstorm) suggesting that in the Belkin tale Pushkin is "polemicizing" with Irving. N. Ia. Berkovskii, "O povestiakh Belkina," in his *Stat'i o literature* (Leningrad: Gosudarstvennoe izdatel'stvo khudozhestvennoi literatury, 1962), 289–92. His argument is developed and modified by Michael R. Katz, "Pushkin's Creative Assimilation of Zhukovsky and Irving," in *The Old and New World Romanticism of Washington Irving*, ed. Stanley Brodwin (New York: Greenwood Press, 1986), 81–89. See also David M. Bethea and

2. Pushkin's *The Bronze Horseman* and Irving's "The Legend of Sleepy Hollow" | 25

Although there is no hard evidence that Pushkin read "The Legend of Sleepy Hollow," the poet would seem to have had ample opportunity to do so. Well before the first Russian translation of Irving's works, his *Sketchbook* became available to the upper crust of the Russian reading public in an 1822 French translation of the fourth edition of Irving's work by Albane Delpeux and Comte Joseph Villetard.[21] Moreover, in April of 1823, the *English Literary Journal of Moscow*, which published parallel texts in English and French, printed an article entitled "The Literature of North America," which included an extensive paraphrase of and excerpts from "The Legend of Sleepy Hollow." The first Russian translation of "The Legend of Sleepy Hollow" was published in issues 11 and 12 of *Moskovskii Telegraf* for 1826. The translator, although not credited in the issues of the journal containing the translation, was the journal's editor Nikolai Polevoi, and the translation was reprinted in his *Novellas and Literary Excerpts* (Povesti i literaturnye otryvki).[22] Pushkin might have read the Irving work in any of these editions.

Although the most persuasive evidence supporting the contention that Irving may have in some sense provided Pushkin with a morphological impetus for his writing of *The Bronze Horseman* remains circumstantial, it is nonetheless convincing. Not only have scholars already argued cogently for Irving's *Sketchbook* as a source for other Pushkin works, but Pushkin wrote all those works on which the influence of Irving has been postulated during roughly the same period, the years bounded by the Boldino autumns of 1830 and 1834. (*The Bronze Horseman* was written during Pushkin's stay at Boldino in

---

Sergei Davydov, "Pushkin's Saturnine Cupid: The Poetics of Parody in *The Tales of Belkin*," *PMLA* 96 (1981): 8–21; A. A. Akhmatova, "Posledniaia skazka Pushkina," *Zvezda* 1 (1933): 161–76; M. P. Alekseev, "Istoriia sela Goriukhina," *Pushkin: Stat'i i materialy* 2 (Odessa, 1926): 70–87; Carl R. Proffer, "Washington Irving in Russia: Pushkin, Gogol, Marlinsky," *Comparative Literature* 20, no. 4 (1968): 329–42.

21 A copy of this translation in two volumes, entitled *Esquisses morales et littéraires, ou Observations sur les Moeurs, les Usages et la Littérature des Anglois et des Américains*, was among the books by Irving contained in Pushkin's library. "The Legend of Sleepy Hollow" (translated as "La legende de la vallée somnifère") appears on pages 271–326 of the second volume of the Delpeux and Villetard translation. B. L. Modzalevskii, "Biblioteka A. S. Pushkina," *Pushkin i ego sovremenniki: Materialy i issledovaniia* 9–10 (1910): 256 (#1018), reports that the second volume is opened only through page 300, but, since the volumes possibly came to Pushkin's possession from A. I. Turgenev, it is not clear who opened the pages. It is therefore not possible to know whether Pushkin read the story.

22 Nikolai Polevoi, *Povesti i literaturnye otryvki* (Moscow: [n. p.], 1829).

November of 1833.) During these years, Pushkin began to evince increasing interest in prose composition, and Irving's works seem to have served him as one source of inspiration. Thus, to return to Jakobson, in his article discussed above, elaborating on Akhmatova's argument for Irving as a source for "The Tale of the Golden Cockerel," he suggests that Irving's "The Legend of the Arabian Astrologer" might in fact have supplied Pushkin with the epithet "the bronze horseman" as well:

> In the model the astrologer tells the sovereign about a metal cockerel, but he makes him a "bronze horseman." Puškin read Irving's tale in 1833, and his first attempt at writing it in verse adjoins the first drafts of the Petersburg story about Evgenij in his manuscript. The figure of the bronze horseman became the main character of that poetic story, and only the cast cockerel remained for the tale, which was not realized until a year later. The combination "bronze tsar," not "bronze horseman," as one reads in Irving, appears in Mickiewicz's "Monument of Peter the Great," which inspired Puškin's description of the Falconet statue. Sometimes another author's work which is the starting point for one of Puškin's creations simultaneously provides a stimulus for another of his related works.[23]

Jakobson's argument here becomes all the more significant in the light of my postulation that another Irving work was crucial to the conception of *The Bronze Horseman*.

While the evidence that Pushkin read "The Legend of Sleepy Hollow" is, to my mind, compelling, I also believe that precisely because the two works represent analogous moments in the evolution of their respective indigenous literary traditions, their juxtaposition would be rewarding on its own merits quite apart from the question of "influence." In other words, invoking the distinction with which I opened this article, I will switch my focus at this point from influence to intertextuality. In this context, the enduring appeal of Pushkin's and Irving's works in their homelands bespeaks the success with which each writer gave artistic expression to the "insoluble antinomies" shaping his native culture as well as his writing career.[24]

---

23   Jakobson, *Puškin and His Sculptural Myth*, 10.

24   Clifford Geertz, "Ideology as a Cultural System," in his *The Interpretation of Cultures* (New York: Basic Books, 1973), 203.

Tellingly, the histories of the critical receptions of *The Bronze Horseman* and "The Legend of Sleepy Hollow" have each been characterized by a persistent difference of opinion, centering on the confrontation between protagonist and horseman. In both cases the related issues of "who wins" and, concomitantly, of what the two rivals, beyond their own persons, represent, has occupied center stage. Critical debates have focused on how the works explore the consequences of historical rupture—the Petrine "revolution" and the American Revolution—as they shape the lives of the tales' "present-day" protagonists. Thus, scholars of *The Bronze Horseman* have been virtually unanimous in viewing the showdown between Evgenii and the statue of Peter the Great as representing the inevitable clash of interests between the individual and the state, while disagreeing sharply on the question of which of the two figures prevails (ethically if not historically) and over where Pushkin's sympathies lie.[25] Scholars of Irving's "Legend" have been equally divided in locating the author's bias with either Ichabod or Brom Bones as incarnations of forces shaping the young American culture. I would suggest that it may well have been precisely the literary embodiment of historical strains with competing claims to legitimacy that attracted Pushkin to Irving's fiction.[26] Key

---

25   Here, of course, I am somewhat oversimplifying. Valerii Briusov identified three major trends in criticism, pointing out that from the beginning critics had been inclined "to see in the images of Evgenii and Peter personifications, symbols of two principles." Briusov, "Mednyi vsadnik," 64–65. David Bethea, in his own thoughtful article on what he terms the "dialogic confrontation" between the traditions of European statuary and Russian heraldry in *The Bronze Horseman*, begins by summarizing Briusov's argument and pointing out that most critics of the poem have tended to "take sides." David M. Bethea, "The Role of the *Eques* in Puškin's *Bronze Horseman*," in *Puškin Today*, ed. David M. Bethea (Bloomington: Indiana University Press, 1993), 117, 99.

26   I would add here in passing a subject certainly worthy of further study. While critics have been inclined in the cases of both works to cast their interpretations in terms of binary oppositions, in each case there is a "third term" that stands in ambiguous relationship to the horseman—the elemental force of nature in *The Bronze Horseman* and the complex of associations surrounding the Hessian mercenary in "Legend." Note, for example, that Richard Gregg has contended in relation to *The Bronze Horseman*: "The basic dynamics of the poem is, then, ternary (not binary, as is commonly claimed)." Richard Gregg, "The Nature of Nature and the Nature of Eugene in *The Bronze Horseman*," *Slavic and East European Journal* 1, no. 2 (Summer 1977): 170. Arguably it is precisely this structural tension between binary and ternary relationships that gives the two works much of their interpretive richness.

concerns in Irving scholarship, then, offer a new perspective from which to read *The Bronze Horseman*.

As in the case of *The Bronze Horseman*, there has been relatively little dispute in the scholarship devoted to Irving's "Legend" over the opposed sociohistorical vectors, tensions created by the emergence of the new American republic, that the story dramatizes. To cite Lloyd M. Daigrepont: "Generally, critics have probed the tale's portrayal of the conflict between civilization (or progress) and the idyllic dream of a new Eden in the American landscape."[27] In one of the passages from "Legend" most frequently adduced by critics in this connection, Irving's tale figures this opposition in terms of the threat posed to the peaceful landscape by flood waters:

> I mention this peaceful spot [Sleepy Hollow] with all possible laud; for it is in such little retired Dutch valleys, found here and there embosomed in the great state of New York, that population, manners, and customs, remain fixed; while the great *torrent* of migration and improvement, which is making such incessant changes in other parts of this restless country, sweeps by them unobserved.[28]

In this context, Donald Ringe directs particular attention to "a fundamental regional conflict—the mutual hostility between New York and New England. [. . .] Ichabod Crane is clearly a Connecticut Yankee invading—and threatening—a New York Dutch society."[29] In his most succinct statement of the competing values that feed this regional enmity, Ringe argues that "to oppose the material values they see in the Yankee desire for change, improvement, and profit, the New York writers affirm a stable society that places its emphasis on order, tradition, and the family values that accompany social stability."[30] In the same vein, Robert V. Wells plumbs Irving's work for "signs of what was going to happen in the nineteenth century when a commercial, industrial world

---

27   Lloyd M. Daigrepont, "Ichabod Crane: Inglorious Man of Letters," *Early American Literature* 19, no. 1 (Spring 1984): 68.

28   Irving, *Sketchbook*, 274 (emphasis mine—C. T. N.).

29   Donald A. Ringe, "New York and New England: Irving's Criticism of American Society," *American Literature* 38, no. 4 (January 1967): 455.

30   Ringe, "New York and New England," 459.

replaced more traditional agrarian patterns."[31] In sum, then, critics have seen Ichabod Crane and Brom Bones, rivals for the hand of Katrina Van Tassel—"whose virtues are those of the settled landscape itself"—as embodiments of two competing social orders, one that cultivates land and lore and the other that consumes it, the former destined by history to be washed away.[32]

Many critics of Irving's "Legend," however, go beyond socio-historical analysis to view the story as more specifically concerned with the plight of American literature and the American writer caught in the forces of social transformation. Certainly, "Legend" invites such approaches, for it is very much a tale about tales, just as Sleepy Hollow itself is a place defined by the origination and preservation of stories:

> From the listless repose of the place, and the peculiar character of its inhabitants, who are descendants from the original Dutch settlers, this sequestered glen has long been known by the name of SLEEPY HOLLOW, and its rustic lads are called the Sleepy Hollow Boys throughout all the neighbouring country. A drowsy, dreamy influence seems to hang over the land, and to pervade the very atmosphere. Some say that the place was bewitched by a high German doctor during the early days of the settlement; others, that an old Indian chief, the prophet or wizard of his tribe, held his powwows there before the country was discovered by Master Hendrick Hudson. Certain it is, the place still continues under the sway of some witching power, that holds a spell over the minds of the good people, causing them to walk in a continual reverie. They are given to all kinds of marvellous beliefs; are subject to trances and visions, and frequently see strange sights, and hear music and voices in the air. The whole neighbourhood abounds with local tales, haunted spots, and twilight superstitions; stars shoot and meteors glare oftener across the valley than in any other part of the country, and the night mare, with her whole nine fold, seems to make it the favourite scene of her gambols.[33]

---

31 Robert V. Wells, "While Rip Napped: Social Change in Late Eighteenth-Century New York," *New York History* 71, no. 1 (January 1990): 18–19. I should note that, in this particular part of his article, Wells is actually talking about "Rip Van Winkle." His article as a whole, however, explores how both of Irving's stories reflect the social transformation of postrevolutionary New York.

32 Allen Guttmann, "Washington Irving and the Conservative Imagination," *American Literature* 36, no. 2 (May 1964): 171.

33 Irving, *Sketchbook*, 272–73.

Yet, as is suggested later in the narrative, Sleepy Hollow stands threatened by the "torrent of migration" shaping life in the New America:

> Local tales and superstitions thrive best in these sheltered, long settled retreats; but are trampled under foot, by the shifting throng that forms the population of most of our country places. Besides, there is no encouragement for ghosts in most of our villages, for they have scarce had time to finish their first nap, and turn themselves in their graves, before their surviving friends have travelled away from the neighbourhood, so that when they turn out of a night to walk the rounds, they have no acquaintance left to call upon. This is perhaps the reason why we so seldom hear of ghosts except in our long established Dutch communities.[34]

Drawing on such passages in Irving's tale, scholars have tended to view the story as a parable of American literary culture, a figuration of the cultural tensions that shaped Irving's own career as a writer. Most frequently, Ichabod Crane emerges from such exegeses as a writer or "ersatz man of letters" defined and ultimately defeated by the bipolar tensions created by the cultural growing pains of the new nation.[35] These pains included the absence of a past comparable to the rich cultural legacy of Europe, the concomitant threat to the stability of ethnic communities rich in folklore posed by the mobility of a frontier-oriented life, the passing of the European patronage system and the growing commercialism (and even "feminization") of American literature, and the challenge posed to imagination by a Protestant ethic privileging practicality and utility.[36] One critic has suggested that it is Brom Bones who is the true bearer of the new American creativity and that the confrontation thus becomes a contest of rival artists.[37] Virtually all these commentators, however,

---

34   Irving, *Sketchbook*, 289.

35   Daigrepont, "Ichabod Crane," 74.

36   See, for example, Terence Martin, "Rip, Ichabod, and the American Imagination," *American Literature* 31, no. 2 (1959): 137–49; Daniel Hoffman, "Prefigurations: 'The Legend of Sleepy Hollow,'" in his *Form and Fable in American Fiction* (New York: Oxford University Press, 1961), 83–96; Robert A. Bone, "Irving's Headless Hessian: Prosperity and the Inner Life," *American Quarterly* 15, no. 2, pt. 1 (Summer 1963): 167–75; Daigrepont, "Ichabod Crane," 68–81. Irving himself cast a jealous eye on the cultural riches of Europe's past in "The Author's Account of Himself" that opens *The Sketchbook* (9): "My native country was full of youthful promise: Europe was rich in the accumulated treasures of age."

37   Daigrepont, "Ichabod Crane," 75–77.

are united in viewing the tale as having a (perhaps unduly) optimistic ending as concerns the prospects for the future of American literature.

We might do well to emulate Irving's critics in suggesting that the prevailing socio-political, historical, and even religious readings of *The Bronze Horseman* may yet not exhaust the interpretive possibilities of the poem. I have argued elsewhere that there is sufficient evidence in Pushkin's poem that Evgenii may be read as a poet figure.[38] I will not repeat that argument here, but will merely adduce briefly the evidence I believe supports a reading that views Evgenii as a "writer" caught in the same net of constraints that conditioned Pushkin's own literary endeavors. Pace any number of scholars on *The Bronze Horseman*, I am not suggesting that Evgenii be read "autobiographically" (although autobiographical parallels between Pushkin and his protagonist support my argument).[39] Evgenii "is" no more Pushkin than the comically preposterous Ichabod Crane "is" Washington Irving. Rather, I am suggesting that Pushkin placed Evgenii in a situation with unquestionable resonances with his own literary context.

In this regard we must first recognize that the confrontation between Evgenii and the tsar, autocrat and subject, constitutes at least as much a *writer's* problem—that is, specifically a defining condition of the literary culture of Pushkin's day—as it does a purely political issue. Pushkin's own tormented relationship with the tsar is too well documented to demand revisitation here, except to recall the extent to which it dominated Pushkin's literary fortunes. In this respect, *The Bronze Horseman* offers a characteristic case in point. Pushkin was counting on the profits from the sale of the works he hoped to produce at Boldino in the autumn of 1833 to ease his ever-precarious financial position, as evidenced by the letter he wrote to the tsar on July 30 of that year requesting leave to absent himself from the capital:

---

38 See Catharine Theimer Nepomnyashchy, "The Poet, History, and the Supernatural: A Note on Puškin's 'The Poet' and *The Bronze Horseman*," in *The Supernatural in Slavic and Baltic Literature: Essays in Honor of Victor Terras*, ed. Amy Mandelker and Roberta Reeder (Columbus: Slavica Publishers, 1988), 34–46 (reprinted in this collection, pp. 2–15—eds.).

39 "Autobiographical" readings of Evgenii rest on the postulation of a "genetic" relationship between *The Bronze Horseman* and poetic fragments, most notably "The Genealogy of My Hero" (Rodoslovnaia moego geroia) and "My Genealogy" (Moia rodoslovnaia), that Pushkin drafted during the early 1830s. See, for example, Lednicki, *Pushkin's Bronze Horseman*.

> In the course of the past two years I have been occupied with historical research alone, not writing a single line of the purely literary. I must spend a month or two in complete isolation, in order to rest up from my very important occupations and to finish a book I began a long time ago, and which will bring me money I need. I am myself sorry to waste time on vain pursuits, but what can I do? They alone bring me independence and a means of living with my family in Petersburg, where my labors, thanks to the sovereign, have a more important and useful goal.[40]

Nicholas I's fundamental objections to the publication of *The Bronze Horseman* dashed Pushkin's hopes. Thus, while Irving lamented the absence of aristocratic patronage of the arts left at the mercy of the growing commercialism of American literature, Pushkin in essence found himself between these two worlds: his dependence on the tsar (a vestige of the old patronage system) and his need to live primarily off his own works in a cultural economy that favored potboiler prose over "gentleman poets."[41] Moreover, Pushkin's distaste for the "rabble" of the reading public, given voice most famously in such works as his "Conversation between the Bookseller and the Poet" (Razgovor knigoprodavtsa s poetom), are echoed in *The Bronze Horseman* as well. If Evgenii is to be viewed as a representative of the "people," then the callous indifference of the Petersburg *narod* to his fate appears all the more jarring, particularly Pushkin's insistence on its mercantile nature:

> В порядок прежний всё вошло.
> Уже по улицам свободным
> С своим бесчувствием холодным
> Ходил народ. Чиновный люд,
> Покинув свой ночной приют,

---

40 *PSS*, 15:70.

41 It is notable in this context that both Irving and Pushkin began as "gentleman" writers and were forced to become "professionals." What might be viewed as a nostalgia for a more aristocratic past is registered in the names of both of their protagonists. Daniel Hoffman observes in this connection: "Ichabod Crane is a sorry symbol of learning, of culture, of sophistication, of a decayed religious faith, of an outworn order in the world. His very name suggests decrepitude: 'And she named him Ichabod, saying, The glory is departed from Israel' (I Sam. iv. 21)." Hoffman, "Prefigurations," 94. In like fashion, the name Evgenii, broken down into its Greek roots, suggests "well-born," which only serves to underscore by contrast the lowly state into which Pushkin's protagonist has fallen.

2. Pushkin's *The Bronze Horseman* and Irving's "The Legend of Sleepy Hollow" | 33

> На службу шел. Торгаш отважный,
> Не унывая, открывал
> Невой ограбленный подвал,
> Сбираясь свой убыток важный
> На ближнем выместить.

> And order was again restored.
> With cold insensitivity
> The masses walked upon the streets
> So recently freed by the waters.
> Emerging from their past night's shelters,
> Officials hurried to their jobs.
> The fearless merchant, not despairing,
> Opened up his plundered cellar
> And counted up his heavy losses
> For which he planned to wreak revenge.⁴²

In the final analysis, Evgenii *is* a "writer," a clerk who "serves" (*sluzhit*) the state for money, a comedown for the scion of a noble family whose name once "pod perom Karamzina / V rodnykh predan'iakh prozvuchalo" (beneath Karamzin's pen / Sounded in native lore). This is a sad commentary on the writer's abasement, not only before the public, but also before the state for his livelihood.⁴³

Let us then turn to the crucial confrontation between Evgenii and the statue. First of all, we should note that Evgenii's challenge to the statue—"Dobro, stroitel' chudotvornyi! . . . Uzho tebe!" (Just wait, proud miracle creator!)—constitutes the sole instance of direct speech in the poem, and his words are specifically addressed to Peter the Great as the miraculous builder of the city, the poser, dare I say, of a creative challenge.⁴⁴ The Bronze Horseman's response to Evgenii's challenge lends itself to two possible interpretations: either the statue really comes alive or the event transpires only in Evgenii's imagination. I would argue, however, that the latter, "naturalistic" explanation yields a richer reading of the poem. If the statue comes alive only in Evgenii's mind, then the poor clerk becomes a poet surrogate who not only forces a reaction from the

---

42 *PSS*, 5:145; Pushkin, "The Bronze Horseman," 154. We should also note that the ships Peter's "window into Europe" brings to his imperial city are, at least by implication, *merchant* ships.

43 *PSS*, 5:138.

44 *PSS*, 5:148; Pushkin, "The Bronze Horseman," 155.

hitherto impassive statue but in essence "rewrites" Peter in the Gothic mode, "displacing" the statue out of material reality into the realm of the poet's fantasy. It would seem, then, that the *poema* presents us with two symmetrical creative acts—Peter's at the beginning and Evgenii's at the end—the juxtaposition of which suggests a mode of being for the writer in the autocratic state. Thus, Pushkin seems to suggest, the creative imagination may yield to political reality on the historical plane—Peter's city will remain standing long after Evgenii's fleeting moment of poetic inspiration has passed. Yet, at the same time, the artistic act—intangible though its fruits may be—has the power to transform, to "displace" the matter of the historical world. In the confrontation between poet and tsar, the poet emerges victorious in the invisible space of the mind.

Let me conclude by reiterating that, hardly surprisingly, both Pushkin and Irving address in what are among their most enduring works the forces that shaped and circumscribed their own careers as writers, standing at the beginning of the emergence of their national literatures on the world stage, haunted by the specter of the over-towering legacy of the western European cultural past. Clearly the threats posed to literature by their respective cultures were different, as history has generously demonstrated. Equally clearly, Pushkin's knowledge of America was limited and his attitude toward the new democracy, as he would express it several years after completing *The Bronze Horseman* and only shortly before his death, mixed grudging admiration with distinct hostility.[45] Yet in Irving, it would seem, he found a kindred spirit, or,

---

45 Pushkin read his best documented sources on the United States—John Tanner, *A Narrative of the Captivity and Adventures of John Tanner during Thirty Years Residence among the American Indians* (French translation, 1835); Alexis de Tocqueville, *De la démocratie en Amérique* (first two volumes, 1836); and Gustave de Beaumont, *Marie, ou l'esclavage aux États-Unis* (1836)—only after completing *The Bronze Horseman*. On Pushkin's attitudes toward America and specifically on his "John Tanner" article, see J. Thomas Shaw, "Pushkin on America and His Principal Sources: His 'John Tanner,'" in his *Collected Works*, vol. 1, *Pushkin: Poet and Man of Letters and His Prose* (Los Angeles: Charles Schlacks, Jr., 1995), 231–59; Glynn Barratt, "Pushkin's America: A Survey of the Sources," *Canadian Slavonic Papers* 15, no. 3 (Autumn 1973): 274–97; B. Mar'ianov, "Ob odnom primechanii k stat'e A. S. Pushkina 'Dzhon Tenner,'" *Russkaia literatura* 1 (1962): 64–67; Mark Al'tshuller, "Pushkin o problemakh demokratii ('Dzhon Tenner')," *Russian Language Journal* 38, nos. 129–30 (Winter-Spring 1984): 69–78; and M. P. Alekseev, "K stat'e Pushkina 'Dzhon Tenner,'" in his *Pushkin i mirovaia literatura* (Leningrad: Nauka, 1987), 542–48. Lednicki, in support of his hypothesis that *The Bronze Horseman* expresses Pushkin's belief that Peter the Great's reforms caused the decline of the old Russian nobility, cites a letter to Petr

perhaps more to the point, a fellow writer caught, like himself, in the growing pains of a young literary culture to which he, like Pushkin after him, gave enduring shape through his works.

Works Cited

Akhmatova, A. A. "Posledniaia skazka Pushkina." *Zvezda* 1 (1933): 161–76.

Alekseev, M. P. "Istoriia sela Goriukhina." *Pushkin: Stat'i i materialy* 2 (Odessa, 1926): 70–87.

———. "K stat'e Pushkina 'Dzhon Tenner.'" In his *Pushkin i mirovaia literatura*, 542–48. Leningrad: Nauka, 1987.

Al'tshuller, Mark. "Pushkin o problemakh demokratii ('Dzhon Tenner')." *Russian Language Journal* 38, nos. 129–30 (Winter-Spring 1984): 69–78.

Barratt, Glynn. "Pushkin's America: A Survey of the Sources." *Canadian Slavonic Papers* 15, no. 3 (Autumn 1973): 274–97.

Barthes, Roland. "The Death of the Author." In his *Image-Music-Text*, translated by Stephen Heath, 142–48. New York: Fontana Press, 1977.

Berkovskii, N. Ia. "O povestiakh Belkina." In his *Stat'i o literature*, 242–356. Leningrad: Gosudarstvennoe izdatel'stvo khudozhestvennoi literatury, 1962.

Bethea, David M., and Sergei Davydov. "Pushkin's Saturnine Cupid: The Poetics of Parody in *The Tales of Belkin*." *PMLA* 96 (1981): 8–21.

Bethea, David M. "The Role of the *Eques* in Puškin's *Bronze Horseman*." In *Puškin Today*, edited by David M. Bethea, 99–118. Bloomington: Indiana University Press, 1993.

Briusov, Valerii. "Mednyi vsadnik." In his *Moi Pushkin*, 63–94. Moscow: Gosudarstvennoe izdatel'stvo, 1929.

Iakovlevich Chaadaev Pushkin wrote but did not send on October 19, 1836 deploring both the "chûte de la noblesse" in Russia and democracy in America: "Voilà déjà 140 ans que la Tabl' o rangakh balaye la noblesse; et c'est l'Emp[ereur] actuel, qui le premier a posé une digue (bien faible encore) contre le débordement d'une démocratie, pire que celle de l'Amérique" (The table of ranks has been sweeping away the nobility for 140 years now, and it is the present emperor who is the first to have put up a dike, still very weak, against the torrent of a democracy worse than that of America). *PSS*, 16:260–61. (Lednicki in *Pushkin's Bronze Horseman*, 65, quotes a very similar excerpt from Pushkin's 1832 outline "On the Nobility" [O dvorianstve]—eds.)

Clendenning, John. "Irving and the Gothic Tradition." In *A Century of Commentary on the Works of Washington Irving (1860–1974)*, edited by Andrew B. Myers, 379–87. Tarrytown: Sleepy Hollow Restorations, 1976.

Daigrepont, Lloyd M. "Ichabod Crane: Inglorious Man of Letters." *Early American Literature* 19, no. 1 (Spring 1984): 68–81.

Fiske, John C. "The Soviet Controversy over Pushkin and Washington Irving." *Comparative Literature* 8, no. 1 (1955): 25–31.

Geertz, Clifford. *The Interpretation of Cultures*. New York: Basic Books, 1973.

Gregg, Richard. "The Nature of Nature and the Nature of Eugene in *The Bronze Horseman*." *Slavic and East European Journal* 1, no 2 (Summer 1977): 167–79.

Guttmann, Allen. "Washington Irving and the Conservative Imagination." *American Literature* 36, no. 2 (May 1964): 165–73.

Hutcheon, Linda. "Literary Borrowing . . . and Stealing: Plagiarism, Sources, Influences, and Intertexts." *English Studies in Canada* 12, no. 2 (1986): 229–39.

Irving, Washington. *The Sketchbook of Geoffrey Crayon, Gent*. In *The Complete works of Washington Irving*, edited by Haskell Springer, general editor Richard Dilworth Rust, vol. 8, 272–97. Boston: Twayne Publishers, 1978.

Iser, Wolfgang. "The Reading Process: A Phenomenological Approach." In *Reader-Response Criticism: From Formalism to Post-Structuralism*, edited by Jane P. Tompkins, 50–69. Baltimore: John Hopkins University Press, 1980.

Jakobson, Roman. "The Statue in Puškin's Poetic Mythology." In his *Puškin and His Sculptural Myth*, translated and edited by John Burbank, 1–44. The Hague: Mouton, 1975.

Kahn, Andrew. *Pushkin's* The Bronze Horseman. London: Bristol Classical Press, 1998.

Katz, Michael R. "Pushkin's Creative Assimilation of Zhukovsky and Irving." In *The Old and New World Romanticism of Washington Irving*, edited by Stanley Brodwin, 81–89. New York: Greenwood Press, 1986.

Lednicki, Wacław. *Pushkin's Bronze Horseman: The Story of a Masterpiece*. Berkeley: University of California Press, 1955.

Mar'ianov, B. "Ob odnom primechanii k stat'e A. S. Pushkina 'Dzhon Tenner.'" *Russkaia literatura* 1 (1962): 64–67.

Martin, Terence. "Rip, Ichabod, and the American Imagination." *American Literature* 31, no. 2 (1959): 137–49.

Modzalevskii, B. L. "Biblioteka A. S. Pushkina." *Pushkin i ego sovremenniki: Materialy i issledovaniia* 9–10 (1910): 1–441.

Nepomnyashchy, Catharine Theimer. "The Poet, History, and the Supernatural: A Note on Puškin's 'The Poet' and *The Bronze Horseman*." In *The Supernatural in Slavic and Baltic Literature: Essays in Honor of Victor Terras*, edited by Amy Mandelker and Roberta Reeder, 34–46. Columbus: Slavica Publishers, 1988. (Reprinted in this collection, pp. 2–15—eds.)

Nikoliukin, A. N. *Literaturnye sviazi Rossii i SShA: Stanovlenie literaturnykh kontaktov*. Moscow: Nauka, 1981.

Pochmann, Henry A. "Washington Irving: Amateur or Professional?" In *Essays on American Literature in Honor of Jay B. Hubbell*, edited by Clarence Gohdes, 63–76. Durham: Duke University Press, 1967.

Polevoi, Nikolai. *Povesti i literaturnye otryvki*. Moscow: [n. p.], 1829.

Proffer, Carl R. "Washington Irving in Russia: Pushkin, Gogol, Marlinsky." *Comparative Literature* 20, no. 4 (1968): 329–42.

Pushkin, A. S. *The Bronze Horseman*. Translated by Catharine T. Nepomnyashchy. In *The Ardis Anthology of Russian Romanticism*, edited by Christine Rydel, 151–55. Ann Arbor: Ardis Publishers, 1984.

———. *Polnoe sobranie sochinenii v shestnadtsati tomakh*. Moscow: Izdatel'stvo AN SSSR, 1937–1959.

Ringe, Donald A. "New York and New England: Irving's Criticism of American Society." *American Literature* 38, no. 4 (January 1967): 455–67.

Shaw, J. Thomas "Pushkin on America and His Principal Sources: His 'John Tanner.'" In his *Collected Works*, vol. 1, *Pushkin: Poet and Man of Letters and His Prose*, 231–59. Los Angeles: Charles Schlacks, Jr., 1995.

Wells, Robert V. "While Rip Napped: Social Change in Late Eighteenth-Century New York." *New York History* 71, no. 1 (January 1990): 4–23.

3

A Note on Curiosity in Pushkin's *The Blackamoor of Peter the Great*

> There is no educated traveler passing through Leiden who has not seen the section of a Negro's *reticulum mucosum* dissected by the famous Ruysch. The remaining part of this membrane was removed by Peter the Great to a cabinet of curiosities in St. Petersburg. This membrane is black; and it is this that gives negroes the inherent blackness that they lose only in the case of illnesses that can tear this tissue, allowing the fat to escape from its cells and causing white patches below the skin.
>
> —Voltaire, *Essay on Universal History, the Manners, and Spirit of Nations*

> My mother's genealogy is even more curious. Her grandfather was a Negro....
>
> —A. S. Pushkin, [The Beginning of an Autobiography]

Curiosity is indeed a curious concept. It is that which prompts us to look beyond established limits. It leads to the opening up of new horizons in knowledge and therefore may represent a challenge to established authority and received opinion. Curiosity may, then, be either good or bad depending on the point of view from which it is apprehended, a function of what Neil Kenny has termed its "extraordinary moral reversibility."[1] In this context, as far as the historical fortunes of the concept are concerned, the seventeenth century witnessed a distinct shift in Western Europe, a shift particularly noticeable in associations of curiosity and travel. Thus, Christian K. Zacher, in his *Curiosity and Pilgrimage,* points to the distinction drawn by medieval Christian thinkers between two understandings of knowledge: *sapientia,* "knowledge of things divine, the attainment of God, the goal Christians must strive for," and *scientia,* "human knowledge, speculative and faulty, inferior to *sapientia*."[2] "Christian thinkers regarded sinful man's pursuit of *scientia* as a flirtation with *curiositas*" and most definitely not a proper motive for pilgrimage: "*curiositas* is a morally useless, dangerous diversion for wayfaring Christians."[3] The age of exploration, though, spurred at least in part by curiosity, placed Europeans in contact with radically different peoples and cultures and thereby gave impetus to the Renaissance rehabilitation of the ancient distinction between *bona* and *mala curiositas.* By the seventeenth century, curiosity had undergone a pronounced change in valence from negative to positive (or at least neutral).[4] One commentator has identified curiosity as "a defining element of the modern age."[5]

I would like to express my appreciation to Robert Maguire, Catherine O'Neil, Ludmilla Trigos, Ronald Meyer, and the two anonymous readers for *The Pushkin Review,* all of whom made very helpful suggestions that have been incorporated into the final version of this article—C. T. N. The epigraph from Voltaire was translated by Professor Nicholas Cronk, Director of the Voltaire Foundation. We are very grateful for his help. This article initially appeared in *Pushkin Review/Пушкинский вестник* 4 (2001): 37–50. Reproduced by permission of Slavica Press and Olga Nepomnyashchy—eds.

1 Neil Kenny, *Curiosity in Early Modern Europe: Word Histories* (Wiesbaden: Harrassowitz Verlag, 1998), 14.

2 Christian K. Zacher, *Curiosity and Pilgrimage: The Literature of Discovery in Fourteenth-Century England* (Baltimore: Johns Hopkins University Press, 1976), 19. See also Dennis Quinn, "Polypragmosyne in the Renaissance: Ben Jonson": "Early and medieval Christian writers condemned curiosity as a vice because, as an excess in the order of learning, it constitutes distraction from the main business of the Christian—salvation of one's soul." *The Ben Jonson Journal: Literary Contexts in the Age of Elizabeth, James and Charles* 2 (1995): 158.

3 Zacher, *Curiosity and Pilgrimage,* 20, 21.

4 Kenny, *Curiosity in Early Modern Europe,* 16. According to Barbara Benedict, "Curiosity is a historical phenomenon that crests when opportunities and commodities that encourage and manifest it crest: the late seventeenth and eighteenth centuries." Barbara Benedict, *Curiosity: A Cultural History of Early Modern Inquiry* (Chicago: University of Chicago Press, 2001), 8.

5 Quinn observes that "the most extensive study of curiosity is that of Hans Blumenberg in *The Legitimacy of the Modern Age.* He, correctly, I think, identifies curiosity as a defining element of the modern age," "Polypragmosyne in the Renaissance," 166.

Even if the secularization of knowledge, travel, and encounters between peoples tipped the balance toward a more positive apperception of curiosity, the term remained slippery, resisting reduction to facile generalizations. Thus, Kenny points to "another kind of semantic reversibility [that] also characterized 'curiosity': its strange capacity, after centuries of mainly denoting desiring subjects, to start denoting desired objects too in the seventeenth century."[6] This blurring of the line between the curiosity of the observer and of the curio, like the "wonder" Stephen Greenblatt identifies as the defining experience of Europeans first encountering and appropriating the New World, suggests the risky, potentially subversive permeability of the boundary between self and other—and the attendant fascination with and commodification of the exotic and monstrous.[7] Thus, Greenblatt observes:

> European voyagers crate up artifacts that they have purchased or stolen or received as gifts, and they take unsuspecting or undefended natives captive, not only in order to serve as interpreters but in order to ship them back for display at home. Such displays—Columbus's Arawaks or Frobisher's Eskimos—appear to have been immensely popular, and by the early seventeenth century could figure as sources of income. Hence Shakespeare's Trinculo dreams about getting the savage Caliban back to England. "Holiday fools," he is sure, will pay handsomely to see the monster: "When they will not give a doit to relieve a lame beggar, they will lay out ten to see a dead Indian" (*The Tempest*, act 2, scene 2, 30–32).[8]

Barbara M. Benedict, writing on curiosity in eighteenth-century Britain, captures the ambiguity of the relationship between the curious spectator and the curious display. She writes of

---

6   Kenny, *Curiosity in Early Modern Europe*, 15.

7   "Wonder effects the crucial break with an other that can only be described, only witnessed, in the language and images of sameness. It erects an obstacle that is at the same time an agent of arousal. For the blockage that constitutes a recognition of distance excites a desire to cross the threshold, break through the barrier, enter the space of the alien." Stephen Greenblatt, *Marvelous Possessions: The Wonder of the New World* (Chicago: University of Chicago Press, 1991), 135. This quote should give some indication of the resonance between curiosity and Greenblatt's "wonder" as well as of the subtlety of his argument about the complexities of the meeting of alien semiotic systems framed by unequal power relations.

8   Greenblatt, *Marvelous Possessions*, 121–22.

> a practice already firmly established in the world of fairs and shows. There, human oddities or "freaks"—limbless artists, giants and dwarves, those with strange appetites or features—already had their curiosity value enhanced by the biographical flourishes provided by their own publicity or by their touts and managers. In print, however, people claiming irregular bodies relied on biography for their claims to marvelous status. [...] These biographical wonders enact through the reader's complicity the thrill of comparison in which observers confirm their normality by contrasting themselves with human marvels.[9]

I would suggest that the very instability of the term "curiosity"—whether it be a spur to voyeurism or the dignified acquisition of knowledge, whether it refer to the observer or the observed, whether it serve commerce, entertainment, scholarship, or art—marks it as a nexus of the growth pains of empire and modernity and of the consequent anxieties about boundaries and even about the very limits of the human in Western Europe at the time.

So what then of Russia and, more specifically, of Pushkin? Yuri Slezkine has suggested that curiosity—the urge to travel, jostle with foreigners, and collect oddities—began in Russia only in the era of Peter the Great:

> Seventeenth-century Muscovites did not travel. They might escape, migrate, or peregrinate, but they did not view movement through space as a worthy pursuit in its own right and did not encourage wonder at things profane or blasphemous. [...] But Peter I's mentors and mercenaries lived in a different world and saw the world differently (because they "observed" it carefully). All creation as they understood it was neatly divided into the "natural" and "artful" (or man-made) varieties, with the recovery of "natural" nature possible only as a result of the elimination of everything "erring" and "altered." "Curiosity" was both a virtue and a profession; "curiosities" were objects remarkably close to the original plan ("primitive") or particularly far removed from it ("monstrous"); and travel was an increasingly well-regarded endeavor to bring curios to the curious.[10]

---

9 Benedict, *Curiosity*, 42–43.

10 Yuri Slezkine, "Naturalists versus Nations: Eighteenth-Century Russian Scholars Confront Ethnic Diversity," in *Russia's Orient: Imperial Borderlands and Peoples, 1700–1917*, ed. Daniel R. Brower and Edward J. Lazzerini (Bloomington: Indiana University Press, 1997), 27, 28.

Slezkine links these impulses with the eighteenth-century preoccupation with classifying the peoples of the earth, and, in Russia, particularly within the empire. Thus, while the Russian *liubopytstvo* (curiosity) and the related calque *kur'ez* may have lacked the rich, theoretically and philosophically loaded history of the analogous terms in Western European languages, by the eighteenth century they would seem to have found themselves similarly balanced between desire and difference, the acquisition of knowledge and the acquisition of property (territorial or otherwise).[11] In the remainder of my argument here I will, moreover, explore the premise that Pushkin's uses of the word *liubopytstvo* in his unfinished novel *The Blackamoor of Peter the Great* expose the contemporary social and personal anxieties that underpin his fictionalized depiction of his great-grandfather's life and times.[12]

To place my argument in context, let me begin with several observations about Pushkin's uses of the word *liubopytstvo* in his work at large. The word *liubopytstvo* occurs eight times in *The Blackamoor of Peter the Great*, as opposed to sixty times in Pushkin's entire *oeuvre*.[13] Most striking, perhaps, is

---

11   For a comparative analysis of the history of the relevant terms in the Romance and Germanic, see Kenny, *Curiosity in Early Modern Europe*. For the Russian case, see two dictionaries that predate Pushkin's time, *Dictionnaire complet françois et russe: Composé sur la dernière édition de celui de l'Académie François*, ed. Ivan Ivanovich Tatishchev (St. Petersburg: De l'Imprimerie impériale, chez J. J. Weitbrecht, 1798), under *curiosité*; and *Slovar' Akademii Rossiiskoi, po azbuchnomu poriadku raspolozhennyi*, part 3: K-N, 2nd ed. (St. Petersburg: Imperatorskaia Akademiia Nauk, 1814), under *liubopytstvo*.

12   For particularly useful and relevant studies of *The Blackamoor of Peter the Great*, see: S. L. Abramovich, "K voprosu o stanovlenii povestvovatel'noi prozy Pushkina: Pochemu ostalsia nezavershennym 'Arap Petra Velikogo,'" *Russkaia literatura* 2 (1974): 54–73; D. I. Belkin, "Zametki o Pushkinskoi traktovke natsional'nogo i obshchechelovecheskogo v obraze afrikantsa Ibragima Gannibala," *Literaturnye sviazi i traditsii* 3: *Mezhvuzovskii sbornik* (Gor'kii, 1972): 52–63; B. L. Bogorodskii, "O iazyke i stile romana A. S. Pushkina 'Arap Petra Velikogo,'" *Uchenye zapiski*, vol. 122 (Leningrad: Leningradskii gosudarstvennyi pedagogicheskii institut im. A. I. Gertsena, 1956), 201–39; Paul Debreczeny, "*The Blackamoor of Peter the Great*: Puškin's Experiment with a Detached Mode of Narration," *Slavic and East European Journal* 18, no. 1 (1974): 119–31; G. A. Lapkina, "K istorii sozdaniia 'Arapa Petra Velikogo,'" *Pushkin: Issledovaniia i materialy* 2 (1958): 293–309; L. S. Sidiakov, "'Arap Petra Velikogo' i 'Poltava,'" *Pushkin: Issledovaniia i materialy* 12 (1986): 60–77; M. G. Kharlap, "O zamysle 'Arapa Petra Velikogo,'" *Izvestiia AN SSSR*, Seriia literatury i iazyka 48, no. 3 (1989): 270–75; D. P. Iakubovich, "'Arap Petra Velikogo,'" *Pushkin: Issledovaniia i materialy* 9 (1979): 261–93.

13   V. V. Vinogradov, ed., *Slovar' iazyka Pushkina* (Moscow: Gosudarstvennoe izdatel'stvo inostrannykh i natsional'nykh slovarei, 1957), vol. 2, 526–27.

the fact that Pushkin employs the word, with only two exceptions, in works of prose. The implicit association between curiosity and narrative evinced by these numbers appears particularly appropriate when we note that in the vast majority of cases in which Pushkin employs the word in his prose fiction or travel notes, curiosity is the prerogative of the first-person narrator or of the narrator's interlocutor, who asks questions that prompt the narrator to tell his story.[14] In other words, it is the narrator's function to satisfy curiosity, which is to say that curiosity is that which drives narrative.

Yet even in this close association with prose Pushkinian curiosity is plagued by a precarious ambiguity. Thus, in at least two of his critical articles, Pushkin takes writers to task for preying on readers' morbid curiosity for sensationalism, implicitly a pitfall of pandering to a popular readership. In the first case, Pushkin abhors what he assumes will be the inevitable success of the publication of the "notes" of a French executioner:

> We do not envy people who, having grounded their calculations on the depravity of our *curiosity*, have devoted their plume to repeating the legends of Samson [Charles-Henri Sanson—eds.], likely illiterate. But let us confess that we, living in an age of confessions, are also with impatience, albeit with disgust, awaiting the *Memoirs of Parisian Executioner*. [...] What will this man tell us who for forty years of his bloody life was present at the last convulsions of so many victims, famous and unknown, saintly and hated? [...] One after another heads fell before us, each pronouncing its last words.... Having sated our cruel *curiosity*, the executioner's book will take its place in libraries to await the inquiries of a future historian.[15]

In the second, "M. E. Lobanov's Opinion about the Spirit of Literature" (Mnenie M. E. Lobanova o dukhe slovesnosti), Pushkin refuses to condemn all of

---

14   Paul Debreczeny points to Pushkin's indebtedness to Sir Walter Scott in creating his naive narrators. Paul Debreczeny, *The Other Pushkin: A Study of Alexander Pushkin's Prose Fiction* (Stanford: Stanford University Press, 1983), 29–30, 63–64. Scott himself had a distinct fondness for the word "curiosity" judging by the frequency of its usage in his novels.

15   Aleksandr Pushkin, "O zapiskakh Samsona," in his *Polnoe sobranie sochinenii v shestnadtsati tomakh*, vol. 11 (Moscow: Izdatel'stvo AN SSSR, 1937–1959), 94–95 (emphasis mine—C. T. N.). Henceforth all references to this edition will be given in parentheses in the text as *PSS*, volume, and page number. (Charles-Henri Sanson [1739–1806] was the royal executioner of France during the reign of King Louis XVI and High Executioner of the First French Republic. The *Mémoires des Sanson* came out in 1830 in Paris—eds.)

French literature because of the excesses of a single group: "Is it possible that [the entire French nation—eds.] has to be responsible for the works of a few writers, mostly young people, using their talent for an evil cause and grounding their selfish calculations in the *curiosity* and nervous excitement of readers?" (*PSS*, 12:69, emphasis mine—C. T. N.) The connection between curiosity and commerce in the literary marketplace threatens not only the content of literature, but the person of the artist as well. And so the most blatant exploitation of curiosity in the interests of art depicted in Pushkin's works figures in *Egyptian Nights* (Egipetskie nochi), in which Charskii, himself squeamish about drawing the attention of society to his calling as an artist, twice in quick succession assures the Italian *improvisatore* that his performance must invariably be a success and therefore make money because it will arouse curiosity: "People's *curiosity* will be aroused," "They will come, don't worry: some out of *curiosity*."[16] Curiosity, then, would seem to be a particularly sensitive gauge of Pushkin's own concerns about the changing social role of the author and literature entailed by the ascendency of prose. Literature—and the artist—for sale to a readership beyond the confines of his immediate circle hovers dangerously close to an exhibit in a freak show.[17]

Given the apparent affinity between curiosity and prose in Pushkin's writings, it is hardly surprising that the word is repeated more frequently in the relatively brief novel *The Blackamoor of Peter the Great*, Pushkin's first extended work of prose fiction, than it is in any of his other works. Moreover, this statistic suggests that Pushkin considered his forebear an especially worthy subject with which to launch his own serious career as a writer of prose fiction, at least in part because Gannibal's exotic foreign origin rendered him a likely object of curiosity in his own right, and, as we shall see, seven of the eight repetitions of the word *liubopytstvo* in *The Blackamoor of Peter the Great* are related directly to the figure of Ibrahim Gannibal. A brief survey of Pushkin's use of the word in his novel will further illuminate the anxieties, both aesthetic and personal, it signals.

---

16   Alexander Pushkin, *Complete Prose Fiction*, trans. and with an introduction and notes by Paul Debreczeny (Stanford: Stanford University Press, 1983), 253. Henceforth all references to this edition will be given in parentheses before the reference to the Russian original. For the original see *PSS*, 8:267.

17   On the literary context in Pushkin's time, see William Mills Todd III, *Fiction and Society in the Age of Pushkin: Ideology, Institutions, and Narrative* (Cambridge, MA: Harvard University Press, 1986), especially "Institutions of Literature," 45–105.

3. A Note on Curiosity in Pushkin's *The Blackamoor of Peter the Great*

In the opening, "Parisian" chapters of the novel, the word is used virtually exclusively to describe the motives of those who gaze on the "Negro" Ibrahim, most particularly women. Susceptibility to the lure of "curiosity" is in fact one of the defining traits of this society: "Wealth, good manners, fame, talent, even eccentricity—all attributes that excited *curiosity*" (12; *PSS*, 8:4, emphasis mine—C. T. N.). The compendium of traits that excite curiosity here is telling, most particularly in anticipation of *Egyptian Nights*, because of the metonymic association of riches, glory, talent, and strangeness. The text makes clear that Ibrahim is first attracted to the Countess precisely because she does not view him with curiosity:

> The Countess greeted Ibrahim politely but without fanfare, which flattered him. As a rule, people looked at the young black man as if he were some strange phenomenon—they surrounded him and showered him with salutations and questions. Their *curiosity* though disguised as courtesy, offended his pride. The sweet attention of women, almost the sole aim of our efforts, not only did not gladden his heart, but filled it with downright bitterness and indignation. He felt that in their eyes he was a kind of rare animal, a peculiar and alien creature who had been accidentally brought into a world that had nothing in common with it. He even envied people who attracted no one's attention, regarding their insignificance as a happy state. (13; *PSS*, 8:4–5, emphasis mine—C. T. N.)

It appears that Ibrahim fears being viewed as a freak, outside the bounds of the human. Of course, as the narrator points out: "quite a few beautiful young women glanced at him with feelings more flattering than mere *curiosity*, though he in his prejudice either did not notice anything, or fancied only flirtation" (13; *PSS*, 8:5, emphasis mine—C. T. N.). This is perhaps the only instance when the narrator's voice departs explicitly from Ibrahim's point of view in the text, underscoring the discrepancy between Ibrahim's understanding of himself as "Other" and his apparent attractiveness as a sexual partner. This discrepancy therefore suggests a certain powerful instability in Ibrahim's image, caught in the space of the exotic between desire, marvel, and disgust, the space into which he projects his own anxieties about how others see him.

There is, however, a marked shift in Ibrahim's relationship to curiosity in the Russian chapters of the novel. Immediately upon his return to Russia, he becomes no longer a potential object of curiosity, but himself an observer of curiosity: "Ibrahim looked with *curiosity* at the newborn capital that had risen from the swamp at the bidding of autocracy" (18; *PSS*, 8:10, emphasis mine—C. T. N.). Ibrahim is here transformed from the object to the subject of the curious gaze. Svetlana Evdokimova has suggested that Ibrahim functions as a "'double' foreigner" in *The Blackamoor of Peter the Great*, rightly underscoring his importance as an observer of the "syncretic," inchoate Petrine epoch simultaneously from inside and from outside.[18] If Ibrahim continually runs the risk in France of being reduced to a curio, in Russia, at least at first, he seems in his new role as subject to be an emblem of the free-wheeling meritocracy of the age, gaining acceptance virtually as kin into the tsar's family and into the society at large.

As the text progresses, Ibrahim becomes a cultural mediator, one who is able to satisfy curiosity (rather than arouse curiosity) because of his superior knowledge. When Peter the Great retires to rest after dining, Ibrahim remains behind with the women of the imperial family: "Ibrahim was left with the Empress and the great duchesses. He did his best to satisfy their *curiosity*, describing the Parisian way of life, the festivities held in the French capital and its capricious fashions" (19; *PSS*, 8:11, emphasis mine—C. T. N.). Shortly thereafter in the text Ibrahim finds himself explaining Petersburg society to the Frenchified Korsakov: "Korsakov showered Ibrahim with questions. Who was the most beautiful woman in Petersburg? Who had the reputation of being the best dancer? What dance was currently in vogue? Ibrahim satisfied his friend's *curiosity* grudgingly" (23; *PSS*, 8:15, emphasis mine—C. T. N.). Here we see clearly how curiosity, specifically the need for explanation, feeds on change and difference within and between cultures. Tellingly, Ibrahim, who himself begins as an object of curiosity because of his origin beyond the boundaries of European culture and because of his status as an outsider in France, in Petrine Russia becomes empowered with the knowledge to satisfy the curiosity of his adopted fellow countrymen and women. His ability to satisfy curiosity thus marks him as an insider, while, as we have noted, his status as an object of curiosity marked him as an outsider in France. Yet an underlying anxiety about curiosity continues to infect the text, imminent in his status as a "go-between," native to neither Russia nor the West—a status that is perilous in the extreme.[19]

---

18   Svetlana Evdokimova, *Pushkin's Historical Imagination* (New Haven: Yale University Press, 1999), 150.

19   I take this term from Greenblatt. See chap. 5, "The Go-Between," of his *Marvelous Possessions*, 119–51.

3. A Note on Curiosity in Pushkin's *The Blackamoor of Peter the Great*

Here we should note that following a tradition that goes back to Pandora and her box, in the overwhelming majority of cases in which *liubopytstvo* is invoked in *The Blackamoor of Peter the Great*, the characters who experience curiosity are female. This fact, I will suggest, exposes an underlying sexual anxiety. The final two incidences of the word *liubopytstvo* in *The Blackamoor of Peter the Great* invoke the stereotypically negative image of the curious, prying woman. In the first instance, Natasha Rzhevskaia falls victim to her desire to learn her fate:

> When the Emperor had locked himself with her father, her heart sank. Some premonition whispered to her that the matter concerned her. When Gavrila Afanasevich sent her off, declaring that he had to speak with her aunt and grandfather, she could not resist the promptings of *feminine curiosity* and quietly stole through the inner apartments to the door of the bedroom. She did not miss one word of the whole horrifying conversation; when she heard her father's last words, the poor thing lost consciousness, and as she fell, she hit her head against the iron-plated chest in which her trousseau was kept. (33; *PSS*, 8:26; emphasis mine—C. T. N.)[20]

Natasha faints when she overhears that her father accepted Peter the Great's matchmaking for *Arap* Ibrahim: "I said that he ruled over us, and it was our duty as his vassals to obey in all things" (32; *PSS*, 8:26). The second instance occurs after Natasha, some time later, having recovered long enough to catch a brief glimpse of Ibrahim, engages in a tête-à-tête with the family's resident dwarf to find out what has happened to her fortunes in the time she has been ill:

> The unlucky beauty opened her eyes and, no longer seeing anyone by her bed, called the maid to her and sent her to fetch the midget. At the same moment, however, the rotund little old elf was already rolling toward her bed like a ball. Lastochka (as the midget was called) had run up the stairs behind Gavrila Afanasevich and Ibrahim as fast as her short legs could carry her, and as she hid behind the door, *in keeping*

---

20   Natasha strikes her head against the chest containing her dowry, thus drawing attention to the "mercantile" aspects of marriage. In this context, see my "The Telltale Black Baby, Or Why Pushkin Began the *Blackamoor of Peter the Great*, But Didn't Finish It," in *"Under the Sky of My Africa": Alexander Pushkin and Blackness*, ed. Catharine Theimer Nepomnyashchy, Ludmilla Trigos, and Nicole Svobodny (Evanston: Northwestern University Press, 2006), 150–71.

with the inquisitive nature of her sex [ne izmeniaia liubopytstvu, srodnomu prekrasnomu polu]. (38; *PSS*, 8:31, emphasis mine—C. T. N.)

Most telling here is the fact that the dwarf, in doubling Natasha's action, also serves as an invocation of the freakish, the marginally human.

At this point, let me return to my assertion of the link between "curiosity" and prose in Pushkin's works. I would argue that Pushkin's first major attempt at prose may conceivably, and even probably, be read as an allegory of the literary process, with the figure of Ibrahim at the center. Pushkin, who at the time when he began writing *The Blackamoor of Peter the Great* had just recently returned from exile at Mikhailovskoe and was himself something of a "curiosity" in Petersburg society, was, of course, aware—even painfully so—of the fragile line dividing the Author's story from the author's story, the narratives generated by the writer as writer from the tales that grow up around the writer's body, both in measure at the mercy of the good faith and competence of the reader. Ibrahim, as an autobiographical fiction, serves to focus the anxiety of the writer balanced between satisfying the curiosity of his readership and risking becoming a curiosity in his own right. In this context, I would direct attention to the first epigraph to this note, a passage from Voltaire's *Essay on Universal History, the Manners, and Spirit of Nations* (Essai sur les moeurs et l'esprit des nations) which encapsulates the more sinister implications of "enlightenment" curiosity about and taxonomies of other peoples.[21] Voltaire's observation makes clear the risk that if one's body attracts curiosity, one will be reduced to a collectible object, a monstrous spectacle. On the other hand, if the writer takes on the role of satisfying the curiosity of others, he might appear little more than a "tout."

Moreover, as the second epigraph to this note demonstrates, Pushkin did indeed view his African heritage as "curious." A number of scholars who have written on *The Blackamoor of Peter the Great* have suggested that Pushkin found his great-grandfather an attractive subject to serve as the focus of an historical

---

21   It is worth noting that Voltaire's novel *L'ingenu*, in which a "native American" finds himself in England and France, allowing the reader to see through his eyes, might have served Pushkin as a model for Ibrahim as a "naive" observer of European civilization. It is telling, however, that the "Huron" in Voltaire's novel turns out to be a European by birth who was raised by native Americans after his parents had been slaughtered. For works by Voltaire contained in Pushkin's library, see B. L. Modzalevskii, "Biblioteka A S. Pushkina," *Pushkin i ego sovremenniki: Materialy i issledovaniia* 9–10 (1910): 360–64.

fiction because the poet drew an analogy of one sort or another between his forebear and himself. However, there has been a definite tendency to downplay or defuse Pushkin's own repeatedly stated belief that his great-grandfather was a "Negro" and therefore insufficient attention has been paid to the aesthetic and psychical implications and metaphorical force of this racial identification as a factor in Pushkin's life and works. Yet I would suggest that beneath the certainly idealized portrayal of Ibrahim in *The Blackamoor of Peter the Great*, and particularly of Ibrahim's relationship with his imperial godfather, which reflected the fact that Pushkin's primary sources on Gannibal's life were family legends and the unremittingly eulogistic "German biography" of Gannibal, lies a darker and more ambiguous reality.[22] This reality, moreover, would have resonated in disturbing ways not only at a transitional moment in Pushkin's literary fortunes, but at a transitional moment in his life as he was contemplating marriage, a situation in which Pushkin could not help but worry that he might find himself in an unenviable position with regard to "curiosity."

In this regard we cannot help but notice that Ibrahim's "Africanness" is unquestionably associated with marginal humanity in the novel, at least as regards the "Blackamoor's" self-perception, as evidenced by his farewell letter to his Parisian mistress: "Why struggle to unite the fate of such a tender and graceful creature with the unlucky fate of a Negro, a pitiful being, scarcely granted the title of a man?" (17; *PSS*, 7:9). Tellingly, Ibrahim places himself in this self-evaluation at the fringes of the human, in the realm of dwarfs (like Lastochka), freaks, and monsters. Studying Peter I as a collector of oddities, Tony Anemone has written of "Peter's unusual, but hardly unique, passions for giants, dwarfs, malformed humans and animals, his love of arranging carnivalesque weddings and funerals for his various 'monsters.'"[23] In the same vein, Nabokov in his study of Abram Gannibal, observes with regard to Gannibal's arrival in Russia that "In Moscow, he [Peter] amused himself with establishing an anatomical and biological museum, with a botanical garden in front of it.

---

22 Gannibal's biography was compiled in German in 1786 by Aleksei Karlovich Rotkirkh, Gannibal's son-in-law. Pushkin partly translated it into Russian. See *PSS*, 12:434–37.

23 Anthony Anemone, "The Monsters of Peter the Great: The Culture of the Kunstkamera in 18th-Century St. Petersburg," *Slavic and East European Journal* 44, no. 4 (2000): 583–602.

The Young Blackamoor was no doubt welcomed as an additional curio."[24] He goes on to suggest a decidedly grotesque reading of the ceremony that would, in the future, allow the poet to claim kinship with the reformer tsar, Gannibal's baptism:

> The ceremony performed on the young Blackamoor, at the Pyatnitski church, in late September or early October, 1707 (not "1705," as the memorial plaque there oddly says), with Peter I as godfather and Christiana Eberhardina, wife of King Augustus II of Poland, as godmother (fide the German biography), was conducted in the rowdy and slapstick atmosphere of Peter's court and smacks of mock marriages between freaks or the elevation of jesters to the rank of governors of Barataria. Indeed, there seems to have been an attempt by some zealous courtiers, a few months before, to marry the Blackamoor: in a letter from Poland, dated May 13, 1707, the tsar writes to Councilor Avtonom Ivanov that he does not wish to have the *arap* conjugated— with, presumably, the daughter of some grandee's Negro servant, or a dwarf, or a Russian female house fool (*domashniaia dura, shutikha*).[25]

While it stretches credibility that Pushkin could have known any of this, there would indeed seem to be a muted echo of the carnivalesque marriage in the associative proximity into which Ibrahim is cast with the dwarf Lastochka in the novel. A scurrilous anecdote included in *Table-Talk* suggests a less than facile attitude on Pushkin's part toward Peter the Great as a "fearless naturalist" as well as toward his great-grandfather's "curious" provenance.[26] It suggests: "Once the young moor who accompanied Peter I on his walk, stopped to satisfy the call of nature and suddenly cried in fright: 'Sire, Sire, my bowel is coming out of me!' Peter came to him and, seeing what was the matter, said: 'Nonsense, this is not a gut but a belly worm.' And he pulled out the worm with his fingers. The anecdote is filthy, but it depicts Peter's habits" (*PSS*, 12:157). At the very least this "anecdote" offers supporting evidence that the figure of the blackamoor was as visceral to Pushkin as it was closely felt. And, of course,

---

24 Vladimir Nabokov, "Appendix One: Abram Gannibal," in Aleksandr Pushkin, *Eugene Onegin*, trans., and with commentary by, Vladimir Nabokov, vol. 3 (New York: Pantheon Books, 1964), 423.

25 Nabokov, "Appendix One: Abram Gannibal," 424–25.

26 I am grateful to Catherine O'Neil for having suggested this reading of this passage to me. The phrasing in quotation marks is hers.

Pushkin's own fears of a marital mismatch were too prescient and are too well documented to detain us here.

In sum, I would conclude that Ibrahim/Abram Gannibal as a locus of curiosity served Pushkin as a potent textual and biographical field on which to put in play his own uncertainties about his place in the world at a moment when his immediate personal, professional, and even political context was in unquestionable flux. That is most certainly why Pushkin turned to the story of his great-grandfather in his first novel. As to why he left the novel unfinished—that is another story.[27]

---

[27] I address the issue of why Pushkin did not finish *The Blackamoor of Peter Great* in "The Telltale Black Baby," focusing my argument on a related, but more relevant context.

Works Cited

Abramovich, S. L. "K voprosu o stanovlenii povestvovatel'noi prozy Pushkina: Pochemu ostalsia nezavershennym 'Arap Petra Velikogo.'" *Russkaia literatura* 2 (1974): 54–73.

Anemone, Anthony. "The Monsters of Peter the Great: The Culture of the Kunstkamera in 18th-Century St. Petersburg." *Slavic and East European Journal* 44, no. 4 (2000): 583–602.

Belkin, D. I. "Zametki o Pushkinskoi traktovke natsional'nogo i obshchechelovecheskogo v obraze afrikantsa Ibragima Gannibala." *Literaturnye sviazi i traditsii 3: Mezhvuzovskii sbornik* (Gor'kii, 1972): 52–63.

Benedict, Barbara. *Curiosity: A Cultural History of Early Modern Inquiry*. Chicago: University of Chicago Press, 2001.

Bogorodskii, B. L. "O iazyke i stile romana A. S. Pushkina 'Arap Petra Velikogo.'" *Uchenye zapiski*, vol. 122, 201–39. Leningrad: Leningradskii gosudarstvennyi pedagogicheskii institut im. A. I. Gertsena, 1956.

Debreczeny, Paul. *The Other Pushkin: A Study of Alexander Pushkin's Prose Fiction*. Stanford: Stanford University Press, 1983.

———. "*The Blackamoor of Peter the Great:* Puškin's Experiment with a Detached Mode of Narration." *Slavic and East European Journal* 18, no. 1 (1974): 119–31.

Dictionnaire complet françois et russe: Composé sur la dernière édition de celui de l'Académie François. Edited by Ivan Ivanovich Tatishchev. St. Petersburg: De l'Imprimerie impériale, chez J. J. Weitbrecht, 1798.

Evdokimova, Svetlana. *Pushkin's Historical Imagination*. New Haven: Yale University Press, 1999.

Greenblatt, Stephen. *Marvelous Possessions: The Wonder of the New World*. Chicago: University of Chicago Press, 1991.

Iakubovich, D. P. "'Arap Petra Velikogo.'" *Pushkin: Issledovaniia i materialy* 9 (1979): 261–93.

Kenny, Neil. *Curiosity in Early Modern Europe: Word Histories*. Wiesbaden: Harrassowitz Verlag, 1998.

Kharlap, M. G. "O zamysle 'Arapa Petra Velikogo.'" *Izvestiia AN SSSR*, Seriia literatury i iazyka 48, no. 3 (1989): 270–75.

Lapkina, G. A. "K istorii sozdaniia 'Arapa Petra Velikogo.'" *Pushkin: Issledovaniia i materialy* 2 (1958): 293–309.

Modzalevskii, B. L. "Biblioteka A S. Pushkina." *Pushkin i ego sovremenniki: Materialy i issledovaniia* 9–10 (1910): 360–64.

Nabokov, Vladimir. "Appendix One: Abram Gannibal." In Aleksandr Pushkin, *Eugene Onegin*, translated by, and with commentary by, Vladimir Nabokov, vol. 3. New York: Pantheon Books, 1964.

Nepomnyashchy, Catharine Theimer. "The Telltale Black Baby, Or Why Pushkin Began the *Blackamoor of Peter the Great*, But Didn't Finish It." In *"Under the Sky of My Africa": Alexan-*

der *Pushkin and Blackness*, edited by Catharine Theimer Nepomnyashchy, Ludmilla Trigos, and Nicole Svobodny, 150–171. Evanston: Northwestern University Press, 2006.

Pushkin, A. S. *Polnoe sobranie sochinenii v shestnadtsati tomakh*. Moscow: Izdatel'stvo AN SSSR, 1937–1959.

Pushkin, Alexander. *Complete Prose Fiction*. Translated by, and with an introduction and notes, by Paul Debreczeny. Stanford: Stanford University Press, 1983.

Quinn, Dennis. "Polypragmosyne in the Renaissance: Ben Jonson." *The Ben Jonson Journal: Literary Contexts in the Age of Elizabeth, James and Charles* 2 (1995): 157–69.

Sidiakov, L. S. "'Arap Petra Velikogo' i 'Poltava.'" *Pushkin: Issledovaniia i materialy* 12 (1986): 60–77.

Slezkine, Yuri. "Naturalists versus Nations: Eighteenth-Century Russian Scholars Confront Ethnic Diversity." In *Russia's Orient: Imperial Borderlands and Peoples, 1700–1917*, edited by Daniel R. Brower and Edward J. Lazzerini, 27–57. Bloomington: Indiana University Press, 1997.

Slovar' Akademii Rossiiskoi, po azbuchnomu poriadku raspolozhennyi. Part 3: K-N. 2nd edition. St. Petersburg: Imperatorskaia Akademiia Nauk, 1814.

Todd, William Mills. *Fiction and Society in the Age of Pushkin: Ideology, Institutions, and Narrative*. Cambridge, MA: Harvard University Press, 1986.

Vinogradov, V. V., ed. *Slovar' iazyka Pushkina*. Vol. 2. Moscow: Gosudarstvennoe izdatel'stvo inostrannykh i natsional'nykh slovarei, 1957.

Zacher, Christian K. *Curiosity and Pilgrimage: The Literature of Discovery in Fourteenth-Century England*. Baltimore: Johns Hopkins University Press, 1976.

4

Katkov and the Emergence of the *Russian Messenger*

In 1856 Mikhail Nikiforovich Katkov founded the *Russian Messenger* (Russkii vestnik), a "thick" journal which soon became one of the most popular publications in Russia.[1] Although the journal survived until 1906, its significance dwindled in the late 1870s, its heyday corresponding roughly to the most brilliant period of the Russian novel. Turgenev, Tolstoy, and Dostoevskii were long-standing contributors to the journal, and on its pages their major novels mingled with the works of many outstanding writers, critics, and literary scholars of the day, including Goncharov, Leskov, Pisemskii, Saltykov-Shchedrin, S. T. Aksakov, Ostrovskii, Fet, Tiutchev, A. K. Tolstoi, Annenkov, A. N. Afanas'ev, and F. I. Buslaev.[2]

Thanks to Marcus Levitt for his great help in the final research and preparation of footnotes for this article—C. T. N. Originally published in *Ulbandus Review* 1, no. 1 (Fall 1977): 59–89. Reproduced by permission of the copyright holder, the journal's editorial board. —eds.

1   For surveys of the history of the *Russian Messenger* see: *Ocherki po istorii russkoi zhurnalistiki i kritiki*, ed. V. G. Berezina et al., vol. 2 (Leningrad: Izdatel'stvo Leningradskogo gosudarstvennogo universiteta, 1965), 217–30; *Entsiklopedicheskii slovar'*, s.v. Russkii vestnik (St. Petersburg: Izdatel'stvo "P. A. Brokgauz i I. A. Efron," 1895), 324–26; *Russkaia periodicheskaia pechat'*, ed. A. G. Dement'ev, A. V. Zapadov, and M. S. Cherepakhov (Moscow: Gosudarstvennoe izdatel'stvo politicheskoi literatury, 1959), 340–43. *Russkii vestnik* hereafter is referred to as *RV*.

2   Two sections of Goncharov's *The Frigate Pallada* (Fregat Pallada) appeared in the *Russian Messenger* under the titles "From Kronstadt to Cape Lizard" (Ot Kronshtadta do mysa Lizarda), and "Sailing in Atlantic Tropics" (Plavanie v Atlanticheskikh tropikakh) in November and May of 1856, respectively. Ostrovskii published his comedy *Your Drink—My Hangover* (V chuzhom piru pokhmel'e) in the first issue of the *Russian Messenger* in January of 1856. Aside from a number of shorter poetic works, Aleksei K. Tolstoi published in the *Russian Messenger* his dramatic *poema Don Juan* (Don Zhuan) in April of 1862; and his historical novel *Prince Serebrianyi* (Kniaz' Serebrianyi) from August to October of 1862. Other writers and poets who published in *The Russian Messenger* were

4. Katkov and the Emergence of the *Russian Messenger*   55

Katkov played a significant role in the development of Russian literature during this crucial period, not only by providing an outlet for publication, but also by giving financial support to writers and by personally influencing their political views. This influence was not always beneficent: Katkov and his editors at times distorted manuscripts and demanded changes to make the works conform to the journal's "line."

Both pre-revolutionary and Soviet scholars have had difficulty in dealing with the controversial figure of Katkov.[3] The editor's odyssey from the ranks of the liberal Westernizers in the period preceding Alexander II's reforms into the reactionary camp of Pobedonostsev in the 1880s, a development paralleled by the increasing conservatism of his journal, largely discouraged Soviet scholarship on the *Russian Messenger*. This brief survey will attempt to gather

---

I. I. Lazhechnikov, Andrei Pecherskii (pseudonym of Pavel Ivanovich Mel'nikov), Evgeniia Tur (pseudonym of Elizaveta Vasilievna Salias de Tournemire), Marko Vovchok (pseudonym of Mariia Aleksandrovna Markovich), Kokhanovskaia (pseudonym of Nadezhda Stepanovna Sokhanskaia), V. S. Kurochkin, D. D. Minaev, M. L. Mikhailov, A. N. Pleshcheev, A. N. Maikov, N. F. Shcherbina, Ia. P. Polonskii, A. M. Zhemchuzhnikov, D. V. Grigorovich, and N. P. Ogarev. During the early 1890s, N. N. Strakhov, K. N. Leont'ev, and V. V. Rozanov all published extensively in the journal. Rozanov published his *Legend of the Grand Inquisitor* ("Legenda o Velikom inkvizitore F. M. Dostoevskogo") from January to April of 1891.

3   One of Katkov's biographers illustrated the differences of opinion about the editor by listing some of the epithets used to describe him: "Some called him the 'creator of Russian publicism,' the 'champion of Russian truth,' the 'bearer of the Russian state idea,' the 'establisher of the Russian enlightenment,' the 'pillar of Russian and Slavic self-knowledge,' the 'golden-tongued apostle of the greatness and glory of Russia,' the 'Russian palladium,' the 'terror of Germany and England,' the 'Russian Thermopylae.' Others gave him derisive and scornful nicknames: the 'thunder thrower of Strastnoi Boulevard,' the 'watchdog of the Russian press,' the 'priest of obscurantism' the 'preacher of sycophantism,' the 'Moscow Menzel,' or even the 'Duke of Alba.'" P. I. Sementkovskii, *M. N. Katkov, ego zhizn' i literaturnaia deiatel'nost'* (St. Petersburg: F. Pavlenkov, 1892), 34. For biographies of Katkov, see: *Mikhail Nikiforovich Katkov i ego istoricheskaia zasluga* (St. Petersburg: Otechestvennaia pol'za, 1889), written by N. A. Liubimov, the managing editor of the *Russian Messenger*; S. Nevedenskii (pseudonym of S. S. Tatishchev), *Katkov i ego vremia* (St. Petersburg: Tipografiia A. S. Suvorina, 1888); Sementkovskii, *M. N. Katkov*; G. Liwoff, *Michel Katkoff et son epoque* (Paris: E. Plon, Nourrit et cie., 1897); Martin Katz, *Mikhail N. Katkov, a Political Biography* (The Hague: Mouton & Co., 1966); Marc Raeff, "A Reactionary Liberal: M. N. Katkov," *Russian Review* 2 (July 1952): 157–67; V. A. Kitaev, *Ot frondy k okhranitel'stvu: iz istorii russkoi liberal'noi mysli* (Moscow: Mysl', 1972); Edward C. Thaden, *Conservative Nationalism in Nineteenth-Century Russia* (Seattle: University of Washington Press, 1964), 38–56.

together the existing information on the journal's history and on its role in the development of Russian literary and intellectual life.

The history of the *Russian Messenger* may be traced back to 1851, when Katkov began his editorial career. Katkov taught philosophy at Moscow University from 1845 until 1850, when the chair of philosophy was abolished in the wave of reaction following the 1848 revolutionary upheavals in Europe. Left without a permanent position, he accepted an offer to assume the editorship of the university's daily newspaper, the *Moscow Gazette* (Moskovskie vedomosti) in February 1851. He apparently soon developed a taste for his new profession and sought to broaden his field of journalistic activity. In 1853 he attempted to purchase the journal *Son of the Fatherland* (Syn otechestva), but the negotiations proved unsuccessful. Learning of Mikhail Pogodin's break with the "young editors" of the *Muscovite* (Moskvitianin) in October 1853, Katkov then tried to gain control of that journal, but again the talks failed.[4] Fearing the loss of the *Muscovite*'s Slavophile orientation, Pogodin refused to turn the journal over to Katkov.

Despite these setbacks, Katkov did not abandon his journalistic ambitions. In 1855, when Alexander II's ascent to the throne heralded an end to the "seven dark years" (*mrachnoe semilet'e*) and an easing of censorship restrictions, Katkov set out to found his own journal.[5] On May 29, 1855, he met with the minister of education, A. S. Norov, and submitted a petition requesting permission to establish a journal under the title *Russian Chronicler* (Russkii letopisets). In his outline of the journal's program, Katkov proposed that it contain a political and a literary department, that it appear weekly, biweekly, or monthly, and that it be accompanied by a daily news sheet entitled *Current Events of the Russian Chronicler* (Tekushchie izvestiia russkogo letopistsa),

---

[4] The "young editors" (*molodaia redaktsiia*) of the *Muscovite* included A. N. Ostrovskii, A. A. Grigor'ev, E. P. Edel'son, B. N. Almazov, T. I. Filippov, and L. A. Mei, as well as the artists P. M. Sadovskii and I. F. Gorbunov. A. F. Pisemskii and P. I. Mel'nikov-Pecherskii were also associated with them. The group existed from 1850 to 1853; it broke up over internal disagreements as well as over a conflict with the "old" board, that is, Pogodin.

[5] On April 6, 1855, Katkov wrote a letter to A. V. Nikitenko in which he asked about censorship conditions: "Tell me, what's the censor like now? It is surmised that there will be a substantial easing of restrictions. Incidentally, isn't it a good time now to begin petitioning for a journal.... Isn't it time for me to begin to petition, so that later I don't find the door locked, like foolish maidens?" Cited in Kitaev, *Ot frondy k okhranitel'stvu*, 52. Receiving an affirmative answer to his query, Katkov went ahead with his plans.

which would print "government decrees and orders, news about military actions and events in the political world, short notes, literary and city news, announcements of new books, etc."⁶ Katkov set forth the aims of the journal concerning its role in literature:

> The editorial board will demand from works of literature that they do not carry the title of literature in vain. A journal cannot create talent, but it can call forth talent and give it direction. In the eyes of the editors, external brilliance will never take the place of internal value. Imagination must be warmed with moral feeling. Petty, empty, and irritating analysis, the daguerreotypical copying of everyday phenomena without depth of experience, without life-creating thought, vain phrase-mongering without belief, without heart, all these things will not only not be printed in the *Russian Chronicler* but will be hunted down in general in literature. The work of the editor is not visible to all, and only he who looks deeper will understand how great is his responsibility and how much both the direction and form of a work can depend on him. The censor excludes that which is against regulations; an editor can do more—he can act positively on the very source of a work.⁷

Katkov's petition met with opposition from the Moscow University authorities on the grounds that there would be a serious conflict of interest between Katkov's position as editor of the *Moscow Gazette* and his work on his own publication, and that the proposed journal would offer damaging competition to the university's newspaper.⁸ Despite the university's objections, Katkov

---

6 Liubimov, *Mikhail Nikiforovich Katkov*, 50.

7 Liubimov, *Mikhail Nikiforovich Katkov*, 52.

8 The *Moscow Gazette*, the only publication in Moscow with the right to print political news, had good reason to fear competition from Katkov's proposed journal. However, Katz reports that, according to the famous Moscow University professor and Westernizer Timofei Granovskii, the opposition mounted by the Moscow University authorities "was directed more at the person of Katkov than at the establishment of a competing journal." Katz, *Mikhail N. Katkov*, 45–46. Liubimov reports that the paper containing the refusal to Katkov's petition lay on the minister of education's desk, but was never signed. Liubimov further suggests that Katkov's case was helped by the intercession of P. A. Viazemskii. On September 7, 1855, Katkov submitted a memorandum to the minister requesting that the decision about his petition to found a journal be considered separately from the question of a daily newsletter. He agreed to leave his post as editor of the *Moscow Gazette* if necessary. Liubimov, *Mikhail Nikiforovich Katkov*, 57–59. Katz, on the other hand, maintains

received permission to print a journal on the condition that he leave his post as editor of the *Moscow Gazette*. The main bureau of the censorship stipulated that the journal could come out not more than once or twice monthly and that the proposed chronicle of military and political events be presented "without any editorial commentary, except that inherent in the selection of news of this kind from periodical publications coming out in Russia."[9] Having been denied permission to publish a daily newsletter and to issue the journal as a weekly, on October 21, 1855, Katkov submitted an application requesting that the name of the proposed journal be changed to the *Russian Messenger* to conform with the alteration of its format. The official decision to allow Katkov's publication was signed by the tsar on October 31, 1855.

On November 15, 1855, an announcement of the upcoming appearance of the *Russian Messenger* was printed in the *Moscow Gazette*. In this advertisement Katkov stressed the fact that the new publication "being a scholarly and literary journal, like all of the journals coming out in our country, is also a political publication, which gives it special importance at the present time when general attention is focused on political events."[10] This was an important selling point for the *Russian Messenger*, since, despite the limitations placed on its political section, it was one of only three journals in Russia that had the right to reprint articles from newspapers, and it was the only one based in Moscow.[11] Katkov further announced that the editorial board of the journal would include E. F. Korsh, P. N. Kudriavtsev, and P. M. Leont'ev.[12]

---

that Katkov's case was won through the intercession of the State-secretary D. N. Bludov. Katz, *Mikhail N. Katkov*, 46.

9   Liubimov, *Mikhail Nikifirovich Katkov*, 64–65.

10 Liubimov, *Mikhail Nikiforovich Katkov*, 67.

11 On June 23, 1855, the minister of education granted to the *Contemporary* and to *Notes of the Fatherland* the right to reprint military news from the *Russian Invalid* (Russkii invalid).

12 Leont'ev's close association with Katkov began in the late 1840s when they both taught at Moscow University. Leont'ev took over the *Moscow Gazette* in 1863. He remained Katkov's co-editor of the *Russian Messenger* managing the journal's finances until his death in 1874. Tatishchev maintains that it was hardly necessary to determine whether Katkov or Leont'ev had written a given article because "both writers were so close in their views, that in this respect neither of them contributed anything individual." He writes: "In this friendly union Katkov possessed the strength of initiative, passion, enthusiasm; in contrast, Leont'ev was a restraining, moderating element. It is very probable that Leont'ev had a softening, pacifying influence on the passionate, impressionable nature of Katkov [...]

4. Katkov and the Emergence of the *Russian Messenger* | 59

The announcement also contained a long list of the journal's prospective contributors.[13]

The announcement of the editorial staff and contributors which Katkov published in the *Moscow Gazette* was indicative of the period in which the journal was founded, the so-called "honeymoon" of Russian liberalism that preceded the reforms of Alexander II. During these years, apparently irreconcilable discords between factions disappeared in the general exhilaration over the expected transformation of Russian society. The *Russian Messenger* served as a rallying point for Moscow liberals, centering around the friends of the late Professor Timofei Granovskii, the members of the circle of A. V. Stankevich.[14] Not only did Katkov's list of prospective contributors include liberals and Westernizers of all shadings and gradations, but also the Slavophiles, who were represented by the Aksakov family.[15] The names of prominent scholars of the day mingled with those of the most promising young writers, notably Turgenev and Tolstoy (listed under the initials L.N.T.).[16] Backed by such an

---

It should be noted that the change in Katkov's views at the end of his life occurred after Leont'ev's death." Nevedenskii, *Katkov i ego vremia*, 112.

13   The list is reprinted in Liubimov, *Mikhail Nikiforovich Katkov*, 67–68.

14   Granovskii died in October 1855 before the journal appeared. After Granovskii's death his followers grouped around A. V. Stankevich, the younger brother of N. V. Stankevich. Katkov, seeking the general support of Moscow liberal circles for his journal, drew close to the Stankevich group. After they gave up plans to found their own journal, discouraged largely by the difficulties Katkov himself had encountered, they accepted Katkov's offer to take part in his journal, and E. F. Korsh and P. N. Kudriavtsev joined the editorial board of the *Russian Messenger*.

15   The Aksakovs were apparently not asked before their names were included in the list of projected contributors to the *Russian Messenger*. Katz reports their initial mixed reactions in *Mikhail N. Katkov*, 46–47. An excerpt from S. T. Aksakov's *Family Chronicle* was published in the first issue of the *Russian Messenger* in January of 1856 and the fifth and last part of his memoirs was published in the July 1856 issue.

16   In a letter written to Katkov sometime around the beginning of 1856, Tolstoy expressed his surprise at finding his name and Turgenev's on the list of prospective contributors to the *Russian Messenger*. Tolstoy claimed that he had given only vague responses to requests from Korsh and Katkov's brother, and reproached Katkov for having treated this as a firm commitment. He ended the letter, however, by saying that he might still publish in Katkov's journal in the future. F. Buslaev, ed., "Perepiska Tolstogo s M. N. Katkovym," in *Literaturnoe nasledstvo*, vols. 37–38, *L. N. Tolstoi*, part 2 (Moscow: Izdatel'stvo AN SSSR, 1939), 189–90. Turgenev apparently promised his story "Phantoms" (Prizraki) to Katkov. The promise precipitated a public confrontation between them: Katkov assumed that

impressive array of talent, Katkov's journal was virtually assured of success from the start.

The first issue of the *Russian Messenger* appeared in January 1856. Through the December 1860 issue, the journal came out twice monthly and consisted of two sections.[17] Literary works and scholarly articles on economic, political, historical, and literary subjects were printed in the first section of the journal. The second section, the "Contemporary Chronicle" (Sovremennaia letopis'), included political news, reviews, and a "miscellany" section. The "line" of the journal came through most clearly in the "Contemporary Chronicle," to which Katkov was a major contributor. From time to time, special departments were created in the "Contemporary Chronicle" for articles dealing with current issues and problems. Thus, in 1858, when the official announcement of the coming reforms made it possible to discuss them more freely in print, a special section was created under the heading "Peasant Question" (Krest'ianskii vopros). Polemical articles with other journals, relatively few during this early period, were also concentrated in the "Contemporary Chronicle."

Katkov selected a very auspicious time to begin his new journal. Aside from the fact that the new feeling of *rapprochement* allowed him to draw on a diversity of talented contributors, he was also setting out in a period of rapid growth in Russian journalism. 150 new newspapers and journals of all types appeared in Russia during the period from 1853 to 1856 compared to only thirty new publications during the years 1851 to 1853, and the role played by newspapers and journals in Russian social and political life grew considerably through the discussion of the "peasant question."[18]

Katkov was also fortunate in drawing the liberal N. F. von Kruze as censor for the *Russian Messenger*. Von Kruze watched over Moscow publications with an eye sympathetic to the spirit of reform, allowing into print materials more

---

    a story by Turgenev entitled "Faust" published in the *Contemporary* in 1857 was in fact "Phantoms" and published a reproach in the *Moscow Gazette*. It touched off an exchange of letters between Turgenev and the *Russian Messenger*, which Katkov published in *RV* 7 (January 1857): 152–58. Turgenev maintained that Katkov's action released him from his promise, and "Phantoms" appeared in the first issue of Dostoevskii's journal *Epoch* (Epokha) in 1864.

17 Each volume consisted of four issues, making six volumes per year. The volumes were numbered from the beginning of the publication.

18 A. V. Zapadov, ed. *Istoriia russkoi zhurnalistiki XVIII–XIX vekov* (Moscow: Vysshaia shkola, 1966), 334.

controversial than could be published in Petersburg. Although he dealt fairly with all the publications under his control, his favorite was apparently the *Russian Messenger*.[19] Throughout 1856–1858, von Kruze repeatedly received warnings from the Moscow censorship committee for allowing questionable articles into print.[20] Finally, in 1858, when the authorities, frightened by the outspoken discussion of the coming reforms in the press, swung temporarily back to the right, von Kruze was removed from his position.

Another circumstance which aided the rapid growth of the *Russian Messenger* in its early years was the split that occurred between the liberal and radical contributors to the *Contemporary* (Sovremennik) in the late 1850s, a split which led the liberals, including Turgenev and Tolstoy, to leave the journal.[21] The consistently pro-reform position of the *Russian Messenger*, added to the

---

19 Kitaev reports: "In his views N. F. Kruze was close to the liberal Westernizers. It is true that he treated the Slavophile publications with sympathetic attention as well, but he showed a preference for the *Russian Messenger*. 'I notice in von Kruze a passion for the *Russian Messenger*,' wrote I. S. Aksakov to A. I. Koshelev in September 1856." Kitaev, *Ot frondy k okhranitel'stvu*, 69.

20 Kitaev, *Ot frondy k okhranitel'stvu*, 68–69. Kitaev cites L. F. Panteleev's memoirs, in which he maintains that von Kruze was responsible for the publication of Saltykov-Shchedrin's *Provincial Sketches*. That *RV* was viewed with suspicion by the authorities during this period is shown by the "Note about different ill-intentioned rumors and ill-intentioned people" (Zapiska o neblagonamerennykh tolkakh i neblagonamerennykh liudiakh) and "List of suspicious people in Moscow" (Spisok podozritel'nykh lits v Moskve) presented by the governor general of Moscow, A. A. Zakrevskii, to the head of the Imperial Chancellery's Third Section, V. A. Dolgorukov. In the former the *Russian Messenger* is singled out along with the journal *Athenaeum* (Atenei) and the *Moscow Gazette* as publications requiring strict surveillance. M. K. Lemke, *Epokha tsenzurnykh reform* (St. Petersburg: Gerol'd, 1904), 1–8. Liubimov reports two confrontations between Katkov and the censorship in 1858 in *Mikhail Nikiforovich Katkov*, 72–115.

21 Worried about possible competition from the newly created *Russian Messenger* and disturbed by the growing dissension between the radicals and liberals on the *Contemporary* staff, sometime in mid-1856 Nekrasov concluded an exclusive contract with Turgenev, Tolstoy, Ostrovskii, and Grigorovich obliging them to publish during 1857 exclusively in the *Contemporary*. The writers were to receive, besides their regular fees, a certain percentage of the subscription monies. The agreement was a failure, and there was no attempt to extend it past the first year. By June 1858 the break between the liberals and the radicals of the critical section headed by Chernyshevskii was complete. Tolstoy considered creating a journal to fight Chernyshevskii, but Turgenev was unwilling to cut his ties with the left. He continued to publish in the *Contemporary* until 1860, and both *Nest of the Gentry* (Dvorianskoe gnezdo, January 1858) and "Hamlet and Don Quixote" (Gamlet i Don-Kikhot; January 1860) appeared there.

fact that it had already by the end of the decade clearly outclassed its paler liberal competitor, the *Notes of the Fatherland* (Otechestvennye zapiski), now made it the logical place for these writers to publish. Tolstoy made his debut in the *Russian Messenger* with *Family Happiness* (Semeinoe schast'e) in 1859, and the novel *On the Eve* (Nakanune) was Turgenev's first work to appear in the journal in 1860.[22]

It was not only the political "line" of the *Russian Messenger* that must have attracted the liberal defectors from the *Contemporary*, but the journal's literary viewpoint as well. One of the major points of contention between the liberals and the radicals on the *Contemporary* staff was Chernyshevskii's vision of the social role of art, elaborated on the pages of the *Contemporary* in such articles as his "Notes on the Gogol Period in Russian literature" (Ocherki gogolevskogo perioda russkoi literatury).[23] In the very first issue of the *Russian Messenger* Katkov answered Chernyshevskii in an article which took the new Pavel Annenkov edition of Pushkin's works as its point of departure.[24] Basing his arguments on the poems from Pushkin's "poet" cycle, Katkov denied the right of the "mob" to dictate to the poet and defended the autonomy of art: "Art must have its own internal purpose, as does everything on earth. This is the basic law of all organization, of each self-sufficient existence, of each activity of the human race."[25] Although the article had a clearly Belinskian ring, maintaining that art and science are but two different types of knowledge and that there is an organic relationship between art and society, Katkov declared himself in no uncertain terms to be against "useful" art:

> We must be careful that instead of a poet we do not saddle ourselves with a phrase-monger or a doctrinaire. The phrase-monger is a type that is good for nothing and is not worth talking about; the doctrinaire is an honorable man, but it would be much better for him to act directly, not resorting to forms of artistic creation. The poem, the story,

---

22 L. N. Tolstoy, *Semeinoe schast'e*, *RV* 20 (April 1859): 435–73, 595–634; I. S. Turgenev, *Nakanune*, *RV* 25 (January 1860): 69–212.

23 N. G. Chernyshevskii, "Ocherki gogolevskogo perioda russkoi literatury," *Sovremennik* 55, no. 2 (1855): 65–132.

24 M. N. Katkov, "Pushkin," *RV* 1 (1856): 155–72 and 306–24; *RV* 2 (1856): 281-310.

25 Katkov, "Pushkin," *RV* 1 (1856): 159. In the "Notes of the *Russian Messenger*" section of the "Contemporary Chronicle" for June 1856, Katkov again defended the autonomy of art. Katkov, "Zametki 'Russkogo vestnika,'" *RV* 3 (June 1856): 213.

the drama, written with a dialectical or oratorical purpose often only harms the thought that called it forth.[26]

The popularity of the *Russian Messenger* grew rapidly in the first five years of its existence, and by 1861 it ranked second in Russia in numbers of subscribers, trailing only the much older *Contemporary*.[27] One of the most popular works published in the *Russian Messenger* in its early years was Saltykov-Shchedrin's *Provincial Sketches* (Gubernskie ocherki), which Nekrasov had rejected for publication in the *Contemporary*.[28] An annoyed Chernyshevskii wrote to Nekrasov on February 7, 1857, about the growth of their Moscow "competitor's" popularity: "The success of the *Russian Messenger* depends more than half on Shchedrin's (Saltykov's) articles—*Provincial Sketches*. [. . .] From no. 16 to the end of the year they dragged on uninterruptedly, producing an effect in every issue. 500 subscribers—that's too few—perhaps 1000 were gained by the *Russian Messenger* by these *Sketches*."[29] Despite the journalistic rivalry between the two publications, the relaxation of the political climate was still such that in 1860 Chernyshevskii could write: "No one is more overjoyed than we are at the brilliant success of the *Russian Messenger*, and no one desires more that this success will continue and grow."[30]

During the early years of the journal's existence, Katkov gradually consolidated his power over the publication. One by one the contributors and editors who differed with him left the journal, and by the early 1860s, Katkov

---

26 Katkov, "Pushkin," *RV* 1 (1856): 314.

27 Liubimov, in *Mikhail Nikiforovich Katkov*, 128, reports that according to the information of the censorship department, in 1862 the *Contemporary* had 7,000 subscribers, the *Russian Messenger* had 5,700, and the *Notes of the Fatherland* and the *Russian Word* (Russkoe slovo) had 4,000 subscribers each. The BrockhausEfron encyclopedia gives the following figures for the same year: the *Contemporary*—6,658, *Russian Messenger*—6,100, *Notes of the Fatherland*—4,500, Dostoevskii's *Time*—4,350, and the *Library for Reading* (Biblioteka dlia chteniia)—3,500. *Entsiklopedicheskii slovar'*, s.v. *zhurnal*.

28 Saltykov-Shchedrin's *Provincial Sketches* was published in *RV* from August of 1856 to August of 1867. For its full publishing history see M. E. Saltykov-Shchedrin, *Sobranie sochinenii* (Moscow: Khudozhestvennaia literatura, 1965), vol. 2, 516–17.

29 N. G. Chernyshevskii, *Polnoe sobranie sochinenii* (Moscow: Khudozhestvennaia literatura, 1949), vol. 14, 338. In this letter Chernyshevskii expresses concern over the competition that the *Russian Messenger* is giving the *Contemporary*.

30 Cited in Kitaev, *Ot frondy k okhranitel'stvu*, 228.

was in full control.³¹ He threw himself into the study of political and economic theory to better prepare for the demands of running a major journal, and he became a firm supporter of English models for political and economic life. The Anglomania of the *Russian Messenger* became so notorious that in 1862 Herzen referred to it as the *Westminster Messenger* (Vestminsterskii vestnik).³²

By 1861, divisions were again opening up between the various factions of Russian society. In that year Katkov reorganized the *Russian Messenger*. The journal became a monthly, and the "Contemporary Chronicle" became a separate weekly publication. To take its place Katkov created a section within the journal under the heading "Literary Review and Notes" (Literaturnoe obozrenie i zametki). In this new section Katkov concentrated the majority of his polemical articles against other journals and journalists. The first major target of Katkov's ire was the *Contemporary*, and the previously cordial relationship between the two publications soon turned to bitter enmity.³³ Katkov then turned his attention to Herzen, who had previously been immune to discus-

---

31 According to Kitaev, the Slavophiles S. T. and I. S. Aksakov left the *Russian Messenger* because Katkov refused to print a review of the *Family Chronicle* by N. P. Giliarov-Platonov. In 1857, Katkov began to polemicize with the Slavophile journal *Russian Conversation* (Russkaia beseda) in a series of "accusatory letters" published under the pseudonym Baiboroda. The polemic, mild in comparison with Katkov's later publicistic attacks, reached its height in March and April of 1857, although the "letters" continued until 1859. Kitaev, *Ot frondy k okhranitel'stvu*, 73–82. Of the liberal Westernizers from the Stankevich circle, Kudriavtsev died, and Korsh and Chicherin left the journal in 1857. Korsh founded the short-lived (1858–1859) journal *Athenaeum*, around which the liberal Westernizers grouped. On the split between the Westernizers in the *Russian Messenger*, see Katz, *Mikhail N. Katkov*, esp. 53–59.

32 Herzen's letter to Turgenev dated February 9, 1862, in A. I. Gertsen, *Sobranie sochinenii v tridtsati tomakh* (Moscow: Izdatel'stvo AN SSSR, 1963), vol. 27, 209.

33 Katkov's attacks on the *Contemporary* began with the creation of the "Literary Review and Notes" section in January 1861, and were at their height during 1861 and 1862, although the *Russian Messenger* and the *Contemporary* remained journalistic adversaries until the latter was closed in 1866. Katkov's most important articles directed against the radicalism of the *Contemporary* included: "Old Gods and New Gods" (Starye bogi i novye bogi, *RV*, February 1861), "Berries of a Field" (Odnogo polia iagody, *RV*, May 1861), "Views on an *Entente Cordiale* with the *Contemporary*" (Vidy na entente cordiale s "Sovremennikom," *RV*, July 1861), "A Few Words About Progress" (Koe-chto o progresse, *RV*, October 1861), "To What Party do We Belong?" (K kakoi prinadlezhim my partii?, *RV*, February 1862), and "A Few Words about One Ironic Word" (Neskol'ko slov po povodu odnogo ironicheskogo slova, *RV*, March 1862). Kitaev, *Ot frondy k okhranitel'stvu*, 228–38; Katz, *Mikhail N. Katkov*, 62–70.

sion in the Russian press.[34] The editor's campaign against the émigré publicist unleashed the anti-Herzen feeling in Russian society, and a number of other journals followed suit.[35] Katkov's role in discrediting Herzen attracted attention in high government circles, including the tsar himself. On November 30, 1862, Katkov and Leont'ev were presented to the emperor and empress at a ball in the great palace of the Kremlin. The imperial couple wished Katkov success and told him that they read the *Russian Messenger* with pleasure.[36]

In February 1862, Turgenev published a second novel in the *Russian Messenger: Fathers and Sons* (Ottsy i deti). The novel elicited wildly differing responses from the critics, their attention centering on the character of Bazarov. The main opponents in the debate were the radical critics Antonovich and Pisarev, the former denouncing Bazarov as a "monster" and a "caricature," the latter hailing the character as a sympathetic portrayal of the "new man."[37] Katkov himself soon entered the debate with articles entitled "Turgenev's Novel and its Critics" (Roman Turgeneva i ego kritiki) and "About Our Nihilism apropos Turgenev's Novel" (O nashem nigilizme po povodu romana

---

34 Disturbed by Katkov's article "To What Party Do We Belong?," Herzen responded in the *Bell* (Kolokol) with an article "To the Senators and Privy Counselors of Journalism" (Senatoram i tainym sovetnikam zhurnalizma). Katkov could not directly respond because of a ban on mentioning the émigré publicist's name in the Russian press. He made oblique references to Herzen in the article "Our Foreign Refugees" (Nashi zagranichnye refugies), printed in *RV* in June of 1862, suggesting that Herzen was responsible for the Petersburg fires in the spring of 1862. Herzen answered Katkov in his article "Bad Weapons" (Durnye oruzhiia). In the meantime, the tsar lifted the ban on attacking Herzen openly. When Katkov received a letter from Herzen demanding that he clarify the insinuations in "Our Foreign Refugees," he held the June issue of the *Russian Messenger* and wrote a response to Herzen. The article, "A Note for the Editor of the *Bell*" (Zametka dlia izdatelia "Kolokola"), was passed by the censorship and printed in great secrecy so that word of the article would not leak out in advance. Kitaev, *Ot frondy k okhranitel'stvu*, 267–74; Lemke, *Epokha tsenzurnykh reform*, 158–61; Nevedenskii, *Katkov i ego vremia*, 136–51.

35 No direct attack on Katkov's article was allowed to appear in the Russian press, although a letter in the *Northern Bee* (Severnaia pchela) protested against the "tone" of "A Note for the Editor of the *Bell*." A number of journals took up the attack against Herzen, including *Our Time* (Nashe vremia), *Son of the Fatherland*, and *Home Conversation* (Domashniaia beseda). Lemke, *Epokha tsenzurnykh reform*, 162–63.

36 Nevedenskii, *Katkov i ego vremia*, 160–61.

37 M. A. Antonovich, "Asmodei nashego vremeni," *Sovremennik* (March 1862): 65–121; D. I. Pisarev, "Bazarov," *Russkoe slovo* (March 1862): section 2, "Russkaia literatura," 1–54.

Turgeneva).[38] In these articles he maintained that the difference of opinion between Antonovich and Pisarev over the character of Bazarov only served to prove that the character was true to life. He then proceeded to use Bazarov as a point of departure for expounding his stand against nihilism as a social phenomenon.

One of the controversies surrounding *Fathers and Sons* is the extent to which Katkov influenced Turgenev during the writing of the novel.[39] Despite claims to the contrary, there is no substantial evidence to prove that Katkov tampered with the manuscript of the novel after the author submitted the final draft for publication.[40] However, seeing in Bazarov an "apotheosis" of his *Contemporary* rivals, Katkov apparently put pressure on Turgenev to make changes in his character so that Bazarov would appear less positive.[41] In any case, the incident illustrates the fact that despite Katkov's defense of the autonomy of art he was not averse to demanding changes from authors and to distorting manuscripts of literary works on both moral and political grounds.

The year 1863 was a turning point in Katkov's journalistic career. He began to lease the *Moscow Gazette* from Moscow University, which put him in control of two most powerful types of publications in Russia, a daily

---

38   Katkov, "Roman Turgeneva i ego kritiki," *RV* 39 (May 1862): 393–424; and "O nashem nigilizme po povodu romana Turgeneva," *RV* 40 (July 1862): 402–26.

39   Scholarly discussions of the issue are surveyed in A. Batiuto, "Parizhskaia rukopis' romana I. S. Turgeneva 'Ottsy i deti,'" *Russkaia literatura* 4 (1961): 57–78.

40   Batiuto, having uncovered what he claims to be a draft of the final manuscript of *Fathers and Sons*, reveals that there is no significant difference between this draft and the version published in the *Russian Messenger*. His argument that Turgenev made additions in the margins of the manuscript which Katkov chose to ignore seems tenuous. Batiuto, "Parizhskaia rukopis'," 51–65.

41   In a letter to Katkov written in Paris in October of 1861, Turgenev speaks of the need for greater rewriting of *Fathers and Sons* than he had expected, concluding: "I hope that after my corrections the figure of Bazarov will become clear to you and will not produce on you the impression of an apotheosis, which was not my intention." I. S. Turgenev, *Polnoe sobranie sochinenii i pisem v tridtsati tomakh* (Moscow: Nauka, 1978–2018), *Pis'ma*, vol. 4, 373 (hereafter *PSS, Pis'ma*). Turgenev speaks again of making changes suggested by Katkov in a letter to him of November 11, 1861 (*PSS, Pis'ma*, 4:378). He continues to discuss changes to *Fathers and Sons* in letters to E. E. Lambert of March 14, 1862 and A. P. Maikov of March 18, 1862 (*PSS, Pis'ma*, 5:28–29, 38). In a letter to A. P. Filosofova of August 30, 1874, Turgenev heartily defended the character of Bazarov (*PSS, Pis'ma*, 13:166).

newspaper and a journal.⁴² The publication in that year of first installments of Fet's "From the Countryside" (Iz derevni), which criticized the reforms from a conservative point of view, was indicative of the *Russian Messenger*'s increasing movement to the right.⁴³ Katkov's chauvinistic stand on the Polish Uprising, which broke out in January 1863, catapulted him to fame both in Russia and abroad as a spokesman for Russian society, while his championship of firm measures to suppress the Poles settled his reputation as a reactionary once and for all.⁴⁴

Despite the growing stigma attached, in liberal circles, to publishing in the *Russian Messenger*, old contributors continued to publish there and new ones joined, some for political and some for financial reasons. Despite his dislike of Katkov, Turgenev published *Smoke* (Dym) in the *Russian Messenger* in March 1867.⁴⁵ He defended his continued association with the journal in a letter to Herzen dated May 22 of the same year:

> The only thing that bothers me are my relations with Katkov, even though they are superficial. But I can say the following: I do not publish my work in the *Moscow Gazette*—I hope that such a misfortune will never come upon me—but in the *Russian Messenger*, which is nothing more than a collection, having no political coloration, and at the present time the *Russian Messenger* is the only journal which is read by the public and can pay. I can't conceal the fact that this explanation

---

42 For the details of the transaction, see Liubimov, *Mikhail Nikiforovich Katkov*, 213–16. After the acquisition in 1863 of the *Moscow Gazette*, the focus of Katkov's attention apparently shifted from the *Russian Messenger*—which was left in the hands of Liubimov—to the newspaper. However, Katkov continued to play an important role in the selection and editing of literary materials to be published in the journal.

43 Fet's "From the Countryside" was published in *RV* in 1862, 1863, and 1864. The last two installments were published in 1868 in *Literary Library* (Literaturnaia biblioteka) and in 1871 in *Zaria* (Dawn).

44 According to Tatishchev, "The events which accompanied this uprising called forth a number of articles by Katkov animated with sincere patriotism, which served as a fully deserved pedestal of his publicistic activity. All of zemstvo Russia listened with great sympathy to the passionate speech of the publicist; his articles also came to the attention of the European press—and Katkov became famous." Nevedenskii, *Katkov i ego vremia*, 163.

45 Turgenev's *Smoke* was published in *RV* in March of 1867. Turgenev also published his "The Story of Lieutenant Ergunov" (Istoriia leitenanta Ergunova) in *RV* in 1868.

is perhaps inadequate, but I have no other. *Notes of the Fatherland* is the *Russian Messenger*'s only rival, and it cannot pay half the money.⁴⁶

Although Tolstoy also thought little of Katkov personally, he continued to publish in the *Russian Messenger* well into the 1870s, demanding and receiving ever higher payment for his works.⁴⁷ After *Family Happiness*, Tolstoy published *The Cossacks* (Kazaki) and *Polikushka* in the journal in 1863.⁴⁸ In 1865 and 1866 the first part of *War and Peace* (Voina i mir) appeared in the *Russian Messenger* under the title *1805* (Tysiacha vosem'sot piatyi god).⁴⁹ Tolstoy broke with Katkov in 1877 over the epilogue to *Anna Karenina*. The novel was serialized in the *Russian Messenger* from 1875 to 1877.⁵⁰ When Katkov received the manuscript of the epilogue, however, he found political sentiments expressed by Levin objectionable and asked the author to make changes.⁵¹ Tolstoy

---

46   Turgenev, *PSS*, *Pis'ma*, 7:201.

47   In an 1861 diary entry Tolstoy wrote: "Katkov is so limited that he suits the public to a tee." Buslaev, "Perepiska," 191. In a November 14, 1865, letter to A. A. Tolstaia, Tolstoy says about Katkov's political views: "Why do you say that I had quarreled with Katkov? Not at all. First, there was no reason, and second, there is as much in common between me and him as there is between you and your water carrier. I am not sympathetic to the idea of forbidding the Poles to speak Polish." L. N. Tolstoi, *Sobranie sochinenii v dvadtsati tomakh* (Moscow: Khudozhestvennaia literatura, 1965), vol. 17, 295. As regards Tolstoy's attitude to the journal itself, in his letter to Katkov offering the editor *1805* the author claimed: "Of [all] journals I would most like to publish in the *Russian Messenger* for the reason that it is the one journal that I read and receive." Buslaev, "Perepiska," 191.

48   Tolstoy's *The Cossacks* was published in *RV* in January and "Polikushka" in February of 1863.

49   Tolstoy's *1805* was published in *RV* in January and February of 1865 and February, March, and April of 1866.

50   Tolstoy's *Anna Karenina* was published in *RV* in January-April of 1875, January-December of 1876, and January-April of 1877.

51   According to Buslaev, "In this last, eighth book, the part of the novel that was originally called the epilogue, Tolstoy touched on what was a burning issue of the time, the freeing of the southern Slavs from the power of the Turks and in general the Slavic question, which at that time was strongly fanned by the Russian government; in this way, Russia was gradually drawn into war with Turkey. Tolstoy, through Levin, expressed in the epilogue his negative attitude to this movement, considering it a fashionable enthusiasm of the idle circles of high society, which had no roots in the masses of the people. Katkov, who supported the official politics of the government, demanded from Tolstoy corresponding changes in his conception of the Slavic question." Buslaev, "Perepiska," 191.

refused, and in place of the epilogue in the May 1877 issue Katkov printed the following notice:

> From the editors. In the previous issue after the novel *Anna Karenina* appeared the statement "ending to follow." But with the death of the heroine, properly, a short epilogue was to follow, about a couple dozen pages, from which the readers could learn that Vronskii, in confusion and grief after the death of Anna, left as a volunteer for Serbia and that all the others are alive and well, and Levin remains in his countryside and gets angry at Slavic committees and volunteers.[52]

In a letter to the editors of the *Russian Messenger* Tolstoy responded in kind:

> The grandiose laconism of the account of the contents of the last part [of *Anna Karenina*] only forces one to regret that the editors wearied the readers for such a long time, for three years, taking up so much space when they could so simply, in the same grandiose tone in which their note was composed, give an account of it. They could have written: There was a lady, she threw over her husband. But, falling in love with another, she began to get angry and threw herself in front of a train. Besides this, there was Levin who got married to a girl and begat a son, and he and his family were healthy all the time.[53]

While some writers published in the *Russian Messenger* for financial reasons, others appear to have been sympathetic toward Katkov's conservative views. This was apparently the case with Aleksei Pisemskii, who published his anti-nihilist novel, *The Troubled Sea* (Vzbalamuchennoe more), in the *Russian Messenger* in 1863.[54] Pisemskii's novel was the first of many representatives of this "genre," which were spawned by Katkov's dogmatic anti-nihilist

---

52   Quoted in Buslaev, "Perepiska," 191.

53   Buslaev, "Perepiska," 191. In July issue of *RV* for 1877 Katkov printed an article on the separate edition of the epilogue to *Anna Karenina* entitled "What Happened after the Death of Anna Karenina?" in which he criticized the novel as unfinished and having no unifying idea. Katkov, "Chto sluchilos' po smerti Anny Kareninoi?," *RV* 130 (July 1877): 462.

54   Pisemskii's the *Troubled Sea* was published in *RV* in March-August of 1863. In an article entitled "The Ideal Editor" (Ideal'nyi redaktor) published in 1861–1862 in the *Library for Reading* under the pseudonym Nikita Bezrylov, Pisemskii clearly had Katkov in mind. P. G. Pustovoit, *A. F. Pisemskii v istorii russkogo romana* (Moscow: Izdatel'stvo Moskovskogo universiteta, 1969), 148.

position and which filled the pages of the *Russian Messenger* during the 1860s and 1870s. Dostoevskii's *The Possessed* (Besy) has been counted as the best of the anti-nihilist novels, while the great majority of them were second-rate attempts at literature.[55]

Another writer of note who published an anti-nihilist novel in the *Russian Messenger* was Leskov, whose *At Daggers Drawn* (Na nozhakh) appeared in the journal in 1870.[56] Leskov came to the journal when his reputation as a reactionary had barred him from publication in all other major journals.[57] He made his debut in the *Russian Messenger* in 1869 with the sketch "The Plodomasov Dwarfs" (Plodomasovskie karliki).[58] In the early 1870s his "The Sealed Angel" (Zapechatlennyi angel), *Cathedral Folk* (Soboriane), and *Family in Decline* (Zakhudalyi rod) also appeared in the journal.[59] However, Leskov's relationship with Katkov and his managing editor Liubimov was far from perfect. The editors distorted his manuscripts, and Katkov took a dislike to and refused

---

55 Among the lesser-known writers who published anti-nihilist novels in *The Russian Messenger* were V. P. Kliushnikov, V. V. Krestovskii, Boleslav Markevich, D. V. Averkiev, and V. G. Avseenko. Markevich, Averkiev, and Avseenko formed part of a "pleiade" of writers which dominated the literary section of *RV* in the mid-1870s.

56 Leskov's *At Daggers Drawn* was published in *RV* in October-December of 1870 and January-October of 1871. For a detailed account of Leskov's relations with Katkov, see William Edgerton, "Nikolai Leskov: The Intellectual Development of a Literary Nonconformist" (PhD diss., Columbia University, New York, 1954), 300–48. Edgerton reports that throughout the time that Leskov was publishing *At Daggers Drawn* in *RV*, he complained in letters about Liubimov's editing of the novel. Edgerton, "Nikolai Leskov," 314.

57 The publication of Leskov's first anti-nihilist novel, *No Way Out* (Nekuda) in the *Library for Reading* in 1864 established the author's reputation as a reactionary. He was boycotted in liberal circles and was unable to publish in any major journal with the exception of *Notes of the Fatherland*, and there only until he broke with Kraevskii in 1867. Edgerton, "Nikolai Leskov," 239–41, 288, 295, 300.

58 Leskov's "The Plodomasov Dwarves" was published in *RV* in February of 1869. This sketch was part of the second version of Leskov's *Cathedral Folk*. Edgerton, "Nikolai Leskov," 323–24.

59 Leskov, "Zapechatlennyi angel," *RV*, January 1873. Leskov later told I. A. Shliapin that under Katkov's influence he had added on a scene at the end in which the Old Believers return to the Orthodox Church because of what appears to be a miracle. Edgerton, "Nikolai Leskov," 334. Leskov's *Cathedral Falk* was published in *RV* in April-July of 1872; and *Family in Decline* in July-October of 1874. Katkov apparently forced Leskov to make extensive changes to *Cathedral Folk*, including eliminating links between the main character, Tuberozov, and Archpriest Avvakum. Edgerton, "Nikolai Leskov," 322–26.

to publish Leskov's *Enchanted Pilgrim* (Ocharovannyi strannik).[60] Leskov's final break with Katkov came in 1874 over changes made by the editor in *Family in Decline,* and at that time Leskov described his relations with the *Russian Messenger*:

> The *Russian Messenger* was the last journal which I could somehow adhere to, where I put up with considerable constraint—now even that is over.... Now I have ended everything with them too; I have no more strength to bear what I bore for so long. Except for "The Sealed Angel," which passed by them for lack of time "in the shadow," I often did not recognize my own works, and, finally, the second part of *Family in Decline,* having appeared in God knows what condition, exhausted or rather ground up the last drops of my patience and of all my spiritual strength.[61]

Dostoevskii's association with the *Russian Messenger* was probably the longest and most important for the history of Russian literature. Like Leskov, he saw his works rudely disfigured at the hands of Katkov and his editorial staff, and the marks of their brutalization of his novels remain to the present day. Yet Dostoevskii published all four of his major novels in the *Russian Messenger* and remained a contributor to the journal until his death in 1881.

Dostoevskii's association with the journal began as far back as 1857 while the author was still in exile. He offered Katkov a story, which was to become the *Village of Stepanchikovo* (Selo Stepanchikovo), and Katkov sent Dostoevskii 500 rubles as an advance. When the story was delivered, however, Katkov did not like it and refused to pay Dostoevskii. The writer and the editor were next brought together as journalistic adversaries, when, during the early 1860s, Dostoevskii's journal *Time* (Vremia) carried on a sharp polemic with the *Russian Messenger*.[62] However, when *Time* was shut down over

---

60 According to Edgerton's "Nikolai Leskov," 339–40, "Katkov did not like the story [*The Enchanted Pilgrim*] and refused to publish it." Edgerton quotes Liubimov's explanation for the journal's decision.

61 Quoted in I. P. Viduetskaia, "Dostoevskii i Leskov," *Russkaia literatura* 4 (1975): 128. On Leskov's break with Katkov over *Family in Decline* see Edgerton, "Nikolai Leskov," 345–46.

62 On the polemic between *Time* and *The Russian Messenger,* see V. S. Nechaeva, *Zhurnal M. M. i F. M. Dostoevskikh "Vremia"* (Moscow: Nauka, 1972), 267–71.

a misunderstanding about an article by Strakhov, "The Fatal Question" (Rokovoi vopros), Katkov helped to clear the matter up with the authorities. The editor published an article in the *Russian Messenger* maintaining the innocence of Strakhov's piece, and in January 1864, the Dostoevskii brothers were able to open a new journal, *Epoch* (Epokha), largely owing to Katkov's intercession.[63]

In 1865, after *Epoch* failed and Dostoevskii had fled abroad to escape his creditors, he was again aided by Katkov. He sent the editor a letter in which he described the plan for *Crime and Punishment* (Prestuplenie i nakazanie) and asked for money.[64] Katkov responded immediately with an advance, as he was to do on numerous occasions in the future when the writer needed money, a fact which at least in part accounts for Dostoevskii's continued loyalty to the *Russian Messenger*.[65] The novel was published in the journal in 1866, but only after Dostoevskii had made extensive changes demanded by Katkov and Liubimov. These changes were centered around the character of Sonia: the prudish editors were offended by Dostoevskii's portrayal of a prostitute as a purveyor of spiritual truth.[66]

---

63 On Strakhov's article and polemics around it, see Konstantin Mochulsky, *Dostoevsky, His Life and Work*, trans. Michael A. Minihan (Princeton: Princeton University Press, 1971), 235; and V. S. Nechaeva, *Zhurnal M. M. i F. M. Dostoevskikh "Epokha"* (Moscow: Nauka, 1975), 7–8. Katkov published an article on "The Fatal Question" in the May 1863 issue of *RV*. According to Nechaeva, in the article Katkov "tried at least to throw light on the intentions of the author of 'The Fatal Question.' But not even naming *Time* and even less Dostoevskii, Katkov directed the whole article against him as his recent journalistic enemy. He wrote about Strakhov that he was not at all a 'disguised Pole,' but a true Russian who 'wanted in this article to declare his patriotic feeling and to serve his people.'" Nechaeva, *Zhurnal M. M. i F. M. Dostoevskikh "Epokha,"* 8. From the pages of the *Contemporary*, Saltykov-Shchedrin and Antonovich polemicized with *Epoch*, accusing Dostoevskii of being afraid of Katkov and submitting to his influence. Nechaeva, *Zhurnal M. M. i F. M. Dostoevskikh "Epokha,"* 183–86.

64 F. M. Dostoevskii, *Polnoe sobranie sochinenii v tridtsati tomakh* (Leningrad: Nauka, 1972–1990), vol. 28, bk. 2, 136–39 (hereafter *PSS*). In this letter Dostoevskii also asks Katkov to forget their disagreement about *The Village of Stepanchikovo*. In a letter to A. E. Vrangel of September 28, 1865, Dostoevskii expressed his fear that both the incident with *The Village of Stepanchikovo* and the polemics which *Time* had carried on with *RV* could prejudice Katkov. Dostoevskii, *PSS*, 28:2:140.

65 On Dostoevskii's financial relations with Katkov, see his letters to Katkov, Vrangel, Liubimov, A. G. Snitkina (Dostoevskaia), and A. N. Maikov, in *PSS*, 28:2:146, 157, 169, 176, 205, 214, and 239.

66 For Dostoevskii's disagreements with *RV* see his letters to Katkov, Liubimov, and A. P. Miliukov (*PSS*, 28:2:145–46, 164, 165–66). In his letter to Miliukov Dostoevskii writes

The Idiot (Idiot) appeared in the *Russian Messenger* in 1868, and *The Possessed* in 1871 and 1872. In *The Possessed* Dostoevskii's epic moral vision again came into conflict with Katkov's prudishness. The editor demanded that the chapter "At Tikhon's" (U Tikhona) be expunged from the novel, objecting to the allusion to a crime against a young girl in Stavrogin's confession.[67] As was the case with *Crime and Punishment*, Dostoevskii's pleas and attempts at compromise came to no avail, and, omitting this key chapter, the author was forced to restructure the entire second half of the novel. Nonetheless, Dostoevskii continued to publish in the *Russian Messenger*. In 1874 he offered Katkov *The Adolescent* (Podrostok), but the editor, already having *Anna Karenina* in hand for the following year, could not afford to take on another work of that magnitude.[68] The *Brothers Karamazov* (Brat'ia Karamazovy) was serialized in the *Russian Messenger* in 1879 and 1880.[69]

Dostoevskii's last novel was also the last flicker of the dying literary prestige of the *Russian Messenger*. Although in the final years of his life Katkov's political power reached its apogee, his reactionary ideas had lost touch with the Russian reading public, and only second-rate writers could be encouraged to publish in his journal. After Katkov's death in 1887, the *Russian Messenger* lost all of its importance, struggling along under various editors as an organ of extreme reaction until its demise in Petersburg in 1906.[70]

---

about Liubimov's objections to the portrayal of a prostitute as an interpreter of the Gospel. For more on this disagreement see Leonid Grossman, *Dostoevsky, His Life and Work*, trans. Mary Mackler (Indianapolis: The Bobbs-Merrill Company, Inc., 1975), 377–78.

67 According to Grossman, it was Katkov and not the censor who was responsible for the changes in *The Possessed*. Grossman, *Dostoevsky, His Life and Work*, 471.

68 The novel appeared in *Notes of the Fatherland* in 1875.

69 Dostoevskii's *The Brothers Karamazov* was published in *RV* in January-November of 1879 and January-November of 1880. A letter from Dostoevskii to V. F. Putsykovich of June 1879 indicates that Dostoevskii ran into problems with the editorial board of *RV* over *The Brothers Karamazov* as well: "In the novel it happened that I adhered to several ideas and positions which, I feared, would not be to their liking [...] and just as I feared, it came to pass: they are nagging at me." Quoted in Viduetskaia, "Dostoevskii i Leskov," 128.

70 After Katkov's death, the journal was continued by his widow, S. P. Katkova, under the editorship of D. N. Tsertelev until the eleventh issue for 1887, when the publication was taken over by F. N. Berg and the company Public Good (Obshchestvennaia pol'za). Berg moved the journal to St. Petersburg where it was published until 1896 when it was moved back to Moscow. From the fourth through the ninth issues for 1896, *RV* came out under the editorship of D. I. Stakheev. It was then acquired by M. M. Katkov, and in 1902 moved back to Petersburg where it went out of business in 1906.

Works Cited

Antonovich, M. A. "Asmodei nashego vremeni." *Sovremennik* (March 1862): 65–121.

Batiuto, A. "Parizhskaia rukopis' romana I. S. Turgeneva 'Ottsy i deti.'" *Russkaia literatura* 4 (1961): 57–78.

Buslaev, F., ed. "Perepiska Tolstogo s M. N. Katkovym." In *Literaturnoe nasledstvo*, vols. 37–38, *L. N. Tolstoi*, part 2, 189-207. Moscow: Izdatel'stvo AN SSSR, 1939.

Chernyshevskii, N. G. "Ocherki gogolevskogo perioda russkoi literatury." *Sovremennik* 55, no. 2 (1855): 65–132.

———. *Polnoe sobranie sochinenii*. Vol. 14. Moscow: Khudozhestvennaia literatura, 1949.

Dostoevskii, F. M. *Polnoe sobranie sochinenii v tridtsati tomakh*. Leningrad: Nauka, 1972–1990.

Edgerton, William. "Nikolai Leskov: The Intellectual Development of a Literary Nonconformist." PhD diss., Columbia University, New York, 1954.

Entsiklopedicheskii slovar'. St. Petersburg: Izdatel'stvo "P. A. Brokgauz and I. A. Efron," 1890–1907.

Gertsen, A. I. *Sobranie sochinenii v tridtsati tomakh*. Vol. 27. Moscow: Izdatel'stvo AN SSSR, 1963.

Grossman, Leonid. *Dostoevsky, His Life and Work*. Translated by Mary Mackler. Indianapolis: The Bobbs-Merrill Company, Inc., 1975.

Katkov, M. N. "Pushkin." *Russkii vestnik* 1 (1856): 155–72 and 306–24; *RV* 2 (1856): 281-310.

Katz, Martin. *Mikhail N. Katkov, a Political Biography*. The Hague/Paris: Mouton & Co., 1966.

Kitaev, V. A. *Ot frondy k okhranitel'stvu: iz istorii russkoi liberal'noi mysli*. Moscow: Mysl', 1972.

Lemke, M. K. *Epokha tsenzurnykh reform*. St. Petersburg: Gerol'd, 1904.

Liubimov, N. A. *Mikhail Nikiforovich Katkov i ego istoricheskaia zasluga*. St. Petersburg: Otechestvennaia pol'za, 1889.

Liwoff, G. *Michel Katkoff et son epoque*. Paris: E. Plon, Nourrit et cie., 1897.

Mochulsky, Konstantin. *Dostoevsky, His Life and Work*. Translated by Michael A. Minihan. Princeton: Princeton University Press, 1971.

Nechaeva, V. S. *Zhurnal M. M. i F. M. Dostoevskikh "Vremia."* Moscow: Nauka, 1972.

———. *Zhurnal M. M. i F. M. Dostoevskikh "Epokha."* Moscow: Nauka, 1975.

Nevedenskii, S. (pseudonym of S. S. Tatishchev). *Katkov i ego vremia*. St. Petersburg: Tipografiia A. S. Suvorina, 1888.

Ocherki po istorii russkoi zhurnalistiki i kritiki. Edited by V. G. Berezina et al. Vol. 2. Leningrad: Izdatel'stvo Leningradskogo gosudarstvennogo universiteta, 1965.

Pisarev, D. I. "Bazarov." *Russkoe slovo* (March 1862): section 2, "Russkaia literatura," 1–54.

Pustovoit, P. G. *A. F. Pisemskii v istorii russkogo romana*. Moscow: Izdatel'stvo Moskovskogo universiteta, 1969.

Raeff, Marc. "A Reactionary Liberal: M. N. Katkov." *Russian Review* 2 (July 1952): 157–67.

Russkaia periodicheskaia pechat'. Edited by A. G. Dement'ev, A. V. Zapadov, and M. S. Cherepakhov, 340–43. Moscow: Gosudarstvennoe izdatel'stvo politicheskoi literatury, 1959.

Sementkovskii, P. I. *M. N. Katkov, ego zhizn' i literaturnaia deiatel'nost'*. St. Petersburg: F. Pavlenkov, 1892.

Thaden, Edward C. *Conservative Nationalism in Nineteenth-Century Russia*. Seattle: University of Washington Press, 1964.

Tolstoi, L. N. *Sobranie sochinenii v dvadtsati tomakh*. Moscow: Khudozhestvennaia literatura, 1960–1965.

Turgenev, I. S. *Polnoe sobranie sochinenii i pisem v tridtsati tomakh*. Moscow: Nauka, 1978–2018.

Viduetskaia, I. P. "Dostoevskii i Leskov." *Russkaia literatura* 4 (1975): 127–36.

Zapadov, A. V., ed. *Istoriia russkoi zhurnalistiki XVIII–XIX vekov*. Moscow: Vysshaia shkola, 1966.

Part II

Russia and the West

5

Jane Austen in Russia: Hidden Presence and Belated Boom

Any consideration of Jane Austen's reception in Russia must begin by acknowledging the seemingly remarkable fact that the first Russian translation of her works occurred only in 1967, with the publication of *Pride and Prejudice* in the Soviet Union.[1] In this chapter I wish to argue that such a belated response, almost a century and a half after her death, may well conceal a more complex reality of Russian contacts with the British novelist, which have so far eluded the official record. Nevertheless, the fact remains that Austen's fiction came to the Russian public very late for a variety of reasons. In this context, the response to her writing provides us with a particularly illuminating case study of the complex transactions between Western and Russian culture over the past two centuries: transactions shaped by the vagaries of history, politics, shifting tastes, values, everyday realities, and gender.

Austen in Nineteenth-Century Russia? The Case of *Eugene Onegin*

The first, indeed the only, published mention of Jane Austen in Russia during her lifetime appeared in a brief notice headed "Short Excerpts, News, and Comments" (Kratkie vypiski, izvestiia i zamechaniia) in the journal *European Herald* (Vestnik Evropy) in June 1816. Opening with a comment on the extent to which the British novel is dominated by women writers, the note points out

---

I would like to thank Jared Ingersoll, Christopher Condill, Edward Kasinec, and Liza Knapp for their help with the research for this chapter—C. T. N. Originally published in *The Reception of Jane Austen in Europe*, ed. Anthony Mandal and Brian Southam (London: Continuum, 2007), 334–49. Used by permission of Bloomsbury Publishing Plc—eds.

1   Jane Austen [Dzhein Ostin], *Gordost' i predubezhdenie*, ed. N. M. Demurova et al, trans. Immannuil Marshak (Moscow: Nauka, 1967).

that: "Apart from the magic names *Edgeworth, Opie, Morgan, Burney, Hamilton*, who have an incredible power over the pockets of buyers, there are many more women novelists, whose talent is known only by the titles of their works." The author then observes: "Now a new novel is garnering true praise: *Emma*, a novel by the author of *Sense and Sensibility, Pride and Prejudice*, 3 Vols," adding that "the unknown woman writer successfully depicts here pictures of quiet family life."[2]

Despite Austen's seeming anonymity and the absence of further mention of her works during the early nineteenth century, a number of Western scholars of Russian literature have since mentioned her in comparative studies of the period, most persistently with regard to Russia's most eminent poet and early prose writer Aleksandr Pushkin, and his masterwork, *Eugene Onegin* (Evgenii Onegin, 1823–31).[3] Maurice Baring, writing in 1910, was certainly among the first, if not the first, to posit a rather general comparison between Pushkin and Austen in suggestively gendered terms:

> Pushkin is remarkable because he combines gifts that are rarely met with in conjunction: the common sense, the reality, the detachment, and the finish of a Miss Austen; the swiftness and masculinity of a Byron; and the form, the lofty form, easy withal and perfectly natural, of a Racine; reaching at times, and should it be necessary, the sublimity of a Milton.[4]

---

[2] "Kratkie vypiski, izvestiia i zamechaniia," *Vestnik Evropy* 87, no. 12 (1816): 319–20.

[3] An important and apparently unique exception to this focus on Pushkin is to be found in Irene Masing-Delic, "Peremena rolei: Pigmalionovskie motivy v 'Emme' Dzhein Ostin i v 'Oblomove' Ivana Goncharova," in *Rossiia i SShA: Formy literaturnogo dialoga* (Moscow: RGGU, 2000), 96–116. She argues, convincingly, for the dependence of Ivan Goncharov's *Oblomov* (1859) on *Emma*. Quite a number of Slavists, in both oral and written communications, have expressed the belief that Tolstoy, probably the Russian master of the family novel, must have been acquainted with Austen's works. However, I am grateful to Galina Alekseeva, Research Director of the museum at Tolstoy's Iasnaia Poliana estate, for confirming that there are no works by Austen in Tolstoy's library, nor is there any mention of Austen in Tolstoy's diaries, letters, or published writings. Given Tolstoy's general knowledge of and interest in English literature, his ignorance of Austen speaks eloquently of her absence in Russia during his lifetime.

[4] Maurice Baring, *Landmarks in Russian Literature* (New York: Barnes and Noble, 1960), 196.

Baring waxes similarly eloquent on the subject of *Eugene Onegin*: "'Oniegin' [sic] is a story of contemporary life told in verse, a novel in verse, the first Russian novel and the best. It has the ease of Byron's 'Don Juan,' the reality of Fielding and Miss Austen, and nevertheless, when the situation demands it, it rises and takes on radiance and expresses poetry and passion."[5] While Baring's hyperbole undoubtedly tells us more about the state of Austen's reception in the West at the time he was writing and about the lengths to which early Slavists would go in conveying their sense of Pushkin's greatness to an Anglophone audience, his perception that Pushkin and Austen adopt compatible approaches to the representation of reality nonetheless strikes a resonant chord.

John Bayley, following Baring, as he himself acknowledges, throws out a number of tantalizing statements: "Though many were written, the novel in verse never achieved real status in the west—Pushkin's is the only masterpiece in the genre—and *Evgeny Onegin* is further compromised in western eyes by the impression that it is in some sense a variant of Byron's *Don Juan*, though a closer parallel would be one of Jane Austen's masterpieces."[6] Bayley further explains,

> As with Jane Austen (whom Maurice Baring perceptively invoked in connection with Pushkin) we are poised between two centuries and their fictional expectations. The eighteenth-century novel retains much of the bravado of opera, stage, and poem; and D'Arcy [sic] and Elizabeth Bennet are happy relations of Onegin and Tatyana on the same kind of stage. It would be ridiculous to follow them to Pemberley; excited by the glitter of the novel's crescendo we play with the idea, only to dismiss it with a smile and a shrug. And yet Jane Austen's earliest critics were struck, and not always favorably, by her faithful imitation of daily living. Pushkin's novel has it too, though neither he nor Jane Austen was concerned to record life in the methodical fashion of the nineteenth-century novel, the novel of realism and naturalism. The stylization of their art conveys the real as part of its insouciance.[7]

---

5   Baring, *Landmarks*, 197–98.

6   John Bayley, *Pushkin: A Comparative Commentary* (London: Cambridge University Press, 1971), 6.

7   Bayley, *Pushkin*, 241.

In like manner, Paul Debreczeny comments on the similarity between the narrative stances of these British and the Russian writers, while recognizing that it is unlikely that Pushkin had read Austen.[8]

More recently, Western commentators have drawn specific attention to parallels between the two novels. Richard Tempest juxtaposes close readings of the scenes from *Pride and Prejudice* and *Eugene Onegin*, in which Elizabeth visits Pemberley in Darcy's absence and Tatiana visits Onegin's estate after his departure. While acknowledging that there is no hard evidence that Pushkin read Austen, Tempest suggests that the problem is worthy of further study.[9] Amateurs, assumedly because less constrained by conventional niceties, have been more willing to underscore the kinship between the two works. In this regard, a letter by one John Bury published in the *Times Literary Supplement* for September 20, 2002 opens with the announcement: "Sir, I don't believe that *Pride and Prejudice* has hitherto been identified as a principal source for *Eugene Onegin*." The author then points to a series of (not always accurate) parallels between the two novels. To give something of the letter's flavor, I will quote here the passage most relevant to my own argument:

> Subsequent to the ball both heroes go through the classic process of withdrawal and return; and for both absence makes the heart grow fonder. While the hero is away, the heroine in both novels visits his country house, and is shown round by the housekeeper—at Pemberley Mrs. Reynolds and at Onegin's house Anisia. The favorite room, or window seat, of the former master (Darcy's father, Onegin's uncle) is shown to the visitor, and she leaves, in both stories, with an entirely new, and unexpected, apprehension of the hero's real nature.[10]

A response by Charles Countinho points out that Vladimir Nabokov's "Commentary" to his translation of *Eugene Onegin* glosses several echoes of Austen in Pushkin's work, seeming to impute them, however, to "descriptive

---

8   Paul Debreczeny, *The Other Pushkin: A Study of Alexander Pushkin's Prose Fiction* (Stanford: Stanford University Press, 1983), 5, 28, 305.

9   Richard Tempest, "The Girl on the Hill: Parallel Structures in *Pride and Prejudice* and *Eugene Onegin*," *Elementa: Journal of Slavic Studies and Comparative Cultural Semiotics* 1, no. 2 (1993): 197–213.

10 John Bury, "*Pride and Prejudice* and *Eugene Onegin*," *Times Literary Supplement* 10 (September 2002): 15.

formulas [...] common to the European novel of the time, whether the locale was Muscovy or Northamptonshire."[11] In fact, Nabokov appears to have overlooked the parallels between *Eugene Onegin* and *Pride and Prejudice*, further raising the question of whether Pushkin knew Austen in his noncommittal observation that "it is curious that Jane Austen was not popular in Tatiana's Russia."[12] Nabokov goes on to point to the existence of early French translations of *Sense and Sensibility* and *Mansfield Park*. Countinho argues that Nabokov had previously spotted the parallels between *Pride and Prejudice* and *Eugene Onegin*, but had dismissed the possibility that Pushkin read Austen. In fact, Nabokov only mentions *Pride and Prejudice* once in his commentary, and that in a decidedly equivocal fashion, commenting that Pushkin uses the word "mechanically" (*mashinal'no*) to describe Tatiana's gesture following Onegin's sermon to her, and Austen writes that Elizabeth answers her aunt "mechanically" during their visit to Pemberley.[13]

The similarities between *Eugene Onegin* and *Pride and Prejudice*, some of which have been pointed out by earlier commentators and others which have hitherto remained unnoted, are indeed striking. In both works the tale, told by an ironic narrator, largely takes place on a modest country estate, and is structured around the paired and contrasted relationships between two sisters from a modest gentry family, a male neighbor, and his aloof friend. The men are bruited about by local gossip as eligible suitors, although the aloof friend, out of overweening *amour propre*, actively hinders the relationship between the male neighbor and the sister he appears destined to wed. The highly symmetrical plot largely turns on an exchange of letters, and pride is the primary hindrance to the consummation of romance. The true heroine of the novel cedes to her sister in beauty and conventional attractions, and is plagued by a silly mother who ill understands her. Reading, writing, marriage, and the *moeurs* of everyday life rather than epic historical events occupy centerstage. The male protagonist is a prideful aristocrat who undervalues the heroine at their first encounter, only to be forced through a painful process of

---

11 Charles Giovanni Coutinho, "*Pride and Prejudice* and *Eugene Onegin*," *Times Literary Supplement* 11 (October 2002): 17; Vladimir Nabokov, "Commentary," in Alexander Pushkin, *Eugene Onegin: A Novel in Verse*, trans. Vladimir Nabokov, vol. 2 (New York: Pantheon Books, 1964), 222.

12 Nabokov, "Commentary," 393.

13 Nabokov, "Commentary," 424.

re-evaluation to come to an understanding of her true worth. The heroine herself misconstrues the hero on first meeting and must learn to understand him better in the course of the novel. At a key moment in the novel, the heroine visits her inamorato's estate in his absence and, from her examination of it, gains a truer vision of his character. In the final analysis, the central intrigue of the novel lies precisely in the process of self-reflection that the heroine undergoes in the course of the plot, a process set in motion by the hero's initial disdain. The heroine emerges a winner in the marriage market and ends the novel in a far higher social station than the one in which she began, having attained the amorous admiration of the suitor who at first disdained her.

As already noted, even those critics who have pointed out parallels between the works of both authors have tended to discount the possibility that Pushkin might have read Austen. There is, after all, no extant trace of Austen in Pushkin's library nor is there any mention of her in his correspondence. I will contend, however, that closer scrutiny of the evidence at hand indicates, at least circumstantially, that Pushkin may have had both the opportunity and the inclination to familiarize himself with Austen's works. While Pushkin's command of English, especially before the 1820s, remains a topic of speculation, there is no question of the fluency of his French from childhood. By 1824, all of Austen's novels had been translated into French, including two 1822 renditions of *Pride and Prejudice*.[14] The latter date is particularly tantalizing, since Pushkin began writing *Eugene Onegin* only a year later. While he was at the time in exile in the south of Russia, it is perfectly plausible that one of the poet's acquaintances, perhaps Countess Elizaveta Vorontsova, the wife of his superior and Pushkin's probable paramour, brought a copy to the cosmopolitan Odessa, where Pushkin began work on his masterpiece.[15] Yet another, even earlier possibility exists that Pushkin might have read the 121-page publication of excerpts from *Pride and Prejudice* in French that appeared in the Swiss periodical, *British Library* (Bibliotheque britannique), in 1813 when Pushkin was a student at the *lycée* at Tsarskoe Selo.

Perhaps the most compelling evidence of the relevance of *Pride and Prejudice* to *Eugene Onegin* is the resonance between the two texts, the fact that

---

14   See Isabelle Bour, "The Reception of Jane Austen's Novels in France and Switzerland: The Early Years, 1813–1828," in *The Reception of Jane Austen in Europe*, ed. Anthony Mandel and Brian Southam (London: Continuum, 2007), 12–33.

15   I am grateful to Irina Reyfman for having suggested this possibility.

5. Jane Austen in Russia: Hidden Presence and Belated Boom

placing Pushkin's novel in dialogue with Austen's enriches our reading of his text. Let me suggest, in this context, what I believe to be two particularly interesting aspects of *Eugene Onegin*, which are thrown into sharp relief by this juxtaposition. The first is that *Eugene Onegin*, like *Pride and Prejudice* and in the spirit of conventional comedy, results in two marriages; however, this is a "happy ending" from which the eponymous protagonist is emphatically excluded at the end, having himself doubly "derailed" the marriage plots in the course of the narrative through his initial rejection of Tatiana's love and his murder of Lenskii in a duel. Second, the very construction of the work hinges on the problem of "reading" character, both in life and art, gaining much of its import from the meta-literary play between the two, while, at the same time, vividly posing the problem of the representation of character, and particularly of character change, in the nascent realist novel.

Let us take the two points together, because they are intimately related. As we have already seen, critics have called attention to the resemblances between two episodes in particular: Elizabeth's visit to Darcy's Pemberley estate and Tatiana's visit to Onegin's estate, and these two analogous scenes serve as touchstones in their similarities and differences. In the first instance, although we have earlier heard much of the wonderful library at Pemberley, it is not the library that draws Elizabeth's attention; rather it is the family portraits and the praise of the housekeeper for Darcy that will predispose her to reconstrue his character in the light of his future actions, especially his "rescue" of her sister Lydia's reputation. This will pave the way further to a final interview in which man and woman, Darcy and Elizabeth, reach a verbal and emotional understanding leading to marriage. In the case of Tatiana's visit to Onegin's estate, on the other hand, the heroine seeks answers in Onegin's books (and the portrait and bust not of the man himself or of his family, but of Byron and Napoleon). Given Onegin's vexed on-again-off-again relationship to reading throughout *Eugene Onegin*, it is hardly surprising that the narrative presents this encounter between Tatiana and Onegin's library as a problem in interpretation, a riddle—and a riddle, moreover, that is significantly recapitulated with Onegin's reappearance in the eighth and final book of his eponymous novel:

> Что ж он? Ужели подражанье,
> Ничтожный призрак, иль еще
> Москвич в Гарольдовом плаще,
> Чужих причуд истолкованье,

> Слов модных полный лексикон?..
> Уж не пародия ли он?[16]
>
> What was he then? An imitation?
> An empty phantom or a joke,
> A Muscovite in Harold's cloak,
> Compendium of affectation,
> A lexicon of words in vogue?...
> Mere parody and just a rogue?[17]
>
> Скажите, чем он возвратился?
> Что нам представит он пока?
> Чем ныне явится? Мельмотом,
> Космополитом, патриотом,
> Гарольдом, квакером, ханжой,
> Иль маской щегольнет иной... (6:168)
>
> In what new guise is he returning?
> What role does he intend to fill?
> Childe Harold? Melmoth for a while?
> Cosmopolite? A Slavophile?
> A Quaker? Bigot?—might one ask?
> Or will he sport some other mask? (198)

As the final interview between Tatiana and Onegin amply demonstrates, the two never seem to attain the ability to communicate, nor is it at all clear that the rather flat reading of Onegin's character at which the prideful Tatiana arrives at the end is indeed accurate or stable.

In this context, what is perhaps most striking—and heartrending—in Tatiana's reproaches to Onegin at their final meeting is her accusation that he is responsible for their missed chance: "And happiness was ours... so nearly! / It came so close!..." (A schast'e bylo tak vozmozhno, / Tak blizko!...; 220; 6:188). Especially viewed in light of the somewhat amazing second chance

---

16 A. S. Pushkin, *Polnoe sobranie sochinenii v shestnadtsati tomakh*, vol. 6 (Moscow: Izdatel'stvo AN SSSR, 1937), 149. Henceforth references to this edition will appear in parentheses in the text.

17 Alexander Pushkin, *Eugene Onegin*, trans. James Falen (Carbondale: Southern Illinois University Press, 1990), 177. Henceforth references to this edition will appear in parentheses in the text.

Austen vouchsafes Elizabeth and Darcy, the impossibility for Tatiana and Onegin of stepping over Lenskii's corpse and back through time is palpable. It focuses vividly both the generic problem of comedy and the narrative problem of character construction I posed above. Do the characters in either novel truly change in the course of the plots and, if so, how should we "read" this change? More important, though, is how change, the passage of time, is thematized in both works. The "comedic" ending of *Pride and Prejudice* offers both reader and characters balance and stability, the satisfaction that they have arrived at a correct "reading" of character, at true meaning, which is a gauge of the possibility of union and continuity. At the end of *Eugene Onegin*, by contrast, we do not truly know which Tatiana is real—the irretrievably lost provincial maiden or the society *grande dame*—or whether her final reading of Onegin is correct or not. Have either of them truly changed? What we do know is that whatever stability (the marriages) is attained at the end comes at the cost of the exclusion of the eponymous protagonist (and of Lenskii as well) from the "comedic" structure. The forms of propriety—and pride—are maintained, but at the terrible expense of recognizing the irrecoverability of the passage of time and the instability of character such a passage entails. I cannot, willy-nilly, help hearing in Tatiana's response something of an answer to Austen, a vindication of pride, if not of prejudice:

> А счастье было так возможно,
> Так близко!... Но судьба моя
> Уж решена. Неосторожно,
> Быть может, поступила я:
> Меня с слезами заклинаний
> Молила мать; для бедной Тани
> Все были жребии равны....
> Я вышла замуж. Вы должны,
> Я вас прошу, меня оставить;
> Я знаю: в вашем сердце есть
> И гордость и прямая честь.
> Я вас люблю (к чему лукавить?),
> Но я другому отдана;
> Я буду век ему верна. (6:188; emphasis mine—C. T. N.)

> And happiness was ours... so nearly!
> It came so close!... But now my fate
> Has been decreed. I may have merely

> Been foolish when I failed to wait;
> But mother with her lamentation
> Implored me, and in resignation
> (All futures seemed alike in woe)
> I married.... Now I beg you, go!
> I've faith in you and do not tremble;
> I know that in your heart reside
> Both honor and a manly *pride*.
> I love you (why should I dissemble?):
> But I am now another's wife,
> And I'll be faithful all my life. (220; emphasis mine—C. T. N.)

Here, Tatiana, having suffered the fate of a marriage without love, which Elizabeth so disdains in her friend Charlotte, ends with what is certainly her kindest "reading" of Onegin: that his heart contains both pride and honor. What interpreting *Eugene Onegin* through, or as a response to, *Pride and Prejudice* suggests, then, is that it is not Onegin's pride that shipwrecks the marriage plot between Onegin and Tatiana, but his "English spleen," his inability to seize the moment, to staunch the passage of time (32; 6:21).

Whether in the end we attribute the convergences between *Eugene Onegin* and *Pride and Prejudice* to the common moment in the evolution of the novel or to a more direct (albeit unverifiable) influence, what is certainly telling is the fact that—at least until very recently—only critics writing from the perspective of the West have drawn comparisons between Austen and Pushkin. As I turn my argument from the possibility of Austen's hidden presence in nineteenth-century Russian literature to the reasons for her "prolonged absence from the Russian literary scene," we need to move beyond the question of historical accident to that of the comparative function and status of the novel in Russia, and its ambivalent relationship to gender and marketplace.[18]

The exclusive "maleness" of the novelists who achieved canonical status in Russian literature stands in particularly sharp relief when viewed in

---

18 For a survey of Austen entries in Russian and Soviet encyclopedias see Gabriella Imposti, "The Reasons for an 'Absence': Jane Austen's Reception in Russia," in *Re-Drawing Austen: Picturesque Travels in Austenland*, ed. Beatrice Battaglia and Diego Saglia (Naples: Liguori, 2004), 374.

relation to the crucial role played by women in the history of British fiction. The stakes are clear in *Eugene Onegin* itself: a work in which a woman—who is not only formed by the reading of novels, but who aggressively takes up the pen to control her own fate—competes with the title character for pride of place in the novel, as well as with the chatty narrator who repeatedly digresses into tongue-in-cheek, yet nonetheless condescending, disquisitions on women readers and writers. For Pushkin, who was making the transition from poetry to prose, from the rarefied realm of the gentleman-poet to the scruffier literary market of journals, the novel as the province of women writers and readers, as a means of diversion and a commodity for sale, was certainly a risky undertaking. This may be why, after a number of false starts, Pushkin only succeeded in completing one prose novel before his death. That novel, *The Captain's Daughter* (Kapitanskaia dochka), moreover, following in the openly acknowledged footsteps of Walter Scott, addressed the important enterprise of portraying the nation's history, to which Pushkin had increasingly directed his energies in non-fiction prose during the final years of his life. By the same token, much of the effort of Russian critics and writers throughout the nineteenth century and even into the twentieth would be expended on establishing the novel as serious business in the life of the nation, in the shaping of Russian society and political destiny, "man's work"—or in renouncing the novel, as did Gogol and Tolstoy, as too unreliable or entertaining for the weighty tasks they set for themselves of transforming society and the soul. It is therefore hardly surprising that the major nineteenth-century Russian novelists would look elsewhere from Austen's "pictures of quiet family life" for models to engage and emulate.

In this context, it is perhaps telling that the only two other published traces of Austen in nineteenth-century Russia, aside from the appearance of cursory encyclopedia entries beginning in 1897, occur in journal articles focusing on British women writers. The first of these mentions of Austen figures in a series of five extensive essays on British literature and journalism in the journal *Fatherland Notes* (Otechestvennye zapiski, 1854), written by Aleksandr Druzhinin: a major critic, the author of one of the earliest Russian literary works devoted to the "woman question," *Polin'ka Saks* (1847), and an Anglophile. Druzhinin asks toward the beginning of the section in question: "For what reason do English letters boast such an abundance of women writers (and first-class writers), while in the remaining countries of Europe, despite all the efforts of diverse persons and the benevolence of male critics, women write little, and if they write, then they write only badly?"[19] Having responded that this phenomenon is owing largely to the education afforded women in Britain, he ends this piece with a virulent attack on "blue stockings" who have, Druzhinin believes, usurped the journal of the Lake Poets, mentioning Austen in passing as a positive counter-example:

> These women, who, however, we shall better call not women writers, but rather writing women, are a sort of plague, a misfortune for British belles-lettres. We will not equate them with Miss Austen, Miss Baillie, Currier-Bell [sic], and the whole pleiad of old and new English writers for anything in the world. They are not women, but dragons, England is not to blame for their existence.[20]

Despite Druzhinin's professed admiration for British women writers, including Austen, gender is clearly not a neutral category in his understanding of the role of women in national literary traditions.

The second mention of Austen presents an apposite counterpoint to Druzhinin's article. It appeared in 1871, in an article entitled "English Women Novelists" (Anglichanki romanistki), also published in *Fatherland Notes* and written by Mariia Konstantinovna Tsebrikova, a prominent female literary critic and progressive advocate of the "woman question." Tsebrikova opens her article by castigating English fiction in general for upholding the social inequality of class structures, partly in the guise of the heroine ever submissive to duty:

> That is why despotic husbands and all mothers jealous of their daughters' naivety so love to give their wives and daughters English novels to read. In these novels everything is so moralistic and orderly; they will not arouse either in wives or daughters any restless strivings, will not summon them to a broad, active life beyond the walls of their native home.[21]

---

19 A. V. Druzhinin, "Pis'mo chetvertoe" of "Pis'ma ob angliiskoi literature," in his *Sobranie sochinenii*, vol. 5 (St. Petersburg: Tip. Imp. Akademii nauk, 1865), 334.

20 Druzhinin, "Pis'mo," 345-46.

21 M. Tsebrikova, "Anglichanki romanistki," *Otechestvennye zapiski* 195, no. 4 (1871): 408. I am grateful to Marianna Murav'eva for having brought this reference to Austen to my attention and for telling me that Anna Filosofova, a relative of Serge Diaghilev who was

5. Jane Austen in Russia: Hidden Presence and Belated Boom

In turning her attention specifically to women authors, Tsebrikova continues in the same vein, as her passing reference to Austen shows:

> Behind the novels of Miss Burney trails an endless round of novels very long, moralistic, and orderly, with very moderate novelistic plots; the novels of Miss Austen, Miss Edgeworth, which educated our hearts and developed our minds in the first years of youth, Miss Edgeworth especially for the common sense of her novels.[22]

As both her criticisms and her discussions of those English women writers she considers exceptions make clear, Tsebrikova favors novels that are in the spirit of contemporary Russian literature: that is, novels that adopt strong social and political stances. It is therefore unsurprising, perhaps, that Austen would not make her way to Russia for almost a century after Tsebrikova wrote these words, until a time when the values of private life and intimate relations would again become the province of the novel in Russia.

Austen and Nabokov

Austen remained all but invisible in Russian culture until well into the second half of the twentieth century, receiving mention only in scattered encyclopedia articles and passingly in surveys of English literature. Austen's quiet brilliance, her preoccupation with the life of the British gentry would hardly seem suited to early twentieth-century Russia, a country wracked by dramatic social change, war, and revolution—its culture dominated, at the high end, by rival groups of Symbolist, Futurist, and Acmeist poets and, at the newly emerging low end, by boulevard romances, "pinkertons," and glossy magazines. The ascension of the Bolshevik government after the October Revolution of 1917 resulted in a hitherto unprecedented degree of state interference in literature. The Stalinist years (1922–1953) were clearly an uncongenial time for Austen to have been discovered in Soviet Russia in earnest, although, as in the case of the early nineteenth century, her works may have been known to an elite few.[23]

---

   born in 1835, had an English governess and mentions in her diary reading Austen for her English lessons.

22 Tsebrikova, "Anglichanki-romanistki," 422.

23 William Mills Todd III has told me that he saw a well-thumbed one-volume edition of Austen's works at Boris Pasternak's *dacha* at Peredelkino, and his observation was

Vladimir Nabokov, in this connection, may be seen as the single, extraordinary exception that proves the rule. Nabokov's extended discussion of Austen's *Mansfield Park* published in his *Lectures on Literature*, based on his teaching at Cornell University beginning in 1948, signals what is certainly the most profound trace left by Austen on twentieth-century Russian culture, albeit in American emigration. While it might be argued that by the time Nabokov wrote his appreciation of Austen, he belonged more to American than to Russian culture, I would counter that, as in approaching the works and legacy of Nabokov in general, it is more fruitful to examine his response to Austen as shaped by—and as a function of—his cultural hybridity.

Thus, when we look at the documented history of Nabokov's decision to include Austen in his "Masters of European Fiction" course, we find that he apparently did not discover Austen in the United States, but was there prompted to a reconsideration of Austen by the urging of his friend Edmund Wilson. In fact, Simon Karlinsky attributes Nabokov's initially negative response to Austen to his Russian background:

> With Jane Austen, who for Wilson shared with James Joyce "the almost unique distinction in English novels of having a sense of form," it was his particular triumph to overcome Nabokov's typically Russian prejudice against women novelists. [...] There was also the fact of Jane Austen's total lack of reputation in Russian culture. Other English women novelists had done quite well in Russia. Ann Radcliffe and the Brontë sisters enjoyed considerable renown throughout the nineteenth century. Mary Elizabeth Braddon's pot-boiler *Lady Aurora Floyd* [sic] was not only unaccountably liked by Tolstoy, but even served as a model for certain episodes in *War and Peace*. Austen, however, was and remains an unknown. The first Russian translation of *Pride and Prejudice* did not come out until the 1960s and it was received without much enthusiasm.[24]

---

confirmed to me in conversation with Pasternak's son, Evgenii Borisovich Pasternak. Pasternak, born in 1890 and therefore of the generation that came of age before the 1917 Revolution, had an excellent command of English and was well versed in British literature and Western European cultural trends. Furthermore, Pasternak's sisters and parents emigrated to Britain before World War II.

24 Simon Karlinsky, "Introduction: 'Dear Volodya, Dear Bunny; or, Affinities and Disagreements,'" in *Dear Bunny, Dear Volodya: The Nabokov-Wilson Letters, 1940–1971*, ed. Simon Karlinsky (Berkeley: University of California Press, 2001), 20.

In fact, Nabokov's original response to Wilson's suggestion that he include Austen in his syllabus was less than enthusiastic, to say the least: "Thanks for the suggestion concerning my fiction course. I dislike Jane, and am prejudiced, in fact, against all women writers. They are in another class. Could never see anything in *Pride and Prejudice*."[25] Here, we should note that Nabokov already admits to familiarity with *Pride and Prejudice*, which is not surprising when we remember that he grew up in an English-speaking household with an Anglophile father and attended Cambridge after his emigration from Russia.

Nabokov's most eloquent response to Wilson's persistence in suggesting that he try *Mansfield Park* is, of course, his inclusion of Austen's novel as required reading in his course. Moreover, when we look more closely at Nabokov's lectures on *Mansfield Park*, we find an intriguing resonance with his own writing. Thus, roughly in the middle of his essay, Nabokov engages in an extensive discussion of the aborted staging of August von Kotzebue's play *Lovers' Vows* adapted by Elizabeth Inchbald, which occupies roughly the middle of Austen's novel: "The whole play theme in *Mansfield Park* is an extraordinary achievement. In chapters 12 to 20 the play theme is developed on the lines of fairy-tale magic and fate."[26]

Nabokov's presentation of the failed production of *Lovers' Vows* as the structural centerpiece of *Mansfield Park* resonates suggestively with the construction of his own novel *Lolita*, which he was writing at the same time as he was rereading Austen and composing his class lectures. Whether it be a case of what Nabokov himself terms a "literary reminiscence" of *Mansfield Park* in *Lolita* or, conversely, a case of Nabokov finding his own artistic practice in his exegesis of Austen, the parallel between the function of *Lovers' Vows* in *Mansfield Park* (as read by Nabokov) and the function of the fictional play *The Enchanted Hunters* in *Lolita* is striking, if devious in a characteristically Nabokovian manner.[27] It is not the play itself that occupies the geographical center of Nabokov's novel, but the Enchanted Hunters Hotel, where Humbert Humbert consummates his affair with Lolita; however, the play does serve as a commentary on the roles of the characters, and the coincidence of the names of the hotel

---

25 *Dear Bunny, Dear Volodya: The Nabokov-Wilson Letters, 1940–1971*, ed. Simon Karlinsky (Berkeley: University of California Press, 2001), 268.

26 Vladimir Nabokov, *Lectures on Literature*, ed. Fredson Bowers (New York: Harcourt, 1980), 30.

27 For the term "literary reminiscence," see Nabokov, *Lectures on Literature*, 26.

and the play underscores the role of artistic fate (Aubrey McFate) in Nabokov's novel. And it would be a "knight's move" worthy of the ludic Nabokov to have taken the spelling of the surname of Lolita's "precursor," Annabel *Leigh*, from the maiden name of Austen's mother, Cassandra *Leigh*, thereby sneaking Austen along with Poe into the genealogy of his nymphet and his novel. There is, finally, a tempting irony in the fact that Nabokov was working on his "Commentary" to *Eugene Onegin* at the very time when he was composing *Lolita* and his *Lectures on Literature*, and there are enough resonances between Nabokov's novel and Pushkin's novel in verse to have led Priscilla Meyer to suggest that "*Lolita* represents a translation through space and time of a Russian literary monument of the 1820s into an American one of the 1950s, a parody of 'paraphrastic' translation at its most extreme, which Nabokov wrote concomitantly with his literal one."[28] The intertextual charge thus comes full circle, and we are left only to wonder that the pedantically vigilant Nabokov failed to see, or acknowledge, the possibility of Pushkin's debt to Austen.

Austen in Soviet Russia and Beyond: The Return of the Everyday

The posthumous response to Austen's works across Europe has followed a rough pattern of discovery and appreciation by an educated elite and later adoption by a popular audience. This has made Austen's reception a bellwether for rival claims both by keepers of high culture and by devotees of mass culture. As Deirdre Lynch has observed:

> Austen's example can also make orthodox ways of accounting for cultural reproduction—our concepts of influence, tradition, literary legitimacy, and canon; our schemes for segregating the literary from the popular—strange and skewed [...] As the disputes about how best to like Austen and the ideas about rescuing her suggest, popularity and marketability appear in some way to threaten Austen's canonicity.[29]

---

28 Priscilla Meyer, "Nabokov's *Lolita* and Pushkin's *Onegin*: McAdam, McEve, and McFate," in *The Achievements of Vladimir Nabokov: Essays, Studies, Reminiscences, and Stories from the Cornell Nabokov Festival*, ed. George Gibian and Stephen Jay Parker (Ithaca: Center for International Studies, Committee on Soviet Studies, Cornell University, 1984), 180.

29 Deidre Lynch, ed., *Janeites: Austen's Disciples and Devotees* (Princeton: Princeton University Press, 2000), 9–10.

5. Jane Austen in Russia: Hidden Presence and Belated Boom | 93

Arguably, albeit in a belated fashion, the Russian reception of Austen has followed a similar trajectory, peaking later and more precipitously in Soviet and post-Soviet Russia in no small part because of the inter-implication of politics and cultural institutions in the USSR and their subsequent implosion in the wake of its collapse.

In light of the historical context, the timing of the publication of *Pride and Prejudice* in the USSR, first in English in 1961 and then in Russian translation in 1967—accompanied by the first relatively extensive article on Austen to be published in the Soviet Union, by N. M. Demurova, which appeared as the introduction to the 1961 English-language *Pride and Prejudice*—makes sense. (The significantly longer introduction to the Russian translation was also written by Demurova.)[30] These publications may be seen as part of what could be termed a gradual return to normality during the Khrushchev and Brezhnev years, after the horrific toll taken on the Soviet population by Stalinist terror, labor camps, and World War II. Despite the fact that socialist realism remained the official aesthetic in the USSR, in Soviet literature during the decades following Stalin's death there was a preoccupation with the everyday, the individual and the private—concerns compatible with the fictive world Austen creates in her novels. Moreover, during the post-Stalin years, there proceeded a gradual reclamation and discovery of foreign and Russian literary works that had been largely inaccessible under Stalin.

The fact that the Anglophone *Pride and Prejudice* appeared in 1961 at the height of the Khrushchev cultural thaw, while the Russian translation of the novel was published in 1967, after the beginning of the crackdown under Brezhnev which ushered in the so-called "era of stagnation," may perhaps be taken as evidence of how little these larger trends were affected by the cultural politics of the moment. Of course, neither version of *Pride and Prejudice* published in the USSR during the 1960s could be considered as a "mass" phenomenon; furthermore, as we have seen, Karlinsky later observed that the translation "was received without much enthusiasm."[31] Austen's by then secure status as a "classic" in the West certainly facilitated the publication of the Russian

---

30 I have been unable to obtain a copy of the Anglophone edition in order to compare the two Demurova articles and am therefore basing my observations on Ekaterina Genieva's bibliography of Austen's Russian reception: Ekaterina Genieva, ed., *Dzhein Osten: biobibliograficheskii ukazatel'* (Moscow: Kniga, 1986), 75.

31 Karlinsky, "Introduction," 20.

translation, as indicated by the fact that it appeared in the prestigious "Literary monuments" (Literaturnye pamiatniki) series from the Academy of Sciences of the USSR. In the wake of these publications, Austen remained largely the property of the hidebound Soviet scholarly establishment: very much, that is, in the realm of the academic. It is perhaps telling in this regard that the translation of *Pride and Prejudice* reportedly took twenty years to complete and was therefore begun in the postwar years, apparently inspired by Somerset Maugham's naming *Pride and Prejudice* one of the ten greatest novels of all time.[32] The translator, moreover, was Immanuil Marshak, a prominent Soviet physicist and son of the renowned translator and writer of children's books Samuil Marshak, who edited the translation-in-progress until his death in 1964.

In her introduction to Marshak's translation, Demurova presents a solid overview of Austen's life, works, and reception based on Anglophone sources. While heralding the Russian translation of *Pride and Prejudice* as filling, "true, only in part, an irritating gap which existed up to the present time in Russian translated literature," Demurova remains silent about the reasons for Austen's neglect in Russia, although she does supply a list of the previous, meagre mentions of Austen in Russia in a footnote.[33] Her silence on this point is particularly striking, since she devotes much of her argument to explaining why Austen has enjoyed such popularity in Britain during the twentieth century.

This silence, read as circumspection, licenses us to draw inferences concerning Austen's belated appearance in Russia from those arguments which Demurova does make. Thus, she is at pains to demonstrate that Austen's works not only transcend the time and social milieu into which their author was born, but look at both with irony. Aside from implicitly smoothing over the issue of Austen's seemingly "alien" class background, Demurova supplies Austen with an excellent pedigree by assigning her a pivotal role in the evolution of the realist novel and by citing a stellar array of British writers in praise of Austen's talent, including those drawing comparisons between Austen and Shakespeare.

---

32   Immanuil Marshak, "Ot perevodchika," in Jane Austen [Dzhein Ostin], *Gordost' i predubezhdenie*, ed. N. M. Demurova et al, trans. Immannuil Marshak (Moscow: Nauka, 1967), 535.

33   N. M. Demurova, "Dzhein Ostin i ee roman 'Gordost' i predubezhdenie,'" in Jane Austen [Dzhein Ostin], *Gordost' i predubezhdenie*, ed. N. M. Demurova et al, trans. Immannuil Marshak (Moscow: Nauka, 1967), 583–84. The quoted phrase is from Demurova, "Dzhein Osten i ee roman," 583.

Thus, despite the fact that it is remarkably free of the political jargon of the day, Demurova's article clearly speaks to its immediate context—both in making a case for Austen's respectability as a world literary figure and in holding Austen and her works up as a standard against which to judge the Soviet present. In the first instance, Demurova discusses at length pressures exerted by the Prince Regent, the future George IV, to influence Austen's writing, about which Demurova concludes: "It required no little courage to stand up to such an attempt."[34] In the second, Demurova finds in Austen's "'mixed' characters [. . .] the key (or, more likely, one of the keys) to an understanding of why the twentieth century 'discovered' Jane Austen for itself."[35] These points could not but take on a particular resonance in late Soviet society, in which writers were routinely subjected to political pressures and where literary characters were to be cast in decidedly black-and-white terms. Finally, we are left with the question of the target audience for Demurova's essay and, by implication, for the translation of *Pride and Prejudice*. In this context, it is perhaps telling that on at least one occasion Demurova refers her readers to Anglophone sources for more on Austen's critical reception.[36] Not only does this underscore the almost complete absence of Russian scholarship on Austen at the time, but it also presupposes a readership of above-average erudition and with library access.

While the next two decades witnessed the appearance of a small coterie of Austen scholars in the USSR, Austen remained far from the mass phenomenon she was in the West. The years 1967–1984 saw some sixty Soviet publications, including two dissertations by T. A. Amelina and M. V. Chechetko in which Austen received some mention.[37] While this seems to be a relatively impressive number, especially taking into account Austen's virtually complete absence from the USSR earlier, a closer look shows that Austen's reception still remained within a fairly circumscribed circle. The figure above includes only twenty substantial, scholarly works devoted exclusively to Austen, almost

---

34 Demurova, "Dzhein Osten i ee roman," 572.

35 Demurova, "Dzhein Osten i ee roman," 564–65.

36 Demurova, "Dzhein Osten i ee roman," 582.

37 T. A. Amelina, "Problema realizma v tvorchestve Dzhein Osten (metod i stil')," abstract (Leningrad: LGU im. A. A. Zhdanova, 1973); M. V. Chechetko, "Realisticheskii roman Dzhein Osten," abstract (Moscow: MGU im. M. V. Lomonosova, 1979).

all of them written by Amelina, A. A. Bel'skii, Chechetko, Demurova, and V. S. Ivasheva, and many of which appeared in highly specialized university publications. Some sixteen considerations of Austen appeared in books on the history of English literature or realism, of which five were written by Bel'skii or Ivasheva. Fifteen publications were reviews of the Russian translation of *Pride and Prejudice* or of Anglo-American studies on or mentioning Austen, while five were translations of comments on Austen by British writers. The remaining items include an encyclopedia article by Bel'skii, a news note on the sale of an Austen manuscript in Britain, and an excerpt of a piece by Austen included in a school anthology.[38] Clearly, Jane Austen was far from a household name in the USSR—at least, until the mid-1980s.

A watershed moment in the reception of Austen's works in the USSR came in the late 1980s, perhaps only coincidentally at the height of glasnost. The years 1986 and 1988 respectively witnessed the publication of two major Austen projects, both spearheaded by the energetic General Director of the Library of Foreign Literature, Ekaterina Genieva. The first of these projects was a bibliography of Austen's works and of foreign and Russian-language publications on Austen, *Jane Austen: A Bio-Bibliographical Index* in the "Writers of Foreign Countries" series, edited and with an introduction by Genieva. The second project, the publication of which extended into 1989, was a three-volume collection of Austen's six completed novels in Russian, compiled and introduced by Genieva, with commentaries by Genieva and Demurova.[39] Thus, by a strange twist of literary history, Jane Austen's works finally became available to the Soviet reading public in the same years as did such long-banned books as Boris Pasternak's *Doctor Zhivago* (1957), Evgenii Zamiatin's dystopian novel *We* (1921–1922), and Aleksandr Solzhenitsyn's *Gulag Archipelago* (1962–1973).

It was, however, only in the wake of the collapse of the USSR in 1991 and the consequent demise of the Soviet cultural establishment, with its attendant artificial inflation of high culture and discouragement of mass entertainment, and the resulting emergence of a market-driven popular culture in post-Soviet Russia, that Austen and her works became a phenomenon in Russia

---

38 A. A. Bel'skii, "Ostin, Dzhein," in *Kratkaia literaturnaia entsiklopediia*, ed. A. A. Surkov, vol. 5 (Moscow: Sovetskaia entsiklopediia, 1968), 486–87.

39 Jane Austen [Dzhein Osten], *Sobranie sochinenii v trekh tomakh*, ed. Ekaterina Genieva, 3 vols. (Moscow: Khudozhestvennaia literatura, 1988–1989).

analogous to and fed by Western "Austen-mania." By the early twenty-first century, not only were all of Austen's works available in Russian, but Anglo-American film adaptations of her fiction had aired on Russian television and websites, while chat-rooms devoted to Austen had appeared on the internet. Austen "chat" in Russia, as in the West, is highly repetitive, emotive, and dominated by a female audience, discussing the relative merits of Austen's novels and of the novels versus the film adaptations, of Colin Firth (a hands-down favorite) and Keira Knightley, of *Bridget Jones Diary* as an adequate or inadequate update of *Pride and Prejudice*, and, most importantly, appropriating Austen in a very personal way as a guide to life and love. Tellingly, a best seller list published in 2003 in the *Weekly Journal* (Ezhenedel'nyi zhurnal), under the heading "What Housewives Read," placed *Pride and Prejudice* eighth, within a field consisting largely of detective fiction by the popular writer Dar'ia Dontsova, non-fiction accounts of women's fantasies and relationships, and the Russian translation of Helen Fielding's *Bridget Jones: The Edge of Reason* (2001).

Perhaps the most revealing indicator of the sea-change in post-Soviet cultural attitudes in Russia is that, while it rarely occurred to Soviet scholars to draw parallels between Austen and Russian writers, and certainly not with her near contemporary Pushkin, at least two Russian-language reviewers of the 2005 film adaptation of *Pride and Prejudice* highlight the parallels between Austen's plot and the plot of *Eugene Onegin*. Alina Rudia quips that "the plot of the film like that of the book takes us back to the age of the beginning of the nineteenth century—a sort of *Eugene Onegin* on British soil."[40] Another reviewer, Svetlana Evsiukova, draws attention to the similar narratives of *Pride and Prejudice* and *Eugene Onegin*, while nonetheless suggesting that there is more at work than simply parallel plots:

> It is not just a matter of the similarity of the plots and characters of *Pride and Prejudice* and *Eugene Onegin*—both Pushkin and Austen employ the clichéd plots of sentimental novels, which at the turn of the eighteenth and nineteenth centuries multiplied in great number. It is a matter of the common, mocking view on literature and life, in good-natured irony and an almost supernatural lightness of style and thought.[41]

---

40 Alina Rudia, "Retsenziia na fil'm," Kino-Teatr, accessed July 13, 2022, https://kino-teatr.ua/news/retsenziya-na-film-96.phtml.

41 Svetlana Evsiukova, "Dzhein Osten, Gordost' i predubezhdenie," accessed July 13, 2022, https://e-motion.tochka.net/6175-dzheyn-osten/.

Thus, after nearly two centuries, the obvious affinities between Austen and Pushkin can finally be acknowledged—at least in the popular press. And why not, when one creative genealogist has given Austen the most impeccable of Russian pedigrees, tracing her back to the legendary first ruler of ancient Rus, Rurik?[42] Austen, it would seem, has at long last found a home on Russian soil!

---

42 "Ostin, Dzhein," Genealogia.ru, accessed June 2006, http://www.genealogia.ru/users/genfamous/descent/Austen.htm (page discontinued—eds.).

Works Cited

Amelina, T. A. "Problema realizma v tvorchestve Dzhein Osten (metod i stil')." Abstract. Leningrad: LGU im. A. A. Zhdanova, 1973.

Austen, Jane [Ostin, Dzhein]. *Gordost' i predubezhdenie*. Edited by N. M. Demurova et al. Translated by Immannuil Marshak. Moscow: Nauka, 1967.

——— [Osten, Dzhein] *Sobranie sochinenii v trekh tomakh*. Translated by Ekaterina Genieva. 3 vols. Moscow: Khudozhestvennaia literatura, 1988–89.

Baring, Maurice. *Landmarks in Russian Literature*. New York: Barnes and Noble, 1960.

Bayley, John. *Pushkin: A Comparative Commentary*. New York: Cambridge University Press, 1971.

Bel'skii, A. A. "Ostin, Dzhein." In *Kratkaia literaturnaia entsiklopediia*, edited by A. A. Surkov, vol. 5, 486–87. Moscow: Sovetskaia entsiklopediia, 1968.

Bour, Isabel. "The Reception of Jane Austen's Novels in France and Switzerland: The Early Years, 1813–1828." In *The Reception of Jane Austen in Europe*, edited by Anthony Mandel and Brian Southam, 12–33. London: Continuum, 2007.

Bury, John. "*Pride and Prejudice* and *Eugene Onegin*." *Times Literary Supplement*, September 10, 2002, 15.

Chechetko, M. V. "Realisticheskii roman Dzhein Osten." Abstract. Moscow: MGU im. M. V. Lomonosova, 1979.

Coutinho, Charles Giovanni. "*Pride and Prejudice* and *Eugene Onegin*." *Times Literary Supplement*, October 11, 2002, 17.

Debreczeny, Paul. *The Other Pushkin: A Study of Alexander Pushkin's Prose Fiction*. Stanford: Stanford University Press, 1983.

Demurova, N. M. "Dzhein Ostin i ee roman '*Gordost' i predubezhdenie*.'" In Jane Austen [Dzhein Ostin], *Gordost' i predubezhdenie*, edited by N. M. Demurova et al., translated by Immannuil Marshak, 538–89. Moscow: Nauka, 1967.

Druzhinin, A. V. "Pis'mo chetvertoe" of "Pis'ma ob angliiskoi literature." In his *Sobranie sochinenii*, 5: 333–47. St. Petersburg: Tip. Imp. Akademii nauk, 1865.

Evsiukova, Svetlana. "Dzhein Osten, *Gordost' i predubezhdenie*." Accessed July 13, 2022. https://e-motion.tochka.net/6175-dzheyn-osten/.

Genieva, Ekaterina, ed. *Dzhein Osten: biobibliograficheskii ukazatel'*. Moscow: Kniga, 1986.

Imposti, Gabriella. "The Reasons for an 'Absence': Jane Austen's Reception in Russia." In *Re-Drawing Austen: Picturesque Travels in Austenland*, edited by Beatrice Battaglia and Diego Saglia, 369–76. Naples: Liguori, 2004.

Jones, W. Gareth. *Tolstoi and Britain*. Washington, D.C.: Berg, 1995.

"Kratkie vypiski, izvestiia i zamechaniia." *Vestnik Evropy* 87, no. 12 (1816): 319–20.

Lynch, Deidre, ed. *Janeites: Austen's Disciples and Devotees*. Princeton: Princeton University Press, 2000.

Marshak, Immanuil, "Ot perevodchika." In Jane Austen [Dzhein Ostin], *Gordost' i predubezhdenie*, edited by N. M. Demurova et al., translated by Immannuil Marshak, 535–37. Moscow: Nauka, 1967.

Masing-Delic, Irene. "Peremena rolei: Pygmalionovskie motivy v 'Emme' Dzhein Osten i v Oblomove' Ivana Goncharova." In *Rossiia i SShA: Formy literaturnogo dialoga*, 96–116. Moscow: RGGU, 2000.

Meyer, Priscilla. "Nabokov's *Lolita* and Pushkin's *Onegin*: McAdam, McEve, and McFate." In *The Achievements of Vladimir Nabokov: Essays, Studies, Reminiscences and Stories from the Cornell Nabokov Festival*, edited by George Gibian and Stephen Jay Parker, 179–211. Ithaca: Center for International Studies, Committee on Soviet Studies, Cornell University, 1984.

Nabokov, Vladimir. *Dear Bunny, Dear Volodia: The Nabokov-Wilson Letters 1940–1971*. Edited by Simon Karlinsky. Berkeley: University of California Press. 2001.

———. *Lectures on Literature*. Edited by Fredson Bowers. New York: Harcourt. 1980.

"Ostin, Dzhein." Genealogia.ru. Accessed June 2006. http://www.genealogia.ru/users/genfamous/descent/Austen.htm (page discontinued—eds.).

Pushkin, Aleksandr. *Eugene Onegin: A Novel in Verse*. Translated by Vladimir Nabokov. 4 vols. New York: Pantheon Books. 1964.

———. *Evgenii Onegin*. In his *Polnoe sobranie sochinenii v shestnadtsati tomakh*, vol. 6. Moscow: Izdatel'stvo AN SSSR, 1937.

Pushkin, Alexander. *Eugene Onegin: A Novel in Verse*. Translated by James E. Falen. Carbondale: Sourthern University Press, 1990.

Rudia, Alina. "Retsenziia na fil'm." Kino-Teatr. Accessed July 13, 2022. https://kino-teatr.ua/news/retsenziya-na-film-96.phtml.

Tempest, Richard. "The Girl on the Hill: Parallel Structures in *Pride and Prejudice* and *Eugene Onegin*." *Elementa: Journal of Slavic Studies and Comparative Cultural Semiotics* 1, no. 2 (1993): 197–213.

Tsebrikova, M. "Anglichanki romanistki." *Otechestvennye zapiski* 195, no. 4 (1871): 403–59.

6

King, Queen, Sui-Mate: Nabokov's Defense against Freud's "Uncanny"

> In the Prefaces I have been writing of late for the English-language editions of my Russian novels (and there are more to come) I have made it a rule to address a few words of encouragement to the Viennese delegation. The present Foreword shall not be an exception. Analysts and analyzed will enjoy, I hope, certain details of the treatment Luzhin is subjected to after his breakdown (such as the curative insinuation that a chess player sees Mom in his Queen and Pop in his opponent's King), and the little Freudian who mistakes a Pixlok set for the key to a novel will no doubt continue to identify my characters with his comic-book notion of my parents, sweethearts and serial selves. For the benefit of such sleuths I may as well confess that I gave Luzhin my French governess, my pocket chess set, my sweet temper, and the stone of the peach I plucked in my own walled garden.
>
> —Vladimir Nabokov, *The Defense* (10–11)

I take as the epigraph to this article the concluding paragraph of Nabokov's 1963 Preface to the English translation of *The Luzhin Defense* (Zashchita Luzhina), titled *The Defense* and published some thirty-five years after the original, which—by Nabokov's account in the same Preface—was begun "in the spring of 1929, at Le Boulon—a small spa in the Pyrenees Orientales where

---

Originally published in *Intertexts* 12, no. 1 (Spring 2008): 1–31. Reproduced by permission of University of Nebraska Press—eds.

I was hunting butterflies—and finished in the same year in Berlin."[1] As Nabokov himself informs us, he makes a point in the prefaces to the English translations of his Russian novels to "address a few words of encouragement to the Viennese delegation," that is, to preempt psychoanalytic readings of his works by poking fun at them *avant la lettre*, so to speak. They are, it would seem, so obvious and trite as to be beneath contempt.

Nabokov's persistent attacks on Freud and his followers—in these prefaces, in interviews, in his fiction and nonfiction, at every conceivable opportunity it seems—have inevitably provoked commentary. Critics generally recognize that these passages have dramatically affected the scholarly and critical reception of Nabokov's works. On the one hand, Nabokov has unquestionably succeeded in scaring off the faint of heart. On the other hand, the very vehemence of Nabokov's protestations could not have failed to draw attention to the infection of the Nabokovian text by Freud as what Michel Foucault in his essay "What Is an Author?" has termed an "initiator of discursive practice." As Geoffrey Green, author of *Freud and Nabokov*, has quipped, "to ban Freud so vociferously is to give him substance, thing-ness within Nabokov's world of textual things."[2] David Larmour, in *Discourse and Ideology in Nabokov's Prose*, challenges in particularly fruitful terms the author's prerogative to dictate the terms of reading.

> If, moreover, in the search for clues to textual ideology, one is to refuse to play the author's game or at least to play it exclusively by his rules, then such interpretive strategies are indeed "fair game." In fact, if we view the attacks on Freud as symptomatic, then the interpreter's attention is drawn to those aspects of the text which the dominant discourse most strenuously negates, denies, and displaces.[3]

I propose in this article to follow Larmour's sage advice and to read *The Defense* against Nabokov's prefatory invections, to suggest that Nabokov's onslaught against what might be termed "pop" Freudian readings of his novel may mask

---

1   Vladimir Nabokov, *The Defense*, trans. Michael Scammell (New York: Vintage, 1964), 7. All further references to this text will appear in parentheses in the text of the article.

2   Geoffrey Green, *Freud and Nabokov* (Lincoln: University of Nebraska Press, 1988), 374.

3   David Larmour, *Discourse and Ideology in Nabokov's Prose* (New York: Routledge, 2002), 68.

a deeper engagement with the Freudian text, specifically with Freud's seminal 1919 article "The Uncanny" (Das Unheimlich).

Before turning to my reading of the match between Nabokov and Freud, as it were, I would like to put forward several larger contextual issues. It might be argued that any modernist writer was up against a series of daunting challenges to the traditional functions of the literary text and to the authority of the author. No less than the survival of literature was at stake, and Freud may be seen as crystallizing these challenges, certainly for Nabokov. Freud raised the question of control of meaning at the same time as the hitherto privileged status of authorial literature appeared to be suffering erosion as a result of incursions by popular culture genres, cinema, not to mention politics, and professional critics—all of which would be assigned ambiguous roles in Nabokov's oeuvre. Nabokov was therefore engaged virtually from the outset of his career with what might have appeared to be, from a pessimistic point of view, a rearguard action in defense of the "artness" of art, which for Nabokov was inextricably bound up with the individuality of the author's voice and perceptions.

Two of the most perspicacious commentators on Nabokov and Freud have framed their arguments about the writer's antipathy to the "Viennese Quack" in terms that resonate with the propositions I have advanced above and with the further argument I make below. Jenefer Shute, in her "Nabokov and Freud: The Play of Power," does, in fact, contend that in "the persistent competition between his [Nabokov's] discourse and Freud's, certain central problematics of the twentieth-century novel are being played out—most importantly, the fictional text's struggle against an encroaching hermeneutics." Nabokov, she maintains, "rejects psychoanalysis as he does all totalitarianism of meaning." However, Freudian discourse is all the more threatening because it always already occupies the space of Nabokov's prose:

> Ironically (as Nabokov. is most acutely aware), this very realm—the realm of imagination, of memory and desire—is precisely that of psychoanalytic discourse; the chosen domain of Nabokov's fiction overlaps, enormously, a region already colonized by Vienna. Memory is Freud's master plot, too; his also the discourse of desire. [. . .] The struggle then is territorial: for Nabokov, it is a battle to reclaim what has been lost to a discourse deadening in its priority. Nabokov's lifelong polemic against Freud has had the paradoxical effect of introducing

him into his every text—but this is because, for the novelist, he is already there. [...]

Freud's text thus compels both respect and resistance because of its power, priority, and proximity. Yet another factor complicates what might otherwise be a simple "anxiety of influence" situation, and that is the persistence of psychoanalytic discourse as a potent system of hermeneutics. [...] Nabokov repeatedly (and preemptively) asserts the inaccessibility of his text to any hermeneutics, above all the Freudian.[4]

Here Shute captures neatly the problem Freud posed to Nabokov—a problem that went far beyond his distaste for critics who might take the license seemingly authorized by Freud to draw grubby, unsavory inferences about Nabokov's private life from his fictions. Freud threatens to intervene between Nabokov's reader and Nabokov's art and, in so doing, to render sterile and automatized what the Nabokovian text envisages as an unbounded dynamic play of (re)reading.

Leland De La Durantaye, in his article "Vladimir Nabokov and Sigmund Freud, or a Particular Problem," adds an important refinement to Shute's argument. He opens his key argument with a pertinent quotation from a Nabokov interview: "Psychoanalysis has something very Bolshevik about it—an inner policing [...] symbols killing the individual dream, the thing itself."[5] "What psychoanalysis shares with Bolshevism—and thereby with totalitarianism," De La Durantaye argues, "is the tendency to negate the singular in favor of the general." He later elaborates: "What most infuriates [Nabokov] is the idea of a system of psychic substitutions. Nabokov regards Freud's vision of the world as not only sexually perverted and socially deranged, but as denying the particular detail its rich, brimming life."[6] Here I would direct the reader back to my

---

4   Jenefer Patricia Shute, *Nabokov and Freud: The Play of Power* (PhD diss., University of California, Los Angeles, 1983), 637, 640–41.

5   Cited in Leland De La Durantaye, "Vladimir Nabokov and Sigmund Freud, or a Particular Problem," *American Imago* 62, no. 1 (2005): 61. Original French quote in "Interview with Anne Guerin."

6   De La Durantaye, "Vladimir Nabokov and Sigmund Freud," 61, 63, One cannot help but think here of the end of the concluding paragraph of *Speak, Memory*, as Nabokov and his wife and their six-year-old son in St. Nazaire on the French coast are making their way to the boat that will take them to the United States: "There, in front of us, where a broken row of houses stood between us and the harbor, and where the eye encountered all

epigraph, the last paragraph of Nabokov's preface to *The Defense*, in which he closes his diatribe against Freud and Freudians with a list of what of he himself has bestowed on his character Luzhin, ending with just such a "particular detail": "the stone of the peach I plucked in my own walled garden." It is indeed in the light of this peach stone that, I argue, we must read *The Defense*.

One final order of business, however, remains before turning to my reading of Nabokov's novel. For the most part, scholars have shown surprisingly little curiosity about when Nabokov might have come to know Freud's ideas and what works by Freud he might have read when, although De La Durantaye does cite the following notation in Nabokov's hand from a note card labeled "Freud" held in the Berg Collection of the New York Public Library: "*Ever since I read him in the Twenties he seemed wrong, absurd, and vulgar to me.*"[7] Much has been made of Nabokov's response to an interviewer's question in which he scoffed at the idea of having undergone psychoanalysis and claimed that his knowledge of Freud was based on "bookish familiarity only."[8] Yet there has been scant acknowledgment of what would seem to be a yawning gap between what might be expected from a reader as sophisticated as Nabokov in terms of direct engagement with any works by Freud he might have read and the rather vulgar, popular Freudian readings he ridicules in his prefaces. We shall return to this point apace.

Here I have to enter the realm of speculation and probabilities. As to when Nabokov first learned of Freud's ideas, the answer is almost certainly at

---

sorts of stratagems, such as pale-blue and pink underwear cakewalking on a clothesline, or a lady's bicycle and a striped cat oddly sharing a rudimentary balcony of cast iron, it was most satisfying to make out among the jumbled angles of roofs and walls, a splendid ship's funnel, showing from behind the clothesline as something in a scrambled picture—Find What the Sailor Has Hidden—that the finder cannot unsee once it has been seen." Vladimir Nabokov, *Speak, Memory: An Autobiography Revisited* (New York: Vintage International, 1989), 309–10.

7   De La Durantaye, "Vladimir Nabokov and Sigmund Freud," 62 (emphasis De La Durantaye's—C. T. N.). While he does raise the relevant questions concerning Nabokov's knowledge of Freud's text, his answer is rather cursory. He specifies only that Nabokov most likely read the *Case of the Wolf-Man* in the 1920s. David G. Cohen, in "My Potential Patients: Origins, Detection, and Transference in *Pale Fire* and Freud's *Case of the Wolf-Man*," *Zembla*, accessed July 24, 2022, https://www.libraries.psu.edu/nabokov/cohen1.htm, implies that Nabokov must have read texts by Freud, and specifically, the Wolf-man, but skirts a direct discussion of which texts when.

8   For example, see Shute, "Nabokov and Freud," 638.

Cambridge.⁹ Nabokov went up to Trinity College, Cambridge in the fall 1919 term. According to John Forrester, at Cambridge, "Freud was all the rage from 1919 on. He [Nabokov] couldn't have avoided it."¹⁰ Nabokov might well have attended the lectures on Freud's conception of dreams delivered to packed audiences in the Psychological Laboratory at Cambridge by W. H. R. Rivers usually on Saturday mornings during the 1920–1921 and 1921–1922 sessions.¹¹ A number of the more talented Cambridge students in Nabokov's age cohort became, at least temporarily, avid Freudians.¹² One figure in particular begs mention here. Despite an absence (at least at the present time) of evidence documenting any association with Nabokov, one member of what constituted itself in 1925 as the Cambridge Psychoanalytic Group presents such a tantalizing series of concurrences with Nabokov as to tempt us into imagining the possibility of some as yet undiscovered connection. I am speaking of Lionel Penrose, who later in life came to be known as a foundational figure in the modern study of human genetics. A year younger than Nabokov, Penrose first heard a lecture on Freud's theory of dreams while working on an ambulance train during the First World War. As he reports in his memoirs, "when the war ended and I went to Cambridge, I tried to study in this new field but it had not penetrated into the University curriculum. The nearest possibility was psychology and this was linked to philosophy and mathematical logic in the

---

9   Stephen Blackwell, in his "Nabokov's Wiener-Schnitzel Dreams: Despair and Anti-Freudian Poetics," *Nabokov Studies* 7 (2002/2003): 131–32, suggests that Nabokov may in fact have authored an anonymous 1919 letter to the *Cambridge Review* ridiculing psychoanalysis.

10 My thanks to John Forrester for this information, which he sent me in an email communication (January 28, 2008).

11 The Lectures were published posthumously as W. H. R. Rivers, *Conflict and Dream* (London: Kegan Paul, Trench Trubner, 1923). I am again grateful to John Forrester for having directed my attention to this work. It should be noted that Rivers was not an uncritical propagandist for Freud's views, and challenged Freud in a sophisticated manner on a number of key points. On this, see the "Preface" to *Conflict and Dream* by G. Elliot Smith (v–ix).

12 According to Forrester, "Nineteen twenty-two was the year of Cambridge in Freud's consulting room." In his "Freud in Cambridge," *Critical Quarterly* 46, no. 2 (2004): 2. For more on the Cambridge Freudians, see this article and Laura Cameron and John Forrester, "Tansley's Psychoanalytic Network: Episode out of the Early History of Psychoanalysis in England," *Psychoanalysis and History* 2, no. 2 (2000): 189–256.

cumbersome academic configuration known as the Moral Sciences Tripos."[13] In 1919 Penrose was giving lectures on Freud's theory of dreams to Cambridge undergraduate societies. Moreover, while, as Brian Boyd maintains, during the first half of 1919 Nabokov wrote at least as many chess problems as he did poems ("in his London notebook there is a chess problem for virtually every poem"), in 1918 Penrose became a founding member of the British Chess Problem Association in London.[14] Although Penrose's son later repeatedly held the title of British Chess Champion, Penrose himself, like Nabokov, excelled at chess problems, rather than at tournament play. Most tempting, however, is the fact that Penrose was one of the first psychoanalytic thinkers to make a connection between the Freudian paradigm and chess.

In the early 1920s, Penrose, like others of his Cambridge acquaintance, went to Vienna to go into analysis. In 1923, he began his analysis with Siegfried Bernfeld. Bernfeld accounted for Penrose's interest in chess problems by suggesting that "he probably projected his infantile family conflicts onto the chessboard."[15] The analyst's proposition apparently triggered a dream in the form of a chess problem.[16] As he interpreted the dream in a paper titled "Psycho-Analysis and Chess," which he delivered at the inaugural meeting of the British Psycho-Analytic Society in 1925, Penrose read the chess pieces as standing in for members of the family circle at a critical moment in his childhood—notably the Black King as his father, the Black Queen as a governess,

---

13 Cited in Forrester, "Freud in Cambridge," 5, from Penrose Papers. Cf. Brian Boyd on Nabokov having possibly begun in the Natural Sciences tripos during his first two terms at Cambridge before going on in Modern and Medieval Languages. Brian Boyd, *Vladimir Nabokov: The Russian Years* (Princeton: Princeton University Press, 1990), 170.

14 Boyd, *Vladimir Nabokov*, 13. In an email to me, Dmitri Nabokov expressed skepticism that his father, "not a 'joiner,'" would have been involved in Penrose's enterprise (personal correspondence, February 1, 2008).

15 Cited in Forrester, "Freud in Cambridge," 8. Originally from "Psycho-Analysis and Chess."

16 The dream in Penrose's words is as follows: "I see before me a certain chess position. It is a problem. White is to checkmate Black in two moves. The location of the pieces is not however quite settled, and I feel as though there may be a misprint in the case of the Black Queen. The White Queen ought to be 'pinning' her, I think, in order that the White Pieces should succeed. As it is, too many moves of Black are unprovided for. But in two cases the nature of the mating move is actually known to me. If the Black Pawn (on the square d6) takes the White Pawn (on c5) I know that the White Queen can then checkmate by moving down to the square b2. If the same Black Pawn simply chooses to move on to d5, the White Queen will mate somewhere else." Cited in Forrester, "Freud in Cambridge," 9.

the White Queen as his mother, and the White King as his maternal grandfather.[17] In the words of John Forrester:

> The most forcefully dynamic aspect of the dream's latent meaning, however, attached to the thought that *in two cases the nature of the mating move is actually known to me*. This referred to his knowledge of the sexual relations between his father and mother, reaction against which was, in Penrose's eyes, the most powerful source of the dream. The "mating position" in the dream depended upon the actions of the Black Pawn, himself. It was thus, he concluded, a dream of omnipotence, a dream that he could affect the "mating" of the King and Queen, whereas in reality he had no such power. As he remarked in his notes, his youngest brother Bernard (born 1903) was not yet born at the time of the events associated with the formation of the dream (though Roland, born 1900, was in the world). He was clearly dating the impulse to master his family constellation through chess as arising *from* the era when his youngest brother was conceived, when he was aged 5. So the notebook page following the outline of the dream chess problem and his associations presents a chronology of the key events in his life, from birth to 1922.[18]

Aside from the striking coincidence that one of the first, if not the first person to pose a connection between the game of chess and Freudian psychoanalysis was studying at Cambridge at the same time as Nabokov, what are we to make of all this? Given what we know of Nabokov's life and acquaintances at this point in time, there seems no possibility that he could have known of Penrose's ideas at the time of writing *The Defense*. Yet, as I hope to show, whether by design or happenstance, the way chess is deployed in the analysis of Penrose's dream to structure meaning dovetails neatly with its function in relation to the characters in *The Defense*.

A further wrinkle in space-time presents itself here. The year 1919 also saw the original German-language publication of Freud's essay "The Uncanny." There is neither evidence nor probability that Nabokov might have read the essay at the time of its first appearance, although his German certainly would have been up to the task by the time that he wrote *The Defense* in 1929. This

---

17 I ask the reader at this point to note the correspondence between the principal figures in Penrose's dream and the major players in Luzhin's childhood—again a striking coincidence.

18 Forrester, "Freud in Cambridge," 10.

proposition, of course, asks that we consider the possibility that Nabokov would have taken the trouble to wade through a text in German by his much-maligned Freud. I submit that, given Nabokov's voracious reading and erudition bordering on, and sometimes crossing over into, pedantry, it does not strain credibility that he might have made the effort.[19] The resonances between the two texts certainly prompt us to imagine the possibility.

"The Uncanny" was written in the summer of 1919, shortly before Freud made the intellectual breakthrough to the death instinct he would elaborate in *Beyond the Pleasure Principle*.[20] In brief, in the essay Freud sets himself the task of defining the "uncanny" (*Unheimlich*) and discovers from an initial survey of dictionary definitions of the word that there is a point at which the *Unheimlich* (literally "unhome-ness") overlaps with its opposite, that which pertains to home (*Heimlich*). That is, if etymology is to be trusted, there is a point at which that what is most familiar and dear becomes threatening and alien. Freud concludes—in no small measure through a reading of E. T. A. Hoffmann's story "The Sandman," a point to which we shall return—that the uncanny represents a response to unresolved childhood trauma, which, because it is unresolved, we are doomed to repeat. It is this repetition, or rather the recognition that we are against our volition repeating the past, which is uncanny, which transforms home into its opposite. Freud's literary demonstration of the uncanny, his reading of the Hoffmann story, makes it clear that the paradigmatic narrative of trauma is the family romance, the child's recognition of his parents' sexuality, and, as a corollary to that recognition, the son's fear that he is doomed to repeat his father. So the Hoffmann story falls into two parts, the second of which is a repetition of the first, which leads the major character, Nathaniel, to go mad and commit suicide to free himself from the cycle of repetition.

---

19   Here we should note that Freud's *Beyond the Pleasure Principle* was published in Russian in the Soviet Union in 1925: Zigmund Freid, *Po tu storonu printsipa udovol'stviia* (Moscow: Sovremennye problemy, 1925). I am grateful to Alexander Etkind for having pointed out this publication to me and for having directed my attention to the fact that, although to date there is no evidence of an early Russian translation of "The Uncanny," he has found references made to the work by Russians in the 1920s. Alexander Etkind, *Eros of the Impossible: The History of Psychoanalysis in Russia*, transl. Noah and Maria Rubins (Boulder: Westview, 1997).

20   On this, see Neil Hertz, "Freud and the Sandman," in *Textual Strategies: Perspectives in Post-Structuralist Criticism*, ed. J. V. Haran (London: Methuen, 1979), 296–321.

I have now placed all the pieces of my jigsaw puzzle out on the table, hopefully in such a fashion that the general outlines of my approach to *The Defense* may be visible. In the simplest terms, I am approaching *The Defense* as a serious, if anxious and ambivalent, response to Freud's "The Uncanny," with chess as a fundamental semiotic system and Hoffmann's "The Sandman," as mediated by Freud, as a significant intertext. Freud's own terms, however, remain primary: the crippling prison of uncontrollable repetition that dooms one to return to a home that is no longer home. For Nabokov, the principal question must be: if one were to accept Freud's terms, might there be a way out of this impasse, this loss of free will and individual self-determination through art, through "the stone of the peach I plucked in my own walled garden"?

The Defense, after all, with its very opening words simultaneously expels its title character from home and threatens him with the seeming inevitability of repeating/replacing his father: "What struck him most was the fact that from Monday on he would be Luzhin. His father—the real Luzhin, the elderly Luzhin, the writer of books—left the nursery with a smile" (15). The catalysts for Luzhin's expulsion from the garden, as it were, are the appearance of the governess—the extra woman in the household—and his father's desire to send him to school to find his talent.[21] When Luzhin attempts to escape from his parents' plans and run back home to hide in the attic, he has his first brush with chess: "Besides books there was a shuttlecock with one feather, a large photograph (of a military band), a cracked chessboard, and some other not very interesting things" (23). This pattern repeats itself at significant moments in the novel.[22] Nabokov himself observes in the preface:

---

21 Luzhin undergoes this initial trauma—which, as we shall shortly see, is endowed with Oedipal guilt by association—at what would seem clearly to be an older age than that to which Freud would date the primal scene of knowledge in the parental bedroom. As any number of critics have noted, one of Nabokov's many disagreements with Freud concerned his repugnance for what he apparently viewed as Freud's sexual abasement of childhood, a period of life Nabokov himself continued to portray as Edenic throughout his life. Luzhin's childhood, then, remains untouched by the family drama, remains in the realm of the prehistory of the novel.

22 I would note in this context that my reading of *The Defense* dovetails at significant points with readings by Boyd and Alexandrov, with the key difference that I impute the forces driving Luzhin not to a supernatural Otherworld, but to the Freudian design against which Nabokov stages a matchup. Brian Boyd, "The Problem of Pattern: Nabokov's *Defense*," *Modern Fiction Studies* 33, no. 4 (1987): 575–604; and Vladimir E. Alexandrov,

> My story was difficult to compose, but I greatly enjoyed taking advantage of this or that image and scene to introduce a fatal pattern into Luzhin's life and to endow the description of a garden, a journey, a sequence of humdrum events, with the semblance of a game of skill, and, especially in the final chapters, with that of a regular chess attack demolishing the innermost elements of the poor fellow's sanity. (8)[23]

The question to be resolved in this article then becomes: how do the chess patterns intersect with patterns of repetition that seem to echo the Freudian text?

To begin to answer this question, let us look at the places in Nabokov's text when Luzhin actually experiences the uncanny, that is, when he experiences a strong sense that he is repeating a past action.[24] The first instance appears to occur on the evening when Luzhin reveals to his father his mastery of chess. Luzhin senior, having returned to the family country house from a tryst

---

"The Defense," in *The Garland Companion to Vladimir Nabokov*, ed. Vladimir E. Alexandrov (New York: Garland, 1995), 75–88.

23 Nabokov then goes on to preempt critics seeking patterns as he will taunt wouldbe Freudians later in the Preface. The following few sentences give a sufficient taste of this tactic: "In this connection, I would like to spare the time and effort of hack reviewers—and, generally, persons who move their lips when reading and cannot be expected to tackle a dialogueless novel when so much can be gleaned from its Foreword—by drawing their attention to the first appearance of the frosted-window theme (associated with Luzhin's suicide, or rather sui-mate) as early as Chapter Eleven, or to the pathetic way my morose grandmaster remembers his professional journeys not in terms of sunburst luggage labels and magic-lantern shots but in terms of the tiles in different hotel bathrooms and corridor toilets" (8–9). And so on in the same vein.

24 The threat and fear of repetition haunt the novel from the outset, and it would be well beyond the space limitations of this article to chart all of the repetitions in the novel (beginning with Luzhin "repeating" his father in the first sentence). It is worth noting, however, what appears to be the first expression of fear of repetition in the chronology of the novel. In the first chapter, Luzhin senior fears to tell his son that he is to be sent to school: "He was afraid, Luzhin senior, that when his son learned why the founders of Russia, the completely featureless Sineus and Truvor, were necessary, as well as the table of Russian words taking the letter "yat" and the principal rivers of Russia, the child would go into the same tantrum as had happened two years before, when slowly and heavily, to the sound of creaking stairs, crackling floorboards and shifting trunks, filling the whole house with her presence, the French governess had first appeared" (17). While, contrary to his father's fears, Luzhin does not repeat a tantrum on this occasion, we do see the onset of yet another repeated pattern in the novel: the destabilization of family dynamics by the introduction of an "extra" woman into the household—whether the governess or Luzhin's aunt or the "lady from Russia," his aunt's acquaintance.

in Petersburg with Luzhin's aunt, proposes that he teach his son how to play chess. Luzhin tries to demur using the excuse that there is no chess set, but his father responds that there might be "some old ones in the attic": "And indeed, by the light of the lamp that his father held aloft, among all sorts of rubbish in a case Luzhin found a chessboard, and again he had the feeling that all this had happened before—that open case with the nail sticking out of its side, those dust-powdered books, that wooden chessboard with a crack down the middle" (63). Luzhin, who goes on repeatedly to defeat his father at chess, is at a loss as to how his father has discovered his passion for chess: "The most obvious explanation did not occur to him, just as sometimes in solving a problem its key turns out to be a move that seemed barred, impossible, excluded quite naturally from the range of possible moves" (63). That the "obvious explanation"—that Luzhin senior is having an affair with the aunt who has divulged the son's secret—does not occur to Luzhin is telling, especially when we remember that from the outset Luzhin senior and the aunt are contrasted by the books that they make available to Luzhin. On the one hand, there are his father's own books with inscriptions that "inspired in him a vague feeling of shame for his father," those same books that threaten to trap him in the figure of the fictional Antosha, as well as unopened classics; on the other hand, "there were two books, both given him by his aunt, with which he had fallen in love for his whole life" (33), the stories of Sherlock Holmes and Jules Verne's *Around the World in 80 Days*. What "thrilled him so about these two books," as Luzhin later realized, "was that exact and relentlessly unfolding pattern" (34). Of course, Luzhin experiences the "uncanny" when his father takes him to the attic to find the chessboard, because, as we have seen, he has gone to the attic and found a chessboard earlier in the novel, during his first attempted flight back home at the end of the first chapter. What we find then is that Luzhin's experience of the uncanny is tied from the outset with unsuccessful flight home, to retreat to a time before his life becomes a complicated chess game and before he appears inexorably doomed to repeat his father. Chess, where Luzhin appears able to defeat all comers, becomes the site of Oedipal rivalry, replacing sex.

Luzhin's second explicit experience of the uncanny comes much later in the novel, in the wake of his meeting with his former schoolmate Petrishchev, who confuses Luzhin with his father's fictional character (197), and of the arrival of his aunt's acquaintance from Petersburg. Here the repeated pattern is described overtly by analogy with chess:

> Just as some combination, known from chess problems, can be indistinctly repeated on the board in actual play—so now the consecutive repetition of a familiar pattern was becoming noticeable in his present life. And as soon as his initial delight in having established the actual fact of the repetition had passed, as soon as he began to go carefully over his discovery, Luzhin shuddered. With vague admiration and vague horror he observed how awesomely, how elegantly and how flexibly, move by move, the images of his childhood had been repeated (country house... town... school... aunt), but he still did not quite understand why this combinational repetition inspired his soul with such dread. (213–14)

Luzhin realizes that, just as earlier he had to devise a defense against Turati's opening, now "he had, if possible, to contrive a defense against this perfidious combination" (214). He now recognizes that the occupations to which at his wife's prompting he has resorted to replace chess must be dropped as dangerous repetitions: "The typewriter, geography and drawing were abandoned, for he knew now that all this was part of the combination, was an intricate repetition of all the moves that had been taken down in childhood" (215–16). Yet despite his precautions, his discards, he soon experiences the uncanny again. Seeking a way to occupy the son of his aunt's acquaintance from Russia, Luzhin discovers in the lining of his jacket a chessboard and "he set out the position of his game with Turati at the point where it had been interrupted" (218). But the child for whom he lays out the board is forgotten until he makes his presence known, and "his terrible little double, little Luzhin, for whom the chess pieces had been set out, crawled over the carpet on his knees. [...] All this had happened once before. [...] And again he had been caught, had not understood how the repetition of a familiar theme would come out in practice" (219).

Luzhin's feeling that "all this had happened once before" evokes his first explicit exposure to his father's sexuality—although that revelation, clear enough to the reader, appears to elude Luzhin. During the soiree to commemorate the first anniversary of the death of his maternal grandfather—a knight's move of sorts to his mother's side of the family, whose male progenitor Luzhin also appears doomed to repeat—Luzhin finds himself in a secluded space upstairs in the family's Petersburg home. This setting echoes the attic to which Luzhin flees when he comes home at the end of the first chapter, but now the secluded space is explicitly identified as a space preoccupied by his father: the elder Luzhin's study. While there, he overhears the violinist, who is taking a break from playing the concert dedicated to his grandfather's music and is apparently speaking with his mistress. This textual/sexual revelation, moreover, coincides with Luzhin's discovery of a chess set, which we as readers only later are given leave to surmise was given to Luzhin senior by Luzhin's aunt, with whom, we soon learn, he is having an affair. Thus, chess and sexuality are linked from this moment, the moment of Luzhin's eavesdropping, but, as we have seen, chess, what the violinist terms, "The game of the gods, infinite possibilities" (43), will take the place of sex for Luzhin as the battlefield for Oedipal struggles with the father figures that proliferate in the novel.[25]

From the moment Luzhin finds the chessboard, he is ever more intensely caught up in the uncanny, by a compulsion to repeat which he conceives as "a continuation of the game that had not been started by him but was being directed with awful force against him" (228), a clear evocation of his interrupted game with Turati. Desperate, Luzhin comes up with one final defense:

> Already the day before he had thought of an interesting device, a device with which he could, perhaps, foil the designs of his mysterious opponent. The device consisted in voluntarily committing some absurd unexpected act that would be outside the systematic order of life, thus confusing the sequence of moves planned by his opponent. It was an experimental defense, a defense, so to say, at random—but Luzhin, crazed with terror before the inevitability of the next move, was able to find nothing better. (242)

This is precisely the defense that will land him in the clutches of his "chess father" (238, 240) and lead to the end of the fatal match in sui-mate: "The device had proved erroneous. This error had been foreseen by his opponent, and the implacable move prepared long ago, had now been made" (246–47).

Valentinov (who is conflated with Turati and fate through the German maid's mispronunciation of his name as "Fati") tries to force Luzhin to repeat the unfinished game with Turati precisely by composing his own script, using the lure of a chess problem, also of his own composition, to tempt Luzhin back into the truncated rivalry—just as Luzhin's father before had tried to "script"

---

25 Note that the primal scene here is placed not in the bedroom, but in the father's study, where (assumedly) he writes his fictions, and is not seen (not an instance of voyeurism), but overheard. One suspects again a significant revision of the Freudian masterplot.

his son in his books about Antosha.²⁶ Luzhin tells his wife on the way to his end: "'The only way out,' he said. 'I have to drop out of the game'" (252). So does Nabokov's game with Freud end in a forfeiture?

Before considering that question further, we need to look at the obverse side of the coin. That is, if Luzhin experiences the uncanny when he finds himself compelled to repeat the past, what of Luzhin's voluntary returns to the past, his attempts to go home? At two key moments in *The Defense*, Luzhin articulates the need to go home. On the first occasion, a voice from outside appears to prompt him when time has been called on his game with Turati, which will ultimately remain unfinished:

> "Go home," whispered another voice insinuatingly and something pushed against Luzhin's shoulder. "What did you say?" he asked again, suddenly ceasing to sob. "Home, home," repeated the voice, and the glass radiance, taking hold of Luzhin, threw him out into the cool dusk, Luzhin smiled. "Home," he said softly. "So that's the key to the combination."²⁷ (141)

On the second occasion, seeking to frustrate the chain of repetitions through an unexpected action and having eluded his wife's vigilance, Luzhin finds himself in a ladies' hairdresser's and resorts to the ruse of claiming to want to buy a wax bust to explain his presence there: "The wax lady's look, her pink nostrils—this also had happened before. 'A joke,' said Luzhin and hastily left the hairdresser's. He felt disgustingly uncomfortable and quickened his step, although there was nowhere to hurry. 'Home, home,' he muttered, 'there I'll combine everything properly'" (244). This latter episode uncannily repeats his experience, while still a schoolboy, of dodging the geography teacher while playing hooky from school to go to his aunt's to learn chess.²⁸ "Only when the teacher, like a blind wind, had swept past him did Luzhin become aware that

---

26 When Luzhin has locked himself in the bathroom in preparation for leaping out the window, among the people he thinks he hears outside the door are "Valentinov, Turati, the old gentleman with the bunch of flowers" (255), all his major rivals in chess. Note that Luzhin senior dies before he is able to complete, or even start, what appears to be a projected novel incorporating Valentinov.

27 The glass is possibly a prefiguration of the window through which Luzhin will plunge at the end.

28 Another chess rival and possible father figure, who, we later learn, was possibly also the geography teacher of his future wife.

he was standing before a hairdresser's window and that the frizzled heads of three waxen ladies with pink nostrils were staring directly at him" (50).[29] In both of these cases, Luzhin is diverted in his attempts to go home—to a home that, after all, no longer exists. In the first instance, he is delivered to the ersatz Russia of his in-laws' home and is then taken off to a sanatorium. Here we find the one place in the novel where the Freudian paradigm is directly addressed. When Luzhin awakes, he does indeed imagine that he has made his way home: "In the window, if you lifted yourself a little, you could see a fence that was also spotted with shadow. 'Evidently I did get home,' said Luzhin pensively" (159–60). In "the autumn beauty of the window," Luzhin experiences "an enigmatic, evasive happiness" (161). Luzhin does appear to "go home" as he undergoes the cure in the sanatorium, but it is clearly not due to the bearded psychiatrist's attempts, distinguished by a woefully misinformed grasp on the details of Russian life in Luzhin's childhood, to subject Luzhin to the "talking cure," to get him to talk about his childhood:

> But Luzhin rarely grew enlivened during these conversations. On the other hand, constantly nudged by these interrogations, his thoughts would return again and again to the sphere of his childhood. It was impossible to express his recollections in words—there simply were no grown-up words for his childish impressions—and if he ever related anything, then he did so jerkily and unwillingly—rapidly sketching the outlines and marking a complex move, rich in possibilities, with just a letter and a number. His pre-school, pre-chess childhood, which he had never thought about before, dismissing it with a slight shudder so as not to find dormant horrors and humiliating insults there, proved now to be an amazingly safe spot, where he could take pleasant excursions that sometimes brought a piercing pleasure. (163–64)

Luzhin finds himself at home in a time before the novel begins, in a time before chess and before words, but, as the remainder of the novel will show, it is not a state of home that can be sustained in the world of the novel. Thus, when Luzhin again tries to go home where he believes he can "combine everything properly," he finds himself trapped in Valentinov's script. So he hurls himself out of the game through the window into eternity, which appears to him through the window in the shape of a chess board: "The window reflections

---

29   These lifeless female figures resonate with the Coppelia theme in Freud's reading of Hoffmann's "The Sandman."

6. King, Queen, Sui-Mate   117

gathered together and leveled themselves out, the whole chasm was seen to divide into dark and pale squares, and at the instant when Luzhin unclenched his head, at the instant when icy air gushed into his mouth, he saw exactly what kind of eternity was obligingly and inexorably spread out before him" (256).

In preparation for his "sui-mate," Luzhin divests himself of the contents of his pockets before saying farewell to his wife:

> Luzhin began to take things out of his pockets—first a fountain pen, then a crumpled handkerchief, then another handkerchief, neatly folded, which she had given him that morning; after this he took out a cigarette case with a troika on the lid (a present from his mother-in-law), then an empty, red cigarette pack and two separate cigarettes, slightly damaged; his wallet and a gold watch (a present from his father-in-law) were removed with particular care. Besides all this there turned up a large peach stone. All these objects were placed on the phonograph cabinet and he checked if there were anything he had forgotten. (251–52)

Of course, the attentive reader knows that what Luzhin has "forgotten" is the chess set still lodged in the lining of his jacket, "and only after several months, when all danger was long, long past, only then was the pocket chess set found again, and by then its origin was obscure" (221).

The implicit invitation—or challenge—to read backward to the origin cannot help but prompt us to look at another passage from the Foreword to the English-language edition of *The Defense* in which Nabokov draws our attention to his structural exploitation of chess designs in the novel. This passage is so important as to justify quotation in full:

> But the chess effects I planted are distinguishable not only in these separate scenes; their concatenation can be found in the basic structure of this attractive novel. Thus toward the end of Chapter Four an unexpected move is made by me in a corner of the board, sixteen years elapse in the course of one paragraph, and Luzhin, suddenly promoted to seedy manhood and transferred to a German resort, is discovered at a garden table, pointing out with his cane a remembered hotel window (not the last glass square in his life) and talking to somebody (a woman, if we judge by the handbag on the iron table) whom we do not meet till Chapter Six. The retrospective theme begun in Chapter Four shades now into the image of Luzhin's late father, whose own past is taken up in Chapter Five when he, in his turn, is perceived recalling his son's early chess career and stylizing it in his mind so as to make of

it a sentimental tale for the young. We switch back to the Kurhaus in Chapter Six and find Luzhin still fiddling with the handbag and still addressing his blurry companion whereupon she unblurs, takes it away from him, mentions Luzhin senior's death, and becomes a distinct part of the design. The entire sequence of moves in these three central chapters reminds one—or should remind one—of a certain type of chess problem where the point is not merely the finding of a mate in so many moves, but what is termed "retrograde analysis," the solver being required to prove from a back-cast study of the diagram position that Black's last move *could not* have been castling or *must* have been the capture of a white Pawn *en passant*. (9–10)

The transparent analogy between Nabokov's "retrograde analysis" and Freud's *Nachträglichkeit*, the reading back from symptoms/repetition to originary trauma, is underscored by the fact that the narrative leap from past into future elides precisely the Oedipal scenario of the father's death before Luzhin senior can assert his artistic priority—and win the rivalry with his son—by rewriting Luzhin into his projected novella *The Gambit*. In this planned work the fictionalized Luzhin, as implicitly dictated by convention (which is, of course, a defeat of priority by repetition), will die young: "Yes, he will die young, his death will be logical and very moving. He will die in bed while playing his last game" (78).[30] Yet the narrator, as echoed by Nabokov in the preface, redirects our attention from masterplot to the detail of the handbag (73, 83) that frames the "retrograde analysis" and apparently belongs to Luzhin's future wife. In this context we should remember that *The Defense*, like E. T. A. Hoffmann's "The Sandman," Freud's exemplary text in "The Uncanny," is structured by a division into two parts in which the second part of the work repeats, as if compelled to do so, the first. That is, having lost his home and his family in the first part of the text, which chronologically precedes the leap into the future, Luzhin is drawn unsuccessfully to reconstitute his family and home in the second part only to find himself undone by the same threat of purloined priority that led to his expulsion from home to begin with.

---

30 Luzhin senior, however, falls short of tracing this death back to its origin: "He started to guide his thought backwards—from this touching and so distinct death back to his hero's vague origin, but presently thought better of it and sat down at his desk to ponder anew" (78).

Thus, in Chapter Six, when the future Luzhina "unblurs" and "becomes a distinct part of the design," we learn how Luzhin and the young woman became acquainted:

> She made his acquaintance on the third day after his arrival, made it the way they do in old novels or in motion pictures; she drops a handkerchief and he picks it up—with the sole difference that they interchanged roles—Luzhin was walking along a path in front of her and in succession shed: a large checked handkerchief that was unusually dirty and had all sorts of pocket debris sticking to it; then a broken and crushed cigarette minus half of its contents; a nut; and a French franc. She gathered up only the handkerchief and the coin and walked on, slowly catching up with him and curiously awaiting some new loss. With the cane he carried in his right hand, Luzhin touched in passing every tree trunk and every bench, while groping in his pocket with his left, until finally he stopped, turned out his coat pocket, shed another coin, and started to examine the large hole in the lining. "Right through," he said in German, taking the handkerchief from her hand ("This also," she said in Russian). "Poor material," he continued without looking up, neither switching to Russian nor showing any surprise, as if the return of his things had been quite natural. (86)

Indulging in "retrograde analysis," we cannot help but be struck by how this episode prefigures Luzhin's actions preceding his final farewell to his wife at the end, emptying his pockets. That their meeting is facilitated more by the exchange of objects than by the exchange of words underscores Luzhin's remarkable, virtually childlike verbal ineptitude, which is a leitmotif of his portrayal throughout and especially of his relationship with his wife. It also reminds us that for Luzhin the exile, perennially homeless, what he carries on his back and in his pockets is what remains of his home and his past. This then encourages us to look for the origins of significant objects in Luzhin's past. In doing so, we find that the two most freighted objects may be traced back to the moment in Chapter Three when Luzhin senior's dalliance with the aunt comes to light, forcing her permanent expulsion from the Luzhin house. Just as the aunt, at Luzhin's insistence and inspired by his conversation with the violinist the preceding evening, is showing Luzhin how to play chess on a board she apparently had given as a gift to his father: "Suddenly she froze, holding a piece in mid-air and looking at the door. 'Wait,' she said anxiously. 'I think I left my handkerchief in the dining room'" (46).³¹ The handkerchief—which would seem to evoke that most famous of literary handkerchiefs signifying the threat of jealousy bred by perfidious rivalry, Desdemona's handkerchief in Shakespeare's *Othello*—and the chess set (albeit both substitutes) are with Luzhin on his dying day, as we have seen. What are we to make of this repetitive design, especially in light of the anomalous peach stone and Freud's "Uncanny"?

Neil Hertz in his suggestive article, "Freud and the Sandman," reads Freud's "The Uncanny" as a symptom of Freud's own anxiety about literary priority of which the preoccupation with the repetition compulsion is a symptom. Freud, who acknowledges from the outset his own unease in venturing into the realm of "aesthetics" in "The Uncanny," in Hertz's reading comes up short against "the desire for representation," "the wish to make a mark, the wish for the power to produce durable representations." Freud, Hertz maintains, is concerned by the dependence of the exposition of psychoanalytic theory on the use of figurative language and, in his discussion of Hoffmann's "The Sandman," he "overstabilize[s]" it, flattens the openness and volatility of the literary text in the service of the Freudian masterplot: "When Freud turns aside from these more literary aspects of the story, he is making a legitimate interpretive move, but it has the effect of domesticating the story."³² I began this article by pointing to the challenge posed by Freudian discourse to modernist writers in general and Nabokov in particular, but Hertz reminds us that the rivalry cuts both ways: when the two fields overlap, they neutralize each other.³³ Given this, "The Uncanny" would seem to be an appropriate textual battleground on which Nabokov might engage Freud at his most vulnerable.

We, as readers, do not know into what posttextual eternity Luzhin departs through the window at the end, because there is no evidence that Luzhin's final vision (unlike that of Cincinnatus at the end of *Invitation to a Beheading*) is situated after rather than before his body dies. We do, however, know what he

---

31   We are also told here of Luzhin's conclusion that "the Queen is the most mobile" (46) of the chess pieces his aunt demonstrates to him. Of the fate of the chess set we learn only, "From that day the chess set remained with him and it was a long time before his father noticed its absence" (47). This clearly prefigures the chess set that will accompany Luzhin to his death.

32   Hertz, "Freud and the Sandman," 309, 304, and 313.

33   Hertz, "Freud and the Sandman," 296.

leaves behind, perhaps as a trace of "the power to produce durable representations": Nabokov's peach stone. Nabokov gifts his inarticulate, but, in Nabokov's own prefatory word, "lovable" (10) character "the stone of the peach I plucked in my own walled garden," the telling detail from the author's past which is a metonym for the incarnation of unrepeatable individuality in the very texture of literature. Perhaps it is inevitable that, like the match between Luzhin and Turati—between "the limpidity and lightness of Luzhin's thought" and "the Italian's tumultuous fantasy" (135)—Nabokov's match with Freud can only end in sui-mate, as Nabokov terms "self-mate" in the preface. This gambit, by which a player forces his own king into checkmate by his rival, suggests a surrender of constricting father figures, just as the more modern term, "self-mate," suggests Luzhin's sterility, his final defense against self-replication, a definitive end to the cycle of repetition, leaving behind only the unique and unrepeatable text of *The Defense* itself.

Works Cited

Alexandrov, Vladimir E. "The Defense." In *The Garland Companion to Vladimir Nabokov*, edited by Vladimir E. Alexandrov, 75–88. New York: Garland, 1995.

Blackwell, Stephen H. "Nabokov's Wiener-Schnitzel Dreams: Despair and Anti-Freudian Poetics." *Nabokov Studies* 7 (2002/2003): 129–50.

Boyd, Brian. "The Problem of Pattern: Nabokov's *Defense*." *Modern Fiction Studies* 33, no. 4 (1987): 575–604.

———. *Vladimir Nabokov: The Russian Years*. Princeton: Princeton University Press, 1990.

Cameron, Laura and John Forrester. "Tansley's Psychoanalytic Network: An Episode Out of the Early History of Psychoanalysis in England." *Psychoanalysis and History* 2, no. 2 (2000): 189–256.

Cohen, David G. "My Potential Patients: Origins, Detection, and Transference in *Pale Fire* and Freud's *Case of the Wolf-Man*." Zembla. Accessed July 24, 2022. https://www.libraries.psu.edu/nabokov/cohen1.htm.

De La Durantaye, Leland. "Vladimir Nabokov and Sigmund Freud, or a Particular Problem." *American Imago* 62, no. 1 (2005): 59–73.

Etkind, Alexander. *Eros of the Impossible: The History of Psychoanalysis in Russia*. Translated by Noah and Maria Rubins. Boulder: Westview, 1997.

Forrester, John. "Freud in Cambridge." *Critical Quarterly* 46, no. 2 (2004): 1–26.

Freud, Sigmund. "Das Unheimliche." *Imago: Zeitschrift für Anwendung der Psychoanalyse auf die Geisteswissenschaften* 5 (1919): 297–324.

———. *Po tu storonu printsipa udovol'stviia*. Moscow: Sovremennye problemy, 1925.

Green, Geoffrey. *Freud and Nabokov*. Lincoln: University of Nebraska Press, 1988.

Hertz, Neil. "Freud and the Sandman." In *Textual Strategies: Perspectives in Post-Structuralist Criticism*, edited by J. V. Haran, 296–321. London: Methuen, 1979.

Larmour, David. *Discourse and Ideology in Nabokov's Prose*. New York: Routledge, 2002.

Nabokov, Vladimir. *The Defense*. Translated by Michael Scammell. New York: Vintage, 1964.

———. *Speak, Memory: An Autobiography Revisited*. New York: Vintage International, 1989.

Pifer, Ellen. "On Human Freedom and Inhuman Art: Nabokov." *The Slavic and East European Journal* 22, no. 1 (1978): 52–63.

Rivers, W. H. R. *Conflict and Dream*. London: Kegan Paul, Trench Trubner, 1923.

Shute, Jenefer Patricia. *Nabokov and Freud: The Play of Power*. PhD diss., University of California, Los Angeles, 1983.

Smith, G. Elliot. "Preface." In W. H. R. Rivers, *Conflict and Dream*, v–ix. London: Kegan Paul, Trench Trubner, 1923.

7

"Imperially, My Dear Watson": Sherlock Holmes and the Decline of the Soviet Empire

> The means of expression *in being different* would express different things—not the same things in different ways. ... We talk as if adaptation were a matter of translation, like passing from one language to another, when in fact it is a matter of passing from one *form* to another, a matter of transposition, of reconstruction.
>
> —Jean Mitry [emphasis in the original—eds.]

In the beginning of the twenty-first century, we have a tendency to take cinematic adaptations of literary works as a matter of course, because they are so ubiquitous a feature of the movie and television industry. Yet any astute scholar of film adaptation recognizes that the transposition of a literary work into film involves a complex semiotic process. Most important, the technical modifications demanded by the differences between the two media—in the simplest terms, the need to convey in pictures what was originally related in words—require different forms of "reading." Equally interesting, in this context, is the fact that the original and the adaptation entail, at least potentially, different

---

The epigraph is cited in James John Griffith, *Adaptations as Imitations: Films from Novels* (Newark: University of Delaware Press, 1997), 25—C. T. N. This article first appeared in *Russian and Soviet Film Adaptations of Literature, 1900–2001: Screening the Word*, ed. Stephen Hutchings and Anat Vernitski (London: RoutledgeCurzon; 2005), 164–77. Reproduced by permission of Taylor and Francis Group, LLC. A division of informa plc—eds.

interpretive communities, to use Stanley Fish's phrase.¹ In other words, each medium carries with it its own "baggage": its own conventions, intertexts, and cultural status. I would submit that the situation becomes even more complicated when the adaptation is also a "translation"—that is, when a literary work produced in one national culture is adapted into cinematic form in another linguistically and politically (taken in the broadest sense of the word) alien environment. In this essay, I would like to take up the challenge to scholars of film adaptation thrown down by James Naremore, who, deploring scholars' preoccupation with "fidelity," has called for "a broader definition of adaptation and a sociology that takes into account the commercial apparatus, the audience and the academic culture industry."² Naremore has maintained, more specifically, that "we need more writing about adaptation of 'low' or pop-cultural texts, and we need to think about how certain texts are adapted cross culturally."³ I would like to explore these issues as they manifest themselves in the Soviet adaptation of the so eminently British adventures of Sherlock Holmes. More particularly, I hope to show that the Soviet transposition and translation of Sir Arthur Conan Doyle's works, which themselves retain the imprint of the socio-political context in which their author wrote, also indelibly bear the marks of their time: the decline of the Soviet empire.

As I suggested from the outset, every adaptation of a well-known literary work carries baggage, but few projects drag with them such a heavy burden as do the adventures of Sherlock Holmes. Over the course of time, over 160 actors have played the character in plays, feature films, made-for-television versions, and on radio, and "S[herlock] H[olmes] has been filmed more times than any other fictional character, ranking second is Dracula."⁴ To complicate matters, there was a pre-cinematic visual and theatrical culture at work in the

---

1   The phrase appears in Fish's essay "Interpreting the Variorum," *Critical Inquiry* 2, no. 3 (1976): 465–85.

2   James Naremore, ed., *Film Adaptation* (New Brunswick: Rutgers University Press, 2000), 10. As most recent commentators on film adaptation have pointed out, the issue of fidelity to the original work, which inevitably privileges the literary work over the film it inspires, remains the primary principle by which not only the popular audience, but even scholars and theorists judge adaptations.

3   Naremore, *Film Adaptation*, 12.

4   Anonymous, "Basic Sherlock Holmes for You Beginners," accessed January 3, 2004, http://www.geocities.com/Hollywood/Derby/3418/basicsherlock.htm (site discontinued—eds.).

construction of Sherlock Holmes in the popular imagination. Thus, among those features of the character of Holmes that have become "canonic," some of his trademark traits are not mentioned in the original stories at all, among them the deerstalker hat, the magnifying glass, the distinctive pipe, and the phrase "Elementary, my dear Watson." The by now iconic hat and magnifying glass appear to have been the inventions of Sidney Padget, in his illustrations for the first editions of the stories published in the *Strand Magazine*.[5] By the same token, the phrase "Elementary, my dear Watson" was evidently used by the first actor to portray Holmes, William Gillette, and was made famous by the film actor probably most closely identified with Holmes even today, Basil Rathbone. Gillette appears also to have introduced the calabash pipe as a Holmes accessory, reputedly because it better suited his face than the more modest variants suggested by the original stories.[6] Arguably, then, the "adapted," largely visual as opposed to verbal Holmes has long since displaced his literary prototype in the mind's eye.

As far as the mark left by the times on the original Holmes stories is concerned, moreover, there is a growing literature on the Sherlock Holmes tales as representations of British imperial ambitions and fears and on Conan Doyle himself as an apologist for empire.[7] Edward Said, in *Culture and Imperialism*, relegates Conan Doyle's works to the "genre of adventure-imperialism," classing the creator of Sherlock Holmes among those writers of his age for whom "empire is everywhere a crucial setting."[8] Among the more interesting analyses of Holmes's imperial resonance are Laura Otis's postulation of Holmes as an "imperial immune system," an antigen against the dangerous infection of the foreign colonial which erupts in crime in the metropolis, Leslie Haynsworth's contention that the counterpoint between Holmes and Watson

---

5   In a 2001 interview Igor' Maslennikov confirmed that he had consulted the Sydney Padget illustrations in making *The Adventures of Sherlock Holmes and Doctor Watson*. Nataliia Rtishcheva, "Igor' Maslenikov: 'Eto zhe elementarno, Vatson!,'" *Moskovskii komsomolets*, April 30, 2000, accessed October 2, 2022, https://www.mk.ru/old/article/2000/04/30/124866-igor-maslennikov-eto-zhe-elementarno-vatson.html.

6   See for example, H. Nisbeth, "What Pipes Did Sherlock Holmes Smoke?," accessed January 3, 2004, http://sherlock-holmes.hypermart.net/ (site discontinued—eds.).

7   For example, see, James Symons, *Conan Doyle: Portrait of an Artist* (London: Mysterious Press, 1987), 69.

8   Edward W. Said, *Culture and Imperialism* (New York: Alfred A. Knopf, 1994), 155, 163.

embodies the tension between the demands of empire abroad and the stability of domestic life at home, and Sheila Sullivan's argument that the Holmes adventures represent an attempt to redefine British imperial pre-eminence in light of rising challenges in the late nineteenth and early twentieth centuries from Germany and the United States.[9] To reiterate here for the sake of clarity, my primary question is not so much the "faithfulness" of the Soviet adaptation to the original Holmes stories, but rather what happens to the adventures of Holmes and Watson when they are transplanted onto Soviet soil. More specifically, what happens to the imperial subtext of the original Holmes stories when they are recreated in a new time, place, and ideological context? Do the Soviet adaptations in any way perform analogous cultural work in their new homeland?

Before exploring the deeper theoretical and exegetical issues raised by the Soviet multi-series adaptation of Conan Doyle's texts to film, let me outline the basic parameters of the project. Between 1979 and 1986, eleven episodes of made-for-television adaptations of some of Sir Arthur Conan Doyle's more famous works were produced for Soviet television. They were directed by Igor' F. Maslennikov, and they featured Vasilii Livanov in the role of Holmes and Vitalii Solomin in the role of Watson. The episodes were grouped into five segments, most of which creatively combined different Holmes stories. The first two episodes aired in 1979, entitled "Acquaintance" and "Bloody Inscription," put together the first of Conan Doyle's Holmes tales, the novel *A Study in Scarlet*, with one of the best-known stories, "The Speckled Band." This adaptation thereby created a fluid cinematic narrative of how the detective and his chronicler took up residence together at 221B Baker Street and used one of Holmes's more celebrated cases as Watson's initiation. Three episodes were aired in 1980—"The Master Blackmailer," "Deadly Flight," and "Hunt for the Tiger,"—

---

9   Laura Otis, "The Empire Bites Back: Sherlock Holmes as an Imperial Immune System," *Studies in Twentieth Century Literature* 22, no. 1 (Winter 1998): 31–60; Leslie Haynsworth, "Sensational Adventures: Sherlock Holmes and His Generic Past," *English Literature in Transition* 44, no. 4 (2001): 459–85; Sheila Sullivan, "Hands across the Water, Crime across the Sea: Gender, Imperialist History, and Arthur Conan Doyle's American," *Victorians Institute Journal* 26 (1998): 95–120. For other interesting discussions of Sherlock Holmes and empire, see Stephen Arata, *Fictions of Loss in the Victorian Fin de Siècle* (Cambridge: Cambridge University Press, 1996); Jon Thompson, *Fiction, Crime, and Empire: Clues to Modernity and Postmodernism* (Urbana: University of Illinois Press, 1993); and Dennis Porter, *The Pursuit of Crime: Art and Ideology in Crime Fiction* (New Haven: Yale University Press, 1981).

based respectively on the stories "The Adventure of Charles Augustus Milverton," "The Final Problem," and "The Adventure of the Empty House." This second series combined one of the later Holmes stories with the tale of the detective's purported demise, plummeting into the Reichenbach Falls locked in a death grip with his archnemesis Dr. Moriarty, and his return by popular demand. In 1981, *The Hound of the Baskervilles* was produced in two episodes, and in 1983, two episodes presented under the title "The Treasures of Agra" united the novel *The Sign of the Four* with one of Conan Doyle's most celebrated stories, "A Scandal in Bohemia," which features the only hint of romance in Holmes's career: the detective's fascination with the adventuress Irene Adler. Finally, in 1986, the final two episodes, under the title *The Twentieth Century Begins*, were aired, the first adapted from the stories "The Engineer's Thumb" and "The Adventure of the Second Stain" and the second—from the stories "His Last Bow" and "The Adventure of the Bruce-Partington Plans." The creation and airing of the series, one of the most popular television events of the Soviet period, spanned the twilight of what I pointedly term here the Soviet Empire, a period that, I would argue, stretches from the invasion of Afghanistan to the beginning of glasnost.

So, the first set of questions that beg our attention concern the meaning of the choice of the adventures of Sherlock Holmes for adaptation in the first place and the more immediate cultural events that would have conditioned the Soviet audience's expectations and reception of the project. Certainly, we should recognize the making of the series as part of the resurgence of detective fiction—especially the works of such "classic" mystery writers as Conan Doyle and Agatha Christie—during the post-Stalin period after decades of being ostracized from official Soviet culture. Also, the late 1960s saw the emergence of the genre of the television mini-series in the USSR, and the earliest and most popular of these productions were adaptations of crime and spy fiction, most notably the first Soviet TV mini-series, the 1966 *The Meeting Place Cannot be Changed* (Mesto vstrechi izmenit' nel'zia), and what remains probably the most popular instance of the genre, the 1973 espionage thriller, *Seventeen Moments in Spring* (Semnadtsat' mgnovenii vesny). We should also note in this regard the airing in the USSR in 1971 of the BBC multi-episode adaptation for television of John Galsworthy's *The Forsythe Saga*, which was so popular with the Soviet viewing audience that it emptied the streets of Moscow during showings. This historic event both demonstrated and whetted an appetite for British period drama on the part of the Soviet public. Comments made by Maslennikov, which highlight the shaping force of generational experience, suggest how these trends converged in the making of *Sherlock Holmes and Doctor Watson*. Maslennikov had the following to say about political engagement in the years after the Khrushchev thaw: "At first I did want to make political films. Iurii Chernichenko and I wrote a screenplay, *Virgin Soil* (*Tselina*), truthful and tough. But we were told: 'What's the matter with you? You want to make a film about victims when Brezhnev was the first secretary there?' From that time on I promised myself not to make films on current events."[10] In a similar vein, when asked by one interviewer whether his wartime childhood had made him want to make movies about war, Maslennikov responded, "No, on the contrary, I wanted people to recover [*chtoby liudi otdokhnuli*] from the war."[11] The Sherlock Holmes project then coincided with the spirit of the time, with the urge to evade the rigors and political disenchantments and pitfalls of the age, or in Maslennikov's words, "Holmes was pure chance. I have no interest in detective literature. I had never seriously read Conan Doyle. It was just a very good screenplay. Iulii Dunskii and Valerii Frid brought it—funny and, most important, it had that which lived and lives in me: playing at being British [*igra v anglichanstvo*]. It's boyishness for adults."[12]

Here we should recognize that the relative cultural space or status occupied by this sort of adaptation in the Soviet Union as opposed to the West was not necessarily the same, and in this respect the question of readership or viewership becomes key. In this context, it would not be amiss to recall that while the driving force of the building and maintenance of empire as well as of the creation and consumption of culture in nineteenth-century Britain was the market, the place of the market in those spheres was arguably taken by ideology in the Soviet Union. While this necessary over-simplification glosses over complexities and nuances, it nonetheless has merit within the context of the subject at hand. The original Holmes stories may be seen as particularly notorious instances of the junction between market, literature, and empire.

---

10   Olga Bakushinskaia, "Igor' Maslennikov: Posle 'Zimnei vishni' muzhchiny nazvali menia predatelem," *Komsomol'skaia pravda*, October 26, 2001, accessed October 14, 2022, https://www.kp.ru/daily/22663/13029/.

11   Nataliia Skliarova, "'Igor' Maslennikov: 'Ot kino, kak ot SPIDa, nel'zia izbavit'sia,'" *Vecherniaia Moskva*, November 14, 2001, 10, accessed June 5, 2023, https://vm.ru/news/23465-igor-maslennikov-ot-kino-kak-ot-spida-nelzya-izbavitsya.

12   Rtishcheva, "Igor' Maslennikov: 'Eto zhe elementarno.'"

Conan Doyle, a savvy observer of consumer demand, conceived the stories as a blatant bid to make money by his pen. He was so spectacularly successful and so resentful that Holmes's celebrity distracted from what he considered his more serious literary labors that he famously killed off his own sleuth. The popular clamor was so vociferous and the financial remuneration so lucrative, however, that Conan Doyle was finally induced to resurrect his hero.[13] To the extent that the popularity of the Holmes stories among the middle-class readership of the day has been convincingly traced, at least in part, to their ability to help readers negotiate the anxieties created at home by the maintenance of empire abroad, we can discern a fairly direct connection between the market at home and the exploitation of foreign resources.[14] In contrast, in the Soviet Union both the production of culture, disengaged from any direct accountability for making a profit, and the expansion of empire were driven, or were perceived as being driven, by very different considerations; ostensibly the empire grew to spread the same project of building communism Soviet domestic culture was to serve.

In attempting, then, to understand whether the Soviet viewer of *The Adventures of Sherlock Holmes and Doctor Watson* took anything more from the experience than pure enjoyment and respite from the unremitting lip service to political seriousness of late Soviet life—whether, that is, the series resonates with the mechanisms and tensions of the maintenance of the Soviet multi-national state—we might better look for relevant comparison not to the original readers of the Holmes stories in nineteenth-century Britain, but to the American public television audience in the late twentieth century. As we know from that experience, the adaptation of literary classics for public television negotiates a liminal cultural space, designed to appeal to an audience with cultural

---

13 Ironically, in interviews, including those cited in this essay, Maslennikov, speaking from the vantage of the post-Soviet Russian market economy in cultural production, has repeatedly compared himself to Conan Doyle in this respect, lamenting the fact that he is so identified as the creator of the Soviet Sherlock Holmes that what he believes to be his more serious work is slighted.

14 Said, for instance, maintains: "And in Europe itself at the end of the nineteenth century, scarcely a corner of life was untouched by the facts of empire, the economies were hungry for overseas markets, raw materials, cheap labor, and hugely profitable land, and defense and foreign policy establishments were more and more committed to the maintenance of vast tracts of distant territory and large numbers of subjugated peoples." Said, *Culture*, 8.

"pretensions."[15] While there would seem to have been something of the same sort of snobbery at play in Soviet culture, we must acknowledge that the Soviet cultural system, quite apart from immediate political considerations, was constituted out of markedly different power relations that were inextricably linked with the Soviet imperial cultural hierarchy. Two points would seem to be most important to make in this connection. The first is the generally acknowledged priority of literature over film in Soviet culture, or, perhaps more accurately, the literariness of Soviet film, which not only had profound effects on the technical realization of cinematic narrative in Soviet film works, but also, arguably, facilitated the blurring of the boundaries between serious and frivolous cultural artifacts. In other words, the relevant cultural divide in the USSR was less between "high" and "low" culture than between unacceptable, excluded cultural products, dissident or otherwise, and those works given the official imprimatur of publication or production. By the same token, the relative lack of discrimination between the personnel, resources, and technical parameters of feature film and made-for-television cinematography in the Soviet Union also served to reshuffle the cultural structure to which we are accustomed in the West. Both of these factors were integrally implicated in the nature of the Soviet system and must be taken into account in the analysis that follows of how we are to understand the semiotic significance of the Soviet rendering of Sherlock Holmes.

One of the most striking aspects of the Soviet adaptation, which speaks to the points just made, is its self-consciousness in locating itself in an ongoing tradition, which is reflected most obviously, first of all, in strategies that draw attention to the fact that the Soviet Holmes is very much the iconic Holmes of the ongoing visual and cinematic tradition and, second, in cinematic quotations. To give just one of the many possible examples of the former, there is a moment toward the beginning of the second series when Holmes poses with his trademark pipe against the window of the Baker Street flat and holds the pose long enough to highlight the traditional Holmes profile. As far as cinematic citation is concerned, toward the beginning of the first series, after

---

15   For a discussion of the recent PBS decision to air a new remake of *The Hound of the Baskervilles* in the "Masterpiece Theater" series, rather than in the "Mystery!" series, thereby conferring on it the status of a literary masterpiece, see, for example, Marilyn Stasio, "Holmes Loses the Hat, and Watson Gets Hip," *New York Times*, Culture section, January 19–25, 2003, 4–5, accessed October 14, 2022, https://www.nytimes.com/2003/01/19/tv/cover-story-holmes-loses-the-hat-and-watson-gets-hip.html.

7. "Imperially, My Dear Watson" 131

Watson has just moved in with Holmes and still does not know the nature of his flat mate's profession, Holmes beckons the new lodger into his room, shows him an array of photographs, and asks if he is acquainted with any of the people in them. Watson somewhat squeamishly responds in the negative, while Holmes maintains that he knows them well. The particularly shady characters exhibited, however, appear all to be shots from vintage films, including Lon Cheney Sr. in his famous make-up for his role in the silent film of *Phantom of the Opera*.[16] This sort of cinematic "in-joke" signals the film's appeal, above and beyond its accessibility to a more general educated audience, to the more rarefied reaches of the creative intelligentsia who might have had the opportunity to see more obscure foreign films and therefore might appreciate the joke. That is, the Holmes films, with their easy familiarity with the foreign cinematic tradition and fondly ironic stance towards their predecessor texts, would seem to be geared to an audience as much of those who produced culture in the Soviet Union as of those who consumed it. Through the same device, moreover, the film draws attention to its artistry as well as to its foreign ancestry: Holmes is as much a fiction as the villains he collects.

Similar instances in which the series acknowledges the temporal and cultural difference inherent in its appropriation of the Holmes tradition include Watson's overblown reaction to the disclosure that Holmes is a detective. In the original scene from *A Study in Scarlet* in which Holmes reveals to a bemused Watson, unable to make sense of the curious array of talents Holmes displays, what his profession is, the revelation entails a relatively lengthy explanation, which begins: "Well, I have a trade of my own. I suppose I am the only one in the world. I'm a consulting detective, if you can understand what that is."[17] The film version, on the other hand, openly acknowledges the fact that it is separated from the original by the legacy of the Conan Doyle stories themselves, by the tradition spawned by the character of Sherlock Holmes. When Holmes finally discloses his profession to Watson—after leaving his new flat mate in uncertainty and hence suspicious for a much longer period of time than in the original novel—Watson is sheepish: the revelation was so obvious that he feels he should have figured it out for himself. This scene underscores the fact that, by the time the television serial was shot, the once obscure,

---

16 This quotation also serves to draw attention to Holmes as himself a master of disguise.

17 A. Conan Doyle, *A Study in Scarlet*, in his *The Complete Sherlock Holmes*, vol. 1 (Garden City: Doubleday, 1930), 24.

virtually unprecedented profession of private detective had become normalized and Conan Doyle's original presentation of it would have seemed affected. Similarly, in the wrap-up scene of "The Speckled Band," the adaptation neatly negotiates a flaw in the original story while at the same time creating a "textual" resonance absent in the prototype. When Holmes explains to Watson how he deciphered the mystery of "The Speckled Band," which depends on the premise that reptiles have the faculty of hearing, Watson breaks in and asks Holmes if he has not read a recent journal article laying out the argument that snakes are deaf. Holmes immediately occupies a backup position provided by the original story. This maneuver functions to establish an affectionate, but ironic distance from the original by acknowledging the obsolescence of Conan Doyle's scientific knowledge and thereby underscoring the pastness of the prototype text in a manner that, as we shall see, resonates most especially with the concluding series of the project. The generally classy stylization that marks the choreography of movement and witty banter throughout the series, rising to its summit in the concluding episodes, has a similar effect.

André Bazin, in his seminal discussion "Adaptation, or the Cinema as Digest," raises the issue of the equation of highbrow culture with difficulty: "The clichéd bias according to which culture is inseparable from intellectual effort springs from a bourgeois, intellectualist reflex. It is the equivalent in a rationalistic society of the initiatory rites in primitive civilizations. Esoterism is obviously one of the grand cultural traditions."[18] While Bazin evokes (and disparages) this distinction specifically to call it into question as an alibi for privileging literature over film in the study of adaptation, his observation serves us well here when we apply it in the opposite direction. In other words, the Soviet adaptation of Conan Doyle's classic popular fictions styled itself a highbrow artefact precisely because it not only triggers elitist cultural knowledge (as in the case of the film citations noted above), but also because of the sophistication of its crafting which, I would argue, demands from the viewer a relationship to the text more commonly associated with the reading of literature or at least of art film.[19] This is particularly notable in the high level of narrative

---

18 Andre Bazin, "Adaptations of the Cinema as Digest," in *Film Adaptation*, ed. James Naremore (New Brunswick: Rutgers University Press, 2000), 22.

19 Maslennikov's repeated allegation that the superiority of his adaptation of the Sherlock Holmes stories lies precisely in the fact that Watson rather than Holmes is his focus is telling in this context. Maslennikov has maintained, "You know why our film is recognized

cohesiveness that binds together the series made of multiple Holmes stories. In sum, unlike the sort of "classy" adaptations of literary works produced for the BBC and US public television, which seek to appeal to a more educated, higher-brow audience by trading on the cultural capital of the source text while at the same time rendering the text more accessible, the Soviet adaptation of the adventures of Sherlock Holmes exhibits aspirations to high culture status in the devices of its own narrative construction which call both for effort and esoteric knowledge on the part of the viewer. While unquestionably enjoyable for and accessible to an uninitiated audience as well (albeit one most likely well read in advance in the Conan Doyle texts), the series of films depends on witty devices to claim an elite cultural space, reminding us of the privileging of high culture, especially the classics of nineteenth-century Realism, which was a hallmark of the Soviet cultural establishment and a means of asserting imperial legitimacy by laying claim to the cultural achievements of the past.

Here, I believe, we reach the heart of the issue we must broach before taking a closer look at the series itself. Precisely because of the political context in which *The Adventures of Sherlock Holmes and Doctor Watson* was created—a context that rested on the absorption into politics of all aspects of Soviet life—the series' very disengagement from contemporary issues must be taken as a significant factor in the way the series was read by its audience. I would argue, in this context, that despite a basic strategy of the film to defuse analogy, the titillation lay precisely in the "imperial nostalgia" in which the adaptation of the original is drenched, the underscoring of its distance from the present in time and space, so that an audience adept at reading between the lines must have found part of the *jouissance* afforded by the cinematic text to lie in a multiplicity of potential relationships to be postulated between the antiquated, bourgeois values of the text and the realities of the Soviet present. As other critics have commented, most notably Maurice Friedburg in his seminal *Russian Classics in Soviet Jackets*, the problem of how to defuse the value systems of pre-revolutionary texts inherently at odds with the ideological premises of the Soviet system was a major and complexly negotiated challenge faced by Soviet

---

as the best? Because in the others there is no Watson—there is no actor who 'played' Holmes in order to illuminate him. Inasmuch as all Conan Doyle's stories are written by the person of Watson, he finds himself in the shadows, out of the picture, his character is inscrutable." Skliarova, "Igor' Maslennikov," 10. In other words, in Maslennikov's version the writer is given pride of place over the detective.

culture.[20] *The Adventures of Sherlock Holmes and Doctor Watson* aestheticizes this challenge by "museumizing" the original tales. In other words, the very painstaking recreation of the stories as period pieces, punctuated by the persistent integration of the exhibition of sculptures and other period art works into the stage sets, has the same effect as does removing a potentially subversive monument to a hero of a deposed culture from a public space into a museum; it would seem to aim at taking that work of art out of dialogue with the present. Ironically, as we shall see, when the trope of the museum is realized in the final instalment of the series, *The Twentieth Century Begins,* it has the effect of laying bare the device, of reclaiming nostalgia as a form of ironic commentary on the loss of innocence that haunts the present.

Given the series' self-reflexivity and self-consciousness, it is not surprising that motifs of gaze, voyeurism, and surveillance are recapitulated and resonate throughout the eleven episodes, culminating, as we shall see, in the concluding sequence of *The Twentieth Century Begins*. In this context, the series, I would argue, walks a fine line between cinematic play and references to the police state. Moreover, not only does Watson find himself at one point a murder suspect (which is not the case in the original story), but suspicion and spying frame the series. Thus, in the first episode before he learns Holmes's true profession, Watson, who claims never to poke his nose in other people's business, imagines, in a scene in a park, that he is under surveillance by Holmes's cronies and himself spies on Holmes and comes to the conclusion that his flat mate is the central criminal mastermind of London. By the same token, in the last episode, based on a story in which Watson does not even appear, Watson again spies on Holmes and decides that he is working as a German spy. When both Holmes and the Baker Street landlady Mrs. Hudson, who has been helping him in disguise, reveal themselves as patriots working in the interests of Britain, Mrs. Hudson highlights for Watson the service that Homes has rendered to Great Britain and notes that she is happy to share in a small way in his glory. While we shall return to a consideration of the concluding episodes of *Sherlock Holmes and Doctor Watson* shortly, let us note here that towards the end of the series, Holmes becomes less private detective and more government agent, working to stave off the threat to empire posed by the looming twentieth century. I would go so far as to contend that Holmes, especially in

---

20 Maurice Friedburg, *Russian Classics in Soviet Jackets* (New York: Columbia University Press, 1962).

7. "Imperially, My Dear Watson" | 135

relation to Watson, becomes a mirror and model for intelligentsia viewers, negotiating the perilous tensions between friendship, trust, patriotism, justice, and integrity, on the one hand, and the invasiveness of the demands of the state, on the other.

As we move to an examination of certain key moments in the series that illustrate how it addresses itself to its viewers, we should note from the outset that there are any number of ways in which the films signal to their audience a rather sophisticated awareness of their status as a translation. The opening credits of *The Hound of the Baskervilles*—which form a clever and elaborate counterpoint to the episodes as do all the framing sequences in the serial—provide a particularly pointed example. A document appears on the screen at the beginning which is meant to represent the manuscript of the Baskerville legend in English, but a grid is placed over the letters, which are decoded into Russian.

To explore further what gets lost—and gained—in translation, let us look first at a simple trace of the pressure of the times on the text—and a reminder of the still very active interference of Soviet censorship in 1979. To make my point, let me first cite the opening paragraphs of *A Study in Scarlet*, which is the beginning of the Holmes corpus:

> In the year 1878 I took my degree of Doctor of Medicine of the University of London, and proceeded to Netley to go through the course prescribed for surgeons in the Army. Having completed my studies there, I was duly attached to the Fifth Northumberland Fusiliers as assistant surgeon. The regiment was stationed in India at the time, and before I could join it, the second Afghan war had broken out. On landing at Bombay, I learned that my corps had advanced through the passes, and was already deep in the enemy's country. I followed, however, with many other officers who were in the same situation as myself, and succeeded in reaching Candahar in safety, where I found my regiment, and at once entered upon my new duties.
>
> The campaign brought honors and promotion to many, but for me it had nothing but misfortune and disaster. I was removed from my brigade and attached to the Berkshires, with whom I served at the fatal battle of Maiwand. There I was struck on the shoulder by a Jezail bullet, which shattered the bone and grazed the subclavian artery. I should have fallen into the hands of the murderous Ghazis had it not been for the devotion and courage shown by Murray, my orderly, who threw me across a pack-horse, and succeeded in bringing me safely to the British lines.

> Worn with pain, and weak from the prolonged hardships which I had undergone, I was removed, with a great train of wounded sufferers, to the base hospital at Peshawar. Here I rallied, and had already improved so far as to be able to walk about the wards, and even to bask a little upon the veranda, when I was struck down by enteric fever, that curse of our Indian possessions. For months my life was despaired of, and when at last I came to myself and became convalescent, I was so weak and emaciated that a medical board determined that not a day should be lost in sending me back to England. I was dispatched, accordingly, in the troopship *Orontes*, and landed a month later on Portsmouth jetty, with my health irretrievably ruined, but with permission from a paternal government to spend the next nine months in attempting to improve it.[21]

Aside from highlighting the centrality of Watson's role as narrator of the stories, a key problem for any film adaptation, this beginning vividly illustrates what Joseph A. Kestner terms "the persistent querying of the Empire in the Sherlock Holmes canon."[22] I have included this passage in full, because it demonstrates precisely how Watson's experiences defending British colonial interests leave him physically broken, literally infecting him with "the curse of our Indian possessions." In the Soviet version, on the other hand, Afghanistan, which the Soviet Union invaded in December 1979, becomes simply "the East" (*vostok*) or, later, "the Eastern colonies" (*vostochnye kolonii*). This minor and apparently predictable alteration nonetheless indicates that the censors saw not only the possibility of a Soviet audience drawing an analogy between one imperial project and the other, but the danger of that analogy. Moreover, especially since this suppression was apparently common knowledge in certain circles at the time, the very word "colonies," substituted for the geographical name, potentially highlights the imperial analogy the censor sought to defuse.[23] In the original it is precisely in Afghanistan that Watson contracts the disease that brings him at the beginning of *A Study in Scarlet* destitute, wasted, and all but friendless to London and to 221B Baker Street and Holmes. In the Soviet version, despite passing references to a wound received abroad,

---

21 Doyle, *Complete*, 15.

22 Joseph A. Kestner, *Sherlock's Men: Masculinity, Conan Doyle, and Cultural History* (Aldershot: Ashgate, 1997), 7.

23 I would like to thank Vitaly Chernetsky for pointing out to me that censoring the mention of Afghanistan was common knowledge.

Watson appears hale and hearty and far from friendless from the beginning, which marks a change in his role throughout to more of an equal to Holmes than a foil. In fact, quite a number of Holmes's lines are actually given to Watson in the series, which is, after all, entitled *The Adventures of Sherlock Holmes and Doctor Watson*, thus giving Holmes's sidekick equal billing up front. In fact, the leitmotif of male pairs or brothers is established in the first scene and runs throughout, displacing the aloof, misanthropic detective of the original from center stage. One episode in particular helps demonstrate how this affects the relationship between Holmes and Watson. Shortly after sending Watson into a funk by deducing the sad decline and demise of the doctor's brother (as he does in the original as well), Holmes, looking out the window of the flat, challenges Watson to deduce what he can about a gentleman passing by. Watson gives it a good shot, but Holmes then adds a startling number of personal details. When Watson professes himself flabbergasted by Holmes's powers, the detective bursts into laughter, claps Watson on the back, and announces that the passing man is his brother (*rodnoi brat*), Mycroft Holmes, who will also come to play a much greater role in the series than he does in the original texts.

As in the original stories, crime most often originates in the series from contact with the foreign, whether East or West. Thus, Jefferson Hope, the murderer in the first two episodes based on *A Study in Scarlet*, is an American who has lost his beloved to the tyrannical and polygamous Mormons. Here, though, I want to draw attention to the portrayal of another "American," a portrayal that departs markedly from the original text, as a comparison of the description of Sir Henry Baskerville from Conan Doyle's story and the filmic adaptation demonstrate:

> Our breakfast table was cleared early, and Holmes waited in his dressing-gown for the promised interview. Our clients were punctual to their appointment, for the clock had just struck ten when Dr. Mortimer was shown up, followed by the young baronet. The latter was a small, alert, dark-eyed man about thirty years of age, very sturdily built, with thick black eyebrows and a strong, pugnacious face. He wore a ruddy-tinted tweed suit, and had the weather-beaten appearance of one who has spent most of his time in the open air, and yet there was something in his steady eye and the quiet assurance of his bearing which indicated the gentleman.

"This is Sir Henry Baskerville," said Dr. Mortimer.[24]

By contrast, Nikita Mikhalkov, who plays Sir Henry in the Soviet production, is an exuberant, opinionated American who first appears in a large and imposing fur coat. (The fur, by the way, which he gives away to the butler Barrymore when he decides to dress like an Englishman, a transformation that does not occur in the original, becomes the mark by which the convict Seldon's body is initially misidentified as Sir Henry's.) Mikhalkov's Sir Henry, first in his fur and later in his chaps, reminds one of nothing more than a cross between Mr. West and his cowboy sidekick Jeddy in Lev Kuleshov's classic silent film *The Adventures of Mr. West in the Land of the Bolsheviks*. Perhaps most interesting in this context is the fact that the ludicrousness of Sir Henry Baskerville's failure as an American to mimic an Englishman successfully, which is periodically underscored, only serves to throw into relief how well Russians in this series are acting "English," perhaps a distant echo of Dostoevsky's Pushkin speech in which the essence of Russianness, and a Russian imperial manifesto of sorts, lies in the Russian ability, as manifested in Pushkin's characters, to "become" the foreign other and therefore function as the great reconciler of nations. Certainly, here, Russians appear more adept at mimicking, even absorbing and thereby appropriating, the foreign than the remarkably inept American. Yet this "talent" inevitably carries with it an anxiety about the instability and permeability of national identity, an anxiety that (as the recurring motifs of disguise, masking and unmasking, betrayal, and eavesdropping suggest) may be symptomatic of *homo sovieticus* of the late Brezhnev period.

The last segment of the series, *The Twentieth Century Begins*, is edgier, darker, and quirkier than the others. After all, the primary mystery in the first episode of this segment, aired at the outset of glasnost, concerns the threat of the making public (*oglashenie*) of a state secret, specifically an immoderate letter written by a ruler which could lead to war if revealed. Moreover, as indicated above, throughout the stories combined here, Holmes acts in the interests of king and country. It is the threatening twentieth century and a nostalgia for a simpler age which preceded it that pervades these episodes from the beginning, as the written text that scrolls down the screen after the opening sequence in the eleventh and final episode makes clear. Punctuated, as the final episodes are periodically, with pictures of goose-stepping troops and

---

24   Doyle, *Complete*, 15.

twentieth-century transport clearly meant to epitomize the inroads of technology on a dying way of life, the sequence ends: "The time of dear old England drowned in Lethe and together with it the Adventures of Sherlock Holmes." Mycroft Holmes appears periodically at his desk, surrounded by technical gimmickry and even in a gas mask, apparently prepared for an imminent outbreak of chemical warfare. As already noted, Mycroft Holmes plays a much larger role in the Soviet series than he does in the original, on occasion, like Watson, being given some of Holmes's lines. By the end, he becomes an incarnation of the state bureaucracy and its technical power rendered threatening by his own machine-like, but also vain, demeanor. The villains in the final episode are all Germans, while Holmes, following the original, poses as an Irish-American, a colonial subject once removed who justifiably works with the Germans to subvert the empire that oppresses his homeland. Of course, as we have seen, just at the moment when Watson, listening in on a conversation between the disguised Holmes and the German spy, is convinced that Holmes has sold out, the denouement reveals Holmes to be on the side of right as always, despite his lack of interest in politics in the early stories.

At this point, toward the end of the final episode, we see the number combination of the German spy's safe automatically tumble to that most significant date, August 1914, identified by Solzhenitsyn and others as the beginning of the end of the Russian empire. Looking back to what Akhmatova called the beginning of the twentieth century from the hindsight of the beginning of the end of the Soviet empire seven decades later, this final segment is fraught with anxieties about the uncertainty of identity and allegiance in the twentieth century and about the dangers and promise (it will bring the movies, after all) of technology. Watson, Holmes, and Mrs. Hudson (the landlady of the Baker Street apartment, who also plays a much larger role here) become ordinary people left behind and powerless to stop the relentless advance of history. The film ends with the director, Maslennikov, himself appearing in a series of frames, screening on an antiquated projector a sequence of a man and woman dancing on a pier over the water. In the end we are brought back to play, but through the prism of a brooding nostalgia for the empire, and the chivalry that was its best defense.

In this regard, the most striking feature of *The Twentieth Century Begins*, as I suggested earlier, is that the trope of the museum becomes the orienting feature of Holmes's portrayal here. As early as the second serial, when Holmes appears to have died along with Moriarty, Mrs. Hudson, in a departure from the original text of "The Final Solution," proposes to preserve Holmes's rooms untouched and create a museum in his memory. In the final episodes, Holmes returns from retirement in the country to the Baker Street apartment which is in the process of being turned into a museum, furniture shrouded in sheets and adorned with a bust of Holmes himself, which is pointedly moved from place to place and posed, confronting Holmes with himself frozen in time and lifeless. He appears as the last outpost of a simpler imperial age and a more innocent and naive belief in the powers of reason and science about to be swept away by the horrors of a century ruled by mass movements, war, and the unleashing of previously unimaginable technological horrors. Holmes, in fact, is brought back from the museum, and contemporary life suffers by comparison.

So, what do *The Adventures of Sherlock Holmes* have to say about the Soviet empire and why was the series so popular? Perhaps because, like the original Conan Doyle stories, the Soviet TV series accepts the mantle of empire, while, perhaps, more so than its predecessor, subverting it. Perhaps, in the end, that is why Watson the chronicler more and more displaces Holmes the deducer and defender as the series progresses.[25] It may be too late to contain the evil forces unleashed by history, but the story still remains to be told—in literature and in film.

---

25 On Watson's role as chronicler eclipsing Holmes in the original stories, see Haynsworth, "Sensational Adventures"; Peter Conroy, "The Importance of Being Watson," in *Critical Essays on Sir Arthur Conan Doyle*, ed. Harold Orel (New York: G. K. Hall, 1992), 36–54; and Kestner, *Sherlock's Men*.

Works Cited

Anonymous. "Basic Sherlock Holmes for You Beginners." Accessed January 3, 2004. http://www.geocities.com/Hollywood/Derby/3418/basicsherlock.htm (site discontinued—eds.).

Arata, Stephen. *Fictions of Loss in the Victorian Fin de Siècle*. Cambridge: Cambridge University Press, 1996.

Bakushinskaia, Olga. "Igor' Maslennikov: Posle 'Zimnei vishni' muzhchiny nazvali menia predatelem." *Komsomol'skaia pravda*, October 26, 2001. Accessed October 14, 2022. https://www.kp.ru/daily/22663/13029/.

Bazin, Andre. "Adaptations or the Cinema as Digest." In *Film Adaptations*, edited by James Naremore, translated by Alain Piette and Bert Cadullo, 19–28. New Brunswick: Rutgers University Press, 2000.

Conroy, Peter. "The Importance of Being Watson." In *Critical Essays on Sir Arthur Conan Doyle*, edited by Harold Orel, 36–54. New York: G. K. Hall, 1992.

Doyle, Conan A. *The Complete Sherlock Holmes*, vol. 1. Garden City: Doubleday, 1930.

Friedburg, Maurice. *Russian Classics in Soviet Jackets*. New York: Columbia University Press, 1962.

Griffith, James John. *Adaptations as Imitations: Films from Novels*. Newark: University of Delaware Press, 1997.

Haynsworth, Leslie. "Sensational Adventures: Sherlock Holmes." *English Literature in Transition, 1880–1920* 44, no. 4 (2001): 459–85.

Kestner, Joseph A. *Sherlock's Men: Masculinity, Conan Doyle, and Cultural History*. Aldershot: Ashgate, 1997.

Naremore, James, ed. *Film Adaptation*. New Brunswick: Rutgers University Press, 2000.

Nisbeth, H. "What Pipes Did Sherlock Holmes Smoke?" Accessed January 3, 2004. http://sherlock-holmes.hypormart.net/ (site discontinued—eds.).

Otis, Laura. "The Empire Bites Back: Sherlock Holmes as an Imperial Immune System." *Studies in Twentieth Century Literature* 22, no. 1 (1998): 31–60.

Porter, Dennis. *The Pursuit of Crime: Art and Ideology in Crime Fiction*. New Haven: Yale University Press. 1981.

Rtishcheva. N. "Igor' Maslennikov: Eto zhe elementarno, Vatson!" *Moskovskii komsomolets*, April 30, 2000. Accessed October 2, 2022. https://www.mk.ru/old/article/2000/04/30/124866-igor-maslennikov-eto-zhe-elementarno-vatson.html.

Said, Edward W. *Culture and Imperialism*. New York: Alfred A. Knopf, 1994.

Skliarova, Nataliia. "Igor' Maslennikov: 'Ot kino, kak ot SPIDa, nel'zia izbavit'sia,'" *Vecherniaia Moskva*, November 14, 2001. Accessed June 5, 2023. https://vm.ru/news/23465-igor-maslennikov-ot-kino-kak-ot-spida-nelzya-izbavitsya.

Stasio, M. "Holmes Loses the Hat, and Watson Gets Hip," *New York Times*, Culture section, January 19–25, 2003, 4–5.

Sullivan, Sheila. "Hands across the Water, Crime across the Sea: Gender, Imperialist History, and Arthur Conan Doyle's American." *Victorians Institute Journal* 26 (1998): 95–120.

Symons, Julien. *Conan Doyle: Portrait of an Artist*. London: Mysterious Press, 1987.

Thompson, Jon. *Fiction, Crime, and Empire: Clues to Modernity and Postmodernism*. Urbana: University of Illinois Press, 1993.

Part III

The Soviet/Post-Soviet Experience

8

Pasternak's *Doctor Zhivago*: The Resurrection of the Living Past

The belated publication of *Doctor Zhivago* (*Doktor Zhivago*) in its homeland obviously rendered open critical response to the novel there all but impossible until the late Soviet period. In the West, scholarship on the novel began to appear immediately after the publication.[1] The central question that has been raised over the years is how the novel should be read, more specifically, what set of criteria should be applied to its analysis and evaluation: should the novel be measured against the conventions of the nineteenth-century realist tradition, most particularly against Tolstoy's epic historical chronicle *War and Peace*, or is *Doctor Zhivago* a "poet's novel," an outgrowth of Pasternak's own early poetry and highly opaque, experimental prose and therefore also of Russia's early twentieth-century poetic culture?[2] It is perhaps not surprising that

---

This article was part of Nepomnyashchy's incomplete book manuscript *The Politics of Tradition: Rerooting Russian Literature after Stalin* and has not been published previously. Permission to publish granted by Olga Nepomnyashchy—eds.

1 Nepomnyashchy was working from the Russian text of Boris Pasternak, *Doktor Zhivago*, first published by the University of Michigan in 1958; and its English translation by Max Hayward and Manya Harari. References to the novel are given in parentheses, first to the Michigan edition, followed by a recent printing of the Hayward-Harari translation (New York: Pantheon Books, 1991), occasionally amended by C. T. N.—eds.

2 On *Doctor Zhivago* and *War and Peace*, see Rimvydas Silbajoris, "Pasternak and Tolstoj: Some Comparisons," *Slavic and East European Journal* 11, no. 1 (Spring 1967): 23–34; Ralph E. Matlaw, "Mechanical Structure and Inner Form: A Note on *War and Peace* and *Dr. Zhivago*," *Symposium* 16, no. 4 (1962): 288–95; John Bayley, "Tolstoy's Legacy. *Dr. Zhivago*," in his *Tolstoy and the Novel* (London: Chatto and Windus, 1966), 294–308; Robert Louis Jackson, "*Doctor Zhivago*: *Liebestod* of the Russian Intelligentsia," in *Pasternak: A Collection of Critical Essays*, ed. Victor Erlich (Englewood Cliffs: Prentice-Hall,

the question of how to approach the novel has so often, whether explicitly or implicitly, been linked with attempts to establish its literary ancestry, for arguably this is how the novel itself poses the question. The text of *Doctor Zhivago* is littered with clues about how it should be read. More importantly, the ways in which the novel describes the nature of cultural continuity are key to understanding how the novel foresees itself as a connecting link in the tradition, as an impetus to the "resurrection" of Russian culture in the wake of the rupture which the novel documents.

Andrei Siniavskii, echoing any number of other commentators on the novel, maintained: "If we approach *Doctor Zhivago* with the yardstick of the traditional realist novel, we inevitably come up against its inferiority, its literary weakness."[3] The "flaws" that critics who have approached the text with this "yardstick" have most frequently discerned in the novel are the welter of improbable coincidences which abound in the plot; the schematic "flatness"—to use E.M. Forster's term—of the characters who at times seems almost interchangeable; the absence of real historical figures, like Napoleon and Kutuzov in *War and Peace*, and the fact that the characters are so frequently kept from the center stage of historical events in a novel that purports to be chronicling a specific historical period. Chronological inaccuracies and inconsistencies mark both references to real historical events and the unfolding of the fictional plot. Isaac Deutscher, one of the novel's most vituperative and least subtle critics, describes a fatal duality in the novel:

> [Pasternak] has not been able to jump the gulf between lyrical symbolism and prose narrative.
>
> This accounts for the incongruity between the various elements that make up *Doctor Zhivago*: on the one side lyrical passages, noble, richly imaginative, refined, and fastidiously polished; and on the other the core of the novel itself, flat, clumsy, labored, and embarrassingly crude.

1978), 137–50; and Krystyna Pomorska, "Doctor Živago," in her *Themes and Variations in Pasternak's Poetics* (Lisse: The Peter de Ridder Press, 1973), 74–90.

3 A. Siniavskii, "Nekotorye aspekty pozdnei prozy Pasternaka," in *Boris Pasternak and His Times: Selected Papers from the Second International Symposium on Pasternak*, ed. Lazar Fleishman (Berkeley: Berkeley Slavic Specialties, 1989), 359. In this article, Siniavskii, while agreeing that Pasternak was deliberately violating conventions in order to achieve artistic effects consistent with the philosophy he espouses in the novel, still finds the novel wanting, labeling it a "brilliant weak novel" (359).

> It is as if the book had been written by two hands: the virtuoso-poet of 65 and a beginning novelist of 16.[4]

One can ask whether these features are "flaws" or if they constitute a consistent pattern of violation of conventional expectations generated by the novel's nineteenth-century predecessors to create a new, internally coherent form validated by the aesthetic stance articulated in the work itself. A careful consideration of the structure of *Doctor Zhivago* in relation to the statements on artistic creation, originality, and influence incorporated into the text support the latter proposition.

Perhaps the best way to begin our exploration of this problem is with Pasternak's own defense of the narrative idiosyncrasies of his novel. In a 1959 interview with Ralph Matlaw he addressed the issues raised by commentators explicitly in relation to his nineteenth-century precursors:

> In the nineteenth-century masters of the novel, Balzac, Stendhal, Tolstoy, if you take away the characters and characterization, the imagery, description and so on, you still have left *causality*, that concept that an action has a consequence. Flaubert's style is the ultimate, merciless verdict on this nineteenth-century causality. For me reality lies not there, but in the multiplicity of the universe, in the large number of possibilities, in a kind of spirit of freedom, a coincidence of impulses and inspirations (not *religious* inspiration, just inspiration—*vdokhnovenie*). [...] Nature is much richer in coincidences than is our imagination. If all these possibilities exist, reality must be the result of choice, of a choice deliberately made. Even in the novel, the totality of the work, the total conception, is important, not the details or the irrationality of details. I have frequently been asked about the coincidences in the book, particularly by young people of fifteen or sixteen, from whom I get many letters. Of course I made the coincidences on purpose, that *is* life, just as I purposely did not fully characterize the people in the book.

---

4   Isaac Deutscher, "Pasternak and the Calendar of the Revolution," in *Pasternak: Modern Judgements*, ed. Donald Davie and Angela Livingstone (Nashville: Aurora Publishers, 1970), 251. Deutscher emphatically believes that *Doctor Zhivago* should be measured against *War and Peace*, and his diatribe comprises a virtual compendium of the criticisms that have been levelled at Pasternak's novel. For one answer to Deutscher, see Irving Howe, "Freedom and the Ashcan of History," in *Pasternak: Modern Judgements*, ed. Donald Davie and Angela Livingstone (Nashville: Aurora Publishers, 1970), 259–68.

> For I wanted to get away from the idea of causality. The innovation of the book lies precisely in this conception of reality.[5]

Here Pasternak provides us with a basic grid within which to explore the binary oppositions that are brought into confrontation throughout the novel and the relationship of this bipolarity to the "duality" of the text. Pasternak's counterpointing of "freedom" and "inspiration" to "causality" entails a series of antinomies that define two diametrically opposed responses to life, one embodied most fully in Zhivago and Lara, the other by Antipov-Strel′nikov. The embracing of life as "freedom" and "inspiration" is associated with the apprehension of history as an organic process as opposed to the perception of history as the inexorable, mechanistic realization of natural law, "causality." Moreover, the organic understanding of the nature of existence carries the associative correlatives of memory, continuity, creativity, and the willingness to submit to the "miracle" of life's unexpectedness and unpredictability. The affirmation of personhood is paradoxically most fully realized in the identification with and consequent dissolution of the individual self in the totality of being. Subordination to "causality," by contrast, leads to the desire to obliterate the past and "remake" life: rupture, destruction, inflexibility, the blind belief in the predictability of history, and the replacement of the individual by the "herd." The relationship between the "irrational details" that make up the texture of *Doctor Zhivago* and the "totality of the work" arguably must be viewed as exegetic. It is precisely those features which endow the novel with cohesiveness, forcing the reader to reinterpret the "irrational details" of the plot on a different plane of meaning. The novel as a whole and the concluding cycle of Zhivago's poems in particular demonstrate the creative response to life which holds the possibility of the reestablishment of cultural continuity not through the reclamation of facts, but through the recovery of the process of signification.

Looking at the sixteen chapters of *Doctor Zhivago* which comprise the prose text of the novel it is not difficult to understand why some critics have been tempted to compare the novel to *War and Peace*. The rich texture of detail, the monumental time span (encompassing some six decades) embracing

---

5   Ralph E. Matlaw, "A Visit with Pasternak," *The Nation*, September 12, 1959, 134. Pasternak gave a similar account of his novel in his August 22, 1959 letter to Stephen Spender, the editor of the journal *Encounter*. Boris Pasternak, *Ob iskusstve* (Moscow: Iskusstvo, 1990), 363–65.

one of the most turbulent periods in modern history, the considerable cast of characters, the vast expanses of space covered, and the essentially chronolinear plot line all suggest correspondences between *Zhivago* and the nineteenth-century historical novel. Yet a closer scrutiny reveals precisely those "flaws" its critics have isolated. Not only does the narrative treat the chronology of the actual historical events with what might best be termed poetic license, but the chronology of the fictional events is riddled with vagueness and discrepancies.[6] By the same token, Pasternak consistently removes his characters from the center of historical events into what seems to be the backwaters of history and away from specific historical moments. Not a single historical personage figures in the novel's sizable cast of characters, thus not allowing the reader to specifically identify place and time. Rather than constituting a technical failure or an intellectual lapse, these deviations from the novel's nineteenth-century precursors serve to relocate and redefine the nature of history. As Viktor Frank comments on the discrepancies in the time structure of *Doctor Zhivago*, "Pasternak worked on the novel for many years, and, of course, it is impossible to explain the clouding [*zatumanivanie*] of the chronology as carelessness, but rather as a conscious intention to dissociate *Doctor Zhivago* from the genre of the novel-chronicle and to relativize time, which lays its net upon the ordinary historical novel."[7] In other words, Pasternak discredits the chronolinear plot line in order to redirect the reader's attention to a very different type of narrative movement which overlies and redefines the apparently linear sequence of the plot, just as he elaborates a new vision of history, which the novel suggests is more consistent with the essence of Tolstoy's views than was Tolstoy himself (465; 454).

In the same vein, we cannot help but draw attention to the marked structural fragmentation of the novel. *Doctor Zhivago* is divided into two parts which are further divided into subsections; twenty-five poems constitute the concluding chapter. The tension created by this highly stylized splintering of the text and the linear flow of the narrative is underscored by the brevity of the chapter subdivisions. The relative paucity of what might be termed "linking"

---

6   For examples of historical inaccuracies in the dating of events in the novel, see Ian Crawford Kelly, "Eternal Memory: Historical Themes in Pasternak's *Doctor Zhivago*" (PhD diss., Columbia University, New York, 1985), 34–38.

7   Viktor Frank, "Realizm chetyrekh izmerenii (perechityvaia Pasternaka)," *Mosty* 2 (1959): 194.

sections, i. e. portions of the narrative in which habitual actions are recounted or any sort of action that takes place over a long period of time represents the focus, and the seemingly disproportionate amount of space devoted to single days in the characters' lives, further fragments the text. The frequency with which these divisions seem to run counter to the logic of the plot breaks up episodes, even interrupting conversations in midstream. Zhivago often disappears from center stage for long periods of time, and when he reappears again, the reader is told little or nothing of what has happened to him in the interim. Conversely, the accounts of two days (in December 1911 and May 1918) provide striking examples of temporal concentration: the first account portrays Lara's attempt on Komarovskii's life at the Sventitskii's Christmas party, and the second, Zhivago's first meeting with Strel'nikov and the later arrival of the family at Varykino. The account of Zhivago's meeting with Strel'nikov is an especially blatant structural disruption of the narrative flow. It begins in Chapter Seven ("On the Road") of Part One and continues into Part Two, spanning all of Chapter Eight ("Arrival").[8] The subdivisions of *Doctor Zhivago* function less like chapters in the traditional novel than like stanzas in a poem, creating a complex interrelationship between the part and the whole, disrupting the "epic" progression of the plot. In a manner more akin to a lyric poem, they focus the reader's attention on the individual moment in time, away from the causal sequence of events to the fullness of life in the present.

One particularly telling incident will serve to illustrate the complexity of the interaction between the structure of the text and the unfolding of the plot. During the winter of 1917–1918, while still in Moscow, Zhivago is called upon to treat the wife of a black-market speculator, who is suffering from typhus. The husband at first believes her ailment to be a nervous disorder triggered by the unexpected chiming of a clock:

> He explained with many digressions that they had recently bought an antique clock. It was a broken-down chiming clock, and they had bought it for a song, merely as a remarkable example of the clockmaker's art (he took the doctor into the next room to see it). They had

---

8   The English translation chooses to place the break between the two major divisions of the novel, Parts One and Two (called volumes—*tom*—in the Russian edition), at the end of Chapter Four, which concludes with the news of the outbreak of the February Revolution. This change would seem to reflect a certain discomfort with the apparent illogic of Pasternak's own break.

even doubted whether it could be repaired. Then, one day, suddenly the clock, which had not been wound for years, had started of itself, played its complicated minuet of chimes, and stopped. His wife was terrified, the young man said; she was convinced that her last hour had struck [*chto eto probil ee poslednii chas*], and now there she was delirious, refused all food, and did not recognize him. (204; 200)

When Zhivago returns home after diagnosing the woman and sending her to the hospital, Tonia tells him of a strange event which occurred in his absence: the alarm clock her father broke a day ago and couldn't repair suddenly began to ring "all by itself." Zhivago's response concludes the chapter subsection: "'My hour for typhus has struck [*Eto moi tifoznyi chas probil*],' said Yury Andreevich laughing. He told her about his patient and the chiming clock" (210; 206).

The next line of the text, which is the first line of subsection fourteen of the sixth chapter, reads: "But he did not get typhus until much later" (210; 206). The phrase "much later" may seem misleading (constituting a subtle example of what Frank calls the "clouding of chronology" in the novel) because the accounts of two incidences of typhus, while completely independent, are situated in close proximity in the text. While in real historical time the two events are several months apart, they are narrated in neighboring sections of the text and therefore are linked in the reader's experience. Only three short paragraphs separate the assertion that Zhivago came down with typhus only "much later" and his coming down with the ailment. In the spatial sequence of the text, then, Zhivago's illness *does* follow almost immediately upon the ringing of the alarm clock. Since *Doctor Zhivago* is a work in which signs and portents are realized with almost monotonous regularity, tension is created between the illusion of the passage of time in the plot as opposed to the physical space of the text. This device recalls Roman Jakobson's observations on the metonymic nature of Pasternak's early prose: "Spatial relations are mingled with temporal ones, and the time sequence loses its compulsory order [. . .] Any contiguity can be construed as a causal series."[9] In the light of Pasternak's

---

9 Roman Jakobson, "The Prose of the Poet Pasternak," in *Pasternak: Modern Judgements*, ed. Donald Davie and Angela Livingstone (Nashville: Aurora Publishers, 1970), 144–45. Since Jakobson wrote this article in 1935, one can relate his observations to *Doctor Zhivago*, as a number of critics have done, only with caution. For an interesting discussion of Jakobson with implications for *Doctor Zhivago*, see Michel Aucouturier, "The Metonymous Hero or the Beginnings of Pasternak the Novelist," *Books Abroad* 44 (1970): 222–27.

comments on causality, contiguity in *Doctor Zhivago* functions not to create a "causal series," but rather as a symptom of the apprehension that the significance of events lies outside of any relationship of cause and effect that might be suggested by temporal sequence.

The juxtaposition of the unanticipated tolling of the two clocks demonstrates both how the structure of *Doctor Zhivago* frustrates conventional narrative expectations and how the text achieves cohesiveness through means other than the sequential unfolding of the events. In this case particularly what is not, properly speaking, a meaningful coincidence in terms of the plot's chronology is rendered significant by the spatial structure of the text. Barry Scherr observed that precisely because Pasternak's use of coincidence illustrates "the wondrous quality of existence, which operates in a manner too mysterious for our reason to fully fathom," it constitutes a formal challenge. He notes that plots usually are structured by events that are causally related, and "Pasternak could hardly have created the series of coincidences that distinguishes his novel had he employed cause and effect." Scherr points out that Pasternak creates "a sense of cohesiveness for a long and involved work" by other means: "His solution was to divide the book into a series of sections, each of which pursues its own themes or set of themes but is bound to the rest through symmetry, parallelism, and various interlocking devices."[10] Arguably, the very nature of coincidence itself provides the paradigm for the structural features of the novel that give coherence to the "irrational details" of the plot.

In one often cited passage about an incident at the front, Pasternak draws attention to the coincidences that abound throughout:

> The man who had just died was Private Gimazetdin; the excited officer who had been shouting in the wood was his son, Lieutenant Galiullin; the nurse was Lara. Gordon and Zhivago were the witnesses. All these people were there together, in one place. But some of them had never known each other, while others failed to recognize each other now. And there were things about them which were never to be known for certain, while others were not to be revealed until a future time, a later meeting. (121; 118)

---

10   Barry P. Scherr, "The Structure of *Doctor Zhivago*," *Proceedings: Pacific Northwest Conference on Foreign Language* 25, part 1 (1974): 274. Gleb Struve gives an account of the novel's coincidences in the "The Hippodrome of Life: The Problem of Coincidences in *Doctor Zhivago*," *Books Abroad* 44 (Spring 1970): 231–36.

Even though the characters are unaware of their connections at this moment in time, their spatial proximity in the text creates the metonymic structure of the narrative, revealing to the reader the overriding importance of coincidence. Textual proximity frequently connects events linked neither by causal nor temporal sequence and creates associative links that uncover their true meaning.

Characters in the novel are largely defined by the appropriateness of their responses to the vicissitudes of experience, by their ability or lack of ability to comprehend their place in the "totality" of life. Angela Livingstone has commented that the novel frequently reports its characters' "erroneous assumption[s]," asking "Why is a correct version of something repeatedly introduced *via* an incorrect one?"[11] One striking example of a character's misunderstanding of his role in the unfolding of events suggests an answer. During the revolutionary autumn of 1905, the railway worker Tiverzin, a coworker of Pasha Antipov's father, wrongly believes that he has singlehandedly started the strike by blowing the whistle: "For many years Tiverzin thought that it was he alone who had stopped work and traffic on the line that night. Only much later, at the trial, when he was charged with complicity in the strike but not with inciting it, did he learn the truth" (32; 32). Precisely because he fails to see the coincidence between his own action and the decision taken in his absence by the strike committee does Tiverzin misapprehend his own role in events. He assumes that he controls what is happening, whereas in reality he is merely an insignificant player in the larger scheme of things. Antipov/Strel'nikov is an even more powerful example of this idea. The narrator observes that while "he possessed an uncommon ability to reason clearly and correctly [. . .] his mind lacked the gift for the unexpected, the power that violates the sterile harmony of empty foresight through unforeseen discoveries that are necessary to the activity of a scholar who lays down new paths" (256–57; 251). Just as Tiverzin's belief that he directs events results from a failure to perceive coincidence, so Strel'nikov's limitation is his lack of the "gift of the unexpected." Later in the novel Zhivago himself articulates this idea, responding to the vapid rhetoric of the partisan leader Liberius with a scathing tirade:

---

11 Angela Livingstone, "'Integral Errors': Remarks on the Writing of *Doctor Zhivago*," *Essays in Poetics* 13, no. 2 (1988): 88.

> Reshaping life! People who can say that have never understood a thing about life—they have never felt its breath, its heartbeat—however much they have seen or done. They look on it as a lump of raw material that needs to be processed by them, to be ennobled by their touch. But life is never a material, a substance to be molded. If you want to know, life is the principle of self-renewal, it is constantly renewing and remaking and changing and transfiguring itself, it is infinitely beyond your or my obtuse theories about it. (347–48; 338)

The inability to apprehend one's role in the unpredictable spontaneity of life ultimately transforms the striving to remake life into destruction and self-destruction, and turns language into the dead letter of political rhetoric divorced both from reality and the personhood of the speaking or writing self.

By contrast, Lara frequently marks the marvelous patterns of coincidence into which life continually shapes itself, by uttering exclamations which draw the reader's attention to the extraordinary nature of intersections between characters, as she does when she learns that Galiullin has served in the army with her husband: "What an extraordinary coincidence [*Kakaia porazitel'naia sluchainost'*]" (128; 125). Lara sees the coincidences as a form of "predestination" (*predopredelenie*), an intervention of higher forces in life. On hearing of Zhivago's meeting with Strel'nikov on the armored train, she exclaims: "But how significant [*znamenatel'no*]! It's as if you were predestined to meet" (306; 296). Likewise, she responds to Zhivago's revelation about Komarovskii's responsibility for his father's death: "What a significant [*znamenatel'naia*] detail! Can it really be true? So he was your evil genius, too? It brings us even closer [*rodnit nas*]! It must be some sort of predestination!" (411; 400).

As for Zhivago's own "gift for the unexpected," it is his submission to the force of life and his ability to perceive and express its significance in his poetry that defines both his destiny and his creativity. Every major turning point in Zhivago's life is marked by the incursion of unforeseen circumstances to which he repeatedly submits and which are often marked by extraordinary coincidences and which are mostly linked, directly or indirectly, with Lara or Evgraf. The most important moments that determine the trajectory of his life show how events carry him, often against his will, to the fulfillment of his destiny.

Zhivago's first encounter with Lara—"the girl from a different circle," as she is identified by the title of the chapter in which she first appears—is initiated by the interruption of an evening concert at the Gromeko home, that is, by the disruption of the ordinary, planned flow of events by the unexpected. While the full force of the young Zhivago's witnessing the aftermath of Madame Guishar's attempted suicide becomes clear only later in the novel, the event is marked as a significant confluence of the characters' fates. During this scene Misha Gordon recognizes Komarovskii as the lawyer who traveled with Zhivago's father on the train and whose malignant influence instigated the latter's suicide. As this is the first time that the unnamed suicide is identified as the elder Zhivago, this revelation discloses that Gordon, later to become Zhivago's friend, had known his father and been present when he died. Gordon's revelation also reveals that Zhivago's father had apparently committed suicide at precisely the moment his son forgot to pray for him.

Zhivago's second vision of Lara also takes place at an interrupted social event, the Sventitskiis' Christmas party in the winter of 1911. The projected course of the evening's events is disrupted, this time twice, and again Zhivago is present at a key moment in the drama of the relationship between Lara and Komarovskii. While Lara's attempt on Komarovskii's life interrupts the festivities the first time, the news of Anna Ivanovna Gromeko's death comes as a second unanticipated incursion, occurring just as Zhivago is about to offer medical help to the distraught Lara. Thus, structural parallelisms between different episodes create resonances between them and shape the text by means unrelated to cause and effect: Zhivago is drawn out of his own "circle," to Lara, by the threat of her mother's death and back to Tonia, away from Lara, by Tonia's mother's death.

The events of the war, revolution, and subsequent civil conflicts—casting the peregrinations of Zhivago and the other characters over immense geographical expanses of Russia—underscore both the disruption of normal life and the extraordinary nature of the coincidences that throw the characters into spatial proximity by forces beyond their control. Zhivago receives word that he has been drafted into the army, which leads to his first separation from his family, just after Tonia gives birth to their son. Wounded at the front, Zhivago finds himself in the same hospital as Galiullin and Lara. There he witnesses yet another significant moment in Lara's life as she learns about her missing husband. Galiullin, who, again coincidentally, served in the same regiment as Antipov, witnessed his disappearance through binoculars and thought that Antipov was killed. However, he tells Lara that her husband was taken prisoner, but she, mistakenly, does not believe that her husband is alive. This curious divergence for the first time raises the issue of what actually

8. Pasternak's *Doctor Zhivago*: The Resurrection of the Living Past

constitutes the "truth"—an issue that is crucial both for the events of the novel and its form.[12]

Zhivago's next major geographical displacement is associated with the appearance in his life of Evgraf, his enigmatic half-brother. Zhivago sees him in his typhoid delirium as the "spirit of his death" (211; 207) who, paradoxically, helps him write poetry (his name, after all, means "good writing"). Zhivago will identify Evgraf in his Varykino diary as "my good genius, my rescuer, resolving all my difficulties. Perhaps in every life there has to be, in addition to the other protagonists, a secret, unknown force, an almost symbolic figure who comes unsummoned to the rescue, and perhaps in mine Evgraf, my brother, plays the part of this hidden benefactor?" (297; 287). Appropriately, given Evgraf's "symbolic" significance, the two are first brought into physical proximity as Zhivago is reading a newspaper, acquired "at that charmed spot, the intersection of Serebriany and Molchanovka" (196; 193), which announces the news of the Bolshevik takeover. Yet it is only when Zhivago comes down with typhus that Evgraf seeks him out and identifies himself to his family. When Zhivago recovers, his wife and father-in-law, supported by Evgraf, make the decision, which Zhivago opposes, but to which he nonetheless submits, to flee Moscow to the estate of Tonia's grandfather in the Urals. The most striking coincidence here is left implicit: both Lara, a native of Iuriatin, and Tonia, whose ancestral estate lies in the environs of Iuriatin, trace their origins to the town that echoes Zhivago's Christian name, Iurii. The drama of his earthly life will reach its culminating point in its environs.

The device underlying these peripeteias of Zhivago's fate is laid bare when Zhivago, wracked by his guilt toward Tonia over his affair with Lara and unreconciled to the necessity of making a final break with Lara, wishes "wretchedly for some impossible, unexpected circumstances to solve his problem for him" (312; 303). Fortuitously, just as Zhivago has postponed yet again the decision to part with his lover, three horsemen overtake him and forcibly conscript him into the partisan guerrillas led by Liberius Mikulitsyn. This incursion of fate takes place at a crossroad marked by a sign advertising mechanical seeders

---

12 In some sense, Pavel Antipov has truly "died" to be "resurrected" as an embodiment of the murderous, mechanical maw of the revolution. As the change in his name suggests, he has come back as a "new man," with all of the living vitality evidenced by the young Pasha's humorous disposition crushed by the weight of the all-embracing "idea" that rules Strel'nikov's actions.

and threshing machines by the firm of Moreau and Vetchinkin (315; 305). The sign, appearing in the novel three times, invokes planting and reaping, life and death. Here it marks Zhivago's final break with his family, who depart for Moscow while he is held captive, and leads to his reunion with Lara after his escape from partisans. As Iuriatin becomes too dangerous for them, they flee to Varykino where they spent their final "stolen" weeks and where Zhivago begins writing down his poems.

As the pattern of coincidences demonstrates, Zhivago is blown about by the circumstances of his life back and forth between the two alternative "circles" embodied in Tonia and Lara who define the poles of his existence: on the one hand, home, family, the accustomed old way of life; on the other, passion, raw being, and poetry.[13] His fate, to which he submits his talent, seems inexorably to lead him away from Tonia to brief, but intense meetings with Lara. This allows him to fulfill his poetic destiny. Tricking Lara into departing with Komarovskii in order to save her daughter, Zhivago, inspired by the afterglow of her presence, turns to writing poetry again: "He was not deliberately striving for such a goal, but this broad vision came of its own accord as a consolation, like a message sent to him by Lara from her travels, like a distant greeting from her, like her appearance in a dream or the touch of her hand on his forehead, and he loved this ennobling imprint" (465; 453). After returning to Moscow, Zhivago is left to live out his remaining years with Marina in the pale reflection of his earlier family.[14] His last, again coincidental meeting with Evgraf, inspires his final burst of writing—coincidentally, in the very room on Kamerger Street where Pasha Antipov rented a room long ago and where Lara visited him—and leads, ultimately, to the consummation of his earthly life in death.

Zhivago's identification of Evgraf as a "symbolic" figure in his life prompts the reader to seek a connection between the pattern of coincidences and the symbolically loaded images that frequently accompany the coincidences in

---

13 In Chapter Five, section fifteen, on the train back to Moscow from Meliuzeevo, Zhivago's thoughts move in two "circles." The first circle includes Tonia, the old order, a desire to return to the past, and the revolution as imagined by idealist youth admiring Blok. The second circle includes the war, Lara, and the "bloody soldiers' revolution."

14 Notably, Zhivago duplicates the pattern of his father's life: like his father, he has three families, only one of which is "legal." In both cases, one family is centered in Moscow, one in Siberia, and one in Paris.

the novel and underscore their significance.¹⁵ The text itself draws our attention to what Ralph Freedman in his discussion of the "lyrical novel" calls "symbolic patterns": "The concept of the lyrical novel is a paradox. [...] [A] lyrical novel assumes a unique form which transcends the causal and temporal movement of the narrative within the framework of fiction. It is a hybrid genre that uses the novel to approach the function of a poem."¹⁶ Like the coincidences in Pasternak's novel, the "symbolic patterns" interimplicated in them serve to give the novel a cohesiveness that runs counter to narrative "causality," forcing the reader to re-evaluate the significance of the "irrational details" of the plot and ultimately Iurii Zhivago himself, whose passivity and apparent lack of will become transformed into an inspired response to the fullness and freedom of life.¹⁷

One passage where Zhivago seems to take a significant action on his own initiative serves to illustrate how patterns of imagery function both structurally and conceptually in a manner similar to coincidences. Zhivago's escape from the partisans is precipitated by his vision of the rowanberry tree that stands at the entrance to the camp. The rowanberry is metaphorically invoked at three other points in the novel.¹⁸ The image first appears in the narrator's description of the dinner table laid out at the Gromeko home on the night when

---

15   The significance of these images is highlighted by their reappearance in Zhivago's final jottings in Moscow before his death: "Whenever his imagination flagged and his work was held up, he spurred it on and whipped it up by making drawings in the margins. These drawings depicted forest cuttings or the intersections of city streets with the advertising column 'Moreau and Vetchinkin. Mechanical seeders. Threshing machines' in the center" (499–500; 488).

16   Ralph Freedman, *The Lyrical Novel* (Princeton: Princeton University Press, 1963), 1. I do not mean to suggest that *Doctor Zhivago* neatly fits Freedman's concept of the lyrical novel. His comments do, however, suggest a productive approach to Pasternak's work.

17   For a detailed analysis of the symbolic temporal patterns in *Doctor Zhivago*, see Catharine Theimer Nepomnyashchy, "The Poetics of Motivation: Time, Narrative, and History in Pasternak, Sinjavskij, and Solzenicyn" (PhD diss., Columbia University, New York, 1987), chapter "Pasternak's *Doktor Živago*: "The Meeting Place of Eternity and Time," 67–159—eds.

18   For productive discussions of the image of the rowan tree, see Irene Masing-Delic, "Zhivago as Fedorovian Soldier," *The Russian Review* 40, no. 3 (1981): 300–316; F. T. Griffiths and S. J. Rabinowitz, "*Doctor Zhivago* and the Tradition of the National Epic," *Comparative Literature* 32, no. 1 (Winter 1980): 63–79; and Maryanne C. Ward, "Eliot and Pasternak: Restoring the Waste Land of Lost Culture and Tradition," *Perspectives on Contemporary Literature* 9 (1983): 3–11.

Zhivago first sees Lara: "Beyond the open side doors of the ballroom the supper table gleamed, white and long as a winter road. The play of light on frosted bottles of red rowanberry cordial caught the eye" (56; 55). The metonymic association of the winter road and the rowanberry graphically presages the reality Zhivago will confront a decade later. It is attributed to the narrator and is in no way associated with the point of view of Zhivago himself, suggesting the imminence of the symbolic patterns that shape the protagonist's destiny in the *realia* of his life. The rowanberry tree appears as a metaphor for the second time in the song of the healer, which Zhivago overhears in the partisan camp. The rowanberry tree is transformed into the beloved of a captive soldier, suggesting a direct parallel with Zhivago's situation. The final figurative evocation of the rowanberry appears in connection with Strel'nikov's suicide, in the last sentence of the main body of the text: "The snow was a red lump under his left temple where he had bled. Drops of spurting blood that had mixed with the snow formed red beads that looked like rowanberries" (476; 464).[19]

These metaphors constitute the larger "rhetoric of images" within which Zhivago's significant encounter with the real rowanberry tree must be read.[20] Suffocated, both literally and figuratively, by the smoke in Liberius's dugout and by the partisan leader's political obtuseness, Zhivago goes out for a "breath of air" (383; 373) and comes upon the rowanberry tree:

> It was half in snow, half in frozen leaves and berries, and it held out two branches toward him. He remembered Lara's strong white arms and seized the branches and pulled them to him. As if in answer, the tree shook snow all over him. He muttered without realizing what he was saying, and completely beside himself: "I'll find you, my beauty, my love, my rowan tree, my own flesh and blood."
>
> It was a clear night with a full moon. He made his way farther into the taiga, to the marked tree, unearthed his things, and left the camp. (385; 375)

---

19 The last two prose chapters, "Conclusion" (Okonchanie) and "Epilogue," are marked by their titles as being after the fact. Structurally, this creates a parallel between the suicide of Zhivago's father at the end of the first chapter of the novel, and the suicide of Antipov-Strel'nikov that closes the narrative.

20 The term "rhetoric of images" most likely refers to Roland Barthes's 1964 essay "The Rhetoric of the Image"—eds.

8. Pasternak's *Doctor Zhivago*: The Resurrection of the Living Past | 159

The rowanberry tree—and, more importantly, Zhivago's perception of the tree as a beckoning image of Lara—functions in a manner analogous to the coincidences and incursions of the unexpected in shaping Zhivago's destiny. Just as he continually surrenders himself to the exigencies thrust on him by life, in this case Zhivago recognizes the symbolic lure of life itself, embodied in the tree as nurturing mother. Here then we can see how Zhivago's talent for life dovetails with his talent for poetry and with his particular scientific talents. As a doctor he is above all a diagnostician, a reader of symptoms, who has a heightened inquisitiveness about the nature of sight and perception. As a poet, his gift is to discover and give poetic form to the symbolic patterns with which life itself presents him, to give expression to the spirit of his age.

The key symbolic image of the novel originates with the candle that Zhivago, on his way with Tonia to the Sventitskiis' Christmas party, sees burning in Pasha Antipov's window, illuminating his conversation with Lara:

> As they drove through Kamerger Street Yura noticed that a candle had melted a patch in the icy crust on one of the windows. The light seemed to look into the street almost consciously [*s soznatel'nost'iu vzgliada*], as if it were watching the passing carriages and waiting for someone.
>
> "A candle burned on the table, a candle burned . . . ," Yura whispered to himself—the beginning of something confused, formless; he hoped that it would take shape of itself. But nothing more came to him. (81–82; 81)

The candle is explicitly described not as a passive object of Zhivago's perceptions, but as a conscious subject that spurs Zhivago's initial conception of the poem "Winter Evening" (*Zimnii vecher*), which will only be written down during his final stay at Varykino some ten years later. The significance of the imagery of the poem, of the candle as the embodiment of Zhivago's destiny, is underscored by the fact that these are the sole lines from Zhivago's poetry recorded verbatim in the prose text.

The candle literally and symbolically marks the intersection, unbeknownst to either of the characters, of Zhivago's and Lara's trajectories in life. It burns in Antipov's room which will become the room where Zhivago will write his last poems and the final resting place of his corpse before his burial—which implicitly suggests an equation between destiny, creativity, and death. It is also the site of the final "meeting" between the two lovers when Lara by chance reappears at the viewing of Zhivago's body. Appropriately, some two decades after Zhivago saw the candle which inspired the conception of the poem, the reader learns about the significance of the candle, both in Zhivago's life and in his poetry, as a symbol of "predestination" (*prednaznachenie*):

> [Lara] strained her memory to reconstruct that Christmas conversation with Pasha, but she could remember nothing except the candle burning on the window sill and melting a round patch in the icy crust on the glass.
> Did she divine that Yury, whose dead body was lying on the table, had seen the candle [*glazok*] as he was driving past, and noticed it, and that from the moment of his seeing its light from the street ("A candle burned on the table, a candle burned. . .") his life took its fatal course [*poshlo v ego zhizni ego prednznachenie*]? (511; 500)

The mention of *glazok* made in the ice by the burning candle and the lines from "Winter Night" here highlight the correspondence between Zhivago's poem and Lara's recollection of the candle.

The nature of creativity is a corollary of the vision of history as initially outlined in *Doctor Zhivago* by Zhivago's uncle, Nikolai Vedeniapin. According to him, history is "as another universe, made by man with the help of time and memory in answer to the challenge of death" (66; 66). This view is developed in the course of the novel in what seems to be a monologue passed from character to character.[21] The mode of transmission and development of Vedeniapin's ideas by other characters and their creative realization by his nephew are, in a sense, part and parcel of the ideas themselves. In other words, Vedeniapin's influence on other characters, again most especially on Zhivago, serves as a paradigm for the practical workings of his conception of history as an ongoing, continuous cultural project. Just as characters are defined by their responses to life, so also are they defined by their responses to ideas, by their "original" or "unoriginal" appropriation of the cultural legacy passed on to them.

The basic lineaments of Vedeniapin's philosophy are laid out early in the novel:

---

21 On the "dialogic" nature of this monologue, see David K. Danow, "Dialogic Poetics: *Doktor Zhivago*," *Slavic Review* 50, no. 4 (Winter 1991): 954–64.

8. Pasternak's *Doctor Zhivago*: The Resurrection of the Living Past

> It is possible to be an atheist, it is possible not to know whether God exists, or why, and yet believe that man does not live in a state of nature but in history, and that history as we know it now began with Christ, and that Christ's Gospel is its foundation. Now what is history? It is the centuries of systematic explorations of the riddle of death, with a view to overcoming death. [...] And then the two basic ideals of modern man—without them he is unthinkable—the idea of free personality and the idea of life as sacrifice. Mind you, all this is still extraordinarily new. There was no history in this sense among the ancients. [...] It was not until after the coming of Christ that time and man could breathe freely. It was not until after Him that men began to live in their posterity. Man does not die in a ditch like a dog—but at home in history, while the work toward the conquest of death is in full swing; he dies sharing in this work. (10; 10)

As a number of scholars have pointed out, Vedeniapin's ideas are indebted to the religious philosopher Nikolai Fedorov (1829–1903) who in his posthumously published lecture notes, titled *The Philosophy of the Common Cause* (Filosofiia obshchego dela), argued that mankind should unite in the "common cause" of resurrecting the dead.[22] Yet while Fedorov placed his hopes on scientific advances and believed in the possibility of literal resurrection, Vedeniapin's understanding of humanity's "common cause" of "overcoming death" is rooted in his conception of history as cultural continuity vouchsafed by the kenotic ideal of the "free personality." Vedeniapin suggests a morphology not only for Zhivago's life and works, but for the text of *Doctor Zhivago* as well. The web of symbolic patterns that lend it structural integrity function as symptoms of the meaningfulness of everyday life. The interconnectedness of human existence, given figurative shape in the coincidences intertwining the characters' lives, becomes an intimation of life lived in history, a window onto the parallel, meaningful dimension of existence, in the narrator's formulation, "a happy feeling that all events took place not only on the earth, in which the dead are buried, but also in some other region which some called the Kingdom of God, others history, and still others by some other name" (13; 13).

---

22 For discussions of Fedorov's ideas in relation to *Doctor Zhivago*, see Masing-Delic, "Zhivago as Fedorovian Soldier"; David Bethea, "Doctor Zhivago: The Revolution and the Red Crosse Knight," chap. 5 in his *The Shape of Apocalypse in Modern Russian Fiction* (Princeton: Princeton University Press, 1989).

The final extended explication of Vedeniapin's ideas is couched in images that recur later both in the novel's prose and in Zhivago's poems. Vedeniapin writes about the ancient world as still connected with nature, still remembering mammoths, dragons, and dinosaurs, remarking that "this ancient world ended with Rome [...] a flea market of borrowed gods, and conquered peoples, a bargain basement on two floors, earth and heaven, a mass of filth convoluted in a triple knot as in an intestinal obstruction" (43; 43). He counters that history begins with Christ:

> And then, into this tasteless heap of gold and marble, He came, light and clothed in an aura, emphatically human, deliberately provincial, Galilean, and at that moment gods and nations ceased to be and man came into being—man the carpenter, man the plowman, man the shepherd with his flock of sheep at sunset, man who does not sound in the least proud, man thankfully celebrated in all the cradle songs of mothers and in all the picture galleries the world over. (44; 43)

Dragons and analogies with ancient Rome reappear in the novel, both marking a return to prehistory, to a time before the replacement of nations and tribes by the dignity of the human person.[23] By contrast to the images of the pagan world, the Christian image cluster of motherhood, birth, and "picture galleries" is reiterated in the poem "Christmas Star." This interpenetration of images highlights the question of the nature of influence, creativity, and originality implicit in the postulation of history as a "common" and continuous project.

Zhivago discovers the absence of originality in his friends when he returns from the front in the interim between the February and October Revolutions:

> Under the old order, which enabled those whose lives were secure to play the fools and eccentrics at the expense of others while the majority led a wretched existence, it had been only too easy to mistake the foolishness and idleness of a privileged minority for genuine character

---

23 Dragons reappear as the hostile force, inspired by the wolves that threaten Lara and Zhivago at Varykino and associated with Komarovskii, with which St. George struggles in the poem "Fairytale." For a discussion of the Roman imagery in the novel, see Irene Masing-Delic, "Capitalist Bread and Socialist Spectacle: The Janus Face of 'Rome' in Pasternak's *Doctor Zhivago*," in *Boris Pasternak and His Times: Selected Papers from the Second International Symposium on Pasternak*, ed. Lazar Fleishman (Berkeley: Berkeley Slavic Specialties, 1989), 372–85.

and originality [*samobytnost'*]. But the moment the lower classes had risen, and the privileges of those on top had been abolished, how quickly had those people faded, how unregretfully had they renounced independent ideas—apparently no one had ever had such ideas! (177; 174–75)

The social inequality of the old regime is censured for creating the illusion of *samobytnost'*—the quality most truly embodied in the novel by Zhivago: "Everything in Yura's mind was still helter-skelter, but his views, his habits, his inclinations were all distinctly his own [*samobytno*]. He was unusually impressionable, and the novelty of his vision was remarkable" (64; 64). Zhivago's ability to judge clearly allows him see the illusory nature of the old life and initially accept the Revolution as the promise of the liberation of the personality, of the creation of true life. Hence he disapproves of the party the Zhivagos throw upon his return to Moscow from Meliuzeevo with the "unheard-of luxury in those already hungry days" of duck and vodka: "But the saddest thing of all was that their party was a kind of betrayal," a denial of the conditions of the time (178; 175).

Later in the novel, back in Moscow shortly before Zhivago's death, the narrative echoes both his uncle's words about history and Zhivago's earlier disappointment at his acquaintances. The narrator passes a scathing judgment on the poverty of thought and corresponding poverty of language of Gordon and Dudorov, now flourishing members of the new Soviet intelligentsia: "To carry on a conversation naturally and intelligently a man must have an adequate supply of words. Of the three, only Yury Andreevich answered this requirement [. . .] The other two were always at a loss for an expression. They did not possess the gift of eloquence. At a loss for words, they paced up and down, puffed at their cigarettes" (492; 481). They unwittingly substitute smoking for their inability to think freely, and their linguistic incapacity creates an atmosphere so suffocating that Zhivago cannot long remain in it. Plagued by "the misfortune of having average taste" (493; 481), they mistake cliche for true sentiment: "These [Dudorov's] reflections appealed to Gordon just because they were so hackneyed. [. . .] It was the very triteness of the feelings and expressions that moved him most; he mistook Dudorov's reflection of prescribed feeling for a genuine expression of humanity" (493; 482). While recording Zhivago's disenchantment with his friends—as well as his increasingly desperate pleas for them to let him leave for a breath of fresh air—the narrator points out: "But he [Zhivago] could hardly say to them: 'Dear friends, how desperately commonplace you are—you and your circle, the names and authorities you always quote, their glamour and art which you so much admire! The only bright and vital thing about you is that you lived in the same time as I did and knew me!'" (493; 481). This passage contains a paraphrase of Christ's words to his apostles who have fallen asleep keeping watch with him which are reiterated in the last of the Zhivago poems, "The Garden of Gethsemane" (Gefsimanskii sad): "On razbudil ikh: 'Vas Gospod' spodobil / Zhit' v dni moi, vy zh razleglis', kak plast" (He awakened them: "God hath granted you to live / During my days on earth, and yet you lie there sprawling"; 565; 558). These inner thoughts of Zhivago about Gordon and Dudorov as lapsed disciples and his recasting of his life as a *Via Dolorosa* in his poem suggest how we are to understand the nature of Zhivago's *imitatio Christi*. It is inextricably rooted in his *samobytnost'* as manifested in his life, thought, and language. And it is his *samobytnost'* that sets Zhivago apart as a threat to the new order.

The originality of Zhivago's language is contrasted to that of the new regime. The narrator comments on the breakdown of language in Russia as early as Chapter Six, describing the situation in Moscow in September 1917: "This was the time to prepare for the cold weather, to store up food and wood. But in those days of the triumph of materialism, matter had become a disembodied concept, and the alimentation and food supply question had taken the place of food and firewood" (186–87; 184). Later, when Zhivago returns to Varykino after his escape from the partisans, he takes the government decrees, which have replaced the theater posters that previously adorned the House of Sculptures facing Lara's apartment, as a specifically linguistic reproach for his initial fascination with the Revolution: "Was it possible that he must pay for that rash enthusiasm all his life by never hearing, year after year, anything but these unchanging, shrill, crazy exclamations and demands, which became progressively more impractical, meaningless [*neudoboponiatnye*, abstruse], and unfulfillable as time went by? Was it possible that because of one moment of overgenerous response he had been enslaved forever?" (391; 381). This "abstruse" language bears no mark of the year in which the posters were written nor of the individual who drafted them; it is even unclear what political party generated them. Their language is completely divorced from reality. Just as the intellectual penury of the Soviet intelligentsia, embodied in Gordon and Dudorov, is mirrored in their verbal insufficiency, so the breakdown of social order in the aftermath of the revolution is reflected in a disruption of the relationship between word and object, language and life. Abstract concepts and theory have taken the place of reality.

This divorce of abstraction from life is incarnated most fully in the figure of Antipov-Strel′nikov. Zhivago tells Lara that he recognizes Antipov-Strel′nikov as "One writ with me in sour misfortune's book [*My v knige roka na odnoi stroke*]" (411; 401), citing Romeo's words about Paris, Juliet's "rightful" husband in Shakespeare's play.[24] Structurally Strel′nikov and Zhivago's lives run a parallel course throughout the text: they both become affianced on the same evening, the evening when Zhivago sees the candle in Antipov's window, and the first mentions of their children and their departures for war succeed one another in the narrative. Yet while circumstances continually throw Zhivago and Lara together, Zhivago and Antipov continually "miss" one another. Zhivago marvels when he first sees Strel′nikov—not yet knowing that he is Lara's husband nor, therefore, into what close proximity fate has thrown them—"How was it possible that he, a doctor, with his countless acquaintances, had never until this day come across anything so definite as this man's personality? How was it that they had never been thrown together, that their paths had not crossed?" If coincidences are the gauge of life's openness to fate, then the life of Strel′nikov—"this man [who] was entirely a manifestation of the will" (254; 248)—is marked by missed chances, by attempts to turn life to his own ends. While Zhivago conceives history "by analogy with the vegetable kingdom" (465; 453), Antipov, in Lara's words, "quarrelled with history" (415; 405), waging his destructive battle from his armored train. As he contemplates the ways to exit from his family life, his appeal to destiny is sidetracked by the blinding lights of a train. For him, a candle, as he tells Zhivago during their final meeting, is associated with revolutionary destruction: "And side by side with this there arose before the eyes of the world the vast figure of Russia bursting into flames like a light [*svechoi*] of redemption for all the sorrows and misfortunes of mankind" (473; 461). Strel′nikov's desire for vengeance against the old world, which Lara describes to Zhivago as "some sort of Roman civic valor" (309; 299), marks him as a throwback to pre-Christian history. While Zhivago's recasting of himself in language is an act of memory, Antipov's renaming of himself is an act of forgetting, an obliteration of his former self, the replacement of the real person Pavel Antipov by the abstraction of "the shooter," Strel′nikov. Lara, in a hurried glimpse she has managed to cap-

---

24 William Shakespeare, *Romeo and Juliet*, Act V, Scene III.

ture of Strel'nikov in Iuriatin, can discern a huge difference between Strel'nikov now and his former self: "It was as if something abstract had crept into this face and made it colorless. As if a living human face had become an embodiment of a principle, the image of an idea" (412; 401). Echoing Strel'nikov's remarks on Lenin (whom Strel'nikov characterizes during his last meeting with Zhivago as avenger for social injustice), Lara's observation, which resonates with her earlier comment that "Strelnikov is his pseudonym—he has an assumed name, like all active revolutionaries" (309; 299), reveals Strel'nikov's—and, for that matter, Lenin's—adoption of false names as a sign of the general despoilment of language, a symptom of the immolation of the individual self on the altar of revolutionary platitude.

Precisely because Strel'nikov's desire to control life would seem to preclude coincidence, the two "coincidental" meetings with Zhivago draw the reader's attention and, together with other structural parallels, mark the opposition between Zhivago and Antipov-Strel'nikov as central to the conception of the novel. These two meetings occur at the end of Book One and at the end of the main body of the text. While Lara in retrospect views both encounters as a form of predestination, from Strel'nikov's point of view they are both failed meetings: in the first case he is looking for an unspecified someone else, and in the second case he arrives too late to see his wife and daughter.

At the crux of the intersection of their fates, as underscored by Zhivago's citation of Shakespeare, stands Lara and what she signifies for each of them. For each man the discovery of Lara's "fall" sets in motion the course of his life. Zhivago is drawn to Lara precisely because she is "fallen," while the revelation of Lara's fall drives Antipov from her and ultimately transforms him into Strel'nikov. In thinking about the past, both Antipov and Lara cast the failure of their marriage in terms of language, attributing it to the "element of artificiality" (108; 107) that enters their lives, the "power of the glittering phrase" (414–15; 404) in Lara's words. Stre'lnikov elaborates Lara's diagnosis in his final conversation with Zhivago, maintaining that his mission was "to pay back in full all the wrongs that she had suffered, to wash her mind clean of those memories so that it should not be possible to return to the past" (473; 462). Strel'nikov thus envisages his mission as precisely the destruction of memory.

Ironically, Zhivago himself, in his brief moment of infatuation with the October Revolution, gave most vivid expression to the Revolution as an act of "surgical" removal, a cutting out of past injustice: "What splendid surgery! You take a knife and with one masterful stroke you cut out all the old stinking ulcers. Quite simply, without any nonsense, you take the old monster of injustice, which has been accustomed for centuries to being bowed and scraped and curtsied to, and you sentence it to death" (198; 194). Zhivago's metaphor of the Revolution as a surgical procedure is, in a sense, rather gruesomely realized in the horrific amputee who, one arm and one leg cut off by the Whites, is sent crawling back to the partisan camp to die. It is the vision of this "bleeding stump of a man" (378; 368), his chopped off arm and leg tied to his back, that sends the disturbed Pamphyl Palykh over the edge, precipitating his murder of his family. What begins in the rhetoric of revolution ends in blood. What initially holds the promise of a new "connectedness" ends in the murderous severing of family ties. Pamphyl Palykh, who can remember neither the name of the officer he gratuitously killed, but who continues to haunt him, nor the place of that murder, becomes the incarnation of the violent force of the masses unleashed by the obliteration of the past, the failure of memory.

Early in the novel, in his improvised lecture to the dying Anna Ivanovna, Zhivago formulates his ideas on immortality and connects it to memory. He begins by rejecting both conventional Christian and Fedorovian conceptions of resurrection. Instead he views rebirth as part of the process of natural renewal. Yet it is to memory, rather than to biological process, that Zhivago devotes the bulk of his remarks:

> This is what your consciousness has breathed and lived on and enjoyed throughout your life—your soul, your immortality, your life in others. And what now? You have always been in others and you will remain in others. And what does it matter to you if later on that is called your memory? This will be you—the you that enters the future and becomes a part of it. (68; 68)

For Zhivago as poet, his poems become the manifestation of his "soul," his "immortality," his "life in others," as underscored by the fact that his words to Anna Ivanovna are reiterated in the concluding scene of the novel: "To the two old [*sostarivshikhsia*, aged] friends [Gordon and Dudorov], as they sat by the window, it seemed that this freedom of the soul was already there, as if that very evening the *future* had tangibly moved into the streets below them, that they themselves *had entered it and were now part of it*. [. . .] And the book they held seemed to confirm and encourage their feeling" (531; 519, emphasis mine—C. T. N.). Likewise, in his meditations on poetry during his last stay at Varykino Zhivago echoes the idiosyncratic conception of symbolism

Pasternak offered in a paper, "Symbolism and Immortality" (Simvolizm i bessmertie), he delivered at a symbolist study circle in 1913.[25] The poet's role in the revelation of the immortality of life lies in his ability to make the reader, separated from him in time and space, re-experience his own experiences. After Lara's departure, Zhivago explicitly casts his poetic project as an act of memory: "I'll put my grief for you in a work that will endure and be worthy of you. I'll write your memory into an image of aching tenderness and sorrow" (464; 452). Even his pain translated into art becomes the "joy of living": "[Zhivago] made a note reaffirming his belief that art always serves beauty, and beauty is delight in form, and form is the key to organic life, since no living thing can exist without it, so that every work of art, including tragedy, expresses the joy of existence" (466; 454). The context in which the passage appears in the novel, together with Zhivago's attempts to give "form" to his experiences in the meter and images of his poetry, implies that form is not what the poet imposes on his experiences, on life, but are the shapes with which life itself supplies him and to which he surrenders. The narrator describes the state of "inspiration" that embraces Zhivago as he writes:

> After two or three stanzas and several images by which he himself was struck, his work took possession of him and he felt the approach of what is called inspiration. [...]
>
> At such moments Yury Andreevich felt that the main part of the work was being done not by him but by a superior power which was above him and directed him, namely the movement of universal thought and poetry in the present historical stage and the one to come. And he felt himself to be only the occasion, the fulcrum, needed to make this movement possible. (448; 437)

The immortalization of self becomes a surrender of self, an immersion in process of life and history.

This understanding of creative process harks back to Zhivago's reception of the candle in Pasha Antipov's window, which "seemed to look into the street almost consciously, as if it were watching the passing carriages and waiting for someone" (81–82; 81). The poet does not find himself in the world around

---

25 See Boris Pasternak, "Symbolism and Immortality" [Synopsis of a Lecture], in *The Marsh of Gold: Pasternak's Writings on Inspiration and Creation*, trans. Angela Livingstone (Brighton: Academic Studies Press, 2008), 40–41—eds.

8. Pasternak's *Doctor Zhivago*: The Resurrection of the Living Past | 169

him: nature, life, finds him. Zhivago's vocation as poet is inherent in his intuitive recognition of the significance of the candle and his translation of that significance into a poetic image just as the transcendent "subjectivity" of the natural world as a "generic and suprapersonal quality" is intimated by Zhivago's and Lara's independently identifying the candle as the sign of Zhivago's predestination.[26]

The episode in which Zhivago sights the candle—or rather the candle sights Zhivago—opens with the reference to his scientific interests: "That winter Yura was preparing a scientific paper on the nervous elements of the retina for the University Gold Medal competition. Though he had qualified only in general medicine, he had a specialist's knowledge of the eye. His interest in the physiology of sight was in keeping with other sides of his character—his creative gifts and his preoccupation with imagery in art and the logical structure of ideas" (80; 79). The connection drawn here, and suggested in "Symbolism and Immortality," between the "physiology of sight" and "imagery in art" anticipates several key statements of Zhivago's views on perception later in the novel. During his captivity by the partisans, Zhivago falls asleep in the forest, and "[t]he dazzle of light and shadow" makes him "invisible as if he had put on a magic cap" (355; 345). When Zhivago awakens, he watches a butterfly disappear, like himself, into its surroundings:

> Folding and unfolding like a scrap of colored stuff, a brown speckled butterfly flew across the sunny side of the clearing. [. . .] Choosing a background with a color like its own, it settled on the brown speckled bark of a pine and became indistinguishable from it, vanishing as completely as Yury Andreevich, hidden by the play of light and shadow, had vanished. (356; 346)

This observation sets in motion a train of thought about "will and purposefulness as superior forms of adaptation; mimicry and protective coloring; the survival of the fittest; and the hypothesis that the path of natural selection is the very path leading to the formation and emergence of consciousness" (356; 346). Zhivago returns to the subject of mimicry once more, when, after his return to Iuriatin, he tells Lara that he expects to be arrested because of his unorthodox views: "Another thing is that I am obsessed by the problem of

---

26 Boris Pasternak, *I Remember: Sketch for an Autobiography*, trans. Manya Harari (New York: Pantheon, 1959), 63.

mimicry, the outward adaptation of an organism to the color of its environment. In this color adaptation is concealed an amazing passage of the inner into the outer." Zhivago explicitly credits his ability to read signs to his "grasp of a situation as a whole," to his organic apprehension of life as a totality (418; 407). The principle of metonymy reveals the association with his remarks on mimicry. Mimicry becomes both a physical manifestation of and a figure for the dissolution of the self in the totality of being, the breakdown of "the Kantian barrier between subject and object," which, as Vedeniapin postulates, holds the promise that "communication between mortals is immortal" (42; 42), that subjectivity is a property of the physical world and can therefore be passed along to others.[27]

In the early autumn of Zhivago's second year of captivity among the partisans, on the same day he observes the disappearing butterfly, he has a vision of Lara that suggests the poet's "divinity." As he watches the chief liaison officer burning papers, he sees the flame as transparent: "The fire with the setting sun behind it was as transparent as the leaves; the flames were invisible and only the waves of shimmering heat showed that something was burning." He associates this invisible flame with Lara: "Here and there the woods were brilliant with ripe berries—bright tassels of lady's smock, brick-red alderberries, and clusters of viburnum, shimmering from white to purple. Whirring their glassy wings, dragonflies as transparent as the flames and the leaves sailed slowly through the air. (353; 343). The passage evokes the Transfiguration of Christ (*Preobrazhenie Gospodne*), celebrated, as Zhivago tells us in the poem "August," on "shestoe avgusta po staromu" (sixth of August by the old style calendar; 548; 540). In the poem Zhivago writes of the "svet bez plameni" (light without flame) that "Iskhodit v etot den' s Favora" (comes on this day from [Mount] Tabor; 549; 541). This image suggests the "invisible fire" (ognia ne bylo vidno; 353; 343) in which the papers are burned. Direct allusions to the Transfiguration follow: "At such moments he felt as if he too were being pierced by shafts of light. It was as though the gift of the living spirit were streaming into his breast, piercing his being and coming out shoulders like a pair of wings [V takie minuty tochno i on propuskal skvoz' sebia eti stolby sveta. Tochno dar zhivogo dukkha potokom vkhodil v ego grud', peresekal vse ego sushchestvo, i paroi kryl'ev vykhodil iz-pod lopatok naruzhu]." (353;

---

27   The quotation about the Kantian barrier comes from Bethea, *The Shape of Apocalypse in Modern Russian Fiction*, 239.

343). The imagery evokes icons portraying Christ's body pierced by rays of light.[28] The use of the verb *preobrazhat'sia* later in the passage supports the connection.

The transfiguration for Zhivago is a transfiguration of the whole of nature, which converges in Lara's image. The transfiguration becomes a moment of direct communication between Zhivago's subjective personality and the world around him in all its vital force, embodied in the figure of Lara. It is a moment that takes Zhivago out of time and space, out of history as it is conventionally understood, and into a transcendent realm of pure existence. It is only a moment, however, and Zhivago immediately returns to the "real" time of historical events: "But everyday, current reality was still there, Russia was going through the October Revolution, and he was a prisoner of the partisans" (353; 343–44). The Transfiguration marks the revelation of Christ's divinity, the voice of God announcing: "This is my beloved Son, in whom I am well pleased; hear ye him" (Matthew 17:5). Similarly, Zhivago's "transfiguration" reveals his "dual nature," his condition of being caught between conventional historical time and the eternity of the fully lived moment, between the "irrational details" of existence and the "totality" of life.

The account of the Transfiguration in the Gospel according to Luke contains the first mention of the crucifixion that lies ahead: "And behold, there talked with him two men, which were Moses and Elijah: Who appeared in glory and spake of his decease which he should accomplish at Jerusalem" (Luke 9:30–31). Zhivago realizes this connection between the Transfiguration and death in "August," in which the poet foresees his death as occurring on the Transfiguration.[29] Resurrection, the completion of the "divine" mission—whether Christ's or the poet's—can only come after death. Zhivago realizes at Anna Ivanovna's funeral that "art has two constant, two unending concerns: it always meditates on death and thus always creates life. All great, genuine art resembles and continues the Revelation of St. John" (91; 90). Fittingly, Evgraf, whom Zhivago first sees as the "spirit of his death" and who at the end arranges

---

28   See, for example, the famous late fourteenth-century icon *The Transfiguration of Christ*, by Theophanes the Greek.

29   According to the "real" chronology of the novel, Zhivago's death seems to take place later in August. The text does not tell us whether his "transfiguration" in the forest takes place on August 6 or not. In both cases, however, it is not the actual dates that are important, but rather the symbolic connection with the holiday created by the poetry and the poetic imagery in the text.

his funeral, will also preserve his poems and become the agent of their "resurrection." While Lara represents the joy that the poet experiences in life, Evgraf represents the possibility of passing on the "immortality" of that experience to others.

Doctor Zhivago is an act of memory, an attempt to reestablish cultural continuity by allowing readers to experience what the writer experienced, to transform death into life, the rupture itself into part of the ongoing process of culture. As the text draws to its close, with Gordon and Dudorov holding the notebook of Zhivago's writings, the evocation of the author's memory at the end of the "story" resonates with its opening:

> On they went, singing "Eternal Memory," and whenever they stopped, their feet, the horses, and the gusts of wind seemed to carry on their singing.
>
> Passersby made way for the procession, counted the wreaths, and crossed themselves. Some joined in out of curiosity and asked: "Who is being buried?"—"Zhivago," they were told.—"Oh, I see. That's what it is."—"It isn't him. It's his wife."—"Well, it comes to the same thing." (3; 3)

The name Zhivago is indeclinable and therefore unmarked for gender. Furthermore, it is homonymous with the accusative/genitive singular of the Church Slavonic form for the "living." In the novel's opening lines the name initiates the complex interimplication of topoi of death and resurrection that runs throughout the novel, culminating in the poems at its end. Thus, the confusion over who is being buried must extend to the title character himself, since he is introduced into the novel with a prefiguration of his death. As scholars have noted, the invocation of the name in this context refers to the angels' words to the women who come to Christ's tomb, only to find it empty: "Why seek ye the living [*zhivago*] among the dead?" (Luke 24:5). Zhivago lives on in memory and in poetry.

The prose text of the novel concludes on an appropriately joyous note: "Thinking of this holy city [Moscow] and of the entire earth, of the still-living protagonists of this story, and their children, they [Gordon and Dudorov] were filled with tenderness and peace, and they were enveloped by the inaudible music of happiness that flowed all about them and into the distance. And the book they held seemed to confirm and encourage their feeling" (531; 519). Yet, as regards the prospects for the "resurrection" of culture at the end of *Doctor Zhivago*, the novel remains ambiguous. Is the Moscow stretching out beneath Gordon and Dudorov the New Jerusalem or the Third Rome? The status of Zhivago's writings, whether or not they have been published, remains unclear. Moreover, the "notebook" (*tetrad'*) remains in the hands of Zhivago's contemporaries and has not yet apparently been passed on to the "children."

The anxiety of transmission inherent in the ending is underscored by the juxtaposition of Zhivago's biological progeny and his artistic legacy. Zhivago's "legitimate" children by Tonia (who bear their grandparents' names) live in Paris. They are unlikely to return to Russia, so their geographical and cultural displacement implicitly problematizes the continuity of the tradition by the Russian diaspora. Zhivago's children by Marina, Capitolina and Claudia, bear "Roman" names, alluding to Vedeniapin's negative view of Rome as prehistory preceding Christianity. His "illegitimate" daughter with Lara, the laundry girl, "Tania Out-of-Turn" (Bezocheredeva) has lost the memory of her origins, which assumedly will be transmitted to her by Evgraf, who, in the novel's final extraordinary coincidence, finds his lost niece while looking for someone else. There nonetheless remains a disturbing rupture between the experiences, and narratives, of father and child. Is poorly educated Tania, who should be his new reader and heir, capable of recovering her father's experiences from his poems? Will Zhivago's poems—or Pasternak's novel—find true heritors to extend the organic continuity, the "historicity" of the Russian cultural tradition?

Works Cited

Aucouturier, Michel. "The Metonymous Hero or the Beginnings of Pasternak the Novelist." *Books Abroad* 44 (1970): 222–27.

Bayley, John. "Tolstoy's Legacy. *Dr. Zhivago.*" In his *Tolstoy and the Novel*, 294–308. London: Chatto and Windus, 1966.

Bethea, David. *The Shape of Apocalypse in Modern Russian Fiction*. Princeton: Princeton University Press, 1989.

Danow, David K. "Dialogic Poetics: *Doktor Zhivago*," *Slavic Review* 50, no. 4 (Winter 1991): 954–64.

Deutscher, Isaac. "Pasternak and the Calendar of the Revolution." In *Pasternak: Modern Judgements*, edited by Donald Davie and Angela Livingstone, 240–258. Nashville: Aurora Publishers, 1969.

Frank, Viktor. "Realizm chetyrekh izmerenii (perechityvaia Pasternaka)," *Mosty* 2 (1959): 189–209.

Howe, Irving. "Freedom and the Ashcan of History." In *Pasternak: Modern Judgements*, edited by Donald Davie and Angela Livingstone, 259–68. Nashville: Aurora Publishers, 1969.

Freedman, Ralph. *The Lyrical Novel*. Princeton: Princeton University Press, 1963.

Griffiths, F. T., and S. J. Rabinowitz. "*Doctor Zhivago* and the Tradition of the National Epic." *Comparative Literature* 32, no. 1 (Winter 1980): 63–79.

Jackson, Robert Louis. "*Doctor Zhivago*: *Liebestod* of the Russian Intelligentsia." In *Pasternak: A Collection of Critical Essays*, edited by Victor Erlich, 137–50. Englewood Cliffs: Prentice-Hall, 1978.

Jakobson, Roman. "The Prose of the Poet Pasternak." In *Pasternak: Modern Judgements*, edited by Donald Davie and Angela Livingstone, 135–51. Nashville: Aurora Publishers, 1969.

Kelly, Ian Crawford. "Eternal Memory: Historical Themes in Pasternak's *Doctor Zhivago*." PhD diss., Columbia University, New York, 1985.

Livingstone, Angela. "'Integral Errors': Remarks on the Writing of *Doctor Zhivago*," *Essays in Poetics* 13, no. 2 (1988): 83–94.

Matlaw, Ralph E. "Mechanical Structure and Inner Form: A Note on *War and Peace* and *Dr. Zhivago*," *Symposium* 16, no. 4 (1962): 288–95.

———. "A Visit with Pasternak," *The Nation*, September 12, 1959, 134.

Masing-Delic, Irene. "Capitalist Bread and Socialist Spectacle: The Janus Face of 'Rome' in Pasternak's *Doctor Zhivago*." In *Boris Pasternak and His Times: Selected Papers from the Second International Symposium on Pasternak*, edited by Lazar Fleishman, 372–85. Berkeley: Berkeley Slavic Specialties, 1989.

———. "Zhivago as Fedorovian Soldier," *The Russian Review* 40, no. 3 (1981): 300–316.

Nepomnyashchy, Catharine Theimer. "The Poetics of Motivation: Time, Narrative, and History in Pasternak, Sinjavskij, and Solzenicyn." PhD diss., Columbia University, New York, 1987.

Pasternak, Boris. *Doctor Zhivago*, translated by Max Hayward and Manya Harari. New York: Pantheon Books, 1991.

———. *Doktor Zhivago*. Ann Arbor: University of Michigan Press, 1958.

———. *I Remember: Sketch for an Autobiography*, translated by David Magarshack and Manya Harari New York: Pantheon, 1959.

———. *Ob iskusstve*. Moscow: Iskusstvo, 1990.

Pomorska, Krystyna. "Doctor Živago." In her *Themes and Variations in Pasternak's Poetics*, 74–90. Lisse: The Peter de Ridder Press, 1973.

Scherr, Barry P. "The Structure of *Doctor Zhivago*." *Proceedings: Pacific Northwest Conference on Foreign Language* 25, part 1 (1974): 274–79.

Silbajoris, Rimvydas. "Pasternak and Tolstoj: Some Comparisons," *Slavic and East European Journal* 11, no. 1 (Spring 1967): 23–34.

Siniavskii, A. "Nekotorye aspekty pozdnei prozy Pasternaka." In *Boris Pasternak and His Times: Selected Papers from the Second International Symposium on Pasternak*, edited by Lazar Fleishman, 359–71. Berkeley: Berkeley Slavic Specialties, 1989.

Struve, Gleb. "The Hippodrome of Life: The Problem of Coincidences in *Doctor Zhivago*." *Books Abroad* 44 (Spring 1970): 231–36.

Ward, Maryanne C. "Eliot and Pasternak: Restoring the Waste Land of Lost Culture and Tradition." *Perspectives on Contemporary Literature* 9 (1983): 3–11.

9

One Day in the Life of Ivan Denisovich and Its Intertexts: Aksakov's "Stepan Mikhailovich's Good Day" and Kataev's *Time, Forward!*

No writer of the post-Stalin period laid a more compelling claim to the mantle of the Russian writer as the conscience of society than Aleksandr Solzhenitsyn. Unconcerned, if not infuriated, by late twentieth-century intellectual trends such as the deconstruction of meaning and the subjective relativity of historiography, Solzhenitsyn devoted his career to reclaiming the suppressed truth about Russia's past, which he saw as a necessary precursor to the spiritual rebirth of his homeland. Little impressed by Western democracy after a decade of exile in Europe and the United States, he became convinced that, as a result of "pluralism," the "Western world" was "paralysed by its inability any longer to distinguish between true and false positions, between manifest Good and manifest Evil" and argued that "In the whole universal flux there is one truth—God's truth."[1] Just as in his pleas to Soviet and later Russian leaders Solzhenitsyn called for a return to a simpler way of life redolent of the nineteenth-century Russian village, so in his fiction he rejected with equal fervor socialist realism and modernist experimentation for the aesthetic of an earlier time with its authoritative narrative voice in the Tolstoyan mode and its full

---

Previously unpublished. Part of Nepomnyashchy's incomplete book manuscript *The Politics of Tradition: Rerooting Russian Literature after Stalin*. Permission to publish granted by Olga Nepomnyashchy—eds.

1   Alexander Solzhenitsyn, "Our Pluralists," *Survey* 29, no. 2 (Summer 1985): 2.

complement of mimetic devices.[2] For him, a writer's worth lay not in formal inventiveness, but rather in the moral weight of his message.

In this article, I focus on the writer's first published work, *One Day in the Life of Ivan Denisovich* (Odin den' Ivana Denisovicha, 1962), which catapulted him to international prominence. In the novella he locates himself as a writer within the Russian tradition and therefore lays the groundwork for his later efforts to recover Russia's past, document the break in cultural continuity that it experienced in the early twentieth century, and return its literature to the time before the rupture. As we shall see, however, Solzhenitsyn locates the breaking point at a different historical moment than do the majority of dissident and dissonant Russian writers of the late Soviet and early post-Soviet periods. For him, the rupture results not only from the Revolution and its aftermath; its seeds also lie in the modernist movements that emerged as a dominant force in Russian culture in the decade before the Bolsheviks seized power.

One Day in the Life of Ivan Denisovich evokes two intertexts that have not been sufficiently explored by commentators: the chapter "Stepan Mikhailovich's Good Day" from Sergei Aksakov's *Family Chronicle* (Semeinaia khronika, 1856) and Valentin Kataev's novel *Time Forward!* (Vremia vpered!, 1932). In the first instance, Solzhenitsyn appears to recognize the predecessor text as a "legitimate" forebear, while in the second, he engages in an active polemic with the earlier text. Notably, like *One Day in the Life of Ivan Denisovich*, each of these texts describes a single day.

"Stepan Mikhailovich's Good Day" as Intertext

There is no self-contained novella- or novel-length one-day narrative in nineteenth-century Russian literature, but there are a few shorter works and sections of works with this narrative form. Of these, the chapter "Stepan Mikhailovich's Good Day" (Dobryi den' Stepana Mikhailovicha) from Sergei Aksakov's *Family Chronicle*, a fictionalized reminiscence of childhood on an estate in Ufa gubernia, seems most likely to have influenced Solzhenitsyn and may have suggested the framework for his narrative of Ivan Denisovich's "good

---

2   See Aleksandr Solzhenitsyn, *Pis'mo vozhdiam Sovetskogo Soiuza* (Paris: YMCA Press, 1974).

day."³ "Stepan Mikhailovich's Good Day" appears at the very end of the first major division of *The Family Chronicle*. Because this entire section of Aksakov's narrative focuses on Stepan Mikhailovich Bagrov, a character modeled on Aksakov's grandfather, readers already have a vivid picture of him by the time they reach the chapter that concerns us: he is a patriarch of almost Biblical proportions, whose rages keep his family and servants in awe and fear. Yet Aksakov prefaces "Stepan Mikhailovich's Good Day" with the disclaimer: "But I'm not going to say any more about the dark side of my grandfather; better I describe for you one of his good, bright days, about which I've heard so much."⁴

As Solzhenitsyn will later recount Ivan Denisovich's day, Aksakov's narrator describes his grandfather's day, tracing the old man's movements from the moment he crawls out of bed until he lies down to sleep again the same night. The narrative follows no causally motivated plot line, but rather derives its order from the sequential unfolding of events in time. As the occurrences of the day play out under the gaze of the temporarily docile Bagrov, the darker side of the old man's nature lies just beneath the surface. The old man's family and servants never forget that his volatile temper could erupt at any moment as they scurry to forestall his whims. The tension between the announced "good day" and the possibility of its disruption marks Stepan Mikhailovich's "good day" as a precursor to Ivan Denisovich's "good day," which likewise includes repeated references to potential threats (punishment cells, searches, illness, starvation). This similarity encourages comparison between the preceding century and the last years of Stalin's reign in which *Ivan Denisovich* is set. However threatening Aksakov's nineteenth-century patriarch may appear, his temper pales in relation to the horrors that Solzhenitsyn's protagonist faces in Stalin's Russia.

---

3   Tolstoy's short story "The Woodfelling" (Rubka lesa, 1855) represents another example of the one-day literary form. Kathryn B. Feuer proposes it as an intertext for *One Day in the Life of Ivan Denisovich*. Kathryn B. Feuer, "Solzhenitsyn and the Legacy of Tolstoy," in *Aleksandr Solzhenitsyn: Critical Essays and Documentary Materials*, ed. John B. Dunlop, Richard Haugh, and Alexis Klimoff, 2nd ed. (New York: Macmillan, 1975), 130. Other examples of pre-revolutionary Russian literary works that feature a narrative that unfolds within one or several days include Tolstoy's *Childhood* (1852), which focuses on two days in the protagonist's life, and a story that the same writer left unfinished entitled "The History of Yesterday" (1851), which was to relate the events of a single day.

4   Sergei Timofeevich Aksakov, *Semeinaia khronika*, in his *Sobranie sochinenii v chetyrekh tomakh* (Moscow: Khudozhestvennaia literatura, 1955), vol. 1, 91.

The social ills of pre-revolutionary Russia become trifles; the past, purely and simply, was better.

Time Forward as Intertext

The first one-day novel in Russian fiction and the only extended one-day narrative to appear in Soviet literature before *One Day in the Life of Ivan Denisovich* is Valentin Kataev's *Time, Forward!*, which drew its title from a line in Vladimir Maiakovskii's 1929 poem The "March of Time" (Marsh vremeni).[5] Kataev's "chronicle," as he himself terms it, is the most artful and eccentric of the production novels that glorified the achievements of the first five-year plan. In the early 1930s, as the Soviet government was consolidating its control over the literary process, writers were exhorted to travel to the far reaches of the Soviet Union to observe, write about, even participate in the building of the new Soviet society. Kataev, ever sensitive to changes in the political climate, was quick to comply, and, in response to a "social command" issued to writers in spring 1931, set off for Magnitogorsk in the Urals, where workers were building a mammoth metallurgical plant. There he found "so much that was amazing" that he ultimately opted to spend almost a year at the site as a representative of *The Workers' News* (Rabochaia gazeta). *Time Forward!* is a product of this trip.[6]

The plot of *Time, Forward!*, which centers on a successful attempt by a brigade of shock laborers to set a world record for the number of mixtures of concrete poured during a shift, is based on actual events. On May 29, 1931, early in Kataev's stay at Magnitogorsk, workers at the construction site entered into a "socialist competition" with brigades in Kuznetsk and Kharkov that focused on similar productivity measures. Kataev helped cover this competition for the newspaper *The Magnitogorsk Worker* (Magnitogorskii rabochii) and drew heavily on the details of it and the personalities involved while writing *Time, Forward!* In his novel, Kataev uses the theme of socialist competition to explore the controversy over increasing tempos of production and, in a broader sense, the question of how technology might redefine humanity's relationship to time—and to the forces of nature in general. Viktor Shklovskii, in his less

---

5   The bulk of the narrative of Andrei Belyi's novel *Petersburg* is confined within a one-day frame.

6   L. Skorino, *Pisatel' i ego vremia: Zhizn' i tvorchestvo V. P. Kataeva* (Moscow: Sovetskii pisatel', 1965), 228.

than enthusiastic review of *Time, Forward!*, recognized "the basic collision of the novel" as "the struggle for speed and the arguments against speed, against the outdistancing of time."[7]

Kataev identifies *Time, Forward!* as an illustration of the conception of time that constituted the underlying logic of the five-year plan as articulated by Stalin: time measured not by clocks, but by tempos and production levels. Launched on October 1, 1928 (although only belatedly approved by the Sixteenth Party Congress in April 1929), the first Soviet plan was originally scheduled to be completed five years later, on September 30, 1933. In 1930, however, Stalin called for Soviet citizens to step up production and fulfill the plan in four years instead of five, and the plan was officially declared at an end on December 31, 1932. The slogan "five in four" was emblematic of the times, expressing a seemingly unbounded faith that human beings, if they pushed themselves (or were pushed) hard enough, could mold time—and therefore the natural world—to their own ends. If time was quantifiable, and therefore relative, anything was possible, even the "overnight" transformation of agrarian Russia into a technologically advanced socialist society. The conception of time as a manipulatable substance owed as much to Russia's sense of inferiority in relation to the West as to Bolshevik scientific utopianism as we see in the speech "On the Tasks of Production Managers" (O zadachakh khoziaistvennikov), which Stalin delivered to industrial managers on February 4, 1931 and which Kataev cites in *Time, Forward!*: "To lower tempos means to fall back, and those who fall back are beaten. But we do not want to be beaten. No, we will not have it! This was the history of old Russia: it was continually beaten because of backwardness."[8] This was Russia's chance to strike back after centuries of humiliation and break with its past. It was not, however, simply a game of catchup. Forging ahead, ostensibly driven by the enthusiasm of Russia's newly "conscious" proletariat fired by Marxism-Leninism-Stalinism, Russia was to surpass its Western rivals, building a superior system.

In *Time, Forward!* this notion of time is most fully embodied in the figure of David Margulies, the novel's central character and the engineer who, as the

---

7   Viktor Shklovskii, "Siuzhet i obraz," *Literaturnaia gazeta*, August 17, 1932, 2.

8   Valentin Kataev, *Vremia, vpered!* (Leningrad: Lenizdat, 1980), 10. In translating passages from the novel, I have relied heavily on the translation: Valentine Kataev, *Time, Forward!*, trans. Charles Malamuth (New York: Farrar & Rinehart, 1933), 11–12. Henceforth page numbers from both editions, Russian first, will be given in parentheses in the text.

9. *One Day in the Life of Ivan Denisovich* and Its Intertexts | 181

primary representative of the positive forces struggling to "outdistance time," decides to go ahead with the record-breaking experiment. The ringing of Margulies's alarm clock at 6:30 on two successive mornings opens and closes the novel, marking the boundaries of the twenty-four-hour time frame within which the plot unfolds. Although the rattle of Margulies's cheap Soviet alarm clock initiates the narrative and we first meet Margulies as he is getting out of bed, Kataev makes it clear that it is not the alarm clock that has roused him: "Margulies was not asleep. He had woken up at six and had outstripped time. It had never yet happened that his alarm clock had really awakened him. Margulies could never entrust to such an essentially simple mechanism as a clock such a precious thing as time" (3; 3). Margulies "didn't own a watch. Somehow he was never able to 'hold onto' one." His acute sense of time derives rather from his observation of the events unfolding around him: "Time was the number of turns of the drum and the pulley, the hoisting of the scoop, the end or the beginning of a shift, the durability of the concrete, the whistle of the mechanism, the opening door of the cafeteria, the knitted brow of the timekeeper, the shadow of the plant moving from east to west and already reaching the railroad track..." (174; 219–220). Margulies equates time with the events that take place in it; it is for him not a metaphysical condition, but rather a medium of production.

Margulies finds his rival and antagonist in Nalbandov, a talented but conservative engineer who opposes Margulies's race against time with the slogan "construction is not a stunt" (stroitel'stvo ne frantsuzskaia bor'ba; 121; 154). Outwardly a dedicated Bolshevik, Nalbandov is in reality an opportunist who enjoys the company of decadent American capitalists and desires Margulies's downfall. The difference between the two engineers' perceptions of time emerges clearly when Nalbandov questions Margulies's decision to diverge from the "recommended" rates of production for the "current year." "Why shouldn't we," Margulies asks, "take advantage of next year's corrections, if we happen to discover them now?" Nalbandov answers with derision: "Oh, so you want to get ahead of time?" and then slams the initiative as "untimely." For Margulies, "It's always timely to move ahead"—particularly since this may help fulfill the plan (187; 235). While time in Aksakov's *Family Chronicle* appears as little more than an inherent, and therefore, neutral condition of narrative, time as a structural element in Kataev's twentieth-century "chronicle" becomes the driving force of events and language, which the human characters must race, conquer, bend to their will: "Time is concentrated. It flies. It interferes. It must be torn away from, leapt out of. It must be outdistanced" (54; 69). The "author" lays bare the device of his own restricted time frame by stepping outside of it and speaking in his own voice. The conflict between Margulies and Nalbandov over the correct tempo of production, can only be resolved seven days after the fact, when samples of the concrete poured during the record-breaking shift have been analyzed for quality in a laboratory. In order to reveal the results of the tests without breaching the restricted time frame of his narrative, Kataev temporarily discards his omniscient narrator and, speaking in his own name, discloses the information in a first chapter *cum* dedication placed not at the beginning of *Time, Forward!*, but rather in the penultimate division of the text:

> The denouement depends on the quality of the concrete.
> The quality of the concrete can be determined in no less than seven days.
> The time of the action of my chronicle is twenty-four hours.
> Thus, the composition would be violated.
> I would have to jump seven days ahead.
> Can this difficulty be solved?
>
> But there is a way out. I include the denouement in the dedication and I place the dedication not at the beginning, but before the last chapter.
>
> Under the banner of a dedication I put the denouement in its place and at the same time release myself from the responsibility of violating the structure. (268; 336–337)

The concrete cubes stand up under pressure, and Margulies is vindicated. The author leaps outside and ahead of time, using his own "technology" to manipulate the temporal structure of his narrative. Just as the work brigades in Magnitogorsk beat time by increasing the amount of concrete they can produce within a strictly defined time period—only to see their records bested immediately by workers at Kuznetsk and the Cheliabinsk tractor plant—so the writer "beats" the time structure of his own narrative.

Aside from the fact that *Time, Forward!* shares the one-day format of *One Day in the Life of Ivan Denisovich*, there are a number of other parallels between the two works that suggest a more than coincidental similarity. To cite only the most obvious correspondences: both *Time, Forward!* and *Ivan Denisovich* focus on the activities of a work brigade laboring on the site of a "socialist city" in an outlying region of the Soviet Union; in both the characters' struggle against the forces of nature is a central issue; and in both characters are defined primarily by their relationship to time. Moreover, a vituperative, if indirect allusion to *Time, Forward!* in Part Six of *The Gulag Archipelago* suggests that Solzhenitsyn may have envisioned *Ivan Denisovich* as a response to socialist realism in general and Kataev's novel in particular. In this section of *Gulag* Solzhenitsyn reserves some of his most trenchant ire for Soviet writers who, capitulating to the exigencies of the Stalinist establishment, painted a Potemkin facade over Soviet literature, masking the horrors of the labor camps. In one passage, after having described the nightmarish journey of a group of wives of "kulaks" into exile, Solzhenitsyn concludes: "This transport was driven to the great Magnitogorsk building operation. Their husbands were brought to join them. Dig away, house yourselves! From Magnitogorsk on, our bards have done their duty and reflected... reality?"[9] Thus, according to Solzhenitsyn, the construction site at Magnitogorsk was in fact an "island" in the Gulag Archipelago and Kataev's depiction of enthusiastic Soviet shock laborers—a blatant falsification of historical fact.[10] In this sense, *One Day in the Life of Ivan Denisovich*, as the first and most scathing exposé of the labor camps to be published in the Soviet Union before glasnost, appears as a counterbalance to *Time, Forward!* and other works that "varnished" Soviet reality. Yet, more than that, Solzhenitsyn in *One Day in the Life of Ivan Denisovich* seems to be arguing against the very basis of the conception of time that Kataev's novel promotes, against the blind faith in progress that forced *homo sovieticus* into a pointless and enslaving race with time. As we shall see, this polemic possesses a profound metaliterary dimension as well.

Time in *One Day in the Life of Ivan Denisovich*

The time frame of *One Day in the Life of Ivan Denisovich* spans seventeen hours, from 5 A.M. to approximately 10 P.M. the same night. Within these temporal boundaries, Solzhenitsyn recounts the events of one day in a Soviet labor

---

9   Aleksandr Solzhenitsyn, *Arkhipelag GULag*, in his *Sobranie sochinenii* (Paris: YMCA-Press, 1980), vol. 7, 361. Here I have used the existing English translation: Aleksandr I. Solzhenitsyn, *The Gulag Archipelago Three*, trans. Harry Willetts (New York: Perennial Library-Harper & Row, 1976), 360.

10 On conditions in Magnitogorsk in the 1930s, see John Scott, *Behind the Urals: An American Worker in Russia's City of Steel* (Bloomington: Indiana University Press, 1989); and Stephen Kotkin, *Magnetic Mountain: Stalinism as Civilization* (Berkeley: University of California Press, 1995).

camp from the point of view of the Russian peasant Ivan Denisovich Shukhov, who is serving the eighth year of his ten-year sentence. For Shukhov this is one of many days, a day like and yet unlike the 3,652 other days in his sentence, and he must muster all the canniness acquired through his years of incarceration to meet its challenges.

Like Aksakov's portrayal of Bagrov's day in the *Family Chronicle*, the narrative of *Ivan Denisovich* is essentially plotless, its events ordered solely by temporal sequence, but like *Time, Forward!* it is a work not only unfolding in time, but *about* time and humanity's relation to time. Shukhov, like Kataev's Margulies, races time, but Shukhov is racing for his survival in a universe controlled and bounded by time. The restriction of the narrative within a one-day frame parallels Ivan Denisovich's spatial confinement. As a close reading of *Ivan Denisovich* demonstrates, moreover, the true nature of Shukhov's imprisonment is not spatial, but temporal: freedom lies not in release from camp, but in escape from the power of time and of the material world it represents.

Like Aksakov and Kataev, Solzhenitsyn opens his narrative with an awakening scene, which establishes the initial time boundary of the narrative: "At five o'clock in the morning, as always, reveille was beaten out—with a hammer against the rail of the staff barrack."[11] The "as always" marks this event as part of the daily routine of the camp, which orders the prisoners' existence: "Shukhov never overslept reveille, always got up on time—before the march to work there was an hour and a half of one's own, not official time [*vremeni svoego, ne kazennogo*], and whoever knew camp life could always earn something" (7). While, on the one hand, time in the form of the camp routine rules Shukhov's life, on the other hand, within certain bounds the prisoner can use his "own" time, as a means of survival, of earning something on the side.

"Shukhov always got up at reveille, but today he didn't get up" (8). This initial break in routine establishes the tension between habitual and out of the ordinary events that defines the texture of the narrative. Departure from routine almost costs Shukhov dearly in this opening scene. Counting on the leniency of the orderly on duty, Ivan Denisovich decides to remain in bed a few extra moments. The expected orderly is not on duty, however, but rather a harsher one, and he threatens to punish Shukhov for his violation of the

---

[11] Aleksandr Solzhenitsyn, "Odin den' Ivana Denisovicha," in his *Sobranie sochinenii* (Paris: YMCA-Press, 1980), vol. 3, 7. Henceforth pages references to this edition will be given in parentheses in the text. All translations are my own.

camp schedule. The punishment is stated in temporal terms as well: "Three days *in the cooler with work as usual!*" (10, Solzhenitsyn's emphasis). Time here becomes a mode of punishment as well as a means of defining the seriousness of an offense. It is not only the duration, however, but also the quality of the punishment that is significant: for Shukhov the "cooler with work as usual" is preferable to the cooler with no work, because it leaves "no time to think" (10). The motif of having "no time" or of "not having enough time" (*nekogda*), of always being rushed and racing against time, recurs throughout *One Day in the Life of Ivan Denisovich* and represents the controlling concern of the protagonist.

Fortunately for Ivan Denisovich, the orderly does not really intend to make him serve his sentence in the cooler; he only needs someone to wash the floor in the staff barrack. This stroke of luck marks the auspicious beginning of Shukhov's "good day." Yet already in these first pages Solzhenitsyn has established the fundamental terms of the zek's existence: the camp authorities use time as a means of control, and the prisoners must adapt to this regimen and, when possible, themselves manipulate time in order to survive.

Shortly before the midday work break, Shukhov has a conversation with Buinovskii, a recent arrival in the camp and former captain in the Soviet Navy, that references both traditional understandings of time and "decree time," an equivalent to daylight saving's time that was employed in the Soviet Union from 1930:

> "It's exactly twelve," announced Shukhov also. "The sun's already at its highest point."
> "If it's at its highest point," retorted the Captain, "that means it's not twelve, but one."
> "Why's that?" Shukhov was amazed. "Any grandfather knows the sun stands highest at lunchtime."
> "That's grandfathers!" the Captain cut in, "but since that time there's been a decree that the sun rises highest at one."
> "Whose decree is that?"
> "The Soviet Government's!" (47–48)

After this conversation, Shukhov cannot keep himself from checking the sky just to see when the whistle blows for lunch break. The authorities control time completely within the camp itself, arrogating to themselves the power to tell time—just as the Soviet state controls time throughout the country through its power to set clocks forward.

Along with his freedom, the prisoner loses the right to "possess" time: "Not even a clock was ticking. Prisoners were not allowed to have timepieces. The bosses kept time for them" (19). Solzhenitsyn's descriptions of how Ivan Denisovich and the other prisoners get along without watches seem to echo, and parody, Kataev's account of Margulies's finely developed sense of time in *Time, Forward!*. Time is measured for the zeks not in terms of the hours of the day, but rather in the divisions imposed on the day by the camp authorities: "None of the zeks ever saw a clock with his own eyes, and what use would they be, clocks? A zek only had to know—is reveille soon? How long until the march to work? Until lunch? Until lights out?" (113). These daily activities, marked by beating on rails or a whistle, form the basis of the camp routine, of camp time, which elapses within natural time, marked by the movements of the sun and moon throughout *Ivan Denisovich*, but nonetheless alienated from it by the intervention of the authorities: "It was said that the evening prisoner count was at nine. Only it never ended at nine, they redid the count a second, and even a third time. You never got to sleep earlier than ten. And reveille, they said, was at five o'clock" (113). The time of day becomes a matter of rumor and conjecture for the prisoners.

Within the camp routine, the authorities bend clock and calendar time to their own ends:

> There wouldn't be a Sunday again this week [*voskresen'ia opiat' ne budet na etoi nedele*], they were embezzling [*zazhilivaiut*] Sunday again. He had expected this and they had expected this: if there were five Sundays in a month, then they were given three, and two they were driven out to work. He'd expected this, but when he heard it—it moved his whole soul, broke it: who wouldn't be sorry for a dear little Sunday? (93)

The phrasing here is interesting. The camp administrators are described as "stealing" Sunday, as if a day of the week were a physical commodity. The system of distributing rations is described in analogous terms. Every five days the productivity of the brigades is assessed and extra rations are allocated to those that meet targets—but only for four of the next five days. On the fifth day everyone receives the same ration: "'Got a good deal' meant that now for five days the bread ration would be good. Five, supposedly, but not five, but only four: of the five days the bosses confiscate [*zakhaltyrivaet*] one" (60). This passage may plausibly be construed as a satirical reference to the Stalinist slogan, mentioned earlier in this chapter, "five in four."

The authorities further constrict existence in the camp by imposing artificial time restrictions and deadlines. When Ivan Denisovich goes to the camp hospital in the morning to try to get released from work, he runs up against such a restriction: "Why are you so late? Why didn't you come in the evening? You know there's no reception in the morning? The list of those released from work is already at the Production Planning Section" (18). As Shukhov knows, the time restrictions in themselves are often empty regulations, but they are another means of constraining the zeks and forcing them to conform to the authorities' definition of time.

Deadlines, the necessity of rushing against time in order to survive, are an inherent element of camp existence. Beating time often represents a matter of life and death: "And then a moment presses, like now, you can't sit around any longer. Like it or not, you'd better hop to it. If we haven't made ourselves a shelter—we'll all perish here" (43). The camp guards intentionally rush the prisoners in order to keep them off balance. This tactic is used on the zeks when they go to pick up packages sent to them from outside: "They rush some so that they'll forget something on the counter. Don't bother going back for it. It won't be there" (93).

Time also becomes a means of creating competition, and therefore dissent and distrust, among the prisoners. After work the zeks huddle in shelters waiting for the march back to camp. None of them wants to be the first to go: "No one comes out immediately after the bell, there's no one stupid enough to freeze there. They all sit in shelters. But the moment comes when all the foremen agree, and all the gangs come out together. If they didn't come to an agreement, prisoners are such a maliciously stubborn people that sitting one another out, they'd sit in the shelters until midnight" (75). The same situation arises at the evening count when no one wants to come out before the others: "and now to freeze an extra ten minutes? We're not fools. You die today, and I'll go tomorrow!" (113). On the other hand, everyone wants to be the first to arrive back at the camp after work (79). The authorities use this type of temporal rivalry to turn the zeks against one another: "Who's a prisoner's worst enemy? Another prisoner. If the prisoners didn't squabble with one another, the bosses wouldn't have any power over them" (88). Time, as manipulated by those in charge of the camp, becomes a divisive force, a measure of the power that the authorities can exercise over the prisoners precisely because the latter are manipulated into submitting to the temporal parameters imposed on them through the system of confinement.

Time is also defined for the zek by his work gang, which constitutes the fundamental structuring unit of life in the camp. The members of Shukhov's gang work together, eat together, and live together in their own corner of the barrack: "Like a large family, it is a family, the work gang" (61). Tiurin, the foreman of Shukhov's gang, is the head of this "family": "For us the foreman is like a father" (71). When Tiurin orders his men back to work before the end of the lunch break, they obey: "That's what a work gang is. Even during working hours a boss can't move a worker, but the foreman says work during a break and it means work. Because he feeds you, the foreman. And besides he doesn't force you to do anything for no reason" (64). The foreman has a certain limited power over time, but ultimately even he must bend to the camp routine, just as Tiurin must finally call a halt to work at the end of the day: "The foreman is a force, but the convoy is a stronger force" (76). Whatever power the foreman may have over the disposition of time within the camp schedule, he is still at the mercy of those in charge of the camp. The work gang, moreover, in Solzhenitsyn's novella, turns out to be nothing more than another method of control. Each gang member's rations and life depend on the work of the others; no one can shirk. Thus, the gang keeps the zeks in line (43).

Beyond the insidious grind of routine, beyond the ever-present threat of the "cooler," lies the sentence. The sentence might seem the primary fixed temporal factor in a zek's life, but in reality it could easily morph from a bounded time period to an endless state: "Shukhov raised his head to the sky and gasped: the sky was clear, and the sun was almost at its highest point. Miracle of miracles: that's how time flew by during work! How many times Shukhov had noticed: the days in the camp flew by—in the blink of an eye. But the sentence itself never moved, it never got less at all" (47).

The experienced zek knows that the authorities can easily slap on another term, and he therefore has little faith in the end of his sentence: "But no one's sentence had ever ended in this camp" (27). Nonetheless, Ivan Denisovich, who is "finishing his term," cannot help but hope: "sometimes you think—your heart jumps: all the same my term is ending, the spindle is unwinding.... Lord! On my own two feet—to freedom?" (49). The true horror of Shukhov's position, of his secret and pitiful desire for an end to his term, is that, as we shall see, life outside is hardly better than life within the confines of the camp.

Ivan Denisovich's struggle for survival is dogged, but Sisyphean; the endless sentence becomes a metaphor for existential imprisonment in time.

Shukhov's existence centers on the struggle for physical survival, and in order to survive, the zek must learn to conserve and exploit time. In manipulating time to their own ends, the prisoners might seem to be placing themselves in opposition to their captors, who exercise total control over their lives, but in reality their attempts—and particularly those of Ivan Denisovich—to claim their "own" time show how they have been co-opted and accept the regimentation of camp time. Just as the authorities "steal" time from the zeks, so the zeks grab moments for themselves within the camp schedule, as, in the morning, they take advantage of the disorganization of the work assigners: "But this moment is ours! While the bosses are figuring everything out, stick in the warmest place possible, sit down, sit, you'll still get a chance to break your back" (35). These pilfered moments seem to make the overall time regimen less oppressive: "And even though the 104th sat barely twenty minutes and the workday—a winter, shortened one—went until six, still it seemed to all of them as if now evening wasn't far away" (38). The zek must move slowly and guard his time if he is to survive. This is the lesson that Buinovskii, lingering for a few moments in the warmth of the mess hall after lunch, is just beginning to learn: "He hadn't been in the camp long, hadn't been long at hard labor. Such minutes, like now, were (he didn't know it) especially important minutes for him, transforming him from a powerful, ringing sea officer into a little-moving, wary zek. Only through this ability to move little would he be able to overcome the twenty-five years of prison allotted to him" (57). As it turns out, however, even the seasoned old camp hand Ivan Denisovich has not truly mastered this principle and remains in thrall to time as defined by the camp.

The moments the prisoner spends eating are the focal point of his day, and they especially must not be rushed: "rushed, food isn't food. It's all wasted, doesn't satisfy" (21). The anticipation of eating blocks out all other concerns and becomes the force governing the zek's existence: "This scoop of gruel was for him now more precious than freedom, more precious than his whole past and future life" (91). These "holy minutes" (101) are the only time within the camp routine the prisoner truly has for himself: "However, he [Shukhov] began to eat it just as slowly, attentively, so that even if the roof were to catch on fire—you shouldn't rush. Not counting sleep, the prisoner lives for himself only ten minutes in the morning at breakfast, five at lunch, and five at supper" (15–16). Eating soothes and provides a respite from the constant pressure of time. "Now nothing bothered Shukhov: not that his sentence was long, not that the day was long, not that there again wouldn't be any Sunday. Now he thought: we'll survive! We'll survive it all, God grant an end to it!" (101).

Yet there is another, no less compelling relationship between food and time established in *Ivan Denisovich*: food is the most urgent necessity for physical survival, and time is a means of acquiring it. Aware of the value of time, Shukhov is extremely jealous of his "own" (*svoe*) time as opposed to "official" (*kazennoe*) time. During his "own" time, the precious hours spent in camp before and after work, Shukhov, as an experienced zek, can earn a little extra. On this particular day, the disappearance of a prisoner after work holds up the march back to camp, and it is the loss of their "own" time that angers Shukhov and the other prisoners: "It's no joke to grab more than half an hour from five hundred men!" (83). Again time is described as if it were a commodity, and, in fact, it becomes a commodity for the prisoners no less than for their jailers, a commodity that can be exchanged for bread. After returning to camp in the evening, Shukhov "sells" time to Caesar, a "well-off" member of his work gang, by agreeing to stand in the package line for him. He tacitly expects to receive Caesar's evening ration in return for his time, or, if Caesar's package has not arrived, to profit by selling his place in line (and, by implication, his time) to someone else (88).

Shukhov never seems to have enough time; he is always racing around trying to "earn something on the side." In the morning after returning to the barrack from the infirmary, for instance, Shukhov rushes to get ready for work (21–22). Shukhov realizes the zek's need to conserve movement, but the pressure of time forces him to break this tenet. Although he knows that "rushing, food isn't food," the desire for an extra serving gets the better of him at lunch: "This minute he should focus all his attention on his food and, taking the thin layer of kasha from the bottom, carefully lift it to his mouth, and there roll it around with his tongue. *But he had to hurry* so that Pavlo would see that he had finished and offer him another kasha" (56, emphasis mine—C. T. N.). This food eaten in haste does not, however, sate Ivan Denisovich's hunger: "Shukhov finished the kasha. Because he had immediately opened his stomach for two—one didn't satisfy him as oatmeal always did" (56). Sometimes Ivan Denisovich seems to rush merely because the habit of trying to beat time has become so ingrained: "Shukhov got some bowls too and shoved them through the hatch, not to get anything extra for himself, but to speed things up" (53).

Nekogda, not having enough time, recurs as a leitmotif throughout Solzhenitsyn's narrative. Although, for instance, Shukhov knows that this camp is much freer than the one he was in before, that you can say anything you want without fear of reprisal, he finds no time to make use of this freedom: "Only there was no time [*nekogda*] to talk much" (105). By the same token, time pressure, or rather the zek's submission to it, drives away all thoughts of the world outside, of the home and family left behind. Like other prisoners, Sukhov routinely refers to the camp and his barrack as "home": "They didn't have any time [*nekogda*] to think about any other home during the day" (88). Shukhov, the narrator later notes, "had still less and less reason to remember the village of Temgenevo and his home cottage. . . . The life here drove him from reveille to lights out, leaving no time for idle memories" (93). The grueling routine of camp life wipes out the zek's past and controls his future, focusing all his attention on the present moment and the struggle to stay alive.

Only at work laying bricks does Shukhov appear to escape temporarily from camp time. In his work Ivan Denisovich reveals himself as the honest Russian peasant he is, drawing satisfaction from the physical labor and a job well done. Pride in his work ultimately brings Shukhov into confrontation with the camp schedule. At the end of the work shift, Shukhov's gang is left with too much mortar, which will freeze and go to waste if it is not used immediately. Shukhov offers to stay behind to finish the job, since his trowel does not have to be turned in. He continues working even after Tiurin tells him not to worry about the mortar, and, even after he has finished, he cannot resist pausing to admire his work even though the delay may anger the convoy (77).

Yet even at work Shukhov rushes, moved by some pressure from inside himself, and the motif of *nekogda* again appears: "Shukhov wanted to find out, but there was no time [*nekodga*]" (70). In another passage, the narrator notes: "The work moved at such a pace—there was no time [*nedosug*] to wipe your nose." (68) Shukhov, moreover, appears constantly to be racing against his partner Kil'digs and the other members of his brigade: he worries that he might "fall behind" (69) and rushes "to grab the plumb before Kil'digs" (64). Kil'digs is much more easygoing in his approach to his work: he "lays bricks the way they weigh medicine in a pharmacy; there's no way to rush the doctor" (72). Ivan Denisovich resents Kil'digs's attitude, ascribing it to the fact that his partner does not live off the gang's rations and therefore his life is not on the line (64). Shukhov envies the better fed and therefore, to his way of thinking, freer Kil'digs. The irony here is that Shukhov also is not working "for himself," but rather for the benefit of his captors. He has indeed been more thoroughly co-opted by the system than has Kil′digs, because he is completely dependent on the food it provides.

Time flies for Ivan Denisovich while he is working, leaving "no time to think": "And all thoughts were swept from his head. Shukhov now didn't remember anything and didn't worry about anything, but only thought—how he should lay the pipe joints and lead it out so it didn't smoke" (44). Such passages suggest that the race with time blots out even more important considerations, that this forgetfulness represents less a release than a narrowing of vision: "And Shukhov no longer saw the distant horizon where the sun was shining on the snow, nor how the workers wandered around the zone from shelters—some to dig holes, which since morning hadn't been dug out, some to strengthen the framework, some to raise rafters in the workshops. Shukhov saw only his wall" (66).

Shukhov's priorities become clear at the evening meal, when he finally finds time to linger and savor his food: "But he had to chew each fishbone and fin thoroughly—to suck out the juice, the beneficial juice. Of course, all of this required time, and Shukhov had nowhere to rush to now, today was a holiday for him: he'd torn away two portions at lunch and two portions at supper. Thanks to such affairs other affairs could be left undone" (102). As he is eating, an old man from the 64th work gang sits down across from him. The old man is a perpetual prisoner: "Shukhov had heard about this old man that he had served countless years in camps and prisons, that he'd served as long as there'd been a Soviet Government and not one amnesty had touched him, and as soon as one ten was finished, they immediately threw him another" (102). The nameless old zek stands out because of the straightness of his back, because of his measured movements and his fortitude; he emerges as an instructive symbol, a model for the survival not only of the body, but of human dignity. Yet Shukhov, who moments before seemingly had all the time in the world, has no time to contemplate this exemplar. As soon as he finishes eating, he is on the run again: "But Shukhov didn't have time [*nekogda*] to examine him long" (103). By the same token, a few moments later he has no time to stop and look at the moon, a marker of natural time which implicitly suggests the possibility of transcending the authorities' control of time: "Shukhov had even less time [*men'she bylo u Shukhova vremeni*] to look at the sky" (103). The true nature of Ivan Denisovich's unfreedom lies in his rush to sustain his physical existence, which leaves him with no time to learn and ponder the meaning of life or to remember: "So you just went on living like this, with your eyes to the ground, and you had no time [*vremeni-to ne byvaet*] to think about how you got in and when you'd get out" (49).

Throughout *Ivan Denisovich*, Shukhov's bunkmate, Aleshka the Baptist, stands in marked contrast to Shukhov. We first meet Aleshka, whispering his prayers, in the opening scene, and, as Shukhov rushes through his day, Aleshka remains always in the background, praying or reading the Gospels. While Shukhov has no time to look at the moon, Aleshka greets the rising of the sun with gladness that intimates his unmediated link with nature and natural time: "The sun rose big, red, as if in a mist. Next to Shukhov Aleshka looked at the sun and was happy, a smile appeared on his lips. His cheeks were sunken, he was surviving on his ration alone, didn't earn anything on the side—what did he have to be happy about?" (33–34). Aleshka remains incomprehensible to Shukhov. Throughout *One Day in the Life of Ivan Denisovich*, as the question posed in the last sentence of the passage just cited demonstrates, we see Aleshka through Shukhov's eyes, through a narrative voice that generally adopts the title character's point of view. Therefore Aleshka is implicitly judged by Shukhov's standards. Not until the end of the day, as the prisoners are lying in their bunks before lights out, does Aleshka speak for himself. The perspective he provides calls Shukhov's standards into doubt.

The scene between Ivan Denisovich and Aleshka opens with an exclamation in the form of a prayer that is voiced by Shukhov: "Thank you, Lord, that another day has passed!" (115). Characteristically, even in this communication formally addressed to God, time remains Shukhov's central concern. Shukhov's prayer reaches Aleshka, who is reading the Gospels: "Look, Ivan Denisovich, your soul wants to pray to God. Why don't you give it freedom [*voli*], eh?" (115–16) Aleshka here alludes to a different kind of freedom: not freedom from the spatial confines of prison, but rather what he views as freedom of the soul. Shukhov's answer shows that his perception of reality is too different from Aleshka's and too tainted by his years in the camps for him to understand. "Because, Aleshka, prayers are like complaints," Shukhov says, referencing the formal petitions for redress that prisoners submitted to the central authorities, "either they don't reach their addressee or they're rejected" (116). Aleshka and Shukhov live in different conceptual realms. Ivan Denisovich comprehends everything in terms of his experience in the camps, and he must translate everything Aleshka says and does into his own linguistic and empirical terms in order to respond. He is a literalist, while Aleshka communicates and views the world in terms of metaphors of faith. This difference emerges again when Aleshka explains why Shukhov's prayers remain unanswered:

> "It's because you pray little, badly, without zeal, and that's why your prayers aren't answered. Prayer must be unremitting! And if you have faith and tell that mountain—move! —it will move." [...]
> "Stop babbling, Aleshka. I've never seen a mountain move. Well, to tell the truth, I've never even seen a mountain. And in the Caucasus when your whole Baptist club prayed—did even one move?" [...]
> "But we didn't pray for that, Ivan Denisovich." (116)

Aleshka's metaphor of the moving mountain becomes for Shukhov a real mountain. Ivan Denisovich is a "doubting Thomas," who demands tangible proof of God's existence before he can believe. Notably, when the Captain asks Shukhov whether or not he believes in God, the latter responds: "And why not? [...] When He thunders up there in the sky how can you help but believe in Him?" (79).

Yet earlier in *One Day in the Life of Ivan Denisovich* Solzhenitsyn provides an ironic comment on Shukhov's attitude toward prayer, which, when juxtaposed with this later scene, calls the zek's whole vision of the world into question. As Shukhov is about to pass through the evening search carrying a piece of saw blade he has found, he prays to God to help him smuggle it past the guards: "Lord! Save me! Don't give me the cooler!" (90). Shukhov is aided in getting through the search by incredible luck, if not divine intervention. Just as the guard is about to feel his second mitten, where the piece of steel is hidden, the order is given to move on to the next column. Now, however, Shukhov has no time for a prayer of thanks: "And he didn't pray again, with gratitude, because there wasn't time [*nekogda bylo*], and besides there was no more need" (90). Shukhov's relationship to God, like his relationship to time, is rooted in his preoccupation with physical survival and material existence.

Aleshka goes on to chide Shukhov for this utilitarian attitude toward prayer, and Shukhov, in his answer, again translates Aleshka's figurative language into the terms of the camp:

> "Out of everything earthly and perishable, the Lord told us to pray only for our daily bread: 'Give us this day our daily bread!'"
> "The ration, you mean?" asked Shukhov. [...]

> "Ivan Denysich! That's not what you should pray for, that they send you a package or that you get an extra portion of gruel. What is important to people is nothing before God! You have to pray for the spiritual [*Molit'sia nado o dukhovnom*]: for the Lord to take evil from our hearts...." (116)

Here Aleshka comes to the crux of the difference between his vision of reality and Shukhov's: Shukhov is constantly racing against time to feed himself. He admires Aleshka's ability to function in the camp. He is impressed by the fact that Aleshka is able to hide his copy of the Gospels so that the guards do not find it: "That's what Aleshka did well: he pushed his little book so deftly into the chink in the wall—they still hadn't found it in a single search" (22). He also admires Aleshka as a willing and obedient worker: "Humble—a treasure in the gang" (70). Ivan Denisovich even admits the superiority of Aleshka's way of doing things: "Aleshka never refused anything, no matter what you asked him to do. If everyone in the world were like that, then Shukhov would be that way too" (74).

In the final analysis, however, Aleshka's approach to life is beyond Shukhov's understanding. He cannot comprehend how someone who lives only on his ration can smile at the sunrise: "For them [the Baptists] the camp rolled like water off a duck's back" (33). Aleshka is not concerned with what "is nothing before God." He prays for his daily bread, lives on his ration or whatever falls to his lot, and, apparently, occupies his time with concern for his soul, rather than for his body. He is content, but Shukhov can only pity him for his helplessness and inability to "earn anything" (119). Aleshka does not worry where his next meal is coming from—God will provide. Ivan Denisovich, on the other hand, spends all his time worrying about sustaining his body. Yet every bit of food he secures, even the piece of sausage given to him by Caesar as he talks with Aleshka, affords him only transitory enjoyment, showing that food and the pleasure, and benefit derived from it are ephemeral.

At its conclusion, the conversation between Aleshka and Ivan Denisovich comes full circle, back to the question of time:

> "In general," he [Shukhov] decided, "no matter how much you pray, they won't take anything off your sentence. All the same you'll sit it out from bell to bell."
>
> "But you shouldn't pray for that!" Aleshka was horrified. "What do you want with freedom? In freedom your last faith will be choked

> by thorns! Be glad you're in prison! *Here you have time to think about your soul!* The Apostle Paul spoke thus: 'Why do you cry and break my heart? I not only want to be a prisoner, but I am ready to die for the name of the Lord Jesus!'"
>
> Shukhov silently looked at the ceiling. He no longer even knew whether he wanted freedom or not. At the beginning he wanted it very much and every evening counted how many days of his sentence had passed, how many were left. And then he got sick of it. And then it became clear that they didn't let the likes of him go home, just drove them into exile. And where his life would be better—here or there—he didn't know.
>
> Only he still wanted to ask God—to go home.
>
> *But they didn't let you go home.* . . . (117–18; emphasis mine—C. T. N.)

Aleshka, freed of concern about his physical being, has time to think about his soul—the time Shukhov never seems to have. More important, he has implicitly achieved liberation from the authorities who define time in the camp. What is truly grim about Ivan Denisovich's situation is not the physical suffering to which he is subjected, but the fact that, in a profound sense, his existence is pointless, because he fails to understand the true nature of his imprisonment. He does not realize that in the outside world, where many villagers from his own home region, dispossessed by collectivization, have been forced to take work as carpet painters and race between cities on airplanes to "save time" (32), the same temporal prison awaits him, the same pressures that keep him from "thinking about his soul." Shukhov no longer knows why or even whether he wants this freedom just as he does not know why he is in prison: "'You see, Aleshka,' Shukhov explained, 'somehow everything's worked out fine for you: Christ ordered you to go to prison and you went. But what did I go to prison for? Because they weren't prepared for war in forty-one, for that? What'd I have to do with it?'" (118). The conversation is cut off at this point by the evening count, but Aleshka has already given his answer earlier in the narrative: "But let none of you suffer as a murderer, or as a thief, or as an evildoer, or as a busybody in other men's affairs. Yet if any man suffer as a Christian, let him not be ashamed, but let him glorify God on this behalf" (22).[12]

Shukhov is imprisoned less by his physical confinement in the camp than by his own preoccupation with his material needs and, therefore, by his sub-

---

12 Aleshka cites 1 Peter 4:15.

jugation by time. He makes clear what matters to him when he enumerates all the good things that have happened to him on this day as the narrative draws to a close: "They hadn't put him in the cooler, they hadn't driven the work gang out to the socialist city, he'd finagled an extra kasha at lunch, the foreman had gotten good rates, he'd enjoyed laying the wall, they hadn't caught him with the saw blade during the search, he'd gotten something off Caesar in the evening and had bought tobacco. And he hadn't gotten sick, he'd recovered" (120). The narrator adds: "There were three thousand six hundred and fifty-three such days in his sentence from bell to bell. The three extra were because of leap years...." (120).

The Ethical and Metaliterary Implications of Solzhenitsyn's Intertexts

The parallels between Ivan Denisovich's race against time in Solzhenitsyn's novella and Margulies's race against time in *Time, Forward!* appear obvious. In simple terms, what separates them is the plus or minus sign that their respective authors place before the efforts of their protagonists to "outdistance" time. While Kataev's novel constitutes an *apologia* for the Stalin Revolution based on the conviction that the new order will free humanity from the "decadent materialism" of the West, Solzhenitsyn casts the race with time as a virtual apotheosis of materialism, the enslavement of human beings by the needs of their bodies.

Just as he places temporal constraints on his narrative in *One Day*, constricting it to a single day, Solzhenitsyn also limits the text's narrative perspective. While virtually all his other works either focus on the experiences of educated characters or have narrators, omniscient or otherwise, who are endowed with above average intellectual resources, the third-person narrative of *Ivan Denisovich* essentially adopts the point of view of the text's title character, a poorly educated peasant who, despite a certain practical shrewdness, has a narrow conceptual horizon. Solzhenitsyn's use of free indirect discourse in *Ivan Denisovich* has misled many critics: succumbing to the sympathy for Shukhov that the text arouses, they view him as an exemplary figure. I would argue this rhetorical stance serves a different purpose. We as readers are lured into empathizing with an unperceptive character—and, more important, with a character who has accepted almost completely the terms of existence imposed on him by the camp—in order to be drawn more profoundly into the atrocity of the experiences described. We can discern the workings of this strategy most clearly in Ivan Denisovich's affirmation that the day he lives through in the course of the narrative is a "good day." The narrative, by encouraging us to identify with the central character, also prompts us to accept his standards of evaluation and to join with him in pronouncing the day "good." This "good," however, makes sense only within the context of the labor camp. By accepting, if only temporarily, Ivan Denisovich's judgment of his day, we too share in the horror of his existence as well as the degradation of his frame of reference, which is so profound that it might allow one to find something "good" in the torment that he faces. Ivan Denisovich is neither "heroic" nor exemplary; he is rather Everyman. Just as his day comes to represent the 3,653 days of his sentence, so he implicitly is merely one of many, better than some and worse than others, and the entire nation is incriminated in the experience of these victims of the Soviet labor camp system.

Returning to the intertexts that, I have proposed, constitute the context for reading *Ivan Denisovich*, we recall that *Family Chronicle* is a fictionalized reminiscence of the past, which, juxtaposed to Solzhenitsyn's novella, prompts us to compare the Russian nineteenth and twentieth centuries, thereby creating a historical perspective for the events recounted in the later work. In contrast, the suppression of historical perspective is an integral aspect of the narrative structure in *Time, Forward!*. The uprooting of characters from their past lives, the focus on their present labors to build the future, constitutes a fundamental condition of the ideology of the text, which associates the "noise of time," a phrase that for Russian readers evokes the work and worldview of the acmeist poet Osip Mandelstam, with the "decadent" civilization of the West, where "history spoke in a stone language of portals, quays, stairways, chapels, basilicas" and where cities "echo" with "legends and conjectures" (124; 157–58).[13] Magnitogorsk, on the other hand, as the wealthy American Ray Rup notes, is a city without a history (124–25; 157–58). The socialist experiment Kataev chronicles represents a break with the past and a new beginning of history. In contrast, *One Day in the Life of Ivan Denisovich* attests, albeit less explicitly than some of Solzhenitsyn's other works, to the cost of the jettisoning of the past that was an integral part of the Stalin terror.

It has been argued that Shukhov stands at the top of the "moral scale" along which Solzhenitsyn ranges the characters in *Ivan Denisovich* because

---

13 Mandelstam titled a collection of autobiographical prose sketches that he published in 1925 *The Noise of Time* (Shum vremeni).

he "holds values not shared by his society—values of an older time."[14] While Shukhov's adherence to a work ethic that places quality and efficiency over the deadlines imposed on him by his gaolers does appear as a vestige of his peasant roots, he has been rendered vulnerable to the machinations of the authorities because he has been torn from the traditional life of the village, just as his fellow villagers have been forced by collectivization to take up the debased "art" of stenciling patterns onto carpets. Aleshka's transcendent values, on the other hand, are implicitly rooted in fidelity to an ongoing tradition represented by the canonical text of the Gospels.

In this context, Solzhenitsyn's apparent choice of *Time, Forward!* as the target of his assault on socialist realism has interesting metaliterary implications. Kataev's "chronicle" is far from a representative work of Stalinist prose. Rather it enjoyed an ambiguous status in the socialist realist canon.[15] Kataev, who earned his literary reputation as a "fellow traveler" in the 1920s, makes ample use of modernist devices in his narrative (rapid fire cuts between visual perspectives, materials, and scenes that recall cinematic montage; marked and self-conscious manipulation of time reminiscent of cinematic flashbacks, flashforwards, and changes in projection speed; the use of exaggerated figurative language and a lyrical style that calls to mind the work of Vladimir Maiakovskii) to an extent that was already becoming unacceptable in official Soviet literature when Kataev was writing *Time, Forward!*. In directing his polemic at Kataev's novel, Solzhenitsyn implicitly suggests a line of continuity connecting the early twentieth-century avant-garde with socialist realism, anticipating the pioneering work of Boris Groys.[16]

By confining his narrative perspective to the point of view of a barely literate peasant, Solzhenitsyn leaves little opportunity for sophisticated discussions of art and literature in his novella, but Ivan Denisovich overhears two conversations between intellectuals that support this association of socialist realism with Russian modernism. Caesar—who, by his ability to fi-

---

14   Gary Kern, "Ivan the Worker," *Modern Fiction Studies* 23, no. 1 (Spring 1977): 16, 20. Kern places Shukhov together with Aleshka at the top of the moral hierarchy in which he views the prisoners as being ranged in *One Day*.

15   When the novel first appeared, it was extensively criticized in the Soviet press, as documented by Skorino, *Pisatel' i ego vremia*, 249–50.

16   Boris Groys, *The Total Art of Stalinism: Avant-Garde, Aesthetic Dictatorship, and Beyond* (Princeton: Princeton University Press, 1992), 9.

nagle for himself a relatively comfortable existence and to set himself apart from the common lot of the prisoners, stands as a condemnation of the artistic intelligentsia—participates in both exchanges, and both concern Sergei Eisenstein, one of the most formally innovative artists to espouse Bolshevik ideology and to continue to create under the Stalin regime. One of these conversations, which focuses on the historical accuracy of Eisenstein's 1925 film *The Battleship "Potemkin"* (Bronenosets "Potemkin"), takes place between the former cameraman Caesar and the former naval officer Buinovskii while the brigade, held up from the evening march back to camp, is waiting for the convoy guards to find the missing prisoner. In it, Caesar's enthusiasm for cinematic artistry and faith in Eisenstein's vision contrasts with Buinovskii's skepticism, which is born of life experience.

> "That's exactly how it was historically!"
> "And then who led them into battle?... Then the larvae on the meat crawl like earthworms. Can they really have been like that?"
> "But you can't show anything smaller with the resources of the cinema!"
> "I think that if they were to bring that meat to us in the camp now instead of our shitty little fish, without washing it, without scraping it off, if they dropped it into a cauldron, we would...." (82)

Buinovskii is cut off by a cry from the zeks heralding the discovery of the missing prisoner, but the conclusion to his sentence is clear: "we would eat the meat." As Gary Kern points out: "a tendentious point is made: the zeks are in worse condition than the sailors who refused to eat the meat, mutinied and heralded the 1905 Revolution."[17] Aside from affirming again the superiority of life under the old regime, the text suggests a connection between the technology of artistic creation and falsification, truth sacrificed to technique. Art's responsibility to reflect life is clearly suggested in this confrontation between artist-technician and seaman in which the veracity of formal device is challenged based on lived experience.

This conversation about Eisenstein must, moreover, be read within the context of an earlier discussion of Eisenstein's work, which Shukhov overhears when he delivers Caesar's lunch ration. While the conversation with Buinovskii concerns a film produced during the relatively relaxed cultural

---

17 Kern, "Ivan the Worker," 8.

conditions of NEP, the earlier exchange focuses on Eisenstein's *Ivan the Terrible* (Ivan Groznyi), which was produced during the mid 1940s, under a fully developed Stalinist system.[18] With his back to Shukhov, who he does not see, Caesar speaks with X-123, an older prisoner with a twenty-year sentence:

> "No, old fellow," said Caesar mildly. "Objectivity requires the recognition that Eisenstein was a genius. Is *Ivan the Terrible* not a work of genius? The dance of the oprichniki with torches! The scene in the cathedral!"
> "Affectation [*Krivlian'e*]!" X-123 said angrily, suspending his spoon in front of his mouth. "There's so much art that it's not art anymore. Pepper and poppy seeds instead of daily bread! And then the vilest political idea—the justification of individual tyranny. A mockery of three generations of the Russian intelligentsia! (He was eating the kasha with an insensible mouth, it was doing him no good.)
> "But what other interpretation would have gotten through?..."
> "Oh, would have *gotten through*? Then don't talk about genius. Say a toady who filled a beastly order. Geniuses do not adjust their interpretations to the taste of tyrants!" (59, Solzhenitsyn's emphasis)

Shukhov clears his throat, hesitantly interrupting the conversation to offer Caesar a bowl of kasha, but Caesar continues the conversation, hardly acknowledging him: "Art is not *what*, but *how*." X-123 responds by challenging this implicit defense of the primacy of form: "The devil take your 'how,' if it doesn't arouse good feelings in me [*k chertovoi materi vashe "kak," esli ono dobrykh chuvstv vo mne ne probudit*]!" (59, Solzhenitsyn's emphasis).

As elsewhere in *Ivan Denisovich*, Solzhenitsyn's "stage directions" prompt the reader to take sides in this argument. Caesar's complete disregard of Shukhov suggests the *intelligent*'s blindness and insensitivity to others (implicitly here the *narod*) and to the reality that surrounds him. Thus, discrediting Caesar's contention that aesthetic value derives purely from the formal properties of a work of art, Solzhenitsyn nudges the reader toward accepting X-123's counterargument. That argument, moreover, is endowed with an unimpeach-

---

18 The two scenes Caesar discusses here are from Part Two of *Ivan the Terrible*, which was condemned during the Zhdanov cultural purge in 1946, and could not be released until 1958. Since *One Day* is set in 1951 and Eisenstein's film seems to have been viewed by only a very small and select political audience before its suppression, Solzhenitsyn appears to take liberties with chronology here.

able literary pedigree; its roots reach back to the two writers James Curtis, adopting Harold Bloom's terminology, has rightly identified as the most formidable "precursors" in the Russian literary tradition: Pushkin and Tolstoy.[19] X-123's concluding words in fact constitute a veiled allusion to Pushkin's 1836 "I erected a monument not built by hands. . . " (Ia pamiatnik sebe vozdvig nerukotvornyi. . .) and to the lyric's third stanza in particular:

> И долго буду тем любезен я народу,
> Что чувства добрые я лирой пробуждал,
> Что в мой жестокой век восславил я Свободу
>   И милость к падшим призывал.[20]

> And long will I be beloved of the people,
> Because I *aroused good feelings* with my lyre,
> Because in my cruel time I praised Freedom
>   And called for mercy for the fallen. (Emphasis mine: C. T. N.)

X-123's paraphrase of Pushkin also recalls Tolstoy's contention in *What is Art* (*Chto takoe iskusstvo*) that all true art is "infectious," that is, arouses ethically appropriate emotions in the reader. The worth of both writer and text rest not on formal virtuosity, but rather on their ability to move the reader.[21] Ironically, Solzhenitsyn views the writer as being no less of an "engineer of human souls" than did Stalin. He simply claims to possess a higher truth, gleaned through bitter experience, and seeks to "infect" the reader with the power of his message.

Solzhenitsyn's rejection of modernism and his defense of the writer's role as a teller of truths and an arbiter of values, which we see reflected in the two conversations about aesthetics that appear in *One Day in the Life of Ivan Denisovich*, found fuller expression in some of the aesthetic statements that he issued later in his career. For example, in a 1993 address to the National Arts Club in New York entitled "The Relentless Cult of Novelty and How It

---

19 James Curtis, *Solzhenitsyn's Traditional Imagination* (Athens: University of Georgia Press, 1984), 31–35.

20 A. S. Pushkin, *Polnoe sobranie sochinenii v shestnadtsati tomakh* (Moscow: Izdatel'stvo AN SSSR, 1937–1959), vol. 3, part 1, 424 (emphasis and translation are mine—C. T. N.).

21 L. N. Tolstoi, *Chto takoe iskusstvo*, in his *Polnoe sobranie sochinenii v dvadtsati tomakh*, vol. 15 (Moscow: Khudozhestvennaia literatura, 1964), 85–89.

Wrecked the Century" Solzhenitsyn attacked the "avant-gardism" and the "relentless cult of novelty" that, he believed, had, since its emergence just before World War II, precipitated a cultural "crisis" as the result of its renunciation of the past and privileging of form over meaning.[22] Although Solzhenitsyn, in this speech, depicts the West as undergoing an "erosion and obscuring of moral and ethical ideals" as a result of this artistic trend, he suggests that Russia has paid the highest price, stopping just short of blaming the Revolution and its aftermath on the Russian avant-garde, which demanded "the classics of Russian literature" be "thrown overboard from the ship of modernity," and relentlessly urged its audience "Forward, forward!." In the phrase "Forward, forward!," Solzhenitsyn seems to allude to both Maiakovskii's and Kataev's cry "Time, Forward!" He argues that the rejection of the cultural past by radical artists such as Maiakovskii and Kataev in the early part of the twentieth century paved the way for Socialist Realism, which he damns as a "pseudoculture" of "ceremonial forms," lacking any real connection with the organic culture of the past.[23]

Such polemical statements on modernism make clear the essential continuity of Solzhenitsyn's artistic stance between the 1960s and the 1990s and serve to articulate what generally is left implicit in early fiction, such as *One Day in the Life of Ivan Denisovich*. Most important here is Solzhenitsyn's identification of the rupture in the "organic" development of the Russian cultural tradition with the emergence of modernism and his understanding of Socialist Realism as akin in spirit to the work of the early twentieth-century avant-garde rather than as a return to the nineteenth-century tradition. While other writers of his generation sought to trace their literary genealogies back to authors of early twentieth-century Russian experimental prose, Solzhenitsyn adheres to a realist aesthetic that harks back to the nineteenth century. In terms of the intertexts I have suggested as a context for *One Day in the Life of Ivan Denisovich*, he claims Aksakov as a legitimate forebear, while rejecting Kataev—along with the repudiation of the past and the consequent striving for progress in life and art through technology and technique he implicitly imputes to him.

---

22 Aleksandr Solzhenitsyn, "The Relentless Cult of Novelty and How it Wrecked the Century," *The New York Times Book Review*, February 7, 1993, 17.

23 Solzhenitsyn, "The Relentless Cult," 3. For more on Solzhenitsyn's views on modernism, see: Richard Tempest, "Aleksandr Solzhenitsyn—(anti)modernist," trans. A. Skidan, *Novoe literaturnoe obozrenie* 3 (2010): 246–63—eds.

Works Cited

Aksakov, Sergei Timofeevich. *Semeinaia khronika*. In his *Sobranie sochinenii v chetyrekh tomakh*, vol. 1, 73–280. Moscow: Khudozhestvennaia literatura, 1955.

Curtis, James. *Solzhenitsyn's Traditional Imagination*. Athens: University of Georgia Press, 1984.

Feuer, Kathryn B. "Solzhenitsyn and the Legacy of Tolstoy." In *Aleksandr Solzhenitsyn: Critical Essays and Documentary Materials*, edited by John B. Dunlop, Richard Haugh, and Alexis Klimoff, 129–46. 2nd ed. New York: Macmillan, 1975.

Groys, Boris. *The Total Art of Stalinism: Avant-Garde, Aesthetic Dictatorship, and Beyond*. Translated by Charles Rougle. Princeton: Princeton University Press, 1992.

Kataev, Valentin. *Vremia, vpered!* Leningrad: Lenizdat, 1980.

Kataev, Valentine. *Time, Forward!* Translated by Charles Malamuth. New York: Farrar & Rinehart, 1933.

Kern, Gary. "Ivan the Worker," *Modern Fiction Studies* 23, no. 1 (Spring 1977): 5–30.

Kotkin, Stephen. *Magnetic Mountain: Stalinism as Civilization*. Berkeley: University of California Press, 1995.

Pushkin, A. S. *Polnoe sobranie sochinenii v shestnadtsati tomakh*. Moscow: Izdatel'stvo AN SSSR, 1937–1959.

Scott, John. *Behind the Urals: An American Worker in Russia's City of Steel*. Bloomington: Indiana University Press, 1989.

Shklovskii, Viktor. "Siuzhet i obraz." *Literaturnaia gazeta*, August 17, 1932, 2.

Skorino, L. *Pisatel' i ego vremia: Zhizn' i tvorchestvo V. P. Kataeva*. Moscow: Sovetskii pisatel', 1965.

Solzhenitsyn, Aleksandr. *Pis'mo vozhdiam Sovetskogo Soiuza*. Paris: YMCA Press, 1974.

———. "The Relentless Cult of Novelty and How it Wrecked the Century." *The New York Times Book Review*, February 7, 1993.

———. *Sobranie sochinenii*. 7 vols. Paris: YMCA-Press, 1980.

———. *The Gulag Archipelago Three*. Translated by Harry Willetts. New York: Perennial Library-Harper & Row, 1976.

——— [Alexander Solzhenitsyn]. "Our Pluralists." *Survey* 29, no. 2 (Summer 1985): 1–28.

Tempest, Richard. "Aleksandr Solzhenitsyn—(anti)modernist." Translated by A. Skidan. *Novoe literaturnoe obozrenie* 3 (2010): 246–63.

Tolstoi, L. N. *Chto takoe iskusstvo*. In his *Polnoe sobranie sochinenii v dvadtsati tomakh*, vol. 15, 44–242. Moscow: Khudozhestvennaia literatura, 1964.

10

Koshkin Dom: Following the Golden Shoelace

> But Pushkin was deliberately writing a novel about nothing.
>
> —Abram Tertz, *Strolls with Pushkin*

In the years before his death in 1997, Andrei Siniavskii was at work on three major projects: a book on Maiakovskii, a compendium of travel sketches, and a novel. Only the novel, entitled *The Cat's House* (or *The House of Cats*, *Koshkin dom*), was completed and published posthumously, in the May 1998 issue of *Znamia*. Siniavskii's widow, Maria Rozanova, ended her afterword to that publication with a short account of the novel's genesis:

> *The Cat's House* was finished in 1995. Then it just sat. In the summer of 1996, the author dismantled the prepared work, changed the order of several chapters, made additions here and there, shortened a great deal, and left some things in variant forms. He did not have time to assemble, to screw together his beloved toy—the text. It fell to me to do it, guided by his plans, remarks and notes. With the help of Natal'ia Rubinshtein, for which I am very grateful to her.[1]

Previously published in *American Contributions to the 13th International Congress of Slavists, Ljubljana, August 2003*, vol. 2: *Literature*, ed. Robert A. Maguire and Alan Timberlake (Bloomington: Slavica, 2003): 139–49. Permission to republish by Slavica Press and Olga Nepomnyashchy—eds.

1 M. V. Rozanova, [Posleslovie], in Abram Terts (Andrei Siniavskii), *Koshkin Dom, Znamia* 5 (May 1998): 149. Henceforth page references to this novel will appear in parentheses in the text.

When the novel was finally published in *Znamia*, it was, as far as I can tell, almost completely ignored by the Russian cultural establishment, whether Siniavskii's friends or foes. I hope to suggest in this article that that neglect, resulting in part from the increasing marketization of post-Soviet cultural institutions, is unwarranted, that *The Cat's House* is a swan song worthy of the stylistic and theoretical virtuosity which have characterized the writings of Abram Tertz from the first.

The Cat's House is subtitled a "long distance novel" (*roman dal'nego sledovaniia*), an echo of the train with which Tertz's novel *Goodnight* (*Spokoinoi nochi*) ends. As this subtitle indicates, like *Goodnight* and Tertz's other later works, *The Cat's House* defies conventional genre classification. It is a fragmented text, which incorporates into its winding way all sorts of verbal flotsam and jetsam, in the process creating a labyrinthine riddle of authorship, exposing the speciousness of any facile distinction between fiction and autobiography. The writer not only includes self-citations from his own texts, real letters received by Siniavskii, and a commentary on Siniavskii's works by the narrator of the novel, but invokes the realia of his own life and approaching death (the latter in a direct address to the reader in the "Prologue," dated December 1996, that is, only two months before Siniavskii's own death). Yet the details and documents of the writer's life incorporated into the text of *The Cat's House* are transformed, or rather troped, rendering their status and significance above all figural rather than documentary.

In essence, then, in this final work of fiction, Tertz revisits one last time the complex of interrelated issues which have preoccupied his prose from the outset of his pseudonymous writing career in the mid-1950s: the intersection in the text of the processes of writing and reading. Tertz's primary mode of exposition and exploration of this fraught territory has from the very beginning of his career been metaphor. The significance of this choice of "dominant" is intimated in the striking passage from Tertz's earliest story "Pkhents" in which the extraterrestrial narrator laments his linguistic alienation:

> How can they understand me when I myself in their language can in no way express my unhuman essence. I do nothing but dodge all over the place and make do with metaphors, but as soon as it comes to what is most important—I fall silent. And I only see the solid, low GOGRY, I hear the swift VZGLYAGU, and the indescribably beautiful PKHENTS overshadows my trunk. Ever fewer and fewer of these words remain in my fading memory. The sounds of human speech

can only approximately convey their construction. And if linguists crowd around and ask what it means, I will say only GOGRY TU-ZHEROSKIP and make a helpless gesture.[2]

Here, I would argue, we are presented with the existential condition of language in which all communication is a form of "translation," a metaphorical approximation, in the idiom of the French deconstructionists a "deferral." In his works, Tertz continually restages this situation by translating the raw material which gives impetus to his prose—whether that raw material be his own life and works or canonic texts of Russian literature and culture—into metaphor. The cat's house itself constitutes a metaphor for the site of reading which entails the series of figures that give coherence to *The Cat's House* and drive its convoluted, fantastic, and phantasmal plot.

The plot of the novel centers on a retired school teacher named Donat Egorovich Bal'zanov. There are quite a number of autobiographical traces in the depiction of Bal'zanov and the other characters in *The Cat's House*. Bal'zanov, for example, bears Siniavskii's father's name and a patronymic that evokes the name of Siniavskii's son Egor. Bal'zanov has a "lady friend" named Nastia, who has an illegitimate son named Andriusha. Not only is Andriusha a diminutive form of Siniavskii's own name, but it is the name of the child whom the narrator of Siniavskii's early story "Icy Weather" (Gololeditsa, published in English as "The Icicle") meets at the end, the child representing the next cycle of reincarnations the tale chronicles. The name thus signals the self-conscious references to Siniavskii's works as well as his life which recur throughout *The Cat's House*. Andriusha's poodle Matil'da, moreover, is apparently inspired by a much beloved poodle of the same name once owned by Siniavskii and his wife. Bal'zanov's closest friend Sasha Surikov, Nastia's brother and a surrogate father of sorts to Andriusha, is nicknamed "Super," short for Superman, because, despite holding a PhD, he devotes his life to being a jack of all trades, helping his friends and suffering from a pronounced weakness for alcoholic beverages. Super is a recognizable literary and cultural type, for he recalls the intellectuals who "dropped out" of Soviet society during the post-Stalin years, turning away from their specializations and taking up menial jobs such as yard keeper, a practice perhaps inspired by Iurii Zhivago as the final

---

2 Abram Terts (Andrei Siniavskii), "Pkhents," in his *Sobranie sochinenii v dvukh tomakh*, vol. 1 (Moscow: SP "Start," 1992), 245.

years of his life are portrayed in Boris Pasternak's eponymous novel. More to the point, perhaps, Super bears an unmistakable resemblance to the Russian folk character Ivan the Fool, as Siniavskii describes him in his book of the same name.[3] However, the character is also based on a figure from Siniavskii's own life.[4] The real life Super (a permanent resident of Moscow) periodically lived with the Siniavskiis in their house in the Paris suburb of Fontenay aux Roses, first assisting Maria Rozanova with the work of the Sintaksis publishing house and later helping to nurse Siniavskii during his final illness. These instances epitomize the complex interplay of autobiography and fiction in the novel. Its complexity begins with the fact that the repeated references to Siniavskii's own biography are generally of a kind that are transparent only to a limited few, a select group of readers with privileged knowledge about the author's life. Far from supporting an arcane, scholarly approach to the text as a form of investigation seeking out "clues" to and from the writer's life, however, the autobiographical traces in *The Cat's House* participate in an intricate aesthetic play which, in the end, invalidates the very method of exegesis they would seem to promote. Thus I hope to show that in a text styled as a mystery novel in which the literary critic as detective relentlessly pursues the elusive criminal, the writer exploits his own biography to deconstruct equally relentlessly the very foundations of literary detection.

To return to Bal'zanov, the retired teacher likes to indulge in the eccentric pastime of wandering through deserted buildings. As the novel proper begins, Bal'zanov has acquired the keys to an "uninhabited house" (*neobitaemyi osobniak*) off the Arbat in Moscow from one of his ex-students who is a policeman, thus initiating the running motif of Bal'zanov's association with law enforcement through the text. There he finds a trove of manuscripts and assorted documents, which set him, as sleuth, off in hot pursuit of a literary evil doer who goes by a host of names, most prominently the "Wizard" (*Koldun*), known also under the name Inozemtsev (which suggests "foreigner" and echoes the word *inoplanetianin* ["being from outer space"], a word that, as we shall see, resonates with the cat imagery presaged by the novel's title). In his search for Inozemtsev, Bal'zanov interrogates the fugitive's wife, Iuliia Sergeevna, a character seemingly largely based on Maria Rozanova, although I suspect that her name

---

[3] I would like to thank Nina Khrushcheva for this observation and, in general, for her thoughtful and extremely helpful reading of an earlier draft of this article.

[4] Although the real Super's surname is not Surikov.

and her portrayal were inspired, at least in part, by the close Siniavskii family friend and outspoken emigre journalist Iuliia Vishnevskaia. In the course of the novel, it becomes evident that the wizard is capable of reincarnating himself, or at least that iniquitous essence that makes him write, into other bodies, in the process destroying the souls of the bodies he occupies (a none too thinly veiled allusion to the controversial metaphor of Pushkin as vampire in *Strolls with Pushkin*).[5] The sorcerer's lives apparently stretch far back into the past, including one incarnation as the eccentric nineteenth-century nobleman Proferansov who competed with his ancestor the town librarian for control of the manuscript of Siniavskii's early novel *Liubimov*. As noted earlier, the cycle of incarnations recalls the early Tertz story "Icy Weather" as well. After donning and discarding a number of other human vessels, including that of an "unknown woman" (*neznakomka*), apparently an allusion to Aleksandr Blok's famous poem of the same name, the villain takes advantage of a face-to-face confrontation with his pursuers to take over the body of Super and fly abroad in his guise. From his refuge in San Francisco, he summons Bal'zanov with as many friends as he chooses to bring with him and dies, apparently once and for all, in the presence of this delegation from Russia.

As indicated earlier, however, it is the clusters of interlocking metaphors for the reading process rather than the plot which drive the text. The principal metaphorical cluster resounds in the title, which *is*, to say the least, overdetermined. The source of the title, *The Cat's House*, which is also the "nickname" of the deserted house which serves as the central site of the plot, is identified in the text (75) as having been inspired by Samuil Marshak's narrative poem of the same name for children.[6] It is the previous dweller in the house and in

---

5   "He [Pushkin] all the more industriously and truthfully devours the souls of others because he doesn't have enough stuffing of his own, because for him impersonation is a way of life and subsistence. [...] Something of the vampire was hidden in so heightened a susceptibility. That's why Pushkin's images have such a luster of eternal youth, of fresh blood, high color, that's why the present manifests itself in his works with such unprecedented force: the whole fullness of existence is crammed into the moment when blood is transfused from random victims into the empty vessel of the one who in essence is no one, remembering nothing, does not love, but only declares to the moment: 'You're beautiful! (You're full of blood!) stop!'—guzzling until he slides off." Abram Tertz, *Strolls with Pushkin*, trans. Catharine Theimer Nepomnyashchy and Slava I. Yastremski (New Haven: Yale University Press, 1993), 83.

6   The basic plot of Marshak's *The Cat's House* tells of a selfish old female cat who callously refuses her kitten nephews shelter and flaunts her riches to her other animal friends.

the writer's body (whose manuscript is among the papers Bal'zanov finds and reads in the course of the novel) who has dubbed it the cat's house because cats appeared to him there. Perhaps, the text allows us to imagine, cats are truly visitors from another planet, and cats "haunt" the text of the novel as a whole even at the most basic level of continual linguistic iteration of related root words. Another text which, although not acknowledged in *The Cat's House*, is certainly an intertextual forebear is E. T. A. Hoffmann's *The Life and Opinions of the Tomcat Murr* (Lebensansichten des Katers Murr, 1819–21), in which two manuscript accounts of the same events from two different points of view, that of the tomcat and of his master, alternate to form the text of the novel or, as the fictional editor explains in the foreword: "When Murr the cat was writing his Life and Opinions, he found a printed book in his master's study, tore it up without more ado and, thinking no ill, used its pages partly to rest his work on, partly as blotting paper. These pages were left in the manuscript—and were inadvertently printed too, as if they were part of it!"[7] Thus, just as Hoffmann's *Little Zaches* (Klein Zaches) clearly served as the impetus for the conception of Tertz's novella *Little Tsores* (Kroshka Tsores, unfortunately rendered in the existing English translation *A Little Jinx*), so Hoffmann's cat certainly stands behind Tertz's *Cat's House*. Taken together, the multiplicitous invocations of cats in the novel would seem to be more suggestive than cohesive. They are a mysterious, otherworldly presence, while at the same time associated with home and childhood. A passage in *Ivan the Fool: An Essay in Russian Popular Belief* (Ivan-durak: Ocherk russkoi narodnoi very) captures these two vectors:

> Figuratively expressed, the folk tale [*skazka*] has the feeling of some internal similarity with the cat. And between them—the folk tale and the cat—there truly is something in common. After all, like the cat, the folk tale, in its being, is tied to habitation, to domestic warmth, to the stove near which in the evenings folk tales were spun. But sitting at

---

When the cat's house burns, she and her butler "Kot Vasilii" (who is invoked in Siniavskii's "Cat's House" as well) are turned away by all but the nephews. The only clear resonance between the two works is that the "cat's house" burns here in the end as well.

7   E. T. A. Hoffmann, *The Life and Opinions of the Tomcat Murr together with a Fragmentary Biography of Kapellmeister Johannes Kreisler on Random Sheets of Waste Paper*, trans. Anthea Bell (London: Penguin Books, 1999), 4. I would like to thank Kirsten Lodge for having recalled this text to my attention.

home, it, like the cat, looks to the forest—aspires to foreign lands and dreams of miracles.[8]

Whatever the multiple resonances of the title of the novel, the cat's house most transparently represents a site of reading, moreover, a place inhabited not only by reader and text, but by reader and author. Significantly, however, the wizard, who recounts in his manuscripts his adventures, including his residence in the cat's house, no longer lives there when Bal'zanov moves in. The author whom Bal'zanov seeks then is to all intents and purposes dead and departed when Bal'zanov and we ourselves, as readers, take up the text of his life. The effect of this displacement as an allegory for signification is heightened by the fact that we read along with Bal'zanov for much of the novel, since a larger part of the papers he discovers in the suitcase in the cat's house are incorporated into the novel of the same title. This strategy has the effect of blurring the boundaries between text and inserted text and between Bal'zanov as reader and the author of the texts he is reading.[9]

What I propose here then is to follow the inserted texts which on occasion edge out the frame story. And here a pair of metaphors proposed by the elusive wizard himself can serve as our guide: "There is an inexhaustible labyrinth in your works.... Like matrioshkas.... But how is it put together? In one is hidden a second, then a third, a fourth.... So what if they're primitive and painted any old way. It's an exit from reality...." (69). However mixed the metaphors, *The Cat's House* is itself both a labyrinth and a matrioshka. As I suggested above, it is not just that the varied texts are inserted into the narrative; they in effect take over the narrative at points, at times even reducing Bal'zanov's function to that of offering "scholarly" commentary on the text being read. To begin with a simple list of what we might term the found fragments of the text, among the papers Bal'zanov comes across in the empty house (in order of their appearance in the novel) are a censored letter lying

---

8   Andrei Siniavskii, *Ivan-durak: Ocherk russkoi narodnoi very* (Paris: Sintaksis, 1991), 52. It would be tempting—but it is beyond the bounds of this article—to explore the resonances between the analogy Siniavskii draws here and Freud's observations on the antinomous meanings of the word *Unheimlich* as a symptom of the return of the repressed in his essay "The Uncanny."

9   Not only does this suggest a paradigm for the effacement of the writer's self by that of the reader in the process of reading, but it also intimates that Bal'zanov and the wizard, like Siniavskii and Tertz, are alter-egos.

on the floor (46), "several frayed pages from an unmarked folio" (48), and the contents of a suitcase, "a pile of faded manuscripts. Letters" (51), including one addressed to "Andrei," which, as we shall see, resonates throughout the work. Among the manuscripts, judging by the title of the third chapter, "The Diaries of the Nobleman Proferansov and Lev Tolstoy," is what appears to be a commentary by the character from *Liubimov* on Tolstoy's obsessive recording of his own life and how the compulsion to document life in art consumed and destroyed the author's life. Proferansov, it appears, is one of the earlier incarnations of Inozemtsev. The inserted texts then appear to follow the course of the author's transmigrations so that the next two chapters are devoted to the wizard's most recent transmigration out of his aging body into that of an up-and-coming young establishment writer, which leads him to move into the writer's home: the cat's house.

In the seventh chapter of thirteen, that is, at the center of the novel, we are presented with yet another group of "nesting" or embedded manuscripts. We learn that Super has left with Nastia a package for Bal'zanov, who is at that time looking particularly for evidence of Inozemtsev's experience in labor camps. Nastia quickly quashes Bal'zanov's hopes that the packet ("There are some not serious camp tales and folk tales. Some sort of article. Or a treatise. Some clippings, letters"; 92) contains Inozemtsev's own writings: "Nastia hastened to disillusion him. No, not Inozemtsev. No, not Superman. Some Siniavskii [writing] about some artist. Who can keep track of them all. It's called *White Epic*. It might as well lie around with you. Your place is safer. Foreign inventions. Both [Siniavskii and the artist] must be dead" (92). The text of the *White Epic*, that is, the text by the obscure writer Siniavskii, occupies all of the first part of Chapter Seven, which is also titled *White Epic*. It is succeeded in the novel by "Chapter Seven (Continuation): Hey, Slavs!" That chapter consists of letters addressed to "Siniavskii" from what I would term pathological ill-wishers.[10]

---

10 I have written elsewhere extensively about the often passionately negative responses Siniavskii's works have inspired in some readers over the years, and Siniavskii's vexed relationship with his own readers is clearly an important context for the portrayal of the relationship between reader and writer in *The Cat's House*. For more on this, see Stephanie Sandler, "Sex, Death and Nation in the *Strolls With Pushkin* Controversy," *Slavic Review* 51, no. 2 (Summer 1992): 294–308; Catharine Theimer Nepomnyashchy, *Abram Tertz and the Poetics of Crime* (New Haven: Yale University Press, 1995), 1–39; Catharine Theimer Nepomnyashchy, "Notes on the Context of Siniavskii's Reception in Gorbachev's Russia," editor's introduction, , *Russian Studies in Literature* 28 (Winter 1991–1992): special issue

In fact they are letters, only slightly modified, including the true names of the signatories, which had been received by Siniavskii himself.[11] Here, then, at the core of the matrioshka-text, we do indeed find documents from the writer's own life. More to the point, we are presented with the writer as reader in the first half of Chapter Seven and with the writer confronted by his readers in the second half of the chapter. Moreover, the letters we find in the middle of *The Cat's House* hark back to the beginning of the work, for not only are fragments of these letters among the papers Bal'zanov finds in the cat's house, but also in the Prologue, ostensibly addressed to the reader by the author of the work *The Cat's House*, the authorial voice seems implicitly to suggest that the novel grows out of self-doubt precipitated by the receipt of letters, apparently the letters embedded in the text of the novel: "And it all began when one abnormal person began to write me letters demanding that I repent before him" (43). The text, therefore, is presented as in some sense being initiated by a real confrontation between reader and writer.

The chapter of *The Cat's House* entitled "The White Epic" appears to take its title from the putative Siniavskii's discussion of a labor-camp artist named Boris Sveshnikov, imprisoned under Stalin, as is evidenced by the following excerpt:

> Sveshnikov begins with the snow in the zone. Before the snow was the camp, prison, biography, but with the snow came the whole world.
>
> Boris Sveshnikov's sketches were done in the camp a long time ago, back in Stalin's time, when Sveshnikov served about ten years. According to the stories, he got lucky one time: he was made the night watchman at a warehouse, and he sketched at night.
>
> And so what came of it? Almost nothing: a white field. A white field, and, in the final analysis, there was nothing to draw on it, to write. A white field, do with us what you will, but stay that way forever and ever—a white field, paper. So that no one will read, leave a trace....
>
> A writer experiences a similar feeling at times. When with a black pen he produces untidy letters on a blank, as yet untouched page. Involuntarily one wishes that the paper—like a white field, like a cover—would overpower the text. You feel sick, are ashamed that you wrote so much. Wouldn't it be better to leave a blank page after you? Perhaps

---

"The Return of Abram Tertz: Siniavskii's Reception in Gorbachev's Russia," ed. Catharine Theimer Nepomnyashchy, 3–11.

11   As I was told by Maria Rozanova in a telephone interview.

only on the edge, for the sake of documentation, to explain what transpired, to stick on a few words. The paper, the landscape will say the rest, the most important.

Sveshnikov's sketches have an inverse sense. Whoever doesn't know that this is about the camps and was sketched in the camps, won't guess. Let it stay that way. Let it remain unknown. That's better: art. Those who know (I almost said the initiates) when they look closely, will make out somewhere a fence, a dump, a barracks, a bath house, the prison: someone has already hanged himself and someone is just sitting biding his time. There are strangely few of these local (camp) associations. These are not sketches from nature, but dreams of eternity, which slide along the glass of nature or history. (92–93)

This section, which is indeed reminiscent of Siniavskii's own labor camp musings *A Voice from the Chorus* (Golos iz khora), constitutes a transparent gloss on the effacement of the artist's—or writer's—autobiographical self when translated into art. The faint traces of the labor camp visible only to "initiates" in Sveshnikov's sketches are equivalent to the embedded references to Siniavskii's life in the text of *The Cat's House*: they are "marginal" to the main sweep of the white field of the text, a blankness that leaves itself open to the play of the reader's imagination. Thus, to quote further from this section of the text of *The Cat's House*:

I should conclude my notes on Sveshnikov with the draft of an idea I've had for a long time, but have still not brought to fruition. No, not about the camp. Not about anything. I've always wanted to write a novel about nothing. To sit down at my desk. . . . touching nothing, thinking about nothing...

. . .and so that the last words would be those with which I began: Gogry! Gogry, gogry, gogry! Tuzheroskip, tuzheroskip! Bu-bu-bu! Miaou-miaou! Tertz! (94)

Aside from the obvious, and I believe correct, insinuation that the novel we are reading is indeed a novel about nothing (a point reiterated in the epilogue; 148), perhaps equivalent to a snow-white field or a blank sheet, I imagine that at least a few readers will recognize the self-citations to Siniavskii's own works in this passage. The first relevant passage, the description of *Evgeny Onegin* from *Strolls with Pushkin*, clearly resonates with the construction of *The Cat's House*: "But Pushkin was deliberately writing a novel about nothing. In *Evgeny*

10. *Koshkin Dom*: Following the Golden Shoelace | 215

Onegin he could think of nothing but shirking his responsibilities as narrator. The novel is made up of poor excuses that draw our attention away to the margins of the verse page and hinder the development of the plot line selected by the writer."[12] By the same token, the words with which the passage cited from *The Cat's House* ends are the words of the first-person narrator of Tertz's first short story, "Pkhents," who claims to be a being who accidentally crashed to earth from outer space. In fact, this passage ends with the concluding words of "Pkhents," with the significant change that the last word, which was "pkhents" in the story, is here replaced by "Tertz."[13] Both of these passages echoing earlier works by Siniavskii broach the evaporation of the autobiographical author "translated"—just as Tertz is Siniavskii's "translation" of himself—into the literary text.

To explore the significance of this claim, let us look back to the Prologue to *The Cat's House*, to the author's reminiscence of his first, much desired and delayed opportunity to read *Robinson Crusoe*:

> And so I sat down in the morning on the low children's bench, which was hewn in labor lessons with her own hands by my older sister Viva and has entered the family collection of furniture-household goods, and plunged into the divine world of travels and adventures. My memory holds a picture, thrown into the aquarium (yes, we, like all normal children, had an aquarium) in the form of a golden shoelace, a saving lasso for the agile Robinson, and we with him, using the aiguilette, make our way onto the abandoned ship, find there a mass of necessary things and food, very useful to every seafarer, planted, as in a fortress, on an uninhabited island. At the end of the road, every wayfarer needs an uninhabited island. (42)

Here we must first of all recognize the echo of this passage in the first mention of the cat's house in the novel, in which it is referred to as an "uninhabited building" (*neobitaemogo osobniaka*), thus underscoring its association with the experience of reading, and echoing the Marshak association and the allusion to an idyllic, childhood encounter with literature. Second, in its invocation of the golden shoelace (*zolotoi shnurok*) this passage initiates what is perhaps the most significant thread (pun intended) in the text, which, it seems, follows

---

12 Tertz, *Strolls with Pushkin*, 92.

13 Tertz, "Pkhents," 250.

wherever "the golden shoelace leads" (44). And so, among the papers in the cat's house, Bal'zanov comes across an enigmatic text which begins:

> "Do you have my beautiful shoe?" "Yes, I have it." "Do you have my golden shoelace?" "No, I don't have it." "Do you have my new handkerchief?" "No, I don't have it." "Do you have my goose?" "No, I have my rooster." "Do you have my silver candelabra?" "I have the tin candelabra."
>
> "Do you have my golden shoelace?" "I have the golden shoelace." (48)

The text continues in the same vein, leading Bal'zanov to try to decode it:

> He began to grow tired of the babbling of the two pretentious burghers. Some sort of puppets, Germans, probably. What do "eagle," "elephants," "candelabra" and twenty-two sparrows have to do with it? And what is this mysterious golden shoelace, which the old burghers now discover they have, then periodically lose? Of course, the old teacher understood that all of this was nothing more than coded signs, masked signals, which were being exchanged not by people, but the words or numbers hidden behind them, if the key is double and the lock has a double turn. It's also possible that each page silently intersects with other pages, and the hidden meaning should become clear at the end of the edition; however, the end wasn't there. (48)

Here we see clearly Bal'zanov's conception of reading, which is to decode, to track down the true meaning behind the cipher that is the text, just as his vocation is to hunt down the author. Yet the golden shoelace will lead Bal'zanov to a very different understanding of the nature of textuality by the end.

Here, though, a slight but relevant detour is in order, for Siniavskii (or, again, Abram Tertz) published a piece entitled, "The Golden Shoelace," in issue number 18 of the journal *Sintaksis* for 1987, that is, relatively early in the glasnost period. The publication opened with a preface lamenting the current state of Russian prose, which, facing a challenge roughly equivalent to that faced by the Futurists early in the century, appeared to be stuck in a dead end. The writer ended this preface with the statement: "As a state that is also a dead end but nonetheless interesting—'the death of the subject, the death of the object,' as has been said here—I want to present a piece of prose on which Abram Tertz is currently working. For me it is to some degree an image of the new Russian prose. The text is called 'The Golden Shoelace'" (183). The text that follows closely resembles the text inserted some ten years later

10. *Koshkin Dom*: Following the Golden Shoelace

into the novel. At the end, however, the following disclaimer appears in the *Sintaksis* text:

> After "The Golden Shoelace" was read and accepted by the meeting so enthusiastically that one well-known Slavist and translator offered to translate it into French right away, M. Rozanova explained in her talk that "The Golden Shoelace" was nothing but a collage made on the basis of an old book, *The Key to Russian Grammar for French People*. Some prose writers present took this trick for an insinuation.[14]

As the juxtaposition with Bal'zanov's practice of reading demonstrates, the golden shoelace retains here some of its satirical force as a send-up of literary scholarship. Yet Tertz plumbs here the deeper issues of the making of meaning as we find at the end of the novel.

The final chapter is entitled "The Thirteenth Chapter and, as the Thirteenth, the Last. *The Golden Shoelace*" (141). After beginning the chapter with the same sort of extended "collage" of conversation exercises rehearsed earlier, the narrator (assumedly the same authorial voice that speaks in the Prologue) concludes:

> And that's it. The end of the investigation. And of the chase. And of the strange happenings. And of wanderings. We haven't caught anyone. Worse, we've lost what we had.... Neither a bird in the hand, nor one in the bush. Of everything with which we set out nothing is left but the 'golden shoelace.' It runs like Ariadne's thread from the Prologue to the Epilogue." (143)

And so, guided through the labyrinth of the text by the gold shoelace, Bal'zanov is left to ponder that particular text:

> Bal'zanov frequently remembered the guiding lamp. How it insisted, just tugged him by the hand—to read over and over "The Golden Shoelace." [...] Untwisted and retwisted "The Golden Shoelace," letting it slip between his fingers, trying to tie up its uncommon knots: *sheet bend and stopper-knot, running knot and figure eight, double seaman's—and* it all came out as *cat's paws*. At first he thought, having noticed in the villainous encoding traces of shameless writings of the most diverse epochs, that he had before him summary material, a sort

---

14   Abram Tertz, "Zolotoi shnurok," *Sintaksis* 18 (1987): 187, note.

> of digest. But one night, during an uncertain, unreliable dream, he experienced a sort of epiphany—so that he even sat up, instantly awakened, on the bed: it wasn't a digest, not a summation—it was a project and a prospectus, a foretext, the foundational text for all the wizards of world literature, sent down by the generalissimus of evil before the beginning of cursed belles letters.
>
> *"Do you have my beautiful shoe?"* O, the trace of the shoe is no accident here. Gogol would come and would take that shoe and make of it Bashmachkin and dress him in a worn-out overcoat so that out of the holes in its sleeves would pour the entire natural school. (144–45)

Here the famous pronouncement attributed to Dostoevskii, "We all came out of Gogol's overcoat," is turned on its head. All literature, Bal'zanov discovers, is spawned not by reality, but by language, by Saussure's *langue*, by language as it exists in its abstract and potential form, by the stuff of grammar books. Two significant moments earlier in the novel serve as especially illuminating contexts for Bal'zanov's revelation at the end. The first is an episode in a manuscript by Inozemtsev which Bal'zanov discovers and reads, and the reader reads along with him. Inozemtsev recounts how in an attempt to find out why objects were disappearing from the Cat's House he set up a surveillance apparatus to film what happened in the house while he was asleep. To his dismay, upon awakening and looking at the film the next morning, he discovered that the thief was not the cats he suspected ("No, cats in the direct sense of the word did not appear there").[15] Instead it is he himself ("I, no, not I, rather my specter," 113), who rises from the bed where Inozemtsev lies sleeping, removes a lithograph by Sveshnikov from the wall, rips it into pieces, and flushes the pieces down the toilet: "However, taking it from under the glass, he did not break the empty mounting" (113). The second episode is the death of Super inhabited by the wizard. The sick man's last words echo the passion of Christ: "Farewell, father is calling me" (138). This echo underscores the sacrificial nature of the wizard's death, suggesting that the literary criminal voluntarily offers himself up to his most dogged literary pursuer and sleuth. The golden shoelace, the empty frame, and the death of the wizard then all replay the "death of the author," the effacement of the author's autobiographical self.[16]

---

15   The Russian suggests an ambiguity untranslatable into English: "Net, koshek v priamom smysle tam ne znachilos'."

16   The possibility remains that the "soul" of the wizard has migrated into Andrei.

10. *Koshkin Dom*: Following the Golden Shoelace

So what are we left with at the end? As at the end of *Strolls with Pushkin*, we are left with the emptiness—like the white blankness of a field of snow or a vacant picture frame—of a text whose author with a capital A has, for all his villainy, offered himself up as a human sacrifice to his critic-pursuer. Yet to reduce this text to a catechism of post-structuralist cliches would be a sad reduction indeed and a betrayal of the text's own performance of the mutual dependence of writer and critic and the permeable boundaries of the self. So let me conclude by suggesting that the true genius (a word I do not use lightly) of this work, like all of Tertz's other works, lies in a trope I might term realizing life in the literary text, that is, performing the converse function of realized metaphor—to transform the realia of the author's life into metaphors that exhaust themselves in the expanse of the text. In the end we are indeed left with only Tertz/Pkhents.

Works Cited

Hoffmann, E. T. A. *The Life and Opinions of the Tomcat Murr together with a Fragmentary Biography of Kapellmeister Johannes Kreisler on Random Sheets of Waste Paper*. Translated and annotated by Anthea Bell, with an Introduction by Jeremy Adler. London: Penguin Books, 1999.

Nepomnyashchy, Catharine Theimer. *Abram Tertz and the Poetics of Crime*. New Haven: Yale University Press, 1995.

———. "Notes on the Context of Siniavskii's Reception in Gorbachev's Russia." *Russian Studies in Literature* 28 (Winter 1991–1992): 3–11.

Rozanova, M. V. [Posleslovie]. In Abram Terts (Andrei Siniavskii), *Koshkin Dom*, *Znamia* 5 (May 1998): 149.

Sandler, Stephanie. "Sex, Death and Nation in the *Strolls with Pushkin* Controversy." *Slavic Review* 51, no. 2 (Summer 1992): 294–308.

Siniavskii, Andrei. *Ivan-durak: Ocherk russkoi narodnoi very*. Paris: Sintaksis, 1991.

Terts, Abram [Andrei Sinyavskii]. *Koshkin Dom*. *Znamia* 5 (May 1998): 41–149.

———. "Pkhents." In his *Sobranie sochinenii v dvukh tomakh*, vol. 1, 233–50. Moscow: SP "Start," 1992.

——— [Tertz, Abram]. *Strolls with Pushkin*. Translated by Catharine Theimer Nepomnyashchy and Slava I. Yastremsky. New Haven: Yale University Press, 1993.

———. "Zolotoi shnurok." *Sintaksis* 18 (1987): 182–87.

11

Tatiana Tolstaia: The Text of Family and the Family in the Text—Genealogy, Gender, and the Rhetoric of Lineage

> While one can do nothing about choosing one's relatives, one can, as artist, choose one's "ancestors."
> —Ralph Ellison

> Genetics? I certainly believe in it. More than that, I believe only in genetics.
> —Tatiana Tolstaia

In this article, I will address how families may infect texts and how they may become texts. What I have in mind here is the intersection and often significant disjunctions between the text of an author's biographical ancestry, the text of an author's literary genealogy, and the portrayal of family in the author's works. My test case here will be Tatiana Tolstaia, whose life, works, and context provide us with a particularly appropriate nexus of the forces that textualize and therefore drive Russian culture.

The epigraphs are taken from Ralph Ellison's "The World and the Jug," *New Leader*, December 9, 1963; and Ol'ga Kabanova, "Tat'iana Tolstaia: literatura—eto razgovor s angelami," *Izvestiia*, January 4, 2000—C. T. N. This article was first published in *New Women's Writing in Russia, Central and Eastern Europe: Gender, Generation, and Identities*, ed. Rosalind Marsh (Newcastle: Cambridge Scholars Publishing, 2012), 355–71. Published with the permission of Cambridge Scholars Publishing—eds.

In 1998 Tolstaia published a volume titled *Sisters* (Sestry), which contained a selection of her own essays and short stories by her sister Nataliia (1943–2010), a writer and specialist in Scandinavian languages at St. Petersburg University. Both the form of this volume and the language that Tolstaia used to describe it in interviews hint at the potential importance of family ties in literature, at the idea of the creation of books as a family affair or something of a cottage industry:

> Our book is a response to what is happening around us. My essays are something intermediate between prose and journalism. We are two completely independent authors. So it is even more curious that when our writings landed under the same cover, there appeared to be an interchange of words, styles, themes. But there is no literary connection between us, only a family connection. The slight madness of this project makes complete sense. At my request, my son produced the dustjacket. And overall, you can observe a family contract.[1]

Tolstaia's tendency to understand literary work as a family affair makes sense given her ancestry. She is, of course, descended from what is perhaps Russia's most illustrious literary family. A distant relative of Lev Tolstoy (1828–1910), she is the granddaughter of Aleksei N. Tolstoi (1883–1945), the "red count," one of a handful of Soviet writers to earn the official designation "living classic" during the Stalin years for his monumental socialist realist historical epics such as *The Road to Calvary* (Khozhdenie po mukam, 1920–42). Tolstaia's title, *Sisters*, is apparently borrowed from the first part of this work.[2] Tolstaia's grandmother, Nataliia Krandievskaia (1888–1963) was a poet and the daughter of the writer Anastasiia Krandievskaia (1865–1938).[3]

---

1   Ol'ga Bondareva, "Sestrichki s"ekhalis' pod odnu oblozhku," *Vechernii klub*, September 3, 1998.

2   Aleksei Tolstoi, "Sestry," first published in the émigré journal *Sovremennye zapiski* 1–6 (1920–21). It was republished thereafter almost annually in the Soviet Union as part of Tolstoi's collected works—eds.

3   Despite Tolstaia's vocal anti-feminism (she has refused to be identified with "women's prose" and has suggested that women are more suited to being editors, academics, and critics than to being fiction writers), her female literary ancestors are clearly important to her, and, for a time, she was reputed to be writing a novel about her grandmother. For Tolstaia's statements on women's writing, see Ol'ga Martynenko, "Malen'kii chelovek—eto chelovek normal'nyi," *Moskovskie novosti*, February 22, 1987, 10; and Peter Barta,

Tolstaia's literary genealogy therefore quite literally began at home. She has described how her ancestors served her as models:

> I read a great deal both of Aleksei Tolstoi and of my grandmother's poetry, and therefore saw how they lived through the period of the formation of their styles, how they searched for their own styles [...] I saw the living process directly. Therefore when, let's say, many people ask whether the fact that my ancestors were famous hindered me.... It didn't hinder me at all. On the contrary, I felt them very deeply from inside—living people before a blank sheet of paper.[4]

Tolstaia, moreover, has insisted on blood as a determining factor in literary style. In interviews she has repeatedly expressed the idea that "when they create a text, people who are genetically close but different in spirit use identical syntactical constructions."[5] Speaking specifically of her grandfather, she notes: "All my childhood I believed that Aleksei Tolstoi was a lousy bastard. The problem was that he had a nasty divorce with my grandmother. But when I read his works, I feel my own intonations. Apparently, I have inherited them genetically."[6]

Yet, while her ancestors provided her with "living" models for the formation of her own literary voice and for her efforts to locate her own writing in the Russian literary tradition, they served her largely as negative exemplars, as instances of the failures and complexities experienced by the Russian writer at the intersection of tradition and politics. She views her grandmother and

---

"The Author, the Cultural Tradition and Glasnost: An Interview with Tatyana Tolstaya," *Russian Language Journal* 44, no. 147–149 (Winter-Spring-Fall 1990): 277. For aggressive attacks on feminism, see Tolstaya, "In a Land of Conquered Men," *Moscow News* 38 (1989), 13; and her "Notes from Underground," *New York Review of Books*, May 31, 1990, 3–7. For a commentary on Tolstaia's skirmishes with Western feminism, see Helena Goscilo, "Monsters Monomaniacal, Marital and Medical: Tatiana Tolstaya's Regenerative Use of Gender Stereotypes," in *Sexuality and the Body in Russian Culture*, ed. Jane T. Costlow, Stephanie Sandler, and Judith Vowles (Stanford: Stanford University Press, 1993), 204–20.

4 Translation from the unpublished transcript of C. T. N.'s interview with Tolstaia in Moscow, February 1990—eds.

5 Larisa Nemchikova, "Kofe s bul'onnymi kubikami," *Vecherniaia Moskva*, August 23, 2001, 6.

6 Larisa Nemchikova, "Priglashenie v druguiu zhizn'," *Vecherniaia Moskva*, January 25, 2001, 9.

great-grandmother as writers out of step with the times, realist writers at a time when Chekhov had already "killed" realism and when realism had been replaced by various manifestations of modernism: "Such writers as Aleksei Tolstoi's mother or my grandmother Krandievskaia's mother—they were the last realist writers with little talent, very little, and they were completely incapable of coming to grips with the new time, which required new paths of expression."[7] As regards her grandfather, Tolstaia has written of him as being a "trained parrot," "useful to Stalin as window-dressing," who sacrificed his talent to socialist realism: "He wanted to sell his soul to the devil, but the devil wouldn't take it: when he attempted to praise the regime his talent abandoned him, and from his superb pen issued an anemic, grey, talentless mush, of no use to anyone."[8] Hardly surprisingly, then, Tolstaia—in accordance with Ralph Ellison's adage cited in the epigraph to this chapter—constructs her own literary genealogy: "of the classics—Bulgakov, Olesha, and Platonov."[9] While she casts her forebears by blood as die-hard realists, her "invented" ancestral tradition is purely modernist.

In her first interview in the Soviet press in 1986, Tolstaia challenged the reigning literary establishment in similar terms, precipitating the first of the controversies that have arisen around her journalistic statements both in Russia and the West. Claiming that she began to write because "I got sick of reading: I didn't like this, I didn't like that," Tolstaia went on, later in the interview,

---

7   C. T. N.'s interview with Tolstaia—eds.

8   Cited from an unpublished manuscript translated by Jamey Gambrell. Tolstaia also discussed her grandfather as a victim of Stalinism in a "meeting with readers" that took place on April 18, 1989 in Moscow, the record of which was published under the title "Vosstanavlivaem litso po cherepu" (We are reconstructing the face based on the skull), in the émigré newspaper *Panorama*, November 3–6, 1989, 12. In her remarks on Aleksei Tolstoi, Tolstaia called for a full publication of his works for the sake of *nasledstvennost'*, which may be roughly rendered into English as the need for "hereditary continuity" in a cultural rather than a biological sense: "As a person with a sense of *nasledstvennost'* [...] I am for showing all that there is." Tolstaia also spoke of her "complicated attitude" to her grandfather. See Tamara Alagova and Nina Efimov, "Interview with Tatyana Tolstaya," *World Literature Today* 67, no. 1 (Winter 1993): 49. Tolstaia demonstrated her knowledge of her grandfather's life and works in a scathing review of a book on Aleksei Tolstoi published after the appearance of her first short story. Tat'iana Tolstaia, "Kleem i nozhnitsami," *Voprosy literatury* 9 (1983): 171–88.

9   Nemchikova, "Priglashenie v druguiu zhizn'," 9. Tellingly, this statement immediately follows Tolstaia's comment cited above from the same interview on her genetic inheritance from Aleksei Tolstoi.

to maintain: "Of course, I don't think about any tradition when I write. But you must agree that it's impossible to write now the way they wrote in the nineteenth century. Open any journal—it's pure Boborykin. And critics are amazed that it's boring. And it should be boring, that's what Boborykins are for...."[10] She thus doubly impugned officially published writers: on the one hand, accusing them of clinging to an outmoded tradition and, on the other, implicitly tracing their lineage to a second-rate writer within that tradition. In a 1987 interview, moreover, she made the inflammatory claim that the novel *Everything is Ahead* (Vse vperedi, 1986) by Vasilii Belov, a leading Russophile writer, was misogynistic.[11] The latter attack especially delayed her acceptance into the conservative Moscow branch of the Writers' Union, of which Belov was a Secretary, and prompted an attack on Tolstaia in the journal *Our Contemporary* (Nash sovremennik), the major publication outlet for the rural prose writers.[12]

In his article, "From the Height of Her Mound: Some Ethical Observations in Connection with a Certain Literary Debut" (S vysoty svoego kurgana: neskol'ko nravstvennykh nabliudenii v sviazi s odnim literaturnym debiutom, 1987), Vladimir Bushin couches his diatribe against Tolstaia, albeit implicitly, in terms of the legitimacy of literary lineage. Moreover, while Bushin directs his attack at Tolstaia's statements in two interviews and claims not to be commenting on her prose, this polemical strategy is clearly meant to undermine her literary stature. The implicit question Bushin poses in his tirade is: who are the true heirs of Pushkin? Who, that is, is truly Russian, who is truly a writer, and who has a right to speak out publicly, to impose their views on "many

---

10 Slava Taroshchina, "Ten' na zakate," *Literaturnaia gazeta*, July 23, 1986, 7. Petr Dmitrievich Boborykin (1836–1921) was a prolific writer whose name, as C. Nicholas Lee points out, has literally become synonymous with bad writing: "His immoderate productivity inspired the verb *boborykat'*: 'to write badly on topical issues.'" C. Nicholas Lee, "Pyotr Dmitrievich Boborykin," in *The Handbook of Russian Literature*, ed. Victor Terras (New Haven: Yale University Press, 1985), 57.

11 Martynenko, "Malen'kii chelovek," 10. Belov's novel is also extremely antisemitic. See Rosalind Marsh, *History and Literature in Contemporary Russia* (Basingstoke: Macmillan, 1995), 81.

12 For a detailed account of the role of Russophile writers in the union, see Catharine Nepomnyashchy, "Perestroika and the Soviet Creative Unions," in *New Perspectives on Russian and Soviet Artistic Culture: Selected Papers from the Fourth World Congress for Soviet and East European Studies, Harrogate, 1990*, ed. John O. Norman (New York: St. Martin's Press, 1994), 131–51.

millions of readers."¹³ Through none too subtle innuendo, he suggests that Tolstaia is not a legitimate heir of the Russian classical tradition, while those she has attacked as Boborykins are.

From the very beginning Bushin pits Tolstaia's biological lineage against the national literary heritage, in his opening sentence citing Tolstaia's statement that "No matter where you look, I have nothing but literary people in my family" (182). Implying that just being born into a literary family does not make one a writer, Bushin goes on, commenting on Tolstaia's assertion that she became a writer because she did not like what there was to read: "If you please, this motif is a bit strange, for both in contemporary and in classical literature, both ours and the world's, all the same there is something even for those who possess famous names to read" (182). As far as Tolstaia's own literary credentials are concerned, he notes with a markedly acerbic undertone the amount of attention the fourteen stories Tolstaia had published to date—which he terms the "mound" from which she surveys Soviet literature (182)—had received from critics, and remarks bitterly on the "complimentary approach" and "formulations" of at least some of Tolstaia's reviewers:

> Just try after that not even to criticize, but just not showing any interest in any publication of T. Tolstaia's, and immediately [...] her admirers [...] will proclaim you that scorned personality for whom the culture of the word is not precious, who would like to ban the unconstrained flight of fantasy in art. Yes, yes, you will immediately be consigned to the camp of the retrogressives, and not only the literary ones. (183)

Thus, what is at issue here is the very nature of glasnost, the danger of allowing competing opinions into the national press, of conferring the prestige and power that accrue to officially published words on those who putatively have not earned them.¹⁴ Bushin claims to be more concerned that such mass

---

13 Vladimir Bushin, "S vysoty svoego kurgana: neskol'ko nravstvennykh nabliudenii v sviazi s odnim literaturnym debiutom," *Nash sovremennik* 8 (1987):184. Henceforth page numbers from this article will be given in parentheses in the text.

14 Like many conservative critics of the time, Bushin avowed himself a supporter of glasnost—and even cited Gorbachev to support his argument at one point in the article (185). He demands that a line be drawn between criticism and slander, defending the "principle affirmed in Russian literature from Belinsky's times: 'criticism is not swearing, and swearing is not criticism'" (185). He essentially accuses Tolstaia—who, in Bushin's words, "considers herself a 'fighter against the old'" (*bortsom so starym*, 185)—of slandering

circulation periodicals as *Literaturnaia gazeta* and *Moskovskie novosti* have rushed to interview a "beginning writer" who "still does not have even a little book, that is, [whose] whole creative baggage could easily fit into a lady's reticule," especially when "it is easy to name many talented writers who have worked in literature for dozens of years who their whole lives were not deemed worthy of such an honor" (183). Tolstaia is too young, too "lightweight" (and too female) to be granted the "honor" of having her words made public. In making her brash statements "from the height of her mound," moreover, she neglects the authority and priority of those who have come before her: "Wanting to become a writer, having decided to come out publicly with an exhortation on such a complex question, how could she not first have pondered what had been said about this by others whose spiritual and creative baggage was somewhat weightier" (183).

The particular bearer of "weightier baggage" whom Bushin periodically cites, rather ludicrously out of context, to validate his argument, is Pushkin. Looking back into the "not so distant past of [our] native people [*rodnogo naroda*]," Bushin maintains that the young generation of the 1930s, "this new generation of our people [*nashego naroda*] [that] was able to comprehend the sorrow of enslaved peoples [*narodov*]" (184), and not Tolstaia, were "Pushkin's fellow countrymen and spiritual heirs" (184). He even goes so far as to suggest that, had she had the chance, Tolstaia would have "edited" Pushkin's *Evgenii Onegin* as well as Gogol's *Dead Souls* and the works of her own "dear [*rodnogo*] grandfather" (184). Bushin's rhetoric, his repetition of the loaded words "people" (*narod*) and "native" (*rodnoi*), suggests that underlying the critic's ire over Tolstaia's purported challenge to authority lies not only a generational and perhaps gender conflict, but a dole of "class antagonism" as well.[15] It is the masses and not this scion of an elite intelligentsia family who are the true heritors of the legacy of Pushkin. Taking issue with Tolstaia's claim in one of her interviews that without knowing ancient Greek and Roman culture one

---

Belov and, by implication, of violating the tradition of Belinskii. Tellingly, he compares the publication of Tolstaia's attack on Belov with the publication of private letters, suggesting that dirty linen should not be washed in public.

15 By the same token, in a diatribe against Tolstaia, the author repeatedly referred to her as "Countess Tolstaia" to satirize the behavior and values of Tolstaia and others of her purportedly effete and snobbish intelligentsia ilk and even Lev Nikolaevich Tolstoy himself. See Lekha Andreev, "Nakrys', ili Kak ia poznal russkuiu literaturu," accessed October 29, 2022, https://fuga.ru/articles/2002/04/tolstaya.htm.

cannot understand Pushkin (and, later in his article, with her attribution of "illiterate patriotism" to a poet who published a false etymology of the word *rodina* [native land]), Bushin maintains that no Russian needs knowledge of any other nation's literature to understand their own national poet:

> It goes without saying, Pushkin absorbed some juices of antiquity and knew the French language as well as French literature very well, but, nonetheless, he is an outgrowth of Russian life and Russian culture, he is profoundly national, his creation is uniquely original, completely independent, and, of course, as a whole understandable to us without recourse to Aristotle or Virgil. (184)

In his assertion that no specialized—or foreign—knowledge is necessary for a (true) Russian to understand Pushkin, in his insistence that the continuers of Pushkin's heritage are the people (narod), and in his sparring with Tolstaia over the issue of "learning" (*obrazovannost'*), over who has the right to confer on or deny individuals the "moral status of educated people" (184), Bushin seems to hark back to proletarian attacks on literary "specialists" in the 1920s, disputing the right of the, perhaps suspiciously cosmopolitan, intellectual elite to priority in Russian culture. "The books of Rasputin and Aitmatov, Belov and Bykov, Astaf'ev and Granin"—peasant writers all, he claims—"are not at all 'pure Boborykin'" (183). These writers are rather, by rhetorical implication, the true heirs of the authority vested in the Russian classical tradition rooted in Pushkin. They—and the people (*narod*) for whom they putatively speak—are Pushkin's true family, the Russian national family.

In his assault on Tolstaia, Bushin passes over in silence Tolstaia's own statements on her place in the literary tradition in a 1986 interview conducted by Slava Taroshchina. In the interview Taroshchina noted that critics have a tendency to try to understand new authors through comparisons to writers of the past: "As soon as a new name appears in literature [...] they immediately try to fit it into some existing schema, to connect it to one of the traditions." She expressed "amazement" at having recently read that Tolstaia "continue[s] the tradition of M. Bulgakov in our literature."[16] Tolstaia responded:

---

16 Taroshchina, "Ten' na zakate," 7. It is worth noting that while Tolstaia's defenders traced literary genealogies for her, her detractors tended to deploy tradition as a weapon against her. Her two most hostile Russian critics, Vladimir Bushin, writing for the Russophile journal *Nash sovremennik*, and Irina Murav'eva in the émigré journal *Grani*, employ cita-

Yes, I was also amazed. I supposedly continue the traditions of Bulgakov, the traditions of Nabokov, of German literature (with which I am unfamiliar), of A. Grin (whom I don't like), generally the traditions of the twenties. The latter, broadly speaking, is not devoid of truth. But it's not a matter of consciously following tradition, rather, in my opinion, it's this. In the literature of the nineteenth century, it seems, all the slots are filled. Try to come up with a new brilliant writer of the nineteenth century—it's difficult. All the seats are taken—the stalls, the gallery, and the standing room. The same, with reservations, can be said of the "Silver Age" of Russian literature. But the Silver Age is, in the main, poetry. But the prose of the twenties gives the sense of a half-empty hall! It is in essence a new prose—style, lexicon, metaphor system, syntax, plot structure—all was different, everything changed, hundreds of possibilities appeared and only a small part of them were realized. It is that literature, that tradition that had just begun to develop, that I like. It's there, in the ruins of that unfinished poetics, that buried treasures may be concealed.[17]

Here, as in her comments on her relatives and on the contemporary "Boborykins" of official Soviet literature, Tolstaia suggests that the nineteenth-century tradition had played itself out, filled up all the seats in running the course of its natural development, and that it is in some sense a falsification of tradition to extend it artificially. In contrast, Tolstaia implicitly views the literature of the 1920s as a broken tradition, cut short by the incursion of socialist realism.[18]

---

tions from the "classics," most notably Pushkin, to bolster their attacks. Bushin, as we have seen, accuses Tolstaia of wanting to rewrite Pushkin, Gogol, and even her own grandfather (184), while Murav'eva links Tolstaia with Aleksei Tolstoi in a "family tradition" the critic describes in less than flattering terms. Irina Murav'eva, "Dva imeni," *Grani* 152 (April-June 1989): 104.

17   Taroshchina, "Ten' na zakate," 7.

18   In two other interviews, Tolstaia made even more explicit her idea that the tradition had been artificially cut off. In the first, she stated: "In the 1920s the discoveries abounded, like mushrooms during a good year. But the discoverers were stopped and no one was left. We are now digging up some of those discoveries. We have to go back to the place where our literature was diverted." Cited in Elena Veselaia, "Is Writing Easier Under Glasnost?," *Moscow News* 26 (1990): 14. In the second, she posed alternatives to the contemporary Russian writer: "We missed a normal and naturally free development of the literary process. Therefore, now, many writers cannot find themselves, because they resemble a person who has suffered a bout of amnesia in relation to the whole literary past. They either try to return to the 1920s and to continue the tradition that was broken off in our country

The terms in which Tolstaia goes on to describe her understanding of her own work as a continuation of that ruptured tradition are particularly telling: "And somehow it is very easy to imagine that there was at that time one more writer, about whom no one knows, who didn't publish a single line, and then he died. And everyone who knew him also died. And his business remained unfinished. Consider that I am [going on] for him."[19]

Tolstaia thus sees herself as a replacement for that which has been lost, forgotten, and prematurely silenced. There is, however, a seemingly fatal disjunction in this formulation of her role in the literary tradition that haunts Tolstaia's prose in the form of those motifs of breaks in continuity, gaps in time and memory that continually confront her characters and narrators, frustrating their attempts to recover the past and make up for its errors. In the images of her prose, then, Tolstaia implicitly raises the question of whether the sixty years of historical experience and cultural oblivion that separate her from her hypothetical ancestor can be bridged, whether the substitution of one object or person for another one that has been irretrievably lost does not leave an inevitable hiatus, which defines the ontology of the Tolstaian text.

Topoi of rupture, silencing, forgetting, and loss thus run throughout Tolstaia's fictions. I would like to focus here on one of her stories in particular that seems to invite a reading as a commentary on Stalinist culture as a breach in, and misappropriation of, the national cultural tradition: "Sleep Soundly, Son" (Spi spokoino, synok). Moreover, as we shall see, the family as the metaphorical basis of the national narrative and its disruption is laid bare in the story.

"Sleep Soundly, Son" explores the consequences of a loss of the truth (and the narrative) of origin, of genealogical amnesia. The story's central character, Sergei, now an adult, was orphaned during the war:

> A child raised in an orphanage, a boy without a name, without a patronymic, without a mother. They had thought up everything, everything for him in the orphanage: a name, a surname, an age. He had no childhood, his childhood had burned up, bombed out at an unknown station, someone's hands had dragged him out of the fire, thrown him on the earth, rolled him, beaten him on the head with a hat, beating out the flame.... He had not understood that that black, stinking hat

---

or to begin from some empty zero." Barta, "The Author, the Cultural Tradition and Glasnost," 274.

19   Taroshchina, "Ten" na zakate," 7.

had saved him—the hat had beaten out his memory [...] Even now, in the middle of the 1970s, an adult, his heart contracted when he passed a store where fur spheres sat round on the shelves. He would stop, look, overcoming himself, strained his memory: Who am I? Where from? Whose son am I? After all, I had a mother, someone gave birth to me, loved me, was taking me somewhere.[20]

The hat, which pursues him into nightmares, becomes a metonym for his lost memory, his lost genealogy, his lost identity. Like the neurotic in Freud's "The Uncanny," Sergei is trapped in a single story, and, having lost all knowledge of the true story of his parentage, continually constructs fictions to fill in the gap left by his lost heritage. In his obsessive fabrication of variations on the same story, Sergei finds more than his match in his mother-in-law, who equally obsessively, retells over and over the account of how a fur coat was stolen from her at a market during the postwar years, and, significantly, Tolstaia opens her narrative about Sergei with his mother-in-law Mariia Maksimovna's story. Both characters are unable to transcend or forget their past losses, and this failure cripples their present lives—especially Sergei's.

We cannot help but be struck from the outset by the incommensurability of the two losses: a fur coat and parents. In meta-literary terms, however, this apparent discordance between trivial and essential appears easily resolvable. We need seek no further than Gogol's "The Overcoat" (Shinel') for the *topos* of obsession with a stolen coat in Russian literature. In case we miss the allusion, at one point in the story, Sergei, having finally grown tired of his mother-in-law's reiteration of the same tale, exclaims to his wife: "Yes, but how many times can it be told! Just think: Akaky Akakievich!" (140; 132–133). This direct invocation of Gogol's pitiful, victimized protagonist, along with the juxtaposition of Sergei's hat with Mariia Maksimovna's fur coat, thus suggests that in "Sleep Soundly, Son," Tolstaia is playing on one of the more famous genealogical statements in the Russian literary tradition, the claim, attributed to Dostoevskii, that "We all came out of Gogol's overcoat." Tolstaia problematizes this tracing of the lineage of Russian literature back to Gogol by associating Sergei's

---

20   Tolstaia, "Spi spokoino, synok," in her *Na zolotom kryl'tse sideli...* (Moscow: Molodaia gvardiia, 1987), 128. Nepomnyashchy's translation. However, when citing other passages from this story, she seems to have relied on the translation by Antonina W. Bouis in Tatyana Tolstaya, *On the Golden Porch* (New York: Vintage, 1990), 131–43. Later references to this translation will be provided parenthetically in the text with English pages numbers first and then Russian second—eds.

hat with a loss of ancestral memory and by raising the question of who in fact stole Mariia Maksimovna's coat, who is the victim and who the thief, and by challenging us with the complicated interconnection between the story of the hat and the story of the coat.[21] There is, in this context, a further disparity between the story of the hat and the story of the coat. While both originate in losses that lead to substitutions, Sergei's story is truly one of loss, while Mariia Maksimovna's is one of substitution, albeit a substitution she construes as an original loss. While the mother-in-law considers herself the rightful owner of the stolen coat, in fact her husband had previously "stolen" it, appropriating it as war booty while he was serving as a military doctor in Germany. After the war Mariia Maksimovna, wearing her coat, goes to the market with her servant Pania to buy a second, everyday coat. She gives her good fur coat to Pania to hold while she is trying on the other coat, and someone absconds with the fur while Pania's attention is distracted. Mariia Maksimovna's "stolen" coat is thus replaced by another, probably also stolen, coat, but one of inferior quality. Pavel Antonovich assumes Pania to be an accomplice in the theft and takes legal action against her. The uneducated Pania, inarticulate in her own defense, is condemned and disappears into oblivion on the other side of the coat, just as Sergei's mother had on the other side of the hat.

Just as the original "theft" of the fur coat results in a substitution, notably of an article made of poorer stuff, so Sergei continually seeks replacements for his lost family among the people he encounters in his post-hat life. While a child in the orphanage, he imagines that first a favorite teacher and then the cook is his lost mother. Later, after he marries into Pavel Antonovich's family, he secretly fantasizes that Mariia Maksimovna is his mother, that in marrying Lenochka he has reconstituted his lost family: "Lenochka had an even, passionless character, as if she were not his wife, but his sister. A mother and a sister—what more could a lost boy dream of?" (138; 131). Yet, as he has decided even earlier in the narrative: "What nonsense, Mariia Maksimovna had no lost son, she had only lost a fur coat" (136; 129). Still, having moved into Pavel Antonovich's family, he considers the possibility that Pavel Antonovich was indeed his father: "And what if Pavel Antonych was Sergei's father? What if he, an elderly man, had had another wife—before Mariia Maksimovna? To leap out

---

21   It is interesting to note in this connection that in his story "The Fur Hat" (Shapka, 1988), Vladimir Voinovich retells Akakii Akakievich's story, making his protagonist a writer and making the relevant article of clothing a fur hat.

of non-being, to acquire a continuous chain of ancestors—Pavel Antonovich, Anton Feliksovich, Feliks Kazimirovich... And why not? A real possibility..." (139; 132). Having himself been held back from stealing as a child, possibly by his mother "from the other side, from behind the hat" (136; 128), Sergei cannot reconcile himself with Pavel Antonovich's theft of the coat. He then conceives the idea that it is Pania—who has vanished, unable to wait for the reappearance of her lost son in the home and whose room he has taken over as his study—who was his mother. Here we should remember that while there is a time lag between Sergei's story of the hat, which takes place during the war, and Mariia Maksimovna's story of the coat, which takes place after, there is an implicit chronological coincidence between the incident of the hat and the original theft of the coat, suggesting that the true equivalence lies there, that Pavel Antonovich's theft and Sergei's dispossession, his amnesia, are interconnected. Sergei, in expanding his fantasy about Pania, himself makes the connection:

> I am her son. Pania is my mother, that's decided, everyone must know. Why did he take the coat from the hook? That coat belonged to Pania's husband, he should have reached it, crawled there, extended his scorched hand toward it—no, he wouldn't have taken it, he wouldn't have stooped to that. But you, high and mighty gentleman, you stooped. And I am married to your daughter. Pavel Antonovich is my father. Otherwise, why does he torment me with the lost fur coat...? (141–42; 133–34)

Thus, through a strange twist of logic, Pavel Antonovich becomes Sergei's father precisely because he has stolen the coat.

The point lies in the fact that Sergei has indeed inherited the deceased Pavel Antonovich's "legacy." Pavel Antonovich is identified as a doctor who "in the twenties and thirties struggled with the plague—and emerged victorious" (137; 130). Echoing the negative associations attached to medical imagery in other Tolstaia stories, Pavel Antonovich's profession suggests a thinly veiled allusion to government purges of suspect individuals and groups during those years. By taking his place in his family and enjoying the fruits of his labors, Sergei becomes Pavel Antonovich's rightful descendant:

> Holding hands tightly, the chain of ancestors walks into the depths, sinking into the dark aspic of time. Stand with us, nameless one, join

> us. Find your link in the chain. Pavel Antonovich, Anton Feliksovich, Feliks Kazimirovich. You are our descendant, you lay on our bed, loved Lenochka without blinking an eye, you ate our sweet rolls—every single currant in them we had to tear away from domestic, attic, and field rats; for you we coughed up horrible phlegm and let our nodes swell, for you we infected camels that spat in our face—you can't get away from us. We built this for you, you nameless and clean boy, this house, this hearth, kitchen, hallway, bedroom, cubby, we lit the lamps and set up the books. We punished those who lifted their hands to steal our property. (142; 134)

His true lineage obliterated, Sergei acquires a substitute one, just as he was endowed with a replacement name at the orphanage. The imposture foisted on him by his amnesia is crowned when, at story's end, he "replaces" Pavel Antonovich—"Serezha, you're shouting so loudly. Just like Pavel Antonovich" (142; 134)—and himself fathers a son named Antosha.

We may then suggest that Tolstaia answers Dostoevskii's assertion that "We all came out of Gogol's overcoat," by charging that official Soviet culture, figured in Pavel Antonovich, "stole" Gogol's overcoat, hijacked the legitimizing *mythos* of the dynastic continuity of Russian classical literature, through an obliteration of memory, a break in cultural continuity. In this context, the surrogate genealogy Sergei inherits through his replacement of Pavel Antonovich appears neither random nor whimsical. Kazimir suggests an allusion to Kazimir Malevich as a representative of the modernist tradition later co-opted by socialist realism. The equally marked name Feliks invokes Feliks Dzherzhinskii, the first head of the Cheka, while Pavel Antonovich represents an inversion of Anton Pavlovich (Chekhov). Thus, Tolstaia seems to implicate the radical artistic avant-garde in the police state, which in turn co-opted "Chekhov," claiming him as a progenitor of socialist realism. The "nameless" link in the chain, which signifies the rupture in the tradition, moreover, fathers Antosha, a name which evokes less Chekhov himself than his early pseudonym, Antosha Chekhonte. Thus the chain of imposture is completed as the story draws to a close: "Sleep soundly, son, you're not to blame for anything at all. The plague corpses in the cemetery are covered with lime, the poppies on the steppe bring sweet dreams, the camels are locked up in the zoos, warm leaves rustle and whisper over your head. What about? What do you care?" (143; 135)

While Antosha is not to blame, his status as the legitimate issue of an illegitimate lineage—or the illegitimate issue of a legitimate lineage— remains ambiguous. Sergei's situation parodies and inverts that of Oedipus. While Oedipus, falling prey to a fiction of origins, replaces his father and enters into incestuous relations with his mother, it is precisely Sergei's fiction of origins that places him in an incestuous relationship with his sister/wife/daughter. Thus, while the revelation of the true solution to the riddle of Oedipus's parentage discloses the tragedy of his situation, the reclamation of Sergei's true parentage, name, and identity hold forth the possibility of a reconstitution of the natural order—but they are irreparably lost.

The story suggests that official Soviet culture rested on the suppression of gaps: Stalinist culture and its successors, in appropriating the pre-revolutionary "realist" heritage, replaced the rupture in the tradition, the cultural amnesia of the Stalin years, with a false line of descent. Viewed in this light, Tolstaia's fictions seek less to reclaim the lost past, to fill in what Gorbachev termed the "blank spots," than to reveal, rehabilitate, and explore the consequences of these gaps. In returning subjectivity to literature in her stories, Tolstaia also brings back the disjunction between inner being and outer world, between ideals and the passage of time that erodes them and makes them unrealizable, between memory and loss, between the text and what lies beyond it, and between word and object—between which subjectivity intervenes. Most important, the disjunctions between word and referent, name and body lead to venal substitutions which threaten the nation as narrative.

Tolstaia's story, then, lays bare the stakes underlying the rhetoric of genealogy employed by Tolstaia in her public statements and by her critics and allies—the same stakes that prompt all of them to return again and again to the complex interpenetration of blood and metaphor, of biological and invented genealogies. Tolstaia's acknowledgement in "Spi spokoino, synok" of the "gap"—of the missing ancestral link—speaks to the rupture in what the American critic Henry Louis Gates, Jr. has called the "signifying chain."[22] In the mythology of Russian culture, beginning with the progenitor of the national tradition Pushkin, it has been the writer's task to safeguard the continuity of language as the glue that holds the nation together. The genealogical

---

22 Thus the "broken" chain of ancestry in Tolstaia's story rather tantalizingly resembles the trope of the relinquished "signifying chain" marking the rupture in cultural tradition experienced in the "Middle Passage" of Africans into American slavery. See Henry Louis Gates, Jr., *The Signifying Monkey: A Theory of African-American Literary Criticism* (Oxford: Oxford University Press, 1988), 136.

rupture Tolstaia chronicles then places the Russian linguistic community at risk, casting about for a new story of shared ancestral values to replace the one that has now been discredited. Genealogy, then, as Bushin's ham-handed attack on Tolstaia unwittingly reveals, becomes a tool for constructing national legitimacy—and for determining who is included in and excluded from the national community. It is easy to see then why the Tolstoi family, with its complex legacies of class and creativity and the colorful figure Tatiana Tolstaia has styled herself, have become a flashpoint for anxieties over the legitimacy of the Russian national family, and it is appropriate that she has become the most eloquent contemporary teller of the national tale—a tale, it would seem, of grandfathers and sisters.

Works Cited

Alagova, Tamara, and Nina Efimov. "Interview with Tatyana Tolstaya." *World Literature Today* 67, no. 1 (Winter 1993): 49–53.

Andreev, Lekha. "Nakrys', ili Kak ia poznal russkuiu literaturu." Accessed October 29, 2022. https://fuga.ru/articles/2002/04/tolstaya.htm.

Barta, Peter. "The Author, the Cultural Tradition and Glasnost: An Interview with Tatyana Tolstaya." *Russian Language Journal* 44, no.147–49 (Winter-Spring-Fall 1990): 265–83.

Bondareva, Ol'ga. "Sestrichki s"ekhalis' pod odnu oblozhku." *Vechernii klub*, September 3, 1998.

Bushin, Vladimir. "S vysoty svoego kurgana: Neskol'ko nravstvennykh nabliudenii v sviazi s odnim literaturnym debiutom." *Nash sovremennik* 8 (1987): 182–85.

Ellison, Ralph. "The World and the Jug." *New Leader*, December 9, 1963.

Gates, Henry Louis, Jr. *The Signifying Monkey: A Theory of African-American Literary Criticism.* New York: Oxford University Press, 1988.

Goscilo, Helena. "Monsters Monomaniacal, Marital, and Medical: Tatiana Tolstaya's Regenerative Use of Gender Stereotypes." In *Sexuality and the Body in Russian Culture*, edited by Jane T. Costlow, Stephanie Sandler, and Judith Vowles, 204–222. Stanford: Stanford University Press, 1993.

Kabanova, Ol'ga. "Tat'iana Tolstaia: Literatura—eto razgovor s angelami." *Izvestiia*, January 14, 2000.

Lee, C. Nicholas. "Petr Dmitrievich Boborykin." In *The Handbook of Russian Literature*, edited by Victor Terras, 57. New Haven: Yale University Press, 1985.

Rosalind Marsh. *History and Literature in Contemporary Russia.* Basingstoke: Macmillan, 1995.

Martynenko, Ol'ga. "Malen'kii chelovek—eto chelovek normal'nyi." *Moskovskie novosti*, February 22, 1987, 10.

Murav'eva, Irina. "Dva imeni." *Grani* 152 (April-June 1989): 99–133.

Nemchikova, Larisa. "Priglashenie v druguiu zhizn'." *Vecherniaia Moskva*, January 25, 2001, 9.

———. "Kofe s bul'onnymi kubikami." *Vecherniaia Moskva*, August 23, 2001, 6.

Nepomnyashchy, Catharine Theimer. "Perestroika and the Soviet Creative Unions." In *New Perspectives on Russian and Soviet Artistic Culture: Selected Papers from the Fourth World Congress for Soviet and East European Studies, Harrogate, 1990*, edited by John O. Norman, 131–51. New York: St. Martin's Press, 1994.

Taroshchina, Slava. "Ten' na zakate." *Literaturnaia gazeta*, July 23, 1986, 7.

Tolstaia, Tat'iana. "Kleem i nozhnitsami." *Voprosy literatury* 9 (1983): 171–88.

———. *Na zolotom kryl'tse sideli. . . .* Moscow: Molodaia gvardiia, 1987.

———. "Vosstanavlivaem litso po cherepu." *Panorama*, November 3–10, 1989, 12–13.

———. [Tolstaya, Tatyana]. "In a Land of Conquered Men." *Moscow News* 38 (1989): 13.

———. [Tolstaya, Tatyana]. "Notes from Underground." *New York Review of Books*, May 31, 1990, 3–7.

———. [Tolstaya, Tatyana]. "Sweet Dreams, Son." In her *On the Golden Porch*, translated by Antonina W. Bouis, 131–143. New York: Viking, 1990.

Tolstaia, Tat'iana, Nataliia Tolstaia. *Sestry*. Moscow: Podkova, 1998.

Veselaia, Elena. "Is Writing Easier Under Glasnost?" *Moscow News* 26 (1990): 14.

Voinovich, Vladimir. *Shapka*. London: Overseas Publications Interchange, 1988.

Part IV

Russian Culture, High and Low

12

Dance as Metaphor: The Russian Ballerina and the Imperial Imagination

> We had an imperial ballet and we returned to an imperial ballet.
>
> —Elizaveta Iakovlevna Surits

Stagings of the imaginary geography of nationhood may take on particular resonance in situations when group identities are rendered vulnerable or contested by rapid social or political change or by encounters with outsiders. At such pivotal moments, dramatic spectacle may become a potent mechanism for working out in symbolic terms shifts in power relations. Ballet has played a remarkably prominent role in the past century in defining Russia for the world outside—from the spectacular debut of Serge Diaghilev's Ballets Russes in Paris in 1909 to the Cold War visits of Soviet ballet troupes to the West decades later. The function of ballet within the Soviet Union to represent and thereby legitimate the consolidation of state power has received less attention. This article attempts merely to start the conversation by suggesting how we might look fruitfully at paradigmatic continuities and discontinuities among the late imperial ballet, the Diaghilev enterprise, and the coming of age of Soviet ballet in the years following the 1917 Revolution in terms of their

---

The Surtis epigraph represents faithful paraphrase of a personal comunication on ballet in Russia before and after the 1917 Revolution (February 6, 2001)—C. T. N. This article originally appeared in *Mapping the Feminine: Russian Women and Cultural Difference*, ed. Hilde Hoogenboom, Catharine Theimer Nepomnyashchy, and Irina Reyfman (Bloomington: Slavica, 2008), 185–208. Published with permission of Slavica Press and Olga Nepomnyashchy—eds.

representation of empire and nation, Russian and foreign. The points of orientation of my argument will be gaze, gender, and the enactment of real power through symbolic imaginaries.

Gaze, Gender, and the Ballerina

In her excellent study *Gendering Bodies/Performing Art: Dance and Literature in Early Twentieth-Century British Culture,* Amy Koritz observes that "the conventions governing gender in ballet tended to maintain strict divisions between gender roles" and that "ballet performance, as opposed to choreography, has traditionally been dominated by women." She asserts that "the cultural position of dance as an eroticized female space catering to male visual pleasure" was defined by the focal role of the ballerina, flanked by the female *corps de ballet,* feeding the male spectator's "fantasy of possession," with the ballerina's male consort (sometimes in Britain danced by a female dancer in travesty) a mere support, no "competitor."[1] This paradigm of the ballerina as an objectified, submissive body vulnerable to the voyeurism and sexual predation of the male spectator is graphically depicted in a late eighteenth-century Russian painting portraying the "training of a serf dancer," in which the male spectator, presumably the patriarch of the estate, gazes through his lorgnette under the hem of the maiden's skirt, her leg conveniently stretched out in a balletic pose to permit a clear view of her "private parts" (see fig. 1).

FIGURE 1. *Education of a Serf Dancer.* By an unknown artist. Late eighteenth century. From the collection of the Bakhrushin Museum.

---

1   Amy Koritz, *Gendering Bodies/Performing Art: Dance and Literature in Early Twentieth-Century British Culture* (Ann Arbor: University of Michigan Press, 1995), 23, 24.

Yet, I would suggest, there is a tension inherent in this paradigm, which becomes progressively more unstable and intense as the role of the ballerina becomes more central in the course of the nineteenth century. A hint of this tension is already evident in the disjuncture between Pushkin's famous conflation of the "dance" of the Onegin stanza with the virtuosity of the ballerina Avdot'ia Istomina (1799–1848) in Chapter One, Stanza XX of *Eugene Onegin*, on the one hand, and his own less than reverent comment in a private letter, from the point of view of a balletomane and connoisseur of the sexual demimonde of the Petersburg ballet of his time, on the other:

> Театр уж полон; ложи блещут;
> Партер и кресла—все кипит;
> В райке нетерпеливо плещут,
> И, взвившись, занавес шумит.
> Блистательна, полувоздушна,
> Смычку волшебному послушна,
> Толпою нимф окружена,
> Стоит Истомина; она,
> Одной ногой касаясь пола,
> Другою медленно кружит,
> И вдруг прыжок, и вдруг летит,
> Летит, как пух от уст Эола;
> То стан совьет, то разовьет
> И быстрой ножкой ножку бьет.[2]

> The theatre's full, the boxes glitter;
> The restless gallery claps and roars;
> The stalls and pit are all ajitter;
> The curtain rustles as it soars.
> And there ... ethereal ... resplendent,
> Poised to the magic bow attendant,
> A throng of nymphs her guardian band,
> Istomina takes up her stand.
> One foot upon the ground she places,
> And then the other slowly twirls,

---

2   Aleksandr Pushkin, *Polnoe sobranie sochinenii v shestnadtsati tomakh* (Moscow: Izdatel'stvo AN SSSR, 1937–1959), vol. 6, 13.

> And now she leaps! And now she twirls!
> Like down from Eol's lips she races;
> Then spins and twists and stops to beat
> Her rapid, dazzling, dancing feet.³

Pushkin's tone is strikingly different in the excerpt from a private letter below.

> Every morning a winged maiden flies to rehearsal past our Nikita's windows, as before telescopes are directed at her and <— —>—but alas... you don't see her, and she doesn't see you. We'll leave the eulogies, my friend. Historically, let me tell you about our doings. Everything is as it was; thank God, there's plenty of champagne—and actresses as well—the one we drink, the other... Amen, amen. (Letter from Pushkin to P. B. Mansurov, St. Petersburg, October 27, 1819)⁴

In the famous stanza from *Eugene Onegin*, we see the ballerina's body "spiritualized" through transformation into light and soaring metaphor, but in the letter, the "actress's" body appears as a very much earthbound site of sexual pleasure and prurience. Similarly, Pushkin's verses cast the theater as a place of aesthetic contemplation, but his letter treats it as a venue for flirtation and voyeurism.

Perhaps most interesting here, however, especially in comparison with the painting of the serf dancer and her master reproduced above, is the scene Pushkin sketches of the ballerina's admirer's frustrated attempts to steal a glimpse through a telescope, for it indicates a complication in the seemingly unambiguously male-dominated hierarchy of scopophilia. There is, after all, power in the ability to attract and hold the admirer's gaze and, even more so, in the refusal to return it. This distinction, I argue, becomes key in understanding how gender and politics, performer and audience intersect in the Russian and Soviet ballet's generation of symbolic capital. The slave, female or feminized, invariably orientalized, poses the would-be possessor with a potentially lethal threat precisely through the ability to attract the desiring gaze. It is this threat that the Russian ballet seems simultaneously to exploit and to neutralize.

---

3   Alexander Pushkin, *Eugene Onegin*, trans. James E. Falen (Carbondale: University of Southern Illinois Press, 1990), 23.

4   Pushkin, *Polnoe sobranie sochinenii*, vol. 13, 11.

The Imperial Precedent

By the latter decades of the nineteenth century, Russian ballet was deeply implicated in the structures of empire and autocracy. The imperial ballet received enormous subsidies from the Emperor to the tune of two million gold rubles every year, and sexual liaisons between royal balletomanes and dancers were a matter of course.[5] The hierarchy of ranks assigned to dancers by the state was analogous to the table of ranks governing the status of civil servants. As the prima ballerina Anna Pavlova recalls: "I left the Ballet School at the age of sixteen; and shortly afterwards I was permitted to style myself *première danseuse*—which is an official title, exactly as [sic] that of *tchinovnik* in government offices."[6]

The isomorphism of ballet and state structure was reinforced by the fact that the ballet audience was indeed, as Anatole Chujoy observes, largely coterminous with the imperial elite:

> At the begining of our century there were nineteen separate courts in St. Petersburg: the Czar's, the dowager Czarina's, and seventeen grand-ducal courts. With the families of the Czar and the grand dukes, courtiers [...] and gentlemen-in-waiting, relatives of these dignitaries, the well-staffed Ministry of the Court, etc., etc., the court comprised several thousand people. In addition, there were his Majesty's Convoy, the Guard Regiments [...] and the naval Guard Equipage. Foreign embassies with their large staffs [...] were also close to the Court and finally there were the aristocratic clubs [...] Now if we consider that of all the theatres in and around St. Petersburg ballet was given regularly only at the Maryinsky, with a seating capacity of some twenty-five hundred, and that the entire ballet season consisted of fifty performances of which forty were by subscription, it follows that there was not much room left for people who [...] were not connected with the Court, the Guard, the Government, the press or the theatre itself.[7]

In essence, by virtue of the fact that it reflected its spectators' own image back at them, the imperial ballet served a legitimating function; it represented the

---

5   Bruce Lincoln, *Between Heaven and Hell: The Story of a Thousand Years of Artistic Life in Russia* (New York: Viking, 1998), 254.

6   A. H. Franks, ed., *Pavlova: A Biography* (New York: Macmillan, 1956), 117.

7   Anatole Chujoy, "Russian Belletomania," *Danse Index* 7 (March 1948): 164.

very power to deploy resources on a massive scale upon which the throne, the court and, indeed, the empire rested. Deborah Jowitt has observed:

> The spectators [at the ballet] looked back at the stage world that flatteringly mirrored theirs in protocol, decorum, and elegance. [...] The parades, grand entrances, and large ensemble dances in the ballets affirmed the power of ceremony. [...] It was natural that even the most frivolous of the spectacles would involve a manipulation of props and costumes as fastidious and elaborate as that of court ceremony and church ritual.[8]

Special dance productions participated in the staging of imperial power even beyond the bounds of the theater. Thus, the Moscow and Petersburg ballet troupes joined forces to perform for the coronation of Nicholas II, and extravagant productions could be staged for visiting foreign dignitaries. In her memoirs the prima ballerina assoluta of the imperial theater, Mathilde Kschessinska, describes one such spectacle produced in 1897:

> The second spectacle, the most brilliant of the three [the other two were staged in the same season for the King of Siam and for Felix Faure, the President of France—C. T. N.], was given on June 28 in honor of Emperor Wilhelm II, but not in a theater, but on Olga's Island, on the upper pond. Places for the spectators were arranged like an amphitheater on the island itself, the stage was constructed on the water, on stilts, and the orchestra was located on an enormous iron caisson, below water level. There were only side decorations on the stage, sidelines, and instead of back scenery the *view* opened out into the distance, on the hills of Babigon. Not far from the stage a little islet was built, decorated with cliffs and a grotto, where I was when the performance began. They presented the one-act ballet *The Adventures of Peleus*, set by Petipa to the music of Delibes and Minkus. The guests were ferried to the island on sloops. Everything was flooded with electric light, and the tableau was truly magical. The ballet began with the grotto, in which I was hidden, opening up, and I stepped onto a mirror, which began to move in the direction of the stage. The impression was created that I was walking on water.[9]

---

8   Deborah Jowitt, *Time and the Dancing Image* (New York: William Morrow and Co., 1988), 243–44.

9   Matil'da Kshesinskaia, *Vospominaniia* (Moscow: Artist, rezhisser, teatr, 1992), 61.

This example demonstrates particularly vividly, I believe, the use of ballet to perform the magnificence of empire, to present the audience with a model for self-validation and emulation and with a narrative of sovereignty.

In this context, Tim Scholl, in his discussion of the significance of the pivotal 1890 Russian staging of *Sleeping Beauty*, suggests how links between *Sleeping Beauty* and the court society of late imperial Russia operated on both literal and figurative planes. On the one hand, the ballet, which in its sumptuousness evoked the luxury of the court, was seen by some contemporaries as an "homage to the Russian court" and members of the Emperor's family frequently attended performances.[10] On the other hand:

> The ballet about a princess who awakens to find herself transported to the next century boded well for those who sought parallels between life and art. That the princess' name was Aurora and the action of the ballet moved from an atmosphere of social upheaval (the wicked fairy Carabosse not only intrudes upon the ballet's court festivities, she brings them to an end) to a dazzling Versailles-like court could only drive these meanings deeper.[11]

The openness of *Sleeping Beauty* to metaphorical reading is especially significant given the fact that it was this ballet in particular, so implicated in the representation of empire, that served as a formative experience for figures who were to play key roles in the Ballets Russes.[12] Russia as marriageable princess who awakens to find her prince and recuperate history vouchsafes the endurance of the Russian imperial line. The Ballets Russes, by contrast, staging Russia for Europe during the fragile interlude between the 1905 Revolution and the Great War, would seem to have posed its foreign audience a riddle, simultaneously alluring and troubling.

Diaghilev Presents: The Russian Sphinx

It is certainly no accident that Serge Lifar, who himself was one of the premier male dancers in Diaghilev's troupe in the 1920s, opens his *History of the*

---

10 Tim Scholl, *From Petipa to Balanchine: Classical Revival and the Modernization of Ballet* (New York: Routledge, 1994), 36.

11 Scholl, *From Petipa to Balanchine*, 21.

12 Scholl, *From Petipa to Balanchine*, 44.

Russian Ballet from Its Origins to the Present Day (Histoire du ballet russe depuis les origines jusqu'à nos jours) with the testimony of a foreigner—Théophile Gautier—on the excellence of Russian ballet training, particularly the training of female dancers, in the nineteenth century. This invocation of the foreign "gaze" as that which bestows authenticity on the "Russianness" of Russian ballet is telling:

> In this way Western European audiences were made fully aware of the high quality of Russian ballet, but did they realize the extent to which it was really *Russian*? In fact, did the Russians know it themselves, and were they not relying on the words of dance historians who claimed that Russian ballet was really nothing more than an offshoot of French ballet, kept in a hothouse safe from the North winds, and guarded even more religiously than in the country of its birth?[13]

The paradigm Lifar adopts here, I would argue, echoes what is perhaps the most fundamental underlying principle of the Ballets Russes endeavor. It is precisely by attracting the admiring gaze of the foreign audience that the Russian ballet becomes legible as a recognizably national art—although, as I will contend further, the narrative of Russianness it performed, onstage and off, draws its force in large measure from the delicate equilibrium between polarities it barely held in check. In fact, it may well be that the very tangible risk that this equilibrium might disintegrate was what made the acting out of nationality such a riveting spectacle.

The "Russian Seasons" in Paris were organized by Diaghilev to showcase abroad artists of the Russian imperial ballet and opera in the summer months of 1908 to 1910. The performances enjoyed remarkable success, a success that permanently changed the history and status of ballet both in Russia and the West. Dance historians have offered a number of explanations for the extraordinary nature of the encounter between Russia and Western Europe, between the Ballets Russes and its prewar, Paris audiences, and certainly no single explanation, but only an appreciation of a complicated intersection of factors can serve in this instance. Here I would highlight the same representational functions we have already surveyed with regard to the imperial ballet: above all, the power to evoke a narrative of imperial opulence in a manner that resonated

---

13 Serge Lifar, *A History of Russian Ballet from Its Origins to the Present Day*, trans. Arnold Haskell (London: Hutchinson, 1954), 10–11 (Lifar's emphasis—C. T. N.).

with the audience's own political, economic, and social pretensions. Thus, just as Scholl pointed to *Sleeping Beauty* as a glorification of the court of the Emperor, so the Ballets Russes seem to have conjured for its more "democratic" European audiences a sort of imperial nostalgia: refined, "severe," noble, tasteful—and sumptuous. As Koritz argues, Diaghilev's troupe reclaimed ballet for high art, moving it from the dance hall into the privileged space of the opera house.[14] Lynn Garafola, moreover, contends that a significant factor in the success of Diaghilev's enterprise was the ability to attract and shape audiences of the rich and powerful, not only royalty: "The elite that actually governed the country was also heavily represented among Diaghilev's public, constituting a political world that was itself an adjunct of Society. [...] Rarely, in modern times, has the audience for any cultural phenomenon assumed so completely the air of a government club."[15] Garafola points to "the role of Diaghilev's early enterprises in a high-level game of international cultural politics" and suggests that it was the exotic character of the Ballets Russes which attracted its very specific audience:

> For these slightly déclassé aristocrats and wealthy foreigners, as for the Franco-Jewish banking/financial network, the "alien" character and undeniable social cachet of Diaghilev's productions mirrored the ambiguities of their own position—the assimilationist aspirations and distinctive tastes that set them apart from the French aristocratic mainstream—while presenting a "racial" and political counterpoint to Wagnerism which in the 1890's and early 1900's reached the acme of its prestige. Diaghilev's annual *Festspiels* celebrated within the context of Latin "cosmopolitanism" the Slavic and "Oriental" legacy of the non-Teutonic East.[16]

Diaghilev himself, in a 1929 interview, spoke of his audience in terms reminiscent of political conquest:

> In 1911 [...] we arrived [in London] for the festivities connected with the coronation of King George V. The organizing committee entrusted

---

14   Koritz, *Gendering Bodies*, 120.

15   Lynn Garafola, *Diaghilev's Ballets Russes* (New York: Oxford University Press, 1989), 304

16   Lynn Garafola, "Toward a New Interpretation of Diaghilev's Ballets Russes, 1909–1914," in *Dance History Scholars Proceedings, Sixth Annual Conference* ([Milwaukee]: Dance History Scholars, 1983), 157.

me with the management of the gala performance at Covent Garden and our "hundred thousand rose performance" is still remembered by everyone present. We issued huge posters announcing that we were buying unlimited quantities of roses, and the large auditorium of Covent Garden and the stage were covered with a carpet of 100,000 roses. The dazzling audience included the ambassadors and ministers of foreign powers, Indian maharajahs, Chinese mandarins, Japanese princes and nobles, African kings, Zulu and Indian chiefs and, of course, King George V and his Court, and indeed everyone who was anyone in society. Thus, in one evening, the Russian ballet conquered the world.[17]

In looking further at the "conquest" by the Ballets Russes of Western Europe in the terms I have set out in this article—gender, gaze, and the metaphorical staging of nationhood—we cannot help but address two overlapping aspects of the Diaghilev troupe's productions—the dramatization of sexual politics and the presentation of the Russian ballet as "oriental"—which have already received considerable attention from historians of dance, music, and fashion.[18] Some of the most fruitful statements on the intersection among gender, sex, and orientalism in the Ballets Russes have come from Lynn Garafola and music historian Richard Taruskin. In her article "Reconfiguring the Sexes," Garafola traces the history of how "Diaghilev's revolution dethroned the ballerina" in favor of the sexually ambiguous ballerino, for which Vaslav Nijinsky served as the prototype.[19] We should note, however, that even this competition for attention did not deprive the ballerina of her metaphorical potency. Taruskin, on the other hand, by placing the orientalist trope in music in historical context, points out that in the pre-Ballets Russes tradition in Russian music, the evocation "not [of] the East, but [of] the seductive East [...] emasculates, enslaves, renders passive. In a word, it signifies the promise or the

---

17 "Around the World with the Russian Ballet: A Previously Unpublished Interview with Serge Diaghilev," *Dance Magazine* (September 1974): 50.

18 Peter Wollen, "Out of the Past: Fashion/Orientalism/The Body," in his *Raiding the Icebox* (Bloomington: Indiana University Press, 1993), 1–34; Emily Apter, "Acting Out Orientalism: Sapphic Theatricality in Turn-of-the-Century Paris," *L'esprit créateur* 34, no. 2 (Summer 1994): 102–16.

19 Lynn Garafola, "Reconfiguring the Sexes," in *The Ballets Russes and Its World*, ed. Lynn Garafola and Nancy Van Norman Baer (New Haven: Yale University Press, 1999), 248. Garafola emphasizes "the antifemale bias implicit in Diaghilev's homosexual radicalism" (267) in her discussion.

experience of *nega* [languor—eds.], a prime attribute of the orient as imagined by Russians." However, he specifies that "*nega*, associated with the orient, is held up as a degenerate counterpart to more manly virtues associated with Russians. It marked the Other—marked it, in fact, for justified conquest." Taruskin concludes with the irony that the "new infusion of semi-Asiatic exotica-cum-erotica, the sex lure that underpinned Diaghilev's incredible success" was a trap of sorts: "The ploy eventually held Diaghilev captive, preventing him from presenting to the West the musical artifacts of the European Russia with which he personally identified."[20]

Arguably the most successful of the Ballets Russes productions evoked sexually charged power struggles between male and female, West and East, master and subordinate. Two of the most spectacular of the early Diaghilev ballets, *Cleopatra* and *The Firebird*, exemplify these tensions particularly vividly. Based loosely on Aleksandr Pushkin's *Egyptian Nights* (Egipetskie nochi), *Cleopatra* made its debut on June 2, 1909, the second night of the fabled first season of the Diaghilev ballet. On this night the stunning Ida Rubinstein, "a trap for the gaze," appeared in the title role.[21] Charles S. Meyer describes her entrance:

> Her very entrance in *Cléopâtre* was designed to arouse the anticipation of the public. First came a grand ritual cortege led by musicians playing on cithara and flutes, followed by dancing fauns, maidens, slaves and attendants. Then, six colossal black slaves entered through the back portal of Bakst's set—a startling interpretation of the interior of an ancient Egyptian temple with huge statues along the side walls and a propylon four columns wide on both sides and two columns deep across the back. The Nubians carried on their shoulders an ebony-and-gold casket, which they set down in the middle of the temple facing the audience. Opened, the casket revealed a mummy swathed in veils which the Nubians lifted and placed center stage. Slaves then began unwinding the veils, removing the first one (red with silver lotuses and crocodiles), then a second (green with the history of the dynasties of the Pharaoh in gold filigree). As the slaves ritualistically removed the

---

20   Richard Taruskin, "'Entoiling the Falconet': Russian Musical Orientalism in Context," *Cambridge Opera Journal* 4, no. 3 (November 1992): 259, 279, 280.

21   Wollen, "Out of the Past," 9.

twelve layers, each more elaborate than the last, the standing figure of Ida Rubinstein—Cleopatra—gradually emerged.[22]

The sumptuousness of the setting is matched by the melodramatic excess of the plot. The Egyptian queen—accompanied by Nijinsky in the role of "her favorite slave, half-man, half-beast, blazing with an erotic fire stoked by her beauty and cold, majestic disdain"—trades sex for death, luring the groom Amoûn away from his faithful love Ta-hor and poisoning him after he enjoys her sexual favors.[23] The emasculating, all-powerful oriental femme fatale in whom political might and lethal beauty (that which draws the gaze) converge, represents a terrifying and titillating tale of the East, overpowering and upstaging the virginal, traditionally tame and white-clad classical ballerina (see fig. 2). According to Benois, moreover, *Cleopatra* "brought the fullest houses."[24]

One of the most successful ballets of Diaghilev's second Paris season, so enduring that it continues to be performed by major companies to this day, *The Firebird*, both complements and, as it were, responds to the

FIGURE 2. *Rubinstein as Cleopatra*, by Leon Bakst. From the collection of Nina and Nikita D. Lobanov-Rostovsky.

---

22   Charles S. Mayer, "Ida Rubinstein: A Twentieth-Century Cleopatra," *Dance Research Journal* 20, no. 2 (Winter 1988): 33.

23   Garafola, "Reconfiguring the Sexes," 249.

24   Benois, *Reminiscences,* 295. Quoted in Kelly Miller, "Anna Akhmatova's 'An Old Portrait' and the Ballets Russes," *Canadian Slavonic Papers* (March-June 2005): 9.

FIGURE 3. Tamara Karsavina, 1911. In the role of the Firebird. E. O. Hoppé Estate Collection/ Curatorial Inc.

disturbing image of the lethal Oriental female presented in *Cleopatra*. Sally Banes, in "*Firebird* and the Idea of Russianness," makes a convincing argument for viewing the ballet as the embodiment of an imperial allegory. It is, she points out, "the story of the unseating of an Asiatic oppressor through the agency of an Oriental woman."²⁵ Banes places the drama danced out in *The Firebird* in the context of Russia's liminal status between Western Europe and its own "East":

> Ivan is as much an autocratic figure as Koshchei, I don't see the liberation in the ballet as democratic, because defeating tyranny can still be compatible with monarchy—especially when the new monarch is backed by nature (or the personification thereof). With the aid of the Firebird, Ivan "liberates" the enchanted oriental kingdom in the most imperial Russian sense: he delivers it into colonial status in his own empire. This he accomplishes with the imprimatur of nature, in the figure of the Firebird—Mother Nature, Mother Russia, but still, paradoxically Asiatic.²⁶

In *The Firebird* Russia achieves a hybrid identity—Western and Eastern, male and female, with its Asian femininity held in check (see fig. 3): "The 'Russian export,' not surprisingly, presents the Russian nation to Western Europe as

---

25   Sally Banes, "Firebird and the Idea of Russianness," in *The Ballets Russes and Its World*, ed. Lynn Garafola and Nancy Van Norman Baer (New Haven: Yale University Press, 1999), 124.

26   Sally Banes, "Firebird and the Idea of Russianness," 131.

Figure 4. Liubov Tchernicheva as Cleopatra in *Cleopatra*, 1918. E. O. Hoppé Estate Collection/ Curatorial Inc.

politically powerful, especially in its suzerainty over its eastern and southern possessions."[27] Yet, in a dream of imperial endurance reminiscent of *Sleeping Beauty,* the ballet in the end pairs Ivan Tsarevich off with "the beautiful Tsarevna [. . .] a 'true' Russian maiden, an ideal of racial purity and national superiority."[28]

I preface my conclusion to this discussion of the Ballets Russes with an image of the ballerina from *Cleopatra* (see fig. 4).

The sphinx-like pose is strangely prescient of a central image of Aleksandr Blok's "The Scythians" (Skify), written in 1918 in the wake of the Bolshevik revolution. Blok's poem, addressed to the West, poses the threat that the Russians—who for centuries "Kak poslushnye kholopy, / Derzhali shchit mezh dvukh vrazhdebnykh ras / Mongolov i Evropy!" (Like obedient slaves / Held a shield between hostile peoples / the Mongols and the Europeans!)—are no longer content passively to accept the European gaze (Vy sotni let gliadeli na Vostok; "You looked for centuries to the East"). Calling on Europe, like Oedipus, to solve the riddle, Blok warns:

> Россия—Сфинкс! Ликуя и скорбя,
>   И обливаясь черной кровью,
>   Она глядит, глядит, глядит в тебя
>   И с ненавистью, и с любовью! . . .

---

27 Sally Banes, "Firebird and the Idea of Russianness," 133.

28 Sally Banes, "Firebird and the Idea of Russianness," 134.

> Russia is a Sphinx! Rejoicing and mourning,
>   And bathed with black blood,
> She looks, looks, looks, at you
>   With hatred and love! . . .[29]

As Blok's metaphor of the sphinx suggests, Russia's liminal status opens for it the possibility of looking either to the East or the West, of being a spectacular lure to the gaze of the West or a specular subject looking on from the East. Ironically, if the Ballets Russes cast its lot with the West by staging Russia as Eastern and feminine, within a few years Soviet ballet would turn to the East, would entrance the Eastern gaze, by abrogating to itself the "Western" attributes of manliness, authority, reason, and enlightenment.

Soviet Ballet Subdues the Orient

Why, after all, did ballet not only survive, but flourish with generous state subsidies throughout the Soviet period? If the extraordinary dominance of Soviet ballet in the later twentieth century makes this development seem inevitable with the blindness of hindsight, we must take ourselves back and remember that ballet, probably the art form most closely tied to royalty and to the pomp and circumstance of court ritual, was on the wane in the West when it was given a new shot of vigor by Russians—by the extraordinary Paris seasons of the Ballets Russes and the subsequent ventures of Diaghilev and his successors and the frenetic missionary work of Anna Pavlova, who inspired a new generation of dancers by taking ballet to remote regions of the world. The harsh conditions in the homeland of Russian ballet after the revolution, though, placed its survival at risk:

> However, the first years after the revolution were very difficult. General devastation in the country, brought about by the First World War and the Civil War, took a toll on the work of theaters. There was no money to pay the salaries of the artists, there was no fuel. The emigration abroad of leading ballerinas, of top dancers, of experienced pedagogues and ballet masters left theaters without direction. The question

---

29 Aleksandr Blok, "Skify," in his *Sobranie sochinenii v vos'mi tomakh* (Moscow: Khudozhestvennaia literatura, 1960), vol. 3, 560–61. The translations are my own—C. T. N.

of closing the Bolshoi Theater in Moscow and other leading theaters was raised pointedly.[30]

A greater risk, moreover, was posed by the challenge of transforming ballet to meet the ideological priorities of the Bolshevik leadership—a challenge rendered all the more daunting by the fact that, given ballet's questionable pedigree, the desirability of its resurrection in the new cultural context was far from uncontested. The answer to the question of why ballet became a vaunted Soviet institution would seem to lie in the convergence of the imperial and Ballets Russes traditions, in the potency of ballet as a means of staging and thereby naturalizing the imperial underpinnings of the internationalist proletarian state.

Let us look then at another pivotal moment, this time in Soviet ballet. *The Red Poppy* (Krasnyi mak) was first staged at the Bolshoi Theater in Moscow in 1927 and is considered a watershed in the evolution of Soviet ballet, the first ballet to adapt the traditional form of dance, with its heavy weight of aristocratic baggage, to ideologically correct content. It is a testimony to the success of the endeavor that the ballet remained in the Soviet repertoire for at least four decades, with the lead role being danced by some of the greatest Soviet prima ballerinas, most notably Galina Ulanova.

The music was written by Reinhold Glière, a composer who was schooled in the tradition of nationalist music promoted by the Mighty Handful and had made his reputation largely with symphonic music before the revolution. Glière turned more concertedly to ballet and opera composition only after the revolution. An early adventure in opera provides a curious, but apropos preface to *The Red Poppy*. In 1923 Glière traveled to the new republic of Azerbaijan to compose the foundation stone of modern Azerbaijani opera, *Sahsenem*, based on Azeri folk motifs and adaptations of traditional Azeri music to Western instruments. The original libretto for the opera was in Russian. It is important to remember that Glière undertook this "Westernizing" mission well before Stalin's "social mandate" sent composers—including Glière—to the various republics of Central Asia to invent musical traditions for them. It is also worth noting in this context that bringing the conventions of Western music to the outlying territories of the empire coming into being was one ac-

---

30   V. Pasiutinskaia, *Volshebnyi mir tantsa* (Moscow: Prosveshchenie, 1985), 144.

tivity through which Russians could unambiguously by their own lights claim the civilizing role of the Westerner.

The Red Poppy, Glière's first successful ballet and the ballet that in a sense made the medium "relevant," was produced at the Bolshoi Theater, symbolic center of Soviet high art.[31] The ballet, which premiered on June 14, 1927, was composed both to honor the tenth anniversary of the Revolution and to commemorate the fiftieth birthday of Ekaterina Geltser, the ballerina who would be the first to dance the lead role of the dancer Toa Xoa.

The basic plot of the ballet (I have conflated accounts of early productions) runs as follows. Act I, Scene 1 opens on the port in a nameless Chinese city. A Soviet ship has docked and is being unloaded by downtrodden Chinese coolies. The famous dancer Toa Xoa is carried onstage in a palanquin and dances a welcoming dance of the fan, but becomes embarrassed when her self-styled fiancé, Li Shan-Fu, who has traveled to Europe and been corrupted by his exposure to European civilization, appears. During the unloading, a coolie collapses under his load and is unable to get up. An overseer begins to beat him. When the coolies try to defend the fallen man, the Englishman who runs the port, Sir Hips, wants to use force to resolve the conflict, but the captain of the Soviet ship orders his sailors to take over the unloading. The coolies are touched by this act of kindness. Toa Xoa gives the captain a bouquet of flowers from which he takes a red poppy and gives it to her or to a coolie "as a symbol of liberty." Li Shan-Fu beats Toa Xoa for consorting "with a Bolshevik." After Toa Xoa departs with Li Shan-Fu and night falls, coolies, Malaysian women, and sailors from different countries perform national dances. The Soviet sailors dance to the popular "Ekh, iablochko."

Act II, Scene 1 takes place in an opium den, where Toa Xoa is dancing. Sir Hips and Li Shan-Fu conspire to get rid of the Soviet captain by using an unsuspecting Toa Xoa, who is falling in love with him, to lure him into the club. The conspirators fall on him with knives, but the Soviet sailors rush to their captain's rescue. The distraught Toa Xoa smokes opium to relieve her sadness.

---

31 Glière made a number of false starts with ballets in the years following the revolution. He composed a ballet entitled *The Zaporosians* (*Zaporozhtsy*), based on Repin's famous painting, as well as a ballet based on Pushkin's *Egyptian Nights* (generally overlooked as the first Soviet Pushkin ballet), which had also provided the impetus for Diaghilev's *Cleopatra*. Neither ballet ever made it to the stage.

Act II, Scenes 2 and 3 consist of two distinct parts of Toa Xoa's opium-induced dream. In the darker, first part Toa Xoa has a dream of monsters and dragons, warriors, priests, and gods of the old China of legend. In the second part, Toa Xoa sees herself in a wonderful land of lotuses, poppies, and butterflies. An apparition of the Soviet captain appears to her, but melts away as she approaches.

In Act III, Scene 1 the villains conspire to poison the Soviet captain at a ball at the house of Li Shan-Fu. When the captain arrives at the ball, Toa Xoa confesses her love for him and begs him to take her away from China. She presents the captain with the poisoned cup, but knocks it out of his hand before he can drink it. The enraged Li Shan-Fu fires at the captain with a revolver, but misses.

In Act III, Scene 2 Toa Xoa watches the Soviet ship departing from the harbor. Li Shan-Fu finds her and, in anger over the failed plot, stabs her. Toa Xoa is surrounded by a group of children, and as she is dying, she urges them to struggle for freedom and hands them a red flower. The ballet concludes with an apotheosis representing the victory of the proletariat, symbolized by an enormous red flower and the incorporation into the orchestral score of the "International."[32]

---

32 In 1949, the ballet was restaged and renamed, significantly in the same year as Glière's other famous, imperial ballet, *The Bronze Horseman* (Mednyi vsadnik), made its debut in both Moscow and Leningrad. On the one hand, this complicates the study of the original ballet, since it is in large measure vestiges of the later version that have survived. On the other hand, the modifications provide ample proof of the political uses of the balletic text in the late Stalinist Soviet Union. The re-choreographed ballet was re-titled *The Red Flower* (Krasnyi tsvetok) so as to mute any reference to opium that might offend the Soviet Union's new Chinese comrades. This renaming appears to be matched in the libretto of the ballet when the dark opening segment of Tao Xoa's dream, clearly an opium-induced hallucination in the original production, may be taken as a simple nightmare in the later version. In another small, but telling detail, the Soviet ship, apparently nameless in the 1927 production, is prominently labeled the *Moscow* in the 1949 production, underscoring the synecdoche of the center for the Soviet whole. Fundamental changes, obviously mirroring the contemporary political reality, were made in the plot and characters of the ballet as well. Tao Xoa's love interest is shifted from the captain of the Soviet ship to a mutinous Chinese coolie named Ma Li Chen, and the heroine dies sacrificing herself to save her lover's life as he leads the other oppressed masses in rebellion.

The Cold War rivalry is blatantly moved to the forefront in *The Red Flower*. Li ShanFu is demoted to the role of a duped pawn at the hands of the major villain, an American arms dealer. Perhaps most strikingly the unloading scene that opens the ballet becomes an open competition between the ever pure Soviet sailors and the arms smuggling Americans,

Two central scenes from the ballet illustrate how gender is deployed in this epic staging of international relations. The first is the energetic dance of the Soviet sailors to the folk tune "Ekh, iablochko," while the second represents the opium-induced dream of the ballerina, returned to center stage in the person of the Chinese music hall dancer Toa Xoa. The juxtaposition of these scenes demonstrates how in The *Red Poppy* key elements of the Ballets Russes productions have been retained in reconfigured form—the Orient enslaved and feminized, driven by passion and hallucination countered by an athletic male cohort in a drama of dominance and submission, Russian and foreign. Soviet Russia, most forcefully in the person of the Soviet ship's captain, stages itself as masculine and Western and, most important, immune to seduction by the oriental dancer—left behind by the new Soviet man who is disciplined to resist the dangerous temptation of returning the fatal gaze of the East.

Tellingly, in the final scene of the ballet, we find the vector of gaze reversed as Toa Xoa looks after the departing ship and its captain, only to be ritually sacrificed, in a sense, to give symbolic birth to the collective of the future. The hallucinatory, potentially lethal passion of the feminized East is vanquished on all fronts by the civilizing mission of Bolshevism. The metaphorical paradigm given shape in the dance therefore evolved in response to policy changes, but, arguably, retained its power to fashion audience conceptions of the master plot of imperial aspiration, even in its proletarian, internationalist guise.

To conclude, what I have tried to show in this article is what Elizabeth Surits expressed so pithily in the epigraph to this article: "We had an imperial ballet and we returned to an imperial ballet." Ballet in the Soviet period became a means of staging the might of the Soviet state metaphorically as well as materially, that is, vanquishing the genii of decadent orientalism unleashed by the Ballets Russes while displaying the Soviet state's virile ability to deploy disciplined athletic male as well as female bodies and massive resources, as had the tsarist government before it, to perform its power. In the final analysis, we see, ballet's intimate relationship with politics never lay very far beneath the surface despite the dramatic metamorphoses in Russia's political fortunes.

---

in which the breakdown of work is triggered when the coolie collapse leads to the breaking open of a freight box to reveal smuggled weapons, a thinly veiled and unmistakably tendentious reference to the arms race. The racial tensions, evident as we have seen in the original as well, here become quite explicitly references to United States racial bigotry.

Works Cited

Apter, Emily. "Acting Out Orientalism: Sapphic Theatricality in Turn-of-the-Century Paris." *L'esprit createur* 34, no. 2 (Summer 1994): 102–16.

"Around the World with the Russian Ballet: A Previously Unpublished Interview with Serge Diaghilev." *Dance Magazine* (September 1974): 48–55.

Banes, Sally. "Firebird and the Idea of Russianness." In *The Ballets Russes and Its World*, edited by Lynn Garafola and Nancy Van Norman Baer, 117–34. New Haven: Yale University Press, 1999.

Benois, Alexandre. *Reminiscences of the Russian Ballet*. Translated by Mary Britnieva. New York: Da Capo Press, 1977.

Blok, Aleksandr. "Skify." In his *Sobranie sochinenii v vos'mi tomakh*, vol. 3, 560–62. Moscow: Khudozhestvennaia literatura, 1960.

Franks, A. H., ed. *Pavlova: A Biography*. New York: Macmillan, 1956.

Garafola, Lynn. *Diaghilev's Ballets Russes*. New York: Oxford University Press, 1989.

———. "Reconfiguring the Sexes." In *The Ballets Russes and Its World*. Edited by Lynn Garafola and Nancy Van Norman Baer, 245–68. New Haven: Yale University Press, 1999.

———. "Toward a New Interpretation of Diaghilev's Ballets Russes, 1909–1914." In *Dance History Scholars Proceedings, Sixth Annual Conference*, 152–65. [Milwaukee]: Dance History Scholars, 1983.

Jowitt, Deborah. *Time and the Dancing Image*. New York: William Morrow and Co., Inc., 1988.

Koritz, Amy. *Gendering Bodies/Performing Art: Dance and Literature in Early Twentieth-Century British Culture*. Ann Arbor: University of Michigan Press, 1995.

Kshesinskaia, Matil'da. *Vospominaniia*. Moscow: Artist. Rezhisser. Teatr, 1992.

Lifar, Serge. *A History of Russian Ballet from Its Origins to the Present Day*, trans. Arnold Haskell (London: Hutchinson, 1954).

Lincoln, Bruce. *Between Heaven and Hell: The Story of a Thousand Years of Artistic Life in Russia*. New York: Viking, 1998.

Mayer, Charles S. "Ida Rubinstein: A Twentieth-Century Cleopatra." *Dance Research Journal* 20, no. 2 (Winter 1988): 33–51.

Miller, Kelly. "Anna Akhmatova's 'An Old Portrait' and the Ballets Russes." *Canadian Slavonic Papers* (March-June 2005): 71–93.

Morley, Iris. *Soviet Ballet*. London: Collins, 1945.

Pasiutinskaia, V. *Volshebnyi mir tantsa*. Moscow: Prosveshchenie, 1985.

Pushkin, A. S. *Polnoe sobranie sochinenii v shestnadtsati tomakh*. Moscow: Izdatel'stvo AN SSSR, 1937–1959.

——— [Alexander Pushkin]. *Eugene Onegin*. Translated by James M. Falen. New York: Oxford University Press, 1990.

Scholl, Tim. *From Petipa to Balanchine: Classical Revival and the Modernization of Ballet.* New York: Routledge, 1994.

Taruskin, Richard. "'Entoiling the Falconet': Russian Musical Orientalism in Context." *Cambridge Opera Journal* 4, no. 3 (November 1992): 253–80.

Wollen, Peter. "Out of the Past: Fashion/Orientalism/The Body." In his *Raiding the Icebox*, 1–34. Bloomington: Indiana University Press, 1993.

13

The Blockbuster Miniseries on Soviet TV: Isaev-Shtirlits, the Ambiguous Hero of *Seventeen Moments in Spring*

> There is another reason why Putin is our president. In him, two beloved characters from [Soviet/Russian] jokes merge: Shtirlits and Vovochka.

Since the collapse of the Soviet Union, as a result of increased access to the Russian audience and more general scholarly trends, Western Slavists have become increasingly interested in manifestations of popular culture during the Soviet period. The relative independence of the Soviet cultural economy from market considerations makes it difficult, if not impossible, to draw a strict line of demarcation between officially generated mass cultural phenomena and genuinely popular entertainment. Nonetheless there is ample evidence that Soviet readers and television viewers, film goers and music lovers sought within the censored culture itself and, at least in the post-Stalin period, found, if in insufficient quantities, cultural products that provided entertainment. Works that offered escape and amusement enjoyed indisputable popularity among the Soviet audience. In this context, I will focus this article on what was arguably one of the most important "low" culture events of the Brezhnev period: the airing in 1973 of the twelve-part miniseries (some fourteen hours of TV viewing), *Seventeen Moments in Spring* (Semnadtsat' mgnovenii vesny). This

---

This article first appeared in *The Soviet and Post-Soviet Review* 29, no. 3 (2002): 257–76. Republished by permission of Brill Pusblishers—eds.

series chronicles the adventures of the fictional Soviet double agent Maksim Maksimovich Isaev, who worked undercover as SS officer Max Otto von Shtirlits in the upper echelons of the Nazi high command during the last months of World War II. As a testimony to the enduring appeal of the series, the June 21, 1998 issue of *Ogonek* carried the following brief news note under the heading "Shtirlits Came Back" (Shtirlits vernulsia) about a guest appearance at a film festival in Sochi by the actor Viacheslav Tikhonov, who played Shtirlits in the series:

> "Shtirlits has arrived!" rejoiced the children and citizens who were meeting the great ones of the world at the "Kinotaur" festival. Shtirlits decorously made his rounds of the crowd, shaking hands. There were so many people who wanted to squeeze the palm of the real live Shtirlits that an incredible crush formed, in which a pickpocket touring in the south had his hand pulled out of joint. The victim was taken to the hospital. A prison one.[1]

In the same vein, a post-Soviet commentator remarked, apparently only partly tongue in cheek: "After a showing of the film in 1995 on Russian Central Television it was noted that, just like twenty years before, city streets were empty during the showing of *Moments* on TV. A drop in the crime level almost to zero was noted in cities, which testifies to the popularity of the film not only among the people, but also in the criminal milieu (what, aren't they people too?)."[2]

This commentary also belongs among what is perhaps the most compelling *post factum* evidence of the original and continuing appeal of this made-for-TV movie, and especially of its central character Shtirlits—that is, its indisputably popular aftermath in the Soviet and post-Soviet periods, culminating in a rather striking presence on the internet. A 2002 article charting popularity on the Russian internet (Runet) by the number of mentions of a given figure on websites, observed that "[Alla] Pugacheva's popularity was comparable to that of Shtirlits," commenting:

---

1   Aleksei Torgashev, Aleksandr Nikonov, Sergei Solovkin, and Viktor Kliukin, "Shtirlits vernulsia," *Ogonek*, June 21, 1998, accessed September 25, 2022, https://www.kommersant.ru/doc/2285811.

2   "K istorii voprosa o Shtirlitse," Kontora brat'ev Divanovykh, access date unknown, http://webideas.com/shtirlits/history.htm (site discontinued—eds.).

But on the whole much more interesting is the presence in the list not of politicians, but of mythical and semi-mythical popular [*narodnye*] personages like Shtirlits, who are the heroes of numerous jokes. Precisely they—Vovochka, Chapaev, Lieutenant Rzhevskii, and Rabinovich—possess the most constant popularity: independent of the political structure and trends in fashion and culture, anecdotes from internet-folklore about Vovochka and other signal figures of the Russian mentality don't go away. The number of entertainment sites like Anekdot.ru or fomenko.ru can only grow, including various sites devoted to each personage separately. For example, it is best to start your acquaintance with the first personage—Shtirlits—with the site in his name (www.geocities.com/stirlits200l.ru [site discontinued—eds.]), where one can become acquainted with the real biography of KGB Colonel Isaev. Then, feeling oneself the spy himself with the aid of a special program (designed to decipher electronic letters written in the Russian language and received in "unreadable" form and also for the decoding and recoding of text files) at the site Shtirlits.ru (www.shtirlitz.ru [site discontinued—eds.]), it is possible to go on to the many anecdotal stories of the adventures of the famous spy at the site "Shtirlitsiada" (ww.webideas.com/shtirlits [site discontinued—eds.]).[3]

Shtirlits jokes apparently appeared shortly after the original airing of the miniseries and continued to proliferate in the late glasnost period when anthologies of jokes began to be published in the Soviet Union.[4] The analogy with Chapaev, another immensely popular Soviet film hero, is exposed on occasion in the jokes themselves, as in the following example:

> "And you, Shtirlits, I would ask to stay."
> For about ten minutes Müller gazed intently at Shtirlits's face.
> "Where could I have seen you before?"—he asked Shtirlits.
> "Perhaps in China?"—Shtirlits tentatively tried to suggest.
> "What year was that? No, before that? Ah! In Russia!"
> "Wait... [Is that you,] Pet′ka?"
> "Vasilii Ivanovich?"

---

3   Iurii Rosich, "Samyi glavnyi geroi Runeta," accessed August 2, 2022, http://rocich.ru/articles/articie.php?sid=251. Another commentator observed that Shtirlits was "the most popular hero of the Soviet people, leaving Chapaev and [Ostap] Bender far behind." Dmitrii Bykov, Vladimir Voronov, and Irina Luk′ianova, "Shtirlits i seichas zhivee vsekh zhivykh," *Sobesednik*, access date unknown, http://www.sobesednik.ru/weekly/23/investigation/288.phtml (site discontinued—eds.).

4   See A. V. Voznesenskii, "O sovremennom anekdotopechatanii," *Novoe literaturnoe obozrenie*, 22 (1996): 393–99.

Moreover, in the late 1980s parodic sequels, brief prose works styling themselves "novels" and featuring Shtirlits and the other characters from the series in irreverent and absurd episodic adventures, began to appear in *samizdat*, then in multiple, often pirated book editions, and later made their way onto the internet as well. These "low" culture spin-offs of the "classic" original (to paraphrase the indignant discourse of some Russian commentators) in part are merely expressions of post-Soviet nostalgia and poke fun at the credulity-stretching ideological purity of Shtirlits and the hackneyed conventions of the series' structure. However, I will argue here that the ubiquity of Shtirlits jokes and parodies also is a function of the popularity of the original series itself. These jokes and parodies expose the series and its "positive hero" as inherently ambiguous and can help us perceive in them the deeply rooted, unvoiced, and perhaps unacknowledged cultural allegiances and anxieties of the Soviet viewing audience.

The character of Isaev-Shtirlits was created by Iulian Semenov, perhaps the most successful Soviet writer of popular fiction of the post-Stalin period.[5] Semenov, who was born in 1931 and died in 1993, began publishing in 1958, but it was after the 1963 publication of his crime novel, *Petrovka, 38* (which took as its title the address of the main police headquarters in Moscow), that Semenov achieved real fame as a popular author. In the wake of the success of *Petrovka, 38*, Semenov began publishing a series of what Soviet critics termed "political chronicles" featuring Shtirlits-Isaev. These works, which mixed fact, in the form of real historical events and documents, and fiction, included the 1969 novel *Seventeen Moments in Spring*.

The figure of Isaev-Shtirlits himself partakes of this same mixture. According to his fictional biography as it unfolds in Semenov's novels, though not in the film, he was born in 1898 in Switzerland, the son of a Moscow law professor and socialist sympathizer forced into emigration. In his youth, Isaev came to know the leading Russian émigré revolutionaries, returned to Russia right after Lenin, and joined the Cheka at the request of Dzerzhinskii himself. The civil war finds him in the Far East. In the 1920s he takes on the identity of

---

5   Richard Stites, *Russian Popular Culture: Entertainment and Society since 1990* (Cambridge: Cambridge University Press, 1992), 152. On Semenov, see also: Walter Laqueur, "Julian Semyonov and the Soviet Political Novel," *Society* 23, no. 5 (July–August 1986): 72–80; A. Vulis, *V mire prikliuchenii: Poetika zhanra* (Moscow: Sovetskii pisatel', 1986), 354–63; V. Kardin, "Sekret uspekha," *Voprosy literatury* 4 (1986): 102–50.

Shtirlits to penetrate the Nazi movement in Shanghai. He is in Yugoslavia in 1941 on the eve of the German invasion of the Soviet Union, and in Krakow in 1944. In *Seventeen Moments in Spring*, he is entangled in the intrigues of the Nazi elite in Berlin in February and March of 1945. The following books chronicle the end of the Third Reich and find Shtirlits in Cold War Europe. Semenov, who openly acknowledged his KGB connections, was apparently given access to secret archives and based his "hero," however loosely, on a real life Soviet spy code-named "Braitenbruch" with the code number A/201. Thus, an article in *Argumenty i fakty* claimed:

> Indeed, the Central Committee of the CPSU advised the writer to transform the German Willy Leman into the Russian Maksim Isaev. Like Shtirlits from the book, Willy Leman was indeed the right hand of Walter Schellenberg, head of the German spy service. He engaged in counterespionage protection of the Reich military industry. Most important was Leman's information on the development of a fundamentally new weapon—"fau" missiles—headed by Werner von Braun in Germany.
> Shtirlits-Leman was held in high esteem both in Moscow and Berlin.[6]

Unlike Shtirlits, however, Leman was arrested by the Gestapo in December 1942 and did not survive the war.[7] In this, as in other things, Semenov had no qualms about "improving" on reality. More to the point, the documentary traces in *Seventeen Moments in Spring* serve to heighten the complex interplay between the reality the series purports to depict and the reality it evokes in the viewer as I hope further discussion will demonstrate.

Semenov himself wrote the screenplay for the television serial of *Seventeen Moments in Spring*, and the miniseries was directed by Tatiana Lioznova. The cast was impressive. As noted above, Isaev-Shtirlits was played by Viacheslav

---

6   "V gostiiakh u 'Shtirlitsev,'" *Argumenty i fakty*, January 1, 1998, accessed August 2, 2022, https://archive.aif.ru/archive/1637804.

7   In the same vein, the obituary of a former intelligence agent recently maintained that she had been the real-life prototype for "radistka Ket": "V Moskve skonchalas' 'radistka Ket,'" *Novoe russkoe slovo*, June 25, 1998, 4. Moreover, a March 1998 article maintained that the Gestapo chief Müller was in fact the prototype for Shtirlits: Igor' Tufel'd, "My govorim—Shtirlits, podrazumevaem ... Miuller?," *Ogonek*, March 22, 1998, accessed September 25, 2002, https://www.kommersant.ru/doc/2285619. The issue also contains an interview with Leonid Bronevoi, the actor who played Müller, on the same subject.

Tikhonov, whose film career spanned more than half a century and included such roles as Prince Andrei Bolkonskii in *War and Peace* and Vsevolod in *Burnt by the Sun* (Utomlennye solntsem). The rest of the distinguished cast included Leonid Bronevoi as Gestapo chief Henrich Müller, Evgenii Evstigneev as Professor Pleishner, Oleg Tabakov as Schellenberg, Rostislav Platt as Pastor Shlag, Iurii Vizbor as Bormann, Leonid Kuravlev as Aisman, Ekaterina Gradova in the film's only major female role as Katia Kozlova (alias Ketrin Kinor or "radistka Ket" [radio operator Ket]), and Efim Kopelian as the voice of Semenov's omniscient third-person narrator. In this context, we should note that Shtirlits jokes frequently and significantly play on a blurring of boundaries between actor and role, life and art, often demanding a comprehensive knowledge of the cast, as in the following examples:

> Shtirlits wakes up in the morning to find his hands and feet bound and begins feverishly trying to remember what happened to him. After long consideration, he resolves: "If people in black come in, that means it's the Gestapo, and I am Shtirlits. If people in green come in, that means I am being held by the NKVD and I am Isaev."
>
> Two men in gray enter, lift him up, and carry him down a succession of corridors. The bound man kicks and hollers:
> "For what?"
> "Last night at the reception, you drank like a pig and then wreaked havoc. Is that how a People's Artist should conduct himself, Citizen Tikhonov?"
>
> ***
>
> Shtirlits shoots Müller in the head. The bullet ricochets on impact and becomes embedded in the wall. "Bullet-proof! [Bronevoi!—the last name of the actor who played Müller—eds.]," thinks Shtirlits to himself.

The permeability of the boundary between the roles and the actors who play them speaks to the extent to which the miniseries may be seen as exposing itself as artifice and thereby subverting its own "ideological purity," a point to which I will return below.

Needless to say, given that I am talking about a film of epic length devoted to espionage, the intrigue chronicled in *Seventeen Moments in Spring* is complex. As the title suggests, the plot is structured around seventeen "moments" or temporally bounded episodes, generally each concentrated on a particular day, beginning with February 2, 1945 and ending with March 24, 1945. These "moments" are unified into a more or less coherent plot by the assignment Shtirlits (code-named "Iustas" in radio transmissions from Moscow) receives from his control back home (code-named Aleks) to check if rumors that someone in the Nazi leadership is trying to negotiate a separate peace with the Western allies are true and, if so, on whose initiative. During the course of the miniseries, Shtirlits indeed discovers that Allen Dulles is negotiating in Berne with General Wolff, who is working on behalf of Himmler. To accomplish his mission, Shtirlits exploits the mutual distrust and atmosphere of general demoralization regnant among the German leadership with the collapse of the Third Reich imminent, throwing in his lot with Bormann to trap Himmler. Shtirlits's task is complicated by the fact that from the beginning of the series we learn that vague suspicions have arisen in the Nazi command around his activities, and he is being investigated by Müller, who is portrayed more as an honest, old-time cop than a vicious Nazi, and who plays a game of cat-and-mouse with Shtirlits throughout. While Müller is depicted as Shtirlits's worthy intellectual opponent, the double agent repeatedly and ultimately outwits him, concocting stories and employing strategies that are implausible, to say the least. Jokes frequently poke fun at Müller's incredible credulity and Shtirlits's consequent invulnerability. Again the examples below "lay bare the device" and reveal the transparency of the conventions on which the series rests:

> Müller was walking through the Reich Chancellery and saw Shtirlits, standing in front of Himmler's door.
> "Shtirlits, what are you doing here?"
> "I am waiting for a tram."
> After walking on a little further, Müller turned around. Shirlits had vanished.
> "I guess he got his tram," thought Müller.

***

> There is a meeting at Hitler's headquarters. Suddenly, Shtirlits comes into the room with a tray of oranges, sets the tray on the table, enters the combination into the safe, reads and photographs all the documents, puts them back, closes the safe, and calmly leaves. After a minute of stunned silence, Hitler comes to and yells:
> "Who was that?"
> "Oh, that was the Russian spy Isaev," answers Müller.

"Why didn't you arrest him and have him shot?!!!" "We have already tried, but he always talks his way out of it. He will just say that he was bringing oranges.

Shtirlits also makes use of several helpers, who generally cause him more trouble than they are worth. His professional contacts are his fellow agent (alias Erwin Kien), a communications specialist, and Kien's wife "Ket," Russians also living in Germany under assumed names. When their apartment is bombed at a crucial moment in the film, the husband is killed, Ket lands in the hospital, and Shtirlits is left without any means of communicating with Moscow. For lack of a better alternative, he recruits Professor Pleishner, a singularly inept agent, who seems to have little other purpose in the plot than to go to Berne and place the Russian code at risk. Then there is Pastor Shlag, whom Shtirlits has released from prison in return for a vague promise of cooperation, with whom he has lengthy philosophical discussions, and whom he later sends to Berne to use his pacifist connections to discredit the peace negotiations. Episodes involving these helpers figure among the most memorable moments in the miniseries (as evidenced by the frequency with which they are lampooned in Shtirlits jokes). Two of the more notable scenes in which these helpers appear deserve mention here. Professor Pleishner, realizing too late that he has missed the danger signal Shtirlits warned him of (two flowerpots in the window of the "safe house" in Berne), finds himself trapped by Nazi agents and, swallowing the cyanide capsule with which Shtirlits has foresightedly supplied him, crashes through the stairway landing window into the street below. Numerous jokes poke fun at the melodramatic prolongation of the scene aggravated by Pleishner's singular dimwittedness as an agent:

> Pleishner was finishing eating the tenth pack of Belomor cigarettes, but the ampule with the poison was still nowhere to be found.
> "I hope I find it in time," thought Pleishner, gazing at the stunned Gestapo agents.
>
> ***
>
> Pleishner threw himself from the window for a fifth time. The poison still did not work.

Ket is pregnant, and Shtirlits asks her to return to Russia to give birth since a woman in childbirth can never hide her nationality, because she will scream out in her native language while in labor. Ket refuses to go home, maintaining valiantly that she will just have to learn to scream in German. The bombing of her apartment building, in which her husband is killed, introduces new complications, however. When the injured Ket gives birth in a hospital, she does indeed scream out in Russian (suggesting that nationality is a biological birthright of sorts), and a nurse reports her to the Gestapo.

> "Couldn't you just give birth?," Müller asks Shtirlits.
> "To what?," Shtirlits replies with interest.
> "That doesn't matter. I just want to know what language you will scream in."

Shtirlits is forced into one of his most "creative" fibs following Ket's arrest: he has to come up with a whopper to explain why his fingerprints are on the Russian radio operator's suitcase. Moreover, in what is unquestionably the most absurd scene in the series, Rolf, interrogating Ket, threatens her baby by holding open the door to the wintry weather outside. Russian audiences apparently did not find ludicrous the assertion that a child bared before an open door would die of exposure in two or three minutes. It would seem, however, as the repeated references in jokes to these and like scenes from *Seventeen Moments in Spring* make clear, that the trope of hyperbolic exaggeration on which these scenes are constructed renders them effective, apparently because they simultaneously acknowledge and lampoon deep-rooted cultural stereotypes. In other words, precisely because it follows its own presumptions to the point of overstatement, the series undercuts its own apparently transparent monology and topples into the very ambiguity on which jokes feed.

Aside from the more preposterous elements of the plot, the narrative structure of the film exhibits certain peculiarities that have also inspired comic rejoinder. As already noted, the title of the miniseries itself foregrounds the passage of time in the film. Apparently to enhance the documentary "feel" of the movie, scenes are flagged with headings giving the precise date and time. This insistence on chronological precision, which might be construed as a device to build suspense, in fact, given the excruciatingly slow pace of *Seventeen Moments in Spring*—and apparently not only to those of us used to the high-paced action of Hollywood-made spy thrillers—borders on the ludicrous. Jokes like the following example lay bare the combination of the slow pace of the film and its continual invocation of time:

> Shtirlits was driving down the Berlin-Munich autobahn. The road was straight—like an arrow. His hands clutched the steering wheel, his eyes looked ahead, and his face did not express a single emotion. Shtirlits was sleeping. He was sleeping with his eyes open—he had gained this ability during his long years as a spy. He slept, but he knew that in exactly three hours and twenty minutes and thirty-eight seconds, he would wake up to hit the brakes at the first gas station.

Other pseudo-documentary techniques serve to break up the linear chronology of the film. Every time a new historical character makes his first appearance, the scene is preceded by a short documentary biography. In the case of the highest-ranking figures—Goering, Goebbels, Himmler, and Bormann—these biographies follow a relatively set pattern including ideologically damning quotes from the historical figures themselves and newsreel clips and are titled "Information for consideration" (Informatsiia dlia razmyshleniia), a phrase apparently of Semenov's own concoction. The entrances of characters such as Müller, Aisman, Schellenberg, and so on, are preceded by the narrator reading from the character's personal dossier (*lichnoe delo*). These dossiers are so repetitive as to make one suspect parody. Even more suspicious is the fact that in bureaucratic form these "personal dossiers" are virtually identical to Soviet Communist Party dossiers.

We should also note that Russia and the Soviet Union—terms that, I believe, it is particularly important to distinguish here—are relegated to the margins in the film. While this is perhaps inevitable in a film in which the bulk of the action takes place in Berlin and Berne, with only a few shots of actors playing Shtirlits's superiors—including Stalin—back in Moscow, it has the effect, intended or not, of endowing the distant homeland with the status of myth. On the one hand, then, the fictional plot is interspersed with newsreel clips of the Red Army's inexorable progress toward Berlin, threatened by the Allies' impending perfidy, which Shtirlits is striving to sabotage. On the other hand, Russia becomes the stuff of nostalgia, relegated to flashbacks, merging with Shtirlits's personal life, with his beloved wife back home, and his solitary celebrations in the privacy of his Berlin house, behind carefully lowered air raid shades, of the Soviet holidays, Red Army Day and International Women's Day. Russia is thus associated with what is most near and dear, with private life and family, that which is either inaccessible or savored only behind closed doors and reduced from geographical reality to emotionally charged symbol, a saccharine sentimentality many Shtirlits jokes exploit.

Usually on February 23 Shtirlits put on his Russian shirt [*kosovorotka*], drank a bottle of vodka, and played the accordion. However, this time he set off for one of Berlin's beer halls and, after forcing the Gestapo men there to form ranks, made them march about and sing revolutionary songs. Only when he got home did he realize how close he came to being discovered that day.

In one sense at least *Seventeen Moments in Spring* is very much about the time in which it was made rather than about the historical period in which it is set. While we learn in a flashback that, earlier in the war, Shtirlits single-handedly and presciently stopped Germany from developing the atom bomb first, thereby implicitly preventing a Nazi victory, we are informed in no uncertain terms virtually from the beginning of the series that for all intents and purposes the war is over, that the defeat of Germany is inevitable whether Shtirlits's current mission succeeds or fails. What is at issue, then, is not World War II, but the alignment of powers during the Cold War, and the noncoincidence of the Iron Curtain with the borders of Germany blurs the lines between enemies and allies in the film, as evidenced by jokes like the following:

Shtirlits never felt nostalgia for his motherland. He was used to Germany, loved Bavarian beer, drove a Mercedes, spoke and even thought in German. But there were so many Soviet spies around that Shtirlits, against his will, had to pretend that he took pleasure in drinking Stolichnaia vodka, smoking Belomor cigarettes, eating tinned beef, and yearning for Russian birch trees....

***

Müller received a report from an informant about Shtirlits. It said: "On the night of May 1, Shtirlits drove outside of Berlin. There, in the forest, in an empty clearing, he drank a bottle of vodka. He set a campfire and got out his balalaika. Then, while playing the balalaika, he began doing a squat dance and singing *chastushki*. After midnight he returned to his apartment, locked the bottle and the balalaika in the safe, and went to sleep."

The next day Shtirlits opened his safe and found—instead of the balalaika and the bottle—a note: "Shtirlits, for shame! You aren't the only one who is nostalgic."

***

> Shtirlits goes into an office and sees Müller in a Red Cavalry hat, seated at his desk and playing a balalaika. "It's true, Shtirlits," Müller pronounces with an air of melancholy, "you are not the only one who longs for the Motherland."

All of this serves to remind us that, by the time *Seventeen Moments in Spring* was written and then transformed into a TV serial, the allies had become adversaries, and Germans had been parsed ideologically into good ones and bad ones. This may help explain not only the number of "good" Germans in the film, who come across much better than the Americans do, but the relatively positive portrayals even of such historical personages and ideological adversaries as Müller.[8]

Quite apart from the Cold War realignment of powers, however, disturbing ambiguities in the representation of identity and national and ideological allegiance are inherent in the very conception of *Seventeen Moments in Spring*, ambiguities that seem to have found resonance, not necessarily on a conscious level, in its original audience. The responses to the series in popular culture, as I hope some of the jokes I have already quoted have suggested, play on these ambiguities and thereby reveal—and draw their humor from—the subversiveness inherent in the original film. (Again, I am not taking a stand here on whether the film was intentionally or unintentionally subversive. In this context, however, I would point out that the only character who actually spouts anything remotely resembling communist ideological rhetoric in the series is also the only character Shtirlits shoots in cold blood: his paid German informant who happily betrays people who help him.)

To clarify the point I am trying to make here, let me note the obvious: everyone in the film speaks Russian. While this was certainly the only practical way of making the film, it has a disconcerting tendency to render the national boundaries between adversaries invisible and therefore implicitly and potentially permeable, as evidenced by the series of Shtirlits jokes concerned with language and nationality:

> Out of all the automobile brands, Shtirlits preferred Mercedes, thereby exhibiting true German patriotism, as was so useful for maintaining his

---

8   One commentator claims this was because Müller himself had actually been a Soviet agent, see Tufel'd, "My govorim—Shtirlits."

cover. Moreover, the Russian spy was very pleased not to be a German spy in Russia: in that case, he would have had to drive a Zaporozhets.

***

Müller calls Shtirlits in and says: "Tomorrow is a communist *subbotnik* [compulsory but unpaid labor day—eds.]. Participation is mandatory."

Shtirlits answers: "Order received!" Then, realizing that he has blown his cover, he sits down at the desk and, under Müller's shocked gaze, writes: "I, Standartenführer von Shtirlits, am really a Soviet spy."

After reading this report, Müller calls Schellenberg and says: "Walter, come and see the inventive things your people are coming up with to get out of participating in the *subbotnik*."

***

Hitler phones Stalin:
"Stalin, did your people take secret documents from my safe?"
"I will find out," says Stalin in a pronounced Georgian accent.
Stalin phones Shtirlits and says, again in a Georgian accent:
"Shtirlits, did you take secret documents from Hitler's safe?"
"Yes, Comrade Stalin."
"Go put them back. People are worrying."

***

Müller was putting together an invitation list for a New Year's banquet at one point.
"Shtirlits, dear fellow, tell me, please, how to spell your last name: does it start with "Sht," "Scht," or "St"?
"It starts with Ш," the spy confidently answered.

***

Shtirlits was walking through the streets of Berlin and suddenly heard Russian being spoken behind him. "Olim Chadashim" [Hebrew for "new repatriates"], Shtirlits thought to himself.

The latter joke in particular, with its anachronistic invocation of Jewish emigration from the Soviet Union in the 1970s and 1980s, throws into relief Shtirlits's peculiar status as himself an émigré of sorts.

Arguably it is the pointedly heroic figure of Isaev-Shtirlits himself that is unquestionably the nexus of the cipher of identity in *Seventeen Moments in Spring*. As the following joke suggests, while Shtirlits's status as a positive hero is indisputable, it is nonetheless problematic:

"Shtirlits," Müller asked at one point. "Would you like to act in a film?"

"Certainly!," Shtirlits affirmed.

"Why?"

"Well, who wouldn't? In films the positive [*polozhtel'nyi*] hero always kills all the bad guys, and as a reward, he gets the thanks of the government and the love of a long-legged blonde with a voluptuous figure."

"Okay, Shtirlits, but how are you so sure you are the positive [*polozhitel'nyi*] hero?"

"Because I positively don't care about anything!" [*mne na vse polozhit'*] Shtirlits enthusiastically announced.

Let me remind you here of what Andrei Siniavskii has to say about the socialist realist positive hero in his essay *What is Socialist Realism*, using an episode from Leonid Leonov's novel *The Russian Forest* as an example:

> The courageous girl Polia is making her way to the front on a dangerous assignment—it takes place during the Fatherland war. For purposes of disguise she is ordered to pretend to be a German sympathizer. In conversation with a Hitlerite officer, Polia plays this role for a while, but with great difficulty: it is morally hard for her to speak like the enemy and not like a Soviet [*govorit' po-vrazheski, a ne po-sovetski*]. Finally, she can no longer hold out and exposes her true face, her superiority over the German officer: "I am a girl of my epoch... perhaps the most ordinary of them, but I am the world's tomorrow... and you would stand up, stand up when you talk to me, if you had the least bit of self-respect! But you sit in front of me, because you're nobody, just a performing horse under the main executioner.... Well, there's no reason to sit now, go to work... take me, show me, where do you shoot Soviet girls here?"

"It is impossible," Siniavskii concludes, "to hide [the positive hero's positive qualities], to mask them; they are written on his brow and sound in his every word."[9]

Clearly, compared with the exemplary—and foolhardy—Polia, Shtirlits presents us with problems. On the one hand, it is true that Shtirlits is so noble that it is virtually written on his brow, and Russians and Germans vie in the film in insisting that "Shtirlits is a good man" [*dobryi*]. Shtirlits's "goodness," however, is of the universal human kind. Thus, what gives him grist for the

---

9   Abram Terts, "Chto takoe sotsialisticheskii realizm," in his *Fantasticheskii mir Abrama Tertsa* (New York: Inter-language Literary Associates, 1967), 421–22.

story that gets him off the hook when his fingerprints are found on the suitcase with the radio in it is that he paused in his spying to help a woman with a baby carriage cross the street. Where ideology is concerned, however, Shtirlits and Polia are poles apart as cultural heroes. What separates them, I would suggest, is more than just the stylistic trappings of distinct artistic periods, late Stalinism and the mid-Brezhnev years. The two characters seem to exemplify different attitudes to the Soviet state power and ideology. V. Kardin, writing in *Voprosy literatury* in 1986, relates an anecdote that throws into relief all of the insidious duplicity inherent in the figure of Shtirlits:

> I remind you of the portraits of Shtirlits one came across a few years ago in women's dormitories. My frontline comrade, invited to a meeting with young people, froze when he caught sight of a photograph of a fascist officer on the wall. I calmed him down, telling him of snapshots of Captain Kloss—the hero of a serial about a Polish agent. Photographs of the fearless captain in the very same greatcoat stand out vividly in a student dormitory in Warsaw....[10]

Kardin adduces this incident to argue that in detective novels ideology gets pushed into the background by the absorbing plot and rendered neutral and therefore harmless, so that one roots for one side or another just as one would at a soccer match. I would suggest that there is more to it than that.

I would argue that the equivocal episode cited above means something much closer to what the horrified frontline veteran saw in it than our commentator will allow, that it does suggest an analogy between Hitler's Germany and the Soviet Union. Let me further advance the proposition that, at least implicitly, in *Seventeen Moments in Spring* the split between Isaev and Shtirlits in some sense invokes a split between Russian and Soviet, that Semenov's super spy represents a paradigm for the survival of the "honest" intellectual in a totalitarian state, striving for professional excellence and basic human decency while hiding his true face from the inhuman state bureaucracy, trusting no one, surrounded by intrigues and enemies, able to be himself only in the solitary confines of his home. Thus, it is hardly surprising that Shtirlits's main opponent, Müller, under his Gestapo exterior just a gritty professional cop with no use for ideology, seems so sympathetic, such a "brother" to his sworn ideological adversary. Writing recently on Savelii Govorkov, nicknamed

---

10   Kardin, "Sekret uspekha," 119.

the "furious" (*Beshenyi*), the superhero protagonist of the series of best-selling thrillers that Viktor Dotsenko began to write in the 1990s, one critic ventured the hypothesis that this new Russian "Rambo" incarnated contemporary myths just as Shtirlits had in his time:

> Earlier, at a time when we had seen our fill of the *Feat of the Espionage Agent*, [...] only one superman—Shtirlits—commanded the reader's (or viewer's) attention. Shtirlits played the piano, in his time studied in the math-physics department, knew heaps of languages, and, in general, knew everything. Shtirlits was a sign of the decline of the empire.[11]

The reference to Superman—and the even more persistent analogy drawn between Shtirlits and James Bond—have repercussions far beyond the intellectually trivial affirmation that both sides in the Cold War had their own culturally specific hero figures. Thus, Umberto Eco in his article, "The Myth of Superman," posits what happens to a mythic hero "fallen" into the time of popular narrative. Eco argues that the episodic, iterative portrayal of Superman in cartoons resolves the narrative paradox of the timeless mythic hero—who "embodies a law, or a universal demand, and therefore must be in part *predictable* and hold no surprises for us"—who is subjected to the temporal mode of popular narrative.[12] I would suggest that the laborious and belabored cinematic conventions on which the portrayal of Shtirlits in *Seventeen Moments in Spring* rests perform the same function: it is Shtirlits's very predictability carried to an absurd degree that allows him to find a cozy home in the popular imagination. Like Superman and James Bond, Shtirlits transcends his time and becomes a cultural paradigm for his society's fears, desires, and anxieties. And, as my final examples should make clear, it is a paradigm that retains a powerful hold over the post-Soviet Russian imagination.

Pavel Ass and Nestor Begemotov, two computer programmers, authored a series of parodic Shtirlits novels in the 1980s and 1990s, which quickly began to circulate through unofficial channels and gained cult popularity on the early Russian internet, ultimately inspiring other authors to add to the project. The first novel in the series, *Shtirlits, or How Hedgehogs Multiply* (Shtirlits, ili

---

11   Vladimir Berezin, "Mifologichekaia epopeia: Beshenyi, Savelii. Professiia—supermen," *Literaturnaia gazeta*, June 11, 1997, 11.

12   Umberto Eco, "The Myth of Superman," in *The Critical Tradition: Classic Texts and Contemporary Trends*, ed. David H. Richter (Boston: Bedford Books, 1998), 867.

Kak razmnozhaiutsia ezhiki), written by Ass and Begemotov in 1986, for all its notoriety, is a rather sophomoric romp of Shtirlits and his German buddies reputedly set at the same time as the original film. A later novel, written by Ass alone, *Shtirlits, or Second Youth* (Shtirlits, ili vtoraia molodost'), is more interesting as an illustration of the tension between time and timelessness adumbrated by Eco. It finds Shtirlits back in Moscow, old and retired, in the post-Soviet age. Through a convoluted series of events, Shtirlits is rejuvenated by a capsule developed for Brezhnev, but too late for the Gensek to take advantage of it. Bormann is already in Moscow, working not for the KGB, but for the GKChB, an even more elite, apparently Russian secret service, and Pastor Schlagg finds himself happily taking care of a beloved hippopotamus as director of the Moscow zoo. Shtirlits summons Pleishner—not the one who fell out of the window, but his twin brother—to come to Moscow and bring a part of the missing party gold he has stashed in a Swiss bank for Shtirlits. Aisman comes, in full SS uniform, at Shtirlits's request as well, and Müller, the eternal bureaucrat, shows up on his own. They pool money and talents to create a commercial spy agency, called the ShRU (by analogy with the TsRU/CIA), and—to make a very long and convoluted story short—Shtirlits ends up foiling a plot on the part of Arab terrorists to steal Lenin's corpse from the mausoleum. This clever spoof demonstrates the vitality of the Shtirlits figure, which, tellingly, outlives the other embalmed bodies and outmoded leader cults in the tale, fed by a nostalgia that blurs the lines between SS and KGB, throwing them all together as "old friends from the front." There is a certain charm about Shtirlits, even gone commercial, that is lacking in the creations of Dotsenko and other writers of popular thrillers from the 1990s. Perhaps it is because these new adventures of Shtirlits hark back to the popular entertainment of childhood and therefore, in Pastor Shlag's zoo, merge with Doktor Aibolit and other figures of the lost, rosy childhood of totalitarianism.

More to the point, however, as *Shtirlits, or Second Youth* shows, the figure of Shtirlits did not lose its mythogenic power in the 1990s and 2000s. By some measures, in fact, the hero's ongoing appeal seemed to pack considerable political energy and hence was easily exploited. I have in mind here the analogies drawn by commentators between Shtirlits and President Vladimir Putin after the latter's election to the Russian presidency in 2000.[13] Commentators, for

---

13 Interestingly enough, in a survey taken before the 2000 election, in answer to the question, "For what hero of film would you vote in the presidential election?," Shtirlits was

instance, invoked the "Shtirlits phenomenon" to explain Putin's sudden rise to power and the feverish adulation that was beginning to surround him, pointing especially to the Putin's stint as a Soviet intelligence agent in East Germany:

> It would seem unnecessary to have to demonstrate that Putin is Shtirlits; it's enough to recall the "German"—in all respects—biography of our Prince: beginning with the fact that every true Petersburger is perceived in Russia as "a bit of a German," and ending with the most natural work with the most natural Germans in the professional line (intelligence, of course, as is appropriate for Shtirlits). For all that inside he is "ours," more precisely "for our side," as he brilliantly demonstrated in Chechnya.[14]

Putin himself, moreover, seemed to encourage such comparisons by claiming that he "decided on a career in the KGB because he was so enamored with the heroic deeds of Soviet detectives and intelligence officers."[15] While the analogy was as often as not invoked merely to dismiss it—"Putin Isn't Your Shtirlits"—the need to deny it continually spoke almost as eloquently as the TV spoofs, anti-Putin rants linking Shtirlits and Putin—or even the joke used as the epigraph to this article.[16] Most evident in these analogies is an element of wishful thinking—perhaps most indicative of the original function of Shtirlits himself—the hope that Putin would prove to be the same sort of decent chap as Shtirlits behind the enigmatic, intimidating, and seemingly alien façade.[17] After all, as one proposal—perhaps only partly in joke—had it, rather than putting back up the monument to Feliks Dzerzhinskii, taken down from Lubianka Square in Moscow in the aftermath of the 1991 failed coup attempt,

---

one the more frequent responses: http://vladimirputin.ru/d7/frames33.htm, access date unknown (site discontinued—eds.).

14   Sergei Zhekov, "Putin i Rossiia," accessed August 2, 2022, http://panorama.ru/works/putin/rossia00.html.

15   Nina L. Khrushcheva, "Homo Sovieticus" [review of *First Person: Conversations with Vladimir Putin*], *Los Angeles Times*, September 24, 2000.

16   For example, in the article of the same name: Sergei Mironov, "Putin—eto vam ne Shtirlits," http://www.komok.ru/article.cfm?c=3&_id=2932 (site discontinued—eds.).

17   Nepomnyashchy followed political events in Russia closely and realized very early on exactly how naive such notions were—eds.

a monument should be erected to Shtirlits, "the sole and inimitable Russian national hero":

> We suggest several variants of the monument: Shtirlits in a forest of birch trees. Shtirlits relates to Vasilii Ivanovich [Chapaev] a joke about a Chukchi. Shtirlits carried the suitcase of a Russian woman pianist. Shtirlits hits a probable antagonist over the head with a bottle of cognac. Shtirlits sits on the spring earth and pets it with his hands. And what figures could be fit on the pedestal! Pastor Shlag on skies. Ket gives birth and cries out "Mama!" Professor Pleishner jumps from the fifth floor, but the poison still doesn't work.[18]

---

18 Bykov, Voronov, and Luk'ianova, "Shtirlits i seichas zhivee vsekh zhivykh."

Works Cited

Vladimir Berezin, "Mifologichekaia epopeia: Beshenyi, Savelii. Professiia—supermen," *Literaturnaia gazeta*, June 11, 1997, 11.

Bykov, Dmitrii, Vladimir Voronov, and Irina Luk'ianova. "Shtirlits i seichas zhivee vsekh zhivykh." *Sobesednik*. Access date unknown. http://www.sobesednik.ru/weekly/23/investigation/288.phtml (site discontinued—eds.).

Eco, Umberto. "The Myth of Superman." In *The Critical Tradition: Classic Texts and Contemporary Trends*, edited by David H. Richter, 865–77. Boston: Bedford Books, 1998.

Kardin, V. (Emil' Kardin). "Sekret uspekha." *Voprosy literatury*, no. 4 (1986): 102–50.

Khrushcheva, Nina L. "Homo Sovieticus" [review of *First Person: Conversations with Vladimir Putin*]. *Los Angeles Times*, September 24, 2000.

Kontora brat'ev Divanovykh. "K istorii voprosa o Shtirlitse." http://webideas.com/shtirlits/history.htm (site discontinued—eds.).

Laqueur, Walter. "Julian Semyonov and the Soviet Political Novel." *Society* 23, no. 5 (July–August 1986): 72–80.

Mironov, Sergei. "Putin—eto vam ne Shtirlits." Access date unknown. http://www.komok.ru/article.cfm?c=3&_id=2932 (site discontinued—eds.).

Rosich, Iurii. "Samyi glavnyi geroi Runeta." Accessed August 2, 2022. http://rocich.ru/articles/articie.php?sid=251.

Stites, Richard. *Russian Popular Culture: Entertainment and Society since 1990*. Cambridge: Cambridge University Press, 1992.

Terts, Abram. "Chto takoe sotsialisticheskii realizm." In *Fantasticheskii mir Abrama Tertsa*, by Abram Terts, 399–446. New York: Inter-language Literary Associates, 1967.

Torgashev, Aleksei, Aleksandr Nikonov, Sergei Solovkin, and Viktor Kliukin, "Shtirlits vernulsia," *Ogonek*, June 21, 1998. Accessed September 25, 2022. https://www.kommersant.ru/doc/2285811.

Tufel'd, Igor'. "My govorim—Shtirlits, podrazumevaem... Miuller?" *Ogonek*, March 22, 1998. Accessed September 25, 2022. https://www.kommersant.ru/doc/2285619.

"V gostiiakh u 'Shtirlitsev.'" *Argumenty i fakty*, January 1, 1998. Accessed August 2, 2022. https://archive.aif.ru/archive/1637804.

"V Moskve skonchalas' 'radistka Ket.'" *Novoe russkoe slovo*, June 25, 1998.

Vulis, A. *V mire prikliuchenii: Poetika zhanra*. Moscow: Sovetskii pisatel', 1986.

Voznesenskii, A. V. "O sovremennom anekdotopechatanii," *Novoe literaturnoe obozrenie* 22 (1996): 393–99.

Zhekov, Sergei. "Putin i Rossiia." Accessed August 2, 2022. http://panorama.ru/works/putin/rossia00.html.

14

Markets, Mirrors, and Mayhem: Aleksandra Marinina and the Rise of the New Russian *Detektiv*

In the 1985 edition of his book on the history of crime fiction, *Bloody Murder,* the British detective novelist Julian Symons maintained that "crime literature [was] almost certainly more widely read than any other class of fiction in the United States, the United Kingdom and many other countries not under communist rule.[1] By the mid-1990s, Symons's exclusion of countries "under communist rule" sounded a particularly piquant note. In the wake of the collapse of censorship, and soon after that the collapse of the Soviet Union itself—and with it of those cultural institutions that had for decades given shape to the literary process in Russia—the *detektiv* became at least as avidly sought after by readers in post-Soviet Russia as it was in the West.[2] As one reviewer observed of the Russian publishing scene at the time: "Any self-respecting publishing

---

I am grateful to my husband, Viacheslav Nepomnyashchy, for his help in finding materials for this article—C. T. N. This article first appeared in *Consuming Russia: Popular Culture, Sex, and Society Since Gorbachev,* ed. Adele Marie Barker (Durham: Duke University Press, 1999), 161–91. Republished by permission of Duke University Press—eds.

1   Julian Symons, *Bloody Murder: From the Detective Story to the Crime Novel: A History,* revised edition (New York: Viking Press, 1985), 16–17.

2   A 1995 survey of Russian readers confirmed the assumption of many commentators that crime and adventure fiction was the most popular book category in Russia: 31.82 percent of male respondents and 26.23 percent of women surveyed identified detective and adventure fiction (*detektivy, prikliucheniia*) as their preferred reading. "Kto vy, pokupateli knig?" *Knizhnoe obozrenie,* August 20, 1996, 3.

house puts out a detective series."³ As dramatic as the realignment of forces in Russian culture was, a brief survey of the history of detective fiction in Russia and the USSR suggests that, like other cultural processes that came to fruition in the glasnost and post-Soviet periods, the surge in detective fiction that took place in the 1990s was long in the brewing.

Russia, of course, lacks a tradition of detective fiction to rival that of Britain or the United States, whose writers have historically dominated the genre. Yet quite apart from the vexed issue of whether *Crime and Punishment* and *The Brothers Karamazov* are too "serious" to be subsumed by the category, by the 1870s, now forgotten writers such as Nikolai Akhsharumov and A. S. Panov were publishing what were then termed "crime novels" (*ugolovnye romany*). And, as O. Krasnolistov tells us, "at the end of the nineteenth and beginning of the twentieth centuries dozens of detective novellas and novels were published in newspapers, journals, and separate editions. A. A. Shkliarevskii, N. P. Timofeev, N. E. Geintse, A. A. Sokolov, and A. M. Pazukhin may be named among the best-known authors of the detective genre."⁴ Nevertheless, detective fiction was generally identified as an "import" from the West, and it experienced its most remarkable periods of popularity in early twentieth-century Russia at transitional moments of social instability when more or less relaxed censorship allowed market considerations to come to the fore. The first spurt came in the wake of the revolutionary upheavals and abolition of censorship in 1905. This "detective boom," which fed on serialized Russian adaptations of the adventures of such favorites as Sherlock Holmes, Nat Pinkerton, and Nick Carter, was short-lived, peaking in 1908 and dropping off precipitously

---

3   T. Kravchenko, "Missis Kholms: Knizhnaia seriia Aleksandry Marininoi," *Russkaia mysl'*, October 23, 1996, http://www.relis.ru/MEDIA/news/lg/texts/43/0405.html (site discontinued—eds.).

4   O. Krasnolistov, "Ot sostavitelia," in *Staryi russkii detektiv: Roman, rasskazy,* issue 1, ed. O. Krasnolistov and E. Mashkirov (Zhitomir: Olesia, 1992), 3. The 4-volume series "Old Russian Detective Fiction" (Staryi russkii detektiv), which was published in Zhitomir in 1992-1993, contained republications of early Russian examples of the genre and brief prefaces that made it clear that the series was aimed at capitalizing on the growing popularity of detective fiction. Facsimile reproductions of early Russian serials of the adventures of Nat Pinkerton, Nick Carter, and Sherlock Holmes also began to appear in the early 1990s in series such as "From the Russian Boulevard Classic" (Iz russkoi bul'varnoi klassiki). On the republication of N. E. Geintse, see Sergei Kamyshan, "'Bul'var' vchera i segodnia," (special for) *Novaia Sibir'*, http://www.sicnit.ru/siberia/55/ liter_04.htm (site discontinued—eds.).

thereafter.⁵ In Russia, as in other countries, the rise of mass fiction aroused emotions little short of horror among the intellectual elite. In a particularly vituperative 1908 article entitled "Nat Pinkerton," Kornei Chukovskii left little doubt as to the issues at stake. Viewing Nat Pinkerton as an emblem of the times, a bastardized offspring of Sherlock Holmes whose fist and greed for financial gain had replaced his predecessor's intellect and devotion to the art of puzzle solving "for art's sake," Chukovskii bemoaned this product of the "savage" taste of the urban petty bourgeoisie (*meshchanstvo*) as a challenge to the intelligentsia's hegemony over culture. With what in the light of hindsight seems almost prophetic acuity, moreover, he linked this looming shift in cultural power relations to a change in the function of the author, to the usurpation of Sherlock Holmes from Arthur Conan Doyle, his "individual creator," by the "nameless authors of the *Adventures of Nat Pinkerton*."⁶

The second spurt in Russian interest in detective fiction came during the relatively freewheeling early years of the NEP, fueled by an unstable and inevitably temporary meeting of literary theory, highbrow parody, a more or less competitive market, and a politically motivated desire simultaneously to encourage literacy and to indoctrinate. The Serapion brother Lev Lunts called on Russian writers to learn plotting from such Western masters as Conan Doyle, while the Formalists studied the plot construction of popular fiction.⁷ In 1923, Nikolai Bukharin purportedly called for the creation of "red Pinkertons" as a counterbalance to the literature of entertainment being issued by private publishing houses and to Western *pinkertonovshchina*, which was presumably designed to distract workers from the revolutionary movement.⁸ The most

---

5   A. F. Britikov, "Detektivnaia povest' v kontekste prikliuchencheskikh zhanrov," in *Russkaia sovetskaia povest' 20–30kh gg.*, ed. V. A. Kovalev (Leningrad: Nauka, 1976), 422. For more on the boom, see: Jeffrey Brooks, *When Russia Learned to Read: Literacy and Popular Literature, 1861–1917* (Princeton: Princeton University Press, 1985), 142.

6   K. I. Chukovskii, "Nat Pinkerton," in his *Sobranie sochinenii v shesti tomakh*, vol. 6 (Moscow: Khudozhestvennaia literatura, 1969), 136, 138. Britikov refers to these anonymous writers as "invisible authors" (*avtory-nevidimiki*). "Detektivnaia povest'," 423.

7   Lev Lunts, "Na zapad! Rech' na sobranii Serapionovykh brat'ev 2-go dekabria 1922 g.," in his *Zaveshchanie tsaria*, ed. Wolfgang Kasack (Munich: Verlag Otto Sagner, 1983), 115–26. See, for example, Viktor Shklovskii, "Novella tain"; and Boris Eikhenbaum, "V poiskakh zhanra."

8   A 1934 Soviet encyclopedia entry likens *pinkertonovshchina* to pornography in "its function of distraction from revolution." P. Kaletskii, "Pinkertonovshchina," *Literaturnaia entsiklopediia* (Moscow: Sovetskaia entsiklopediia, 1934), vol. 8, 645.

touted of these "ideological" detective fictions, apparently inspired directly by Bukharin's challenge, was Marietta Shaginian's *Mess-Mend: A Yankee in Petrograd* (Mess-Mend: Yanki v Petrograde, 1923), published under the pseudonym Jim Dollar.[9] Although the serially published novel was a commercial success, critics judged this attempt (and others like it) to combine entertainment and ideology a failure, and this judgment and the formidable cultural biases from which it sprang in effect guaranteed that detective fiction would remain on the periphery of Soviet literature.

Detective fiction all but ceased to exist in the Soviet Union under Stalin's rule. Beginning already in the 1920s, even such "classics" as the works of Conan Doyle were removed from libraries along with other objectionable "boulevard" literature, and with the shutting down of private publishing houses, detective fiction was no longer published.[10] The reasons for its disappearance were deeply rooted in the driving forces of the culture of socialist realism. The suppression of crime literature and other popular fiction, first of all, stands as a testimony to the curious marriage of politics and highbrow culture that blossomed under Stalin and persisted under his successors. As I noted above in relation to Chukovskii's comments on the pre-revolutionary burgeoning of crime fiction, the mass appeal of popular fiction posed a very real threat to the intelligentsia's control over culture. And, as has become eminently clear in the light of the virtual collapse of the educated elite's preeminent status in post-Soviet Russia, despite the unquestionable sufferings endured by members of that group at the hands of the Soviet regime, the intelligentsia survived as a coherent group throughout the Soviet period in no small measure as a result of the regime's artificial inflation of the role of high culture. From the point of view of the political powers that be, literature considered escapist distracted readers from more serious ideological concerns, and the detective novel in

---

9   On the "Red Pinkerton" in general and *Mess-Mend* in particular, see Britikov, "Detektivnaia povest'"; Robert Russell, "Red Pinkertonism: An Aspect of Soviet Literature of the 1920s," *SEER* 60, no. 3 (1982): 390–412; Kaletskii, "Pinkertonovshchina," 645–49; Carol Avins, *Border Crossings: The West and Russian Identity in Soviet Literature 1917–1934* (Berkeley: University of California Press, 1983), 48–60; Katerina Clark, *Petersburg: Crucible of Cultural Revolution* (Cambridge, MA: Harvard University Press, 1995), 173–82; and Samuel D. Cioran, "Translator's Introduction," in Marietta Shaginian, *Mess-Mend: Yankees in Petrograd*, trans. Samuel D. Cioran (Ann Arbor: Ardis, 1991), 7–21.

10 My thanks to Evgeny Dobrenko for sharing his knowledge and insights concerning detective fiction in the Soviet Union.

particular seemed to incarnate harmful values. As any number of commentators on detective fiction have pointed out, the formula of the genre intrinsically upholds the prevailing social order by exposing and extirpating deviance. In traditional Western detective fiction, crime is directed against private property or rooted in the private realm of passion. In the former case, the unmasking and punishment of the criminal becomes an affirmation of the capitalist structure, while in the latter, crime appears as a universal aspect of human nature. Both sources of crime would have been equally inimical to Soviet socialist utopian ideology, which identified the origins of crime as social and therefore "curable," and moreover, traced them to the injustices of the very capitalist system upheld by Sherlock Holmes and his confreres. Detective fiction did manage, however, to survive in the safe haven of children's literature; for example, in Anatoly Rybakov's *The Dagger* (Kortik, 1948). Rybakov's novella—which, in the spirit of the "red Pinkerton," combines an adventure-packed mystery plot with the story of the origins of the Komsomol—was read with apparent pleasure by generations of Soviet adolescents at least up until the glasnost period.[11]

With the coming of the cultural "thaw" after Stalin's death, the detective novel for adults returned to the Soviet Union as well. Among the most popular Soviet writers of the genre were Arkadii Adamov and Iulian Semenov, both of whom began publishing in the late 1950s; Lev Ovalov (pseudonym of Lev Shapovalov), whose *Adventures of Major Pronin* (Prikliucheniia maiora Pronina) came out in 1957; the brothers Arkadii and Grigorii Vainer, who had achieved substantial popularity by the late 1960s; and Nikolai Leonov, who published his first *detektiv* in 1970. Like their Western counterparts, these writers created series detectives, including Ovalov's Major Pronin, Adamov's Vitaly Losev, the Vainers' Pal Palych Znamenskii, and Leonov's Lev Gurov. The most spectacularly successful of these creations (in the Soviet period, at least) was Semenov's double agent Maksim Isaev, who, in the course of the political thrillers chronicling his adventures, infiltrated the Nazi high command

---

11   In the general realm of crime fiction under Stalin, we might also note the autobiographical cycle, *Notes of an Investigator* (Zapiski sledovatelia), by Lev Romanovich Sheinin, who worked in the USSR Prosecutor's Office and participated in the Nuremburg trials, and such postwar, Cold War spy novels as Nikolai Nikolaevich Shpanov's *Incendiaries* (Podzhigateli, 1949). Shpanov turned to writing detective fiction in the 1950s, creating the series hero Colonel Nil Kruchinin.

as Max Otto von Shtirlits.¹² Isaev-Shtirlits, as played by the actor Viacheslav Tikhonov, was further popularized in the television serial *Seventeen Moments of Spring* (Semnadtsat' mgnovenii vesny), based on the 1968 Semenov novel of the same name. Works by the Vainer brothers were also adapted for the screen, including the TV movie *The Meeting Place Cannot Be Changed* (Mesto vstrechi izmenit' nel'zia), based on their 1975 novel *Era of Mercy* (Era miloserdiia), which offered a glimpse at the seamier side of life in the USSR during the postwar years.

Detective fiction by foreign authors also reappeared in the Soviet Union in the decades after Stalin's death. A 1971 *Literaturnaia gazeta* article expressed concern that virtually all foreign literature published in Soviet journals consisted of detective fiction, pointing out that fifteen works by Agatha Christie alone had appeared in Soviet journals between 1966 and 1970.¹³ One commentator remarked that the predominance of detective fiction in translated literature testified to a "great demand for the detective genre" among Soviet readers, especially when viewed in the light of the fact that "home-produced detective fiction" (*otechestvennye detektivy*) was being issued even in the 1960s in large print-run editions. He concluded that since the time when such "red Pinkertons" as Shaginian's *Mess-Mend* had been sold in editions mounting to "tens and hundreds of thousands of copies," the demand for such works not only had not decreased, but seemed to have increased.¹⁴ V. Kardin, writing during the first glimmerings of glasnost in 1986, provided some rather sobering statistics: only 5–6 percent of readers, including schoolchildren whose reading demands are largely dictated by the academic program, regularly

---

12 Semenov, whose real name was Liandres, achieved wide popularity in the USSR with his novel *Petrovka, 38* (1963), which takes its title from the address of central Moscow police headquarters. Of Semenov, Richard Stites writes: "Semenov is immensely popular (some 35 million copies of his sixty or so books in print, many of them filmed) and immensely wealthy." Richard Stites, *Russian Popular Culture: Entertainment and Society since 1900* (Cambridge: Cambridge University Press, 1992), 152. On Semenov, see also Walter Laqueur, "Julian Semyonov and the Soviet Political Novel," *Society* 23, no. 5 (1986): 72–80; A. Vulis, *V mire prikliuchenii: Poetika zhanra* (Moscow: Sovetskii pisatel', 1986), 354–63; V. Kardin, "Sekret uspekha," *Voprosy literatury* 4 (1986): 102–50.

13 G. Andzhaparidze, "Bogachi-filantropy i belye 'mersedesy'. Chto i kak my perevodim," *Literaturnaia gazeta*, January 20, 1971, 13.

14 Britikov, "Detektivnaia povest'," 434.

turned to the classics, "the leader of literature."[15] The article suggests that detective fiction, on the other hand, enjoyed a level of popularity in the USSR comparable to that in the West. Thus Kardin goes on to say that "only 10–15 percent of booksellers' orders" for such reading matter were being met, despite the fact that "detective fiction is issued in enormous print runs, published in the mass series Military Adventures [Voennye prikliucheniia], Feat [Podvig], and others."[16] In sum, whatever illusions Western scholars may have entertained about the reading habits of Soviet Russians—illusions most likely fed by a lack of credible statistics for patterns of reading and wishful thinking on the part of the intelligentsia who monopolized the national literary press—well before glasnost Russians were reading a great deal of detective fiction, and were clamoring for more.

The easing and eventual curtailment of censorship along with the increasing orientation of the Soviet publishing industry toward market considerations during the glasnost period created conditions favorable to satisfying the demand for popular reading matter. However, Soviet writers who had made their reputations earlier found that the changing circumstances constituted more a crisis than a windfall. Although some Soviet detective novelists, notably Semenov, jumped on the glasnost bandwagon, most writers in the genre found themselves in a situation faintly analogous to but unquestionably far worse than that of such Western Cold War best-selling authors as John Le Carre.[17] Having had to justify its existence to a cultural establishment wary of entertaining literature as well as to conform to rigid oversight by the Ministry of Internal Affairs (MVD), Soviet detective fiction had been ideologically tendentious and populated by squeaky-clean "positive heroes" who represented the now discredited political system and the police force now exposed

---

15   Kardin, "Sekret uspekha," 103.

16   Kardin, "Sekret uspekha," 108.

17   Richard Stites points out that in the glasnost period, "Semenov began publishing his own books, a journal, and a newspaper and branching out into various enterprises [...] Detective and science fiction writers, including the Strugatskys and the Vainers, joined forces in the *Detective Story and Political Novel* [Detektiv i politika], edited and published by Semenov, containing crime stories, spy thrillers, documents from the Stalin terror, and pro-Gorbachev commentary, thus closing the ranks of practitioners of urban popular fiction along liberal lines." *Russian Popular Culture*, 181. As late as 1994, after Semenov's death, republications of the writer's works were still in fifth place on the best-seller list for the year. "Chempiony izdavaemosti 1994 goda," *Knizhnoe obozrenie*, January 10, 1995, 3.

as riddled with corruption.[18] Of the writers of "canonical" Soviet *detektivy*, only Nikolai Leonov, having successfully recast his inspector Lev Gurov as a "superman" struggling against the forces of the Mafia, remained among the top bestsellers in Russia in 1996.[19] It is thus hardly surprising that by the summer of 1991, hurriedly translated editions of the works of Western writers—foremost among them Agatha Christie and the British author of sensational crime fiction James Hadley Chase—had not only begun to edge out the returning "serious" literature of émigré and previously proscribed Soviet writers from the tables of street vendors in Moscow, but had far outpaced their Soviet counterparts in popularity as well.[20] After the initial dominance of translated literature, however, works by such Russian émigré writers as Eduard Topol' and Fridrikh Neznanskii began to make inroads in the market.[21] The most

---

18   On official oversight, see Larisa Isarova, "Beskonechnye kilometry detektivov: Koe-chto o deval'vatsii populiarnogo zhanra," *Literaturnaia gazeta*, April 12, 1989, 3. On the difficulties posed to Soviet detective novelists by the changed political and social conditions in Soviet and post-Soviet Russia, see Roman Arbitman, "Dolgoe proshchanie s serzhantom militsii. Sovremennyi rossiiskii detektiv: izdatel' protiv chitatelia," *Znamia* 7 (1995): 201–7; Geilii Riabov's introduction to the anthology *Imenem zakona: Sovremennyi sovetskii detektiv* (Moscow: Sovetskii pisatel', 1989), 3–6; Viktor Toporov, "Pretenzii k poterpevshim" [review of Arkadii and Grigorii Vainer, *Ob"ezzhaite na dorogakh sbitykh koshek i sobak* and *Poterpevshie pretenzii ne imeiut*], *Literaturnoe obozrenie* 2 (1987): 65–69; and Tat'iana Kravchenko, "Losev. Syshchik i dolgozhitel': Sovetskii sledovatel' i postsovetskoe vremia," *Literaturnaia gazeta*, July 12, 1995, 4. For a more optimistic view, see the article by Iuliia Latynina (who herself writes detective novels under a male pseudonym) published along with Kravchenko's: "Plokhoi khoroshii detektiv: On podchiniaetsia zakonam rynka, no ne zakonam tusovki," *Literaturnaia gazeta*, July 12, 1995, 4.

19   One reviewer argued that Leonov benefited from the liberation from overly narrow subject matter afforded by the new political situation. Grigorii Revzin, "Sherlok Kholms i Sancho Pansa. Klassicheskii detektiv: Igra po pravilam" [review of Nikolai Leonov, *Polnoe sobranie sochinenii v 12 tomakh*], *Ex Libris NG*, February 20, 1997.

20   See Tinatin Zurabishvili, "Liubimye pisateli rossiian," *Knizhnoe obozrenie*, February 14, 1995, 3.

21   Roman Arbitman, arguing that Russian writers living in their home country were unable to free themselves from the hold of the Soviet tradition of detective fiction, placed his hopes for the future of the genre in Russia on émigré writers. In this context, aside from Topol' and Neznanskii, he named Lev Gurskii, who made his debut with four novels published in 1995–96. Arbitman, "Dolgoe proshchanie." The nomination of Gurskii's political thriller *Change of Places* (Peremena mest), about a plot to replace the Russian president with an impostor, for the Small Booker (Malyi Buker) Prize in 1995 caused something of a scandal because it challenged the still hard line between "high" and "low" culture in Russia. According to one reviewer, "many people believe Arbitman to be the

interesting development, however, was the appearance, beginning in the early 1990s, of a new generation of "home-grown" Russian writers, who by mid-decade were more and more frequently topping the best-seller lists (themselves a product of the commercialization of the book market).[22]

Nancy Condee and Vladimir Padunov have aptly termed this radical change in the landscape of Russian literature, driven by a dramatic surge in interest in and availability of all types of formulaic fiction, "the wholesale social displacement of the cult of high culture."[23] This marginalization of the former cultural elite and the collapse, or near collapse, of the government-sponsored institutions that supported its ostensible cultural predominance, along with the sensational proliferation of new publishers and publications, landed—or stranded—Russian readers in an unfamiliar land governed by different rules and unaccustomed road signs.[24] Readers who took what they could get under the old system suddenly had to get used to making choices, especially given burgeoning book prices and wages eroded by inflation. On the other hand, with big money being made in the popular publishing industry, publishers vied with one another to find new advertising come-ons to lure readers—still unused to high-pressure sales tactics—into parting with their money.

For example, the generic designation *detektiv* (perhaps best translated by Symons's equally ecumenical "crime fiction"), as defined by the assortment

---

author of both Gurskii's novels." Anna Lapina, "Fokus udalsia: 'U nas tut chastnyi detektiv, a ne politicheskii triller', ili Bestseller dlia uzkogo kruga," *Novaia Sibir'*, April 21, 1997.

[22] Arbitman argues that this phenomenon was spurred by the fact that publishers had exhausted the supply of Western fiction not covered by copyright and were unwilling to pay high royalties for more recent works by Western writers ("Dolgoe proshchanie," 202). Lev Gurskii suggests that the Russian reader had just grown heartily sick of "foreign names and unfamiliar cities, 'magnums' and 'thompsons,' Texas rangers and corrections to someone else's constitution." Lev Gurskii, "Nol' tselykh piat' desiatykh" (review of Vitalii Babenko, "Nul'"), *Literaturnaia gazeta*, June 11, 1997, 11. The prospect of sharing, if only in some small measure, in the soaring profits in the publishing industry must also have motivated some Russians to try their hand at detective fiction. A number of *intelligenty* write *detektivy* under pseudonyms, and, in some cases, works attributed to one pseudonymous author are written by a number of different people.

[23] Nancy Condee and Vladimir Padunov, "The ABC of Russian Consumer Culture: Readings, Ratings, and Real Estate," in *Soviet Hieroglyphics: Visual Culture in Late Twentieth-Century Russia*, ed. Nancy Condee (Bloomington: Indiana University Press, 1995), 141.

[24] Notably, the venerable institution of the "thick" journal was kept alive in the 1990s, largely by support from the Soros Foundation.

of books jumbled together in such series as Lokid's "Contemporary Russian Detective Fiction" (Sovremennyi rossiiskii detektiv) or Eksmo's "Black Cat" (Chernaia koshka) series, covers a wide range of formula fiction from thrillers (*boeviki*), even *superboeviki*, and political thrillers to action novels (*ostrosiuzhetnye romany*), murder mysteries, and even what at least one critic has categorized as the "woman's roman noir" (*chernyi zhenskii roman*).[25] There is, of course, considerable "leakage" not only between these subdivisions of the *detektiv*, but between the *detektiv* and such other popular genres as fantasy, science fiction, and the romance novel. Nonetheless, the gamut remains broad enough that all works grouped together under a given heading will hardly appeal to all readers. One reviewer deplored in particularly vivid terms the plight of the Russian fan of popular fiction in the 1990s:

> Take a look at any bookstand—you'll be dazzled by the distorted physiognomies and black muzzles of pistols aimed right at the forehead of the potential reader. And all the same bright, loud, cellophane.... Red-blueblack with gold. By the way, very often the picture on the cover has no relationship whatsoever to the text located under that very cover. And the selection of names in series looks just as absurd as their format. Buying books in one and the same series, you may run into quite a powerful *detektiv*, or you may get "something" in a poke. And, truly, it's a shame when Viktor Dotsenko and Aleksandra Marinina stand right next to each other in a stand with identical cellophane covers. If some neophyte happens to buy Dotsenko, he'll shrug his shoulders on the fifth page and won't buy any more books in that series. And too bad. That series is not filled with Dotsenko alone. The opposite can happen: Marinina's intelligent *detektivy* will hardly be to the taste of potential readers of Dotsenko.[26]

Viktor Dotsenko and Aleksandra Marinina do in fact represent the opposite poles of the spectrum covered by the *detektiv* in Russia as it existed in the 1990s. While reviewers and her publisher's advertising copy dubbed Marinina the "Russian Agatha Christie," the hero at the center of Dotsenko's serial novels—a returning Afghan veteran named Savelii Govorkov ("he's Rex, a.k.a. the rabid" [*on zhe Reks, on zhe beshenyi*]) who singlehandedly battled the forces

---

25   Sergei Mitrofanov, "Samaia strashnaia skazochnitsa Rossii," *Ex Libris NG*, March 6, 1997.
26   Kravchenko, "Missis Kholms."

of the Russian Mafia—was persistently labeled the "Russian Rambo."[27] Aside from suggesting the effectiveness of invoking Western models to help orient the Russian reader in the confusing early post-Soviet book landscape, these slick clichés, even if only loosely accurate, conveyed some idea of the distance between Dotsenko's *superboeviki* and Marinina's murder mysteries.[28] Even more interesting, by April 1997, according to *The Book Review* (Knizhnoe obozrenie), Marinina and Dotsenko were locked in a "best-seller race" for the status of top-selling writer in Russia. Moreover, while Dotsenko had held that position virtually unchallenged for some three years, Marinina seemed to be taking the lead.[29]

Aleksandra Marinina is the pseudonym of Marina Alekseeva, a police lieutenant colonel who holds a doctorate in jurisprudence and worked in crime analysis and prognostication at the Moscow Juridical Institute until 1998.

---

27 See, for example, Mitrofanov, "Samaia strashnaia"; and the advertisement announcing Marinina's collected works at the end of an edition of one of her novels: "We present to your attention the complete collected works of the Russian Agatha Christie—A. Marinina." Aleksandra Marinina, *Svetlyi lik smerti* (Moscow: Eksmo, 1997). Dotsenko commented on his hero's reputation as a Russian Rambo in a 1996 interview: [G. Nezhurin and O. Pogorelova], "Viktor Dotsenko: 'Esli by seichas Khristos vernulsia k nam na zemliu . . . vriad li on stal by podstavliat' vragu vtoruiu shcheku,'" *Knizhnoe obozrenie*, July 30, 1996, 10. A 1998 interview with Marinina revolved completely around comparisons between the Russian writer and the grande dame of British detective fiction. Notably, however, the questions and Marinina's answers to them addressed only biographical, as opposed to textual, similarities and differences between the two writers. Vlada Vasiukhina, "Dva litsa Aleksandry Marininoi," *Ogonek*, September 20, 1998, accessed August 23, 2022, https://www.kommersant.ru/doc/2286056.

28 Unfortunately, there are to date no Russian reader surveys studying preference by individual author. However, Dotsenko has identified his most "grateful readers" as veterans of the Afghan war: L. Goriunova and G. Borisov, "Samyi blagodarnyi moi chitatel'—'afgantsy'...," *Knizhnoe obozrenie*, April 15, 1997, 6. Alla Shteinman, director of a publishing house specializing in women's detective literature (which she claims men refer to as "*tetki-press*" or "hag press"), suggested in an interview that, hardly surprisingly, the primary audience for *boeviki* consists of men: G. Nezhurin, "Alla Shteinman: 'Umenie vzglianut' na situatsiiu s iumorom i samoironiei tol'ko pribavliaet nam shansov vyigrat',''' *Knizhnoe obozrenie*, September 3, 1996, 6. Arguably, however, the works both of Dotsenko and Marinina, albeit in very different ways, reflect anxiety over changing gender roles in post-Soviet Russian society.

29 By 1996 Marinina had begun to sign contracts with Western publishers for translations of her books, and the *New York Times* dubbed her "Russia's most successful current crime writer." Alessandra Stanley, "The World: In Its Dreams; Russia Solves Its Crime Problem," *New York Times*, March 15, 1998, 4.

Marinina began writing fiction in 1991, when she coauthored a *detektiv* on the narcotics Mafia that was published in the journal *Police* (Militsiia) in 1992. The first two works she wrote on her own, introducing the policewoman who has become her signal character, both of which appeared in spring 1995, were also published in *Police*. Only at the end of 1995 did Lokid and Eksmo, major publishers of detective fiction, approach her and take over as her primary publishers. By 1997 she had published eighteen novels and novellas, which in Russia by the late 1990s had sold copies running into the double-digit millions.[30] Like many other detective novelists, Marinina produces books with remarkable speed. In early interviews, she noted that she wrote them on the computer at work, at home, and on vacation, thinking through the twists of her convoluted plots as she rode to work on public transport, all the while observing as readers devoured her books.[31] Claiming that the enormous print runs of her books affected her little, since she was paid flat-rate honoraria, Marinina maintained in early interviews that her newfound literary fame had changed her life hardly at all: "Marinina-Alekseeva as before arrives at work around nine, and leaves at seven, rides the subway, wears civilian clothes, which in style and color in no way stick out from the general picture of police surroundings, and the only thing she has allowed herself in her words, from what she has earned

---

30 By early 1998, the *New York Times* put the figure at ten million copies: Stanley, "The World: In Its Dreams," 4. Most of the biographical information given here is taken from an interview with Marinina: Igor' Semitsvetov, "Aleksandra Marinina: 'Prestupnikov ia opisyvaiu osobenno liubovno,'" *Ogonek*, May 12, 1997, accessed August 23, 2022, https://www.kommersant.ru/doc/2285012. The proliferation of editions and perhaps even obfuscation on the part of publishers make it hard to determine the order in which Marinina's books were written. Moreover, Marinina revealed in a recent interview that she coauthored her first book *Six-winged Seraphim* (Shestikrylyi Serafim) with a colleague named Aleksandr and that the two decided to use a common pseudonym composed out of their first names: Aleksandra Marinina. Vasiukhina, "Dva litsa Aleksandry Marininoi."

31 Semitsvetov, "Aleksandra Marinina: 'Prestupnikov ia opisyvaiu.'" In Marinina's novel *The Radiant Face of Death* (Svetlyi lik smerti), Tat'iana Obraztsova—an episodic character who works as a senior investigator for the St. Petersburg branch of the MVD and who also writes best-selling detective novels under the pseudonym Tat'iana Tomilina and, like Marinina herself, is called the "Russian Agatha Christie"—sees a woman, who will later turn out to be a murder victim, reading one of her books on the metro. This sight leads her to muse on her readership: "As a whole the category of her readers was roughly: all women and men over forty." Aleksandra Marinina, *Svetlyi lik smerti* (Moscow: Eksmo, 1997), 36–37.

as a writer is to buy a new fur coat."³² The purported normality, even austerity, of Marinina's life, despite her meteoric rise to fame as a writer, led reviewers to compare her with the main character of her books. In this context, one commentator observed: "Although in fact I do not exclude the possibility that the author of best sellers, whose publishers, if they are not complete fools, must seriously play her up, aiming, potentially, at movie rights as well, could shape her image literally on the fly."³³

Marinina, then, like other best-selling authors in Russia in the post-Soviet era, herself became a salable commodity. Thus, a journalist who attended a "presentation" of a ten-volume edition of Marinina's works in the late 1990s noted that while a great deal was made of Marinina during the evening, including the revelation of "incredibly touching details" of her biography, almost nothing was said about the books that were being "presented":

> At the buffet reception that same literary agent and assistant director of the MVD juridical institute Nathan Zablotskis openly announced that the presentation was part of a big Eksmo advertising campaign, completely devoted not to the books, but to the author. Its component parts include visits by Marinina on television programs of the most diverse character, from Oleinikov's *My Cinema* to cosmetics shows, and the publication of biographical sketches in various publications. The main task is to obtain a recognition reaction [*reaktsii uznavaniia*] from the reading masses. By a remarkable coincidence, Marinina's presentation to journalists took place in the "Tolstoy" hall, and the buffet afterward—in the "Pushkin" hall. Probably, the Eksmo people have the idea that the fashionable detective lady [*modnaia detektivnaia dama*] should take her place in those ranks, not in the sense of the classic quality of her prose, but by [the principle of] automatic association: fruit-apple, detective fiction-Marinina.³⁴

This commodification of the author arguably represents the other side of the coin of the anonymity of authorship deplored by Chukovskii early in the

---

32   Mitrofanov, "Samaia strashnaia." In early 1998, Alekseeva's popularity as a novelist finally prompted her to resign from her job. Stanley, "The World: In Its Dreams," 4.

33   Mitrofanov, "Samaia strashnaia."

34   Aleksandr Gavrilov, "Radost' uznavaniia: Izdateliam vygodnee torgovat' liud'mi, chem knigami," *Ex Libris NG*, May 19, 1997.

twentieth century. (Tellingly, it has also been rumored that Marinina has become a "collective.")

In the game of images, moreover, it is all the better if the author's image resembles that of her series detective, which in the given case happens to be so. Marinina's "heroine" is Anastasiia Kamenskaia, like her creator a police lieutenant colonel who works as an analyst (*analitik*). Kamenskaia, however, works not in an institute, but at 38 Petrovka, the central police headquarters in Moscow. Kamenskaia's character is based on the premise that she remain in her Petrovka office, drinking cup after cup of coffee and chain smoking, while her male colleagues do all the legwork of gathering evidence and interviewing suspects. She then solves what are generally devilishly complex crimes by subjecting the material the men gather to cold, machinelike logic combined with an extraordinary imagination, which allows her to (re)construct multiple narratives based on the evidence and ultimately arrive at the "correct" story. While the premise that Kamenskaia works solely out of her office is in fact honored more in the breach, her crime busting is always a function of intellect rather than force, and she fires a gun only at target practice to focus her thoughts. In fact, her physical vulnerability is underscored by the fact that she suffers from chronic back problems and periodic attacks of low blood sugar. Dogged in her pursuit of criminals, Kamenskaia is pathologically lazy away from her job. We are repeatedly told that she can barely drag herself out of bed in the morning, and it takes quantities of her beloved coffee and linguistic exercises in the shower to get her going. (Kamenskaia knows five languages fluently and spends her vacations translating Western detective novels into Russian.) She is particularly "lazy"—and generally incompetent—when it comes to anything that might be termed "women's work," especially cooking. Not only does every male in her life seem to know his way around a kitchen better than she does, but virtually all of them—from her husband, her wheelchair-bound ex-lover, and her stepfather to her colleagues and even the criminals she is tracking—end up cooking for her. Kamenskaia's most distinctive feature, however, is her thoroughly nondescript appearance, underscored by her own conviction that she is physically (and, at least implicitly, sexually) unattractive, a judgment confirmed by the lack of interest she generally inspires in men on first meeting. On the other hand, her face is a "blank slate," a "gift" that allows her, with the aid of makeup, mimicry, and stylish clothing (she generally wears jeans, sweatshirts, and sneakers), to transform herself, quite literally beyond recognition, into a strikingly seductive alter ego. Kamenskaia, however, uses her talent for "disguise" (that is, she uses makeup) only in police work, refusing to dress herself up for those close to her, whether it be her mother or the men in her life. In her demand that people take her as she is, whether it is a question of physical appearance or the way she chooses to prioritize her life, Kamenskaia is consistently classified as different from "normal" Russian women.

While Marinina clearly drew on her own autobiography for her conception of her heroine, she equally clearly took more than a hint or two from the detective fiction she claims to have loved all her life. In one interview she maintained that she aims to combine detective mystery with the romance novel in the manner of Sidney Sheldon, and she named Georges Simenon and the Vainer brothers as her favorite writers in her own genre.[35] Her texts, however, make passing references to other Western models that have left their imprint on her characters and plot structures. Kamenskaia certainly owes her image as a sedentary intellect safely ratiocinating within an interior space locked off from the outside world of crime and criminals in part to Sherlock Holmes's "smarter brother," Mycroft, and in part to Rex Stout's Nero Wolfe, who also passed on to her his proverbial laziness, if not his bulk or refined palate. Marinina's use of an ongoing cast of characters, and particularly her focus on a police team (the "Department for Particularly Dangerous Crimes") whose members—with Kamenskaia as their intellectual center—share the investigative labor, are reminiscent of the 87th Precinct police procedurals of Ed McBain, whose works Kamenskaia translates when on vacation from her police duties. As far as female models are concerned, the persistent invocations of Agatha Christie by critics would seem to have little more than "brand name" value, identifying Marinina as a woman writer of puzzle murder mysteries. More pertinent, perhaps, is a passing reference to the far less well-known American mystery writer Charlotte Armstrong. Particularly interesting in this context is Armstrong's technique of more or less explicitly casting her detective fictions as reworked fairy tales.[36] In what is probably the first work in the Kamenskaia series, *Coincidence* (Stechenie obstoiatel'stv), Kamenskaia's ability to transform herself from a mousy, sexually unappealing physical nonentity

---

35   Semitsvetov, "Aleksandra Marinina: 'Prestupnikov ia opisyvaiu.'"

36   Ed McBain's Matthew Hope novels are also tales of detection cast as reworked fairy tales, as their titles suggest: *Goldilocks* (1978), *Rumpelstiltskin* (1984), *Snow White and Rose Red* (1985), *Cinderella* (1986). It may not be too much to suggest that detective narratives, with their promise of happy endings, are in a sense fairy tales for adults.

into a femme fatale is implicitly compared to the fairy-tale-like transformation of Hans Christian Andersen's ugly duckling into a swan and to Cinderella's (Zolushka's) transformation into a desirable mate for a prince.[37] This fairy-tale element in the portrayal of Kamenskaia (which sometimes seems almost to resemble a female variant on Clark Kent as alter ego for Superman, at least as far as sexual prowess is concerned) runs throughout the series and certainly accounts for some of the appeal of Marinina's fiction to female readers.

Although it would be problematical to identify Marinina as a "feminist" writer in any recognizably Western sense of that word, viewing her works in the light of some Western scholarship on feminist detective fiction may help explain her popularity with contemporary Russian readers. Sandra Tome, for example, suggestively contrasts the hard-boiled feminist detective fictions Sue Grafton and Sara Paretsky began writing in the 1980s with what she terms "the feminist mystery after feminism" of the early 1990s, taking as her examples of the latter the British television series *Prime Suspect*, the Patricia D. Cornwell novel *Postmortem*, and the American big-box-office film *The Silence of the Lambs*.[38] She begins by pointing out that it is a fundamental principle of feminist detective fiction to locate the origin of crime in patriarchal social structures. "Moments of metaphoric confusion or mistaken identity" render the female murder victim and the female detective "dangerously interchangeable":

> Within the terms of this feminist polemic, *all* women are subordinated objects, a fact that is driven home precisely through the confusion of the detective—the traditional repository of knowledge and authority in the mystery narrative—with the female murder victim, the one whose knowledge has been annihilated. Frequently, the confusion is literalized as the detective herself becomes a target of the killer; she becomes the victim whose murder she is trying to redress.[39]

---

37 The text makes explicit reference to "Zolushka," and Kamenskaia's "pseudonym" is Larisa Lebedeva (from the Russian word meaning "swan").

38 Tome's argument is not without problems even within the context of the Western works she chooses to treat as exemplary. For instance, she passes over in silence the fact that Grafton and Paretsky continued to write in the 1990s. This lapse and others, however, do not affect the applicability of her arguments here.

39 Sandra Tome, "Questing Women: The Feminist Mystery after Feminism," in *Feminism in Women's Detective Fiction*, ed. Glenwood Irons (Toronto: University of Toronto Press, 1995), 47. For a complementary argument, see Glenwood Irons, "New Women Detectives:

Grafton's and Paretsky's detectives, Kinsey Milhone and V. I. Warshawski, rebel against these repressive institutions, Tome argues, by becoming private eyes—loners and outsiders. As in the fictional worlds of male predecessors such as Raymond Chandler and Dashiel Hammett, crime in feminist detective novels is endemic to the social fabric, not an aberration, a temporary disturbance of the order restored by the intellectual victory of Holmes and his successors in classic British detective fiction. "The hard-boiled detective contents himself or herself with defeating a small portion of the chaotic element, usually, in the genre's tradition of individualism, one on one." In the case of the female "dick," "her defeat of the criminal each time is what allows her to entertain options, like living and working alone, since it illustrates to her, and to us, the possibility of her altering the conditions of her victimization."[40]

In contrast, in the "feminist mysteries after feminism" of the 1990s the female detective functions not as an outsider, Tome says, but rather as a member of a large law enforcement agency. Her vulnerability is underscored by the nature of the crimes themselves, serial acts of sex and violence by men against women, depicted in gruesome detail. While, for example, Clarice Starling's pursuit of investigative threads on her own in *The Silence of the Lambs* leads in the end to the criminal, this dangerous "autonomy" almost puts her in the place of the victim and motivates her return to the protective embrace of "her 'normal' FBI family with its more 'normal' father figure." The moral, Tome argues, is that "the threatening, even gothic, nature of the criminal acts, together with an emphasis on the female detective's helplessness in the face of them, ensures that packing up and lighting out is never a real option. Full of stalkers, serial killers, and cannibals, the world the detective inhabits is, we are told, too dangerous for a woman working on her own."[41] The price the female detective must pay for protection in the 1990s, Tome concludes, is the sacrifice of her personal life, which is marred by threatening and abusive relations with men, to her professional life, and of her self-definition as a woman to her self-definition as a professional law enforcement officer, "one of the guys." This inconsistent compromise with the male establishment, Tome concludes,

---

G is for Gender-Bending," in *Gender, Language, and Myth: Essays on Popular Narrative*, ed. Irons (Toronto: University of Toronto Press, 1992), 127–41.

40 Tome, "Questing Women," 52.

41 Tome, "Questing Women," 53–54.

leaves the female detective trapped in cramped spaces, suffering from claustrophobia.[42]

I have rehashed Tome's argument at some length because I believe that an examination of the ways in which Marinina's works follow—or, perhaps more to the point, depart from—the paradigms Tome describes can lead us to one source of their appeal in the form of the anxieties they simultaneously express and neutralize. Kamenskaia certainly shares with her Western opposite numbers the vulnerable status of the female detective as potential victim. In *Coincidence*, not only is the murder victim clearly an alter ego for Kamenskaia, but in the second half of the book, Kamenskaia, in what is apparently her first field assignment, is set up as bait to catch the professional hitman-killer and almost becomes his next victim. In Marinina's second book, *Playing on Another's Field* (Igra na chuzhom pole), one of the murder victims is clearly a surrogate for Kamenskaia. In *Death for the Sake of Death* (Smert' radi smerti) she again becomes the target of professional hitmen. In *Death and a Little Love* (Smert' i nemnogo liubvi), the novel in which Kamenskaia marries her longtime boyfriend, the bride who takes her place in line at ZAGS when Kamenskaia refuses to go through the full marriage ritual is murdered. Brutal crimes against women abound, in at least two cases lingering as haunting evidence of Kamenskaia's failures. Thus, at the end of *Another's Mask* (Chuzhaia maska), after Kamenskaia has brilliantly unraveled a devilishly clever and convoluted series of murders, a rape remains unsolved, a synecdoche for the rampant and random abuse of women afoot in the society. Even more disturbingly, at the end of *Death and a Little Love*, a female rape victim is brutalized and held hostage as a pawn in the duel of wits between Kamenskaia and the male murderer, who resolves to kill the woman by slowly draining the blood from her body. Kamenskaia ingeniously succeeds in keeping the criminal engaged in a telephone conversation with her, thereby distracting him so the male SWAT team can take him by surprise. Despite Kamenskaia's valiant efforts, neither the criminal nor his victim survives. Tellingly, however, Kamenskaia clearly identifies with the male murderer rather than with his female victim—and is more upset by his death as well.

As the latter episode should make clear, Marinina's works fit snugly into neither of Tome's paradigms for the feminist detective novel, although they do display a closer affinity to the 1990s texts Tome examines. Kamenskaia is,

---

42 Tome, Questing Women," 56–60.

after all, not a private detective but a representative of the police. She is, moreover, surrounded by a protective male collective. And although Tome argues that the woman detective must struggle to gain acceptance from her initially misogynistic male colleagues, Kamenskaia, by the time we meet her, is viewed not with hostility or even mere tolerance but with respect by the men in her department. Most notably its head, Viktor Alekseevich Gordeev (affectionately nicknamed "Kolobok" by his subordinates), Kamenskaia's mentor-father figure recognized her talent, brought her into his team from the suburban police force, and guides her career with wise paternal advice. Kamenskaia also enjoys the respect of Iura Korotkov, her closest co-worker, who confides the vagaries of his love life to her, and Misha Dotsenko, the youngest member of the team, who stands so in awe of Kamenskaia's superior intellect that he can bring himself neither to address her by the host of diminutives—Nastia, Asia, Nasten'ka—employed by her other male colleagues nor to use the familiar form of address with her. Tellingly, any hostility Kamenskaia may experience from co-workers outside her department is ascribed not to her gender but to the nature of her unfamiliar position as an *analitik* who remains holed up in her office doing mental labor rather than going into the field. It is only when Kamenskaia leaves the protective confines of her office that she finds herself at risk. More significantly, when Kamenskaia herself becomes a potential victim, it is almost always when she is "disguised" as a sexually alluring female. The implicit moral is that it is specifically sexual autonomy that turns woman into victim.

In any case, whenever Kamenskaia is in danger there is always at least one male conveniently around to save the day; and when she does find herself in a one-on-one confrontation with a villain, her protective male collective is never far away. For example, her male colleagues are there to monitor her nightlong vigil with the hitman who plans to take her life in *Coincidence* as well as her verbal duel with the murderer in *Death and a Little Love,* which takes place over the telephone from the safety of her office. If, as Tome argues, Western female detectives of the 1990s suffer from claustrophobia, constricted by their entrapment within male institutional structures, Kamenskaia suffers from agoraphobia—she cannot stand being in crowds. The fact of the matter is that Kamenskaia is in her element when she is in her office safely surrounded by solicitous men.

Marinina's portrayal of Kamenskaia's private life departs even more markedly from Tome's feminist detective paradigms. Although her relationships with her sister-in-law, Dasha, and Korotkov's girlfriend, Liusia, are cordial, Kamenskaia has no close female friends, and her relationship with her mother, Nadezhda Rostislavovna, a renowned linguistics scholar, is doubly distant, first of all because the latter has spent most of her time in Sweden, and, second, because when she visits and finally returns to Russia, she persistently tries to reform her daughter's inattention to her appearance, dislike of social functions, and "improper" eating habits.[43] In contrast, as far as the men in her life are concerned, Kamenskaia is singularly blessed. In place of the wicked stepmother of fairy tales, she has a good stepfather, who has also worked for the police his whole life and who more than makes up for her absent father, serving at home, as Gordeev does at work, as Kamenskaia's mentor. Aleksei Chistiakov, a brilliant mathematician, Kamenskaia's boyfriend in the earlier works and later her husband, has been devoted to Kamenskaia since the two met while students. He weathered with fortitude the one passionate affair Kamenskaia has had in her life, and although he himself gets carried away from time to time (at least before the marriage) by bursts of lust, he becomes bored with his sexual partners after two or three days and realizes yet again that Kamenskaia, despite her persistent refusals to marry him over a period of some fifteen years, is the only woman for him. Then there is Kamenskaia's half-brother, Aleksandr, her father's son by his second wife. A successful businessman and physically a male carbon copy of his half-sister, Aleksandr is as devoted to Kamenskaia as her stepfather and boyfriend/husband are. These men, especially Chistiakov, form the same type of protective buffer around Kamenskaia outside her office as her male colleagues do on the job. Her physical vulnerability away from work is particularly underscored by her chronic back problems, bouts of which set in whenever she carries anything heavy (generally groceries) and leave her immobilized on the floor of her apartment, sometimes for days, dependent on Chistiakov to minister to her needs. Moreover, although Kamenskaia initially lives alone, insisting that she and Chistiakov keep their separate apartments even after their marriage (a plan that falls by the wayside in later books), the risk this attempt at geographical autonomy places her in is highlighted when the door of her apartment is rigged to explode when she enters.

Kamenskaia refuses to put on makeup or fashionable clothing to please the men in her life, insisting that they accept her as she is, which they are all

---

43 Kamenskaia's mother returns to Russia and to her husband, apparently for good, in *The Stylist* (Stilist).

more than willing to do. In fact, Chistiakov, her stepfather, and her half-brother seem at times to know her better than she knows herself, and with predictable regularity manage to anticipate her every need.[44] Thus, Kamenskaia finally capitulates and agrees to marry Chistiakov not because she is suddenly overwhelmed by passionate love for him, but because he realizes that she would prefer that he spend their vacation money on a computer she needs for her work. Moreover, he is so certain that she will choose the computer over the trip that he goes out and buys the computer before he hears her answer. When he presents her with this *fait accompli*, she realizes that no one will ever love her and accept her as he does, including, as the none too subtle symbolism of the computer suggests, understanding that her work will always come first. For all their compatibility (Chistiakov is as much of a workaholic as Kamenskaia) and mutual comprehension, their marriage is at best sexually pallid and implicitly infertile.

That female sexuality amounts to little more than an impetus to depersonalization is made clear in *The Stylist*, when Kamenskaia is reunited in the course of a criminal investigation with her old flame, the one passionate love of her life, exactly a year after her marriage. Despite the fact that she initially feels the old attraction and that her former lover, who has been crippled and confined to a wheelchair, claims now to love her, she finds she is no longer interested in him because he does not understand who she truly is, that is, does not comprehend her devotion to her work. By the same token, she discounts the attraction a private detective, with whom she has a one-night stand in *Coincidence*, claims to feel for her, writing it off to her disguise. Kamenskaia shies away from sexual allure, it would seem, because it renders her interchangeable rather than unique. Only her professional persona offers her protection and a distinct identity.

It is hardly surprising that the roots of crime in Marinina's works can be traced to the same anxieties that drive Kamenskaia's professional and private lives, and in this Marinina differs most sharply from her feminist contemporaries in the West—as well as from her male Russian contemporaries, whose

---

44   In this context, Janice A. Radway's speculation on one of the reasons women may turn to romance novels may apply to Marinina's female readers as well: "[A woman] may well turn to romance reading in an effort to construct a fantasy-world where she is attended, as the heroine is, by a man who reassures her of her special status and unique identity." Janice A. Radway, "Women Read the Romance: The Interaction of Text and Context," *Feminist Studies* 9, no. 1 (1983): 62.

heroes expend their energy battling the Mafia and corrupt politicians. As we have seen, Tome argues that the interchangeability of the female detective with the female murder victim serves as an indication of the vulnerability of women to crime that has its origin in patriarchal institutions. By contrast, in Marinina's tangled plots, in which the true villain is often not the murderer and motives are frequently multiple and confused, it is more difficult to categorize criminals and victims by gender—although, as we shall see below, gender is far from irrelevant. Murders virtually never happen in the singular in Marinina's works, although even what appear to be serial killings by maniacs are never quite what they seem. Arguably, then, the function of the multiple murder plot in Marinina's fiction is somewhat different from that of sexually motivated serial crimes by men against women, which, as Tome points out, expose the female detective's vulnerability. In Marinina's fictions certainly one motivation for abandoning the classic detective novel's focus on a single murder is to demonstrate Kamenskaia's particular gift for synthesizing plots, for tracing the logical links between apparently disparate acts.[45] On a deeper level, however, the multiple murder seems to be the inevitable consequence and most appropriate demonstration of the origins of crime in Marinina's works. Thus, virtually without exception, murder in Kamenskaia's world is inextricably linked with the villain's acceptance of the dehumanizing premise that people, regardless of gender, are interchangeable—on the basis of their physical appearance. Thus, in *Playing on Another's Field* the victims are all "stars" of "snuff films" chosen solely on the basis of their physical resemblance to the female relatives who have inspired murderous rage in the "clients" who order the films; in *Another's Mask* all three of the murders involve the substitution of one identical twin for another; in *Death and a Little Love* the victims are selected because they are brides, identically dressed in white; and in *The Stylist* the fourteen victims of sodomy and murder are all adolescent boys of Semitic appearance who bear a striking physical resemblance to one another.

Marinina can hardly be considered a political writer, especially when viewed in the context of the lurid political thrillers being penned by her male compatriots. Nonetheless, in some of her books the source of the impulse to dehumanize others from which murder emanates is implicitly traced to lapses in the Soviet past that are tied to the post-Soviet present by the thread of financial gain, charting a disturbing continuity between the systemic abuses, earlier

---

45 I am indebted to Richard Borden for this observation.

political and later economic, of the two periods. The political critique is most pointed in *Death for the Sake of Death*, which, uncharacteristically for Marinina, borders on dystopian science fiction. On her new computer, Kamenskaia discovers a curious pattern of high incidence of crime in one region of Moscow balanced symmetrically by a correspondingly low incidence of crime in another region. The two areas form a perfect figure eight with a research institute at the center. Kamenskaia's suspicions that the beneficent ray the institute claims to be testing has a reverse effect, transforming ordinary citizens into violent criminals, turns out to be true. The post-Soviet military industrial complex, desperate for vicious soldiers to fight in Chechnya and rebuild the crumbled empire, and the Mafia, which has invested money in the project, vie both in their indifference to the innocent victims of the experiment and in safeguarding the secret of the negative effects of the ray from Kamenskaia's prying. In case we miss the allegory of the ray as a figure of the Soviet utopian experiment gone wrong, creating a link between the political powers of the past and the economic powers of the present, the researcher in charge of the project is a virulent misanthropist whose hatred of all others was bred by his childhood in a cramped Soviet barracks. The money he will get from selling the ray to the highest bidder will allow him to flee to seclusion from the people his Soviet past has taught him to despise. Equally suggestive of allegory is the schizophrenia of the murderer in *Death and a Little Love,* whose incipient mental illness causes him, despite his brilliant intellect, to be rejected from the police force, which, as Kamenskaia says, is mired in dirt and compromise. Unable to leave behind the world of childhood where good and evil were clear and distinct, his twisted sense of justice leads him into particularly sadistic crime. In *Playing on Another's Field* the link between past injustice and present crime is explicit. The ringleader behind the snuff film enterprise is in fact a seemingly innocuous old lady, a crippled Jewish piano teacher. In a twist at the end of the book, we learn that under Stalin she was denied a brilliant career as a concert pianist because of her deformity, and that she suffered for her Jewishness during the campaign against cosmopolitanism and the Doctor's Plot. Embittered and in need of money, since she will only instruct talented students and takes no payment, she has turned to particularly horrible crime. Musing on the woman's equally talented accomplice, a gifted composer and filmmaker, Kamenskaia pointedly, if rhetorically, asks: What is wrong with a society that cannot make use of such talent? The message is clear: the political ills of the past continue to be visited on the present in the form of violent, economically motivated crime.

Economics, like politics, devalues human beings, rendering them expendable and replaceable. In other words, while the old Soviet system turned people into political chattel, the new market chaos transforms individuals—and, in Marinina, perhaps especially women and writers—into commodities, valued according to their salability.

Yet if Kamenskaia's forays into the crimes of the past to solve the crimes of the present carry a political charge, it is one that, as a rule, is heavily personalized, psychologized—and gendered. The hand holding the gun, the preferred murder weapon in Marinina's works, is virtually always male.[46] In a number of cases, moreover, a male murderer tries to frame a woman for his evildoing. In *Another's Mask* a romance novelist, who kills his twin brother in order to assume his identity and thereby elude and delude both his publishers and his overbearing mother, tricks a mentally unstable, infatuated female fan into committing the murder. The murderer in *Death and a Little Love*, who claims his motive in killing brides was to commit a perfect crime and therefore prove the police wrong in their rejection of him, constructs a devious scenario leading the police to an older woman, and stages her supposed suicide by shooting her in the mouth when her eyes are closed waiting for him to kiss her. Thus, women stand at greater risk not only as victims, but also as potential fall guys for male violence.[47]

---

46   Men also hold most other "phallic" weapons such as knives and syringes.

47   In the 1997 novel, *Male games* (Muzhskie igry), Marinina genders crime explicitly male in a way that comes quite close to Tome's paradigm for the 1990s. As the story opens, Gordeev has been promoted and has been replaced by a new male head of the department. The typically complex plot begins as an investigation of what is apparently a series of serial murders. Kamenskaia's suspicions fall on a female ex-basketball player named Anna Lazareva. As the investigation progresses, however, she begins to question Lazareva's guilt and even whether the murders were actually committed by a single person. The plot thickens as Kamenskaia finds herself embroiled in a parallel murder investigation that seems to lead directly to her own beloved stepfather, and her antipathy to her new boss grows so overwhelming (primarily because he will not allow her to stay in her office and do mental labor rather than going out into the field) that she considers leaving her job and even her profession. In the end, she discovers that all the murders are linked to a complex scheme, located in a special institute funded by the government, to take power in Russia. Her new boss, rather than her stepfather, turns out to be implicated, and, as she learns at the end, Gordeev, who has only pretended to leave the department, and General Zatochnyi, another recurring father-mentor figure, have used her without her knowledge to uncover the threads of the conspiracy. Although Kamenskaia's faith in her stepfather is vindicated, she finds that she—no less than Lazareva, who dies in the course of the novel—has been

Given the dangers posed by traditional female roles, it is hardly surprising that Kamenskaia retreats to the safety of androgyny.[48] It is, after all, precisely Kamenskaia's refusal to look or act like other women (along with her superior intellect, of course) that constitutes her uniqueness, her non-exchangeability. Kamenskaia's ambiguity in terms of gender classification manifests itself particularly markedly in relationship to her wedding in *Death and a Little Love*. She insists on wearing black to her wedding, the color putatively gendered male by contrast with bridal white in the twisted logic of the murderer, and refuses to go through the full ZAGS ritual; both departures from "normal" female behavior by implication save her life when the woman who takes her place in line is killed apparently in her stead. Shortly before the wedding, moreover, Kamenskaia has a conversation with her half-brother, Aleksandr, significantly stage-managed in such a way that the two siblings, who "strikingly resemble one another," talk not face-to-face but to their reflections in a mirror.[49] While Sandra Gilbert and Susan Gubar may take issue with Bruno Bettelheim about who speaks from the mirror in "Snow White," the symbolism here is clear. Aleksandr Kamenskii becomes Anastasiia's male alter ego; he pointedly asks her if she is sorry she is getting married, if she really would not prefer to be following up a lead in a police investigation rather than going to ZAGS—a question Kamenskaia declines to answer so as not to have to lie. Shortly thereafter, Korotkov, convinced that Kamenskaia was the intended victim of the ZAGS murderer, presses on her, despite her protests, his service revolver. Hiding from her new husband the danger that may hang over her, she confides in Aleksandr:

> "Remember that there is a pistol lying in my purse. I would hardly be able to use it."
> "Why?"

---

a pawn in "male games." It is worth noting that at the point of her lowest ebb in the novel, Kamenskaia "remakes herself" in the front of the mirror. This episode appears particularly compelling when we bear in mind that as we learn in an earlier book it was Kamenskaia's stepfather who was originally the "voice in the mirror" from whom Kamenskaia learned both that she was plain and that her plainness represented a gift for disguise, and therefore detection.

48 There are positive female characters who are able to combine motherhood with careers and even the ability to cook—Dasha, Liusia, and Gordeev's wife—but they are episodic.

49 Aleksandra Marinina, *Smert' i nemnogo liubvi* (Moscow: Eksmo, 1996), 23.

> "I don't know," she shrugged her shoulders. "I'd get flustered, frightened, what does it matter what... I'm not used to it."
>
> "You want me to use it?"
>
> "God forbid! Under no circumstances. Just remember that I have it. And if something should happen, watch out that my purse isn't torn away from me or that I don't throw it someplace myself. Who knows what I might do out of fear. By the way, once again, if something happens—remember that it is very effective to hit someone on the head with a purse with a pistol in it. It's certain I wouldn't be able to do that, but you'll take care of it."[50]

Curiously, this gun, which warrants so much comment at the beginning, in flagrant violation of Chekhov's famous dictum that a gun once brought onstage must be fired in the course of the play, is never mentioned again and plays no further role in the plot, which in fact ends with another gun *not* going off. This pointed emasculation of the archetypal phallic symbol of the hard-boiled private "dick's" manhood, squirreled away in a lady's purse, and nonetheless only to be wielded by a man, raises doubts that the female detective suffers from narrative as well as investigative impotence.

If, as Gilbert and Gubar provocatively suggest, a pen is a metaphorical penis, do we have a confusion, whether deliberate or inadvertent, of metaphors here? If guns belong in the hands of men, what of writing implements? Put in other terms, if, as Tome suggests, the female detective's vulnerability threatens to undermine her authority, what are we to say of the female detective novelist's *authority,* especially under conditions, such as those inherent in 1990s Russia, in which the traditional role of the Russian writer is being undermined by the commercialization of literature?[51] Not only do members of the creative intelligentsia—sometimes, as we have seen, portrayed as cripples—play central roles

---

50   Marinina, *Smert' i nemnogo liubvi,* 40.

51   While space constraints make it impossible to discuss further here the fascinating relationship between sleuthing and storytelling, not only in Marinina but in the works of other female writers who have created female detectives, it is worth noting that Kamenskaia's talent for detection is repeatedly attributed as much to imagination—to the ability to conceive diverse plots to fit the evidence—as it is to reason. Moreover, we learn that Kamenskaia wrote poetry when she was young, and in *Coincidence,* in a faked biography, she attributes her poems to the female murder victim. In *The Stylist* she demands that her former lover return those poems to her. As discussed in the text, issues of plagiarism and authorship are central to both of those works.

in most of Marinina's fictions, but, more important, issues of authorship figure prominently in a significant number of her works. In *Coincidence* the motive for murder originates in plagiarism, in a man's public claim to authorship of a manuscript in fact written by the female murder victim, who is "bumped off" so that her threatened revelation that the now highly placed political figure—who, as it turns out, is also a power in an international drug syndicate—did not write his own dissertation will not lead to closer scrutiny of his other past dealings. Interestingly enough, the female author's motivation in revealing the deception is not pride of authorship. Rather she wrote what should have been her own doctoral dissertation for attribution to someone else in return for the promise of a payment that would have solved her perennial problems with separate living space and thereby put her romantic life in order. Her anger is aroused, then, not by the original misattribution of the manuscript, but by the fact that the "orderer" (*zakazchik*) "stiffed" her, destroying her dreams for a successful love life. Yet Marinina's repetition of the identical term, *zakazchik*, for the party who orders both the dissertation and the murder of its authoress suggests a curious—and distinctly non-Barthesian—metaphorical as well as literal "death of the author." The author, in a sense, consigns herself to death when she agrees simultaneously to sacrifice her career to her love life and to sell her rights to authorship. No longer the product of a "unique" talent, writing becomes a commodity valued merely for the status it imparts to its owner, who, in the given case, can barely rehash its contents intelligibly.

The nature of authorship as defined by the post-Soviet publishing industry is central to the narrative of both *Another's Mask* and *The Stylist*, and in both the impetus to murder is driven by publishers' attempts to bilk authors of their fair share of the enormous profits their best-selling books are generating. In *Another's Mask* the issue of the interconnection of gender and authorship again comes into play. A persistent "red herring" in the case is the suggestion that the putative murder victim, a wildly popular Russian romance novelist, could not have written the books credited to him because it is unlikely that a man could have such a sensitive understanding of female psychology. His wife does indeed claim to be the true author of the books in her negotiations with publishers after her husband's apparent death, insisting that her husband was merely a front, his image as an attractive male being a major selling point for the books. Yet Marinina fans our essentialist biases only to explode them at the end. The books were indeed written by the man, who was not murdered at all, but has merely usurped "another's mask." In *The Stylist* Kamenskaia's ex-lover works as a translator not of Western, but Eastern detective novels. Yet, as it turns out, he is a translator only in the loosest sense. In rendering them into Russian, he completely reworks the texts of a phenomenally productive Japanese graphomaniac with a knack for plotting but no literary talent. Together, and unbeknownst to either, the writer and his "translator" have become the fantastically successful best-selling Japanese "author" Otori Mitio. As it turns out, it was his publishers who arranged to have "the stylist" beaten and left a virtually helpless cripple to keep him from emigrating from Russia. He is too valuable a commodity to be allowed to get away. As this play with the fine line between author and translator underscores, authorship in the new Russia is a risky and potentially violent business, not because of what the author has to say, but because of what he or she might have to sell.

The world of Marinina's fictions, on the face of it, would hardly seem to offer comfort to the reader of pulp. Behind the facade of a friendly neighbor and loving husband may lurk a vicious serial killer, and the course of true love is more likely to end in disillusionment or murder than in happy endings. Far from allowing her readers to escape to exotic climes, Marinina rooted her plots and characters firmly in the beleaguered everyday life of 1990s Russia, where politicians were corrupt or ineffectual and police lived from paycheck to paycheck, watching their meager wages dwindle with inflation. Yet, if we accept the answer to highbrow critics who dismiss popular fiction as pablum for the uneducated and intellectually lazy masses—that, on the contrary, it fulfills a need—then the sales of Marinina's books in the 1990s suggest that they offered a wide spectrum of readers, which seemed to cross boundaries of gender and class, something they not only wanted but needed.[52] The key to her works' popularity perhaps lay at least partly in their overt confrontation with the anxieties and threats posed by the instability of life in early post-Soviet Russia, which were thereby rendered manageable and therefore less frightening. As Umberto Eco has pointed out, it is the very "iterative" nature of formulaic fiction, its predictability, that allows it to offer respite from unsettling *realia*, an argument that goes far toward explaining why such fictions enjoy

---

52 See, for example, Radway's arguments concerning the romance novel in "Women Read the Romance" and in her book, *Reading the Romance: Women, Patriarchy, and Popular Literature* (Chapel Hill: University of North Carolina Press, 1984).

particular popularity at moments of social instability.[53] After all, it is reassuring that there are honest cops willing to work long hours and forgo the big bucks offered for private security work just for the sake of bringing criminals to justice. Moreover, even if Kamenskaia does not always solve cases fast enough to save the innocent, she inevitably arrives at the correct solution in the end, and the problems she solves are—as in all true detective fictions—riddles of identity, revealing the true person behind the public mask, a particularly consoling message at a time when radically changing values unsettled long-held assumptions about definitions of the self. For those with a taste for romance, Marinina holds out the hope that, no matter how plain you may be, there is a possibility of finding your true soul mate; and for those fond of intellectual challenge, devious and complicated plots abound. As one male reviewer, apparently of intelligentsia persuasion, observed, his attention was first drawn to Marinina's books when:

> one day in the subway I caught sight of two young people who were reading with enthusiasm a new book issued in the "pocket book" series and, to all appearances, written by a woman. What amazed me was that in external appearance these young people did not resemble at all not only readers of women's novels, but any readers at all. No, I don't mean to say that it seemed to me that they didn't know how to read, I would have found it easier to imagine them rather with a plasterer's handbook or the magazine *Radio*, but under no circumstances with "pulp fiction" [*chtivom*].[54]

His interest piqued, he read all these "women's" novels for himself, concluding, "Now everyone reads Marinina."[55]

---

53   See, Umberto Eco, "The Myth of Superman," in his *The Role of the Reader: Explorations in the Semiotics of Texts* (Bloomington: Indiana University Press, 1979), 117–22.

54   Mitrofanov, "Samaia strashnaia."

55   Mitrofanov, "Samaia strashnaia."

Works Cited

Andzhaparidze, G. "Bogachi-filantropy i belye 'mersedesy'. Chto i kak my perevodim." *Literaturnaia gazeta*, January 20, 1971, 13.

Arbitman, Roman. "Dolgoe proshchanie s serzhantom militsii. Sovremennyi rossiiskii detektiv: izdatel' protiv chitatelia." *Znamia* 7 (1995): 201–7.

Avins, Carol. *Border Crossings: The West and Russian Identity in Soviet Literature 1917–1934*. Berkeley: University of California Press, 1983.

Britikov, A. F. "Detektivnaia povest' v kontekste prikliuchencheskikh zhanrov." In *Russkaia sovetskaia povest' 20-30kh gg*. Edited by V. A. Kovalev, 408–53. Leningrad: Nauka, 1976.

Brooks, Jeffrey. *When Russia Learned to Read: Literacy and Popular Literature, 1861–1917*. Princeton: Princeton University Press, 1985.

"Chempiony izdavaemosti 1994 goda." *Knizhnoe obozrenie*, January 10, 1995.

Chukovskii, K. I. "Nat Pinkerton." In his *Sobranie sochinenii v shesti tomakh*, vol. 6, 117–49. Moscow: Khudozhestvennaia literatura, 1969.

Cioran, Samuel D. "Translator's Introduction." In *Mess-Mend: Yankees in Petrograd*, by Marietta Shaginian, 7–21. Ann Arbor: Ardis, 1991.

Clark, Katerina. *Petersburg: Crucible of Cultural Revolution*. Cambridge, MA: Harvard University Press, 1995.

Condee, Nancy, and Vladimir Padunov, "The ABC of Russian Consumer Culture: Readings, Ratings, and Real Estate." In *Soviet Hieroglyphics: Visual Culture in Late Twentieth-Century Russia*. Edited by Nancy Condee, 130–72. Bloomington: Indiana University Press, 1995.

Eco, Umberto. "The Myth of Superman." In *The Role of the Reader: Explorations in the Semiotics of Texts*, by Umberto Eco, 107–24. Bloomington: Indiana University Press, 1979.

Gavrilov, Aleksandr. "Radost' uznavaniia: Izdateliam vygodnee torgovat' liud'mi, chem knigami." *Ex Libris NG*, May 19, 1997.

Goriunova, L., and G. Borisov. "Samyi blagodarnyi moi chitatel'—'afgantsy.' . . . " *Knizhnoe obozrenie*, April 15, 1997, 6.

Gurskii, Lev. "Nol' tselykh piat' desiatykh" [review of Vitalii Babenko, "Nul'"]. *Literaturnaia gazeta*, June 11, 1997, 11.

Isarova, Larisa. "Beskonechnye kilometry detektivov: Koe-chto o deval'vatsii populiarnogo zhanra." *Literaturnaia gazeta*, April 12, 1989, 3.

Irons, Glenwood. "New Women Detectives: G is for Gender-Bending." In *Gender, Language, and Myth: Essays on Popular Narrative*. Edited by Glenwood Irons, 127–41. Toronto: University of Toronto Press, 1992.

Kaletskii, P. "Pinkertonovshchina." In *Literaturnaia entsiklopediia*, vol. 8, 645–49. Moscow: Sovetskaia entsiklopediia, 1934.

Kamyshan, Sergei. "'Bul'var' vchera i segodnia." Access date unknown. (Special for) *Novaia Sibir'*. http://www.sicnit.ru/siberia/55/ liter_04.htm (site discontinued—eds.).

Kardin, V. [Emil' Kardin]. "Sekret uspekha." *Voprosy literatury* 4 (1986): 102–50.

"Kto vy, pokupateli knig?" *Knizhnoe obozrenie*, August 20, 1996.

Kravchenko, Tat'iana. "Losev. Syshchik i dolgozhitel': Sovetskii sledovatel' i postsovetskoe vremia." *Literaturnaia gazeta*, July 12, 1995, 4.

———. "Missis Kholms: Knizhnaia seriia Aleksandry Marininoi." *Russkaia mysl'*, October 23, 1996. http://www.relis.ru/MEDIA/news/lg/texts/43/0405.html (site discontinued—eds.).

Krasnolistov, O. "Ot sostavitelia." In *Staryi russkii detektiv: Roman, rasskazy*. Edited by O. Krasnolistov and E. Mashkirov, vol. 1, 3–4. Zhitomir: Olesia, 1992–1993.

Lapina, Anna. "Fokus udalsia: 'U nas tut chastnyi detektiv, a ne politicheskii triller,' ili Bestseller dlia uzkogo kruga." *Novaia Sibir'*, April 21, 1997.

Laqueur, Walter. "Julian Semyonov and the Soviet Political Novel." *Society* 23, no. 5 (1986): 72–80.

Latynina, Iuliia. "Plokhoi khoroshii detektiv: On podchiniaetsia zakonam rynka, no ne zakonam tusovki." *Literaturnaia gazeta*, July 12, 1995, 4.

Lunts, Lev. "Na zapad! Rech' na sobranii Serapionovykh brat'ev 2-go dekabria 1922 g." In his *Zaveshchanie tsaria*, edited by Wolfgang Kasack, 115–26. Munich: Verlag Otto Sagner, 1983.

Marinina, Aleksandra. *Smert' i nemnogo liubvi*. Moscow: Eksmo, 1996.

———. *Svetlyi lik smerti*. Moscow: Eksmo, 1997.

Mitrofanov, Sergei. "Samaia strashnaia skazochnitsa Rossii." *Ex Libris NG*, March 6, 1997.

Nezhurin, G. "Alla Shteinman: 'Umenie vzglianut' na situatsiiu s iumorom i samoironiei tol'ko pribavliaet nam shansov vyigrat'.'" *Knizhnoe obozrenie*, September 3, 1996.

[Nezhurin, G., and O. Pogorelova]. "Viktor Dotsenko: 'Esli by seichas Khristos vernulsia k nam na zemliu . . . vriad li on stal by podstavliat' vragu vtoruiu shcheku.'" *Knizhnoe obozrenie*, July 30, 1996.

Radway, Janice A. *Reading the Romance: Women, Patriarchy, and Popular Literature*. Chapel Hill: University of North Carolina Press, 1984.

———. "Women Read the Romance: The Interaction of Text and Context." *Feminist Studies* 9, no. 1 (1983): 53–78.

Revzim, Grigorii. "Sherlok Kholms i Sancho Pansa: Klassicheskii detektiv: Igra po pravilam" [review of Nikolai Leonov, *Polnoe sobranie sochinenii v 12 tomakh*]. *Ex Libris NG*, February 20, 1997.

Riabov, Geilii. Introduction to *Imenem zakona: Sovremennyi sovetskii detektiv*, 3–6. Moscow: Sovetskii pisatel', 1989.

Russell, Robert. "Red Pinkertonism: An Aspect of Soviet Literature of the 1920s." *SEER* 60, no. 3 (1982): 390–412.

Semitsvetov, Igor'. "Aleksandra Marinina: 'Prestupnikov ia opisyvaiu osobenno liubovno.'" *Ogonek*, May 12, 1997. Accessed August 23, 2022. https://www.kommersant.ru/doc/2285012.

Stanley, Alessandra. "The World: In Its Dreams; Russia Solves Its Crime Problem." *New York Times*, March 15, 1998.

Stites, Richard. *Russian Popular Culture: Entertainment and Society since 1900*. Cambridge: Cambridge University Press, 1992.

Symons, Julian. *Bloody Murder: From the Detective Story to the Crime Novel: A History*. Rev. ed. New York: Viking Press, 1985.

Tome, Sandra. "Questing Women: The Feminist Mystery after Feminism." In *Feminism in Women's Detective Fiction*. Edited by Glenwood Irons, 46–63. Toronto: University of Toronto Press, 1995.

Toporov, Viktor. "Pretenzii k poterpevshim" [review of Arkadii and Grigorii Vainer, *Ob"ezzhaite na dorogakh sbitykh koshek i sobak* and *Poterpevshie pretenzii ne imeiut*]. *Literaturnoe obozrenie* 2 (1987): 65–69.

Vasiukhina, Vlada. "Dva litsa Aleksandry Marininoi." *Ogonek*, September 20, 1998. Accessed August 23, 2022. https://www.kommersant.ru/doc/2286056.

Vulis, Abram. *V mire prikliuchenii: Poetika zhanra*. Moscow: Sovetskii pisatel', 1986.

Zurabishvili, Tinatin. "Liubimye pisateli rossiian." *Knizhnoe obozrenie*, February 14, 1995.

Selected Publications by Catharine Theimer Nepomnyashchy

Books

Nadezhda Azhgikhina and Ketrin Taimer-Nepomniashchaia [Catharine Theimer Nepomnyashchy]. *Tni dnia v avguste*. Moscow: MediaMir, 2014.

Hilde Hoogenboom, Catharine Theimer Nepomnyashchy, and Irina Reyfman, eds. *Mapping the Feminine: Russian Women and Cultural Difference*. Bloomington: Slavica Publishers, 2008.

Catharine Theimer Nepomnyashchy, Nicole Svobodny, and Ludmilla Trigos, eds. *"Under the Sky of My Africa": Alexander Pushkin and Blackness*. Evanston: Northwestern University Press, 2006.

Contains Catharine Theimer Nepomnyashchy and Ludmilla A. Trigos, "Introduction: Was Pushkin Black?," 3–45.

Contains Catharine Theimer Nepomnyashchy, "The Telltale Black Baby, or Why Pushkin Began *The Blackamoor of Peter the Great* but Didn't Finish It," 150–71.

Catharine Theimer Nepomnyashchy. *Abram Tertz and the Poetics of Crime*. New Haven: Yale University Press, 1995.

Published in Russian as *Abram Terts i politika prestupleniia*. Translated by E. Ishunina, I. Kirilova, E. Panasova, and T. Funtusova. Ekaterinburg: Izdatel'stvo Ural'skogo universiteta, 2003.

Abram Tertz (Andrei Sinyavsky). *Strolls with Pushkin*. Translated by Catharine Theimer Nepomnyashchy and Slava Yastremski. Introduction by Catharine Theimer Nepomnyashchy. New Haven: Yale University Press, 1993.

Republished in 2017 by Columbia University Press as part of the Russian Library series in a revised and expanded edition that includes a memoir about Nepomnyashchy and Yastremski by Michael Naydan as well as a translation of "Puteshestvie na Chernuiu rechku" that was planned by Nepomnyashchy and Yastermski, begun by Yastremski, following Nepomnyashchy's death, and then finished by Naydan.

Scholarly Articles and Book Chapters

"Examining Lensky's Body: Forensic Pedagogy." In *Teaching Nineteenth-Century Russian Literature: Essays in Honor of Robert L. Belknap*. Edited by Deborah Martinsen, Cathy Popkin, and Irina Reyfman, 287–301. Boston: Academic Studies Press, 2014.

"Adaptation in Contexts: A Tale of Two Annas." In *Tolstoy on Screen*. Edited by Lorna Fitzsimmons and Michael A. Denner, 317–37. Evanston: Northwestern University Press, 2014.

"The Émigré Alter-Ego: Émigré Literary Criticism." In *A History of Russian Literary Theory and Criticism: The Soviet Age and Beyond*. Edited by Evgeny Dobrenko and Galin Tihanov, 269–86. Pittsburgh: University of Pittsburgh Press, 2011.

Russian version published in *Istoriia russkoi literaturnoi kritiki: Sovetskaia i postsovetskaia epokhi*. Edited by Evgenii Dobrenko and Galin Tikhanov, 608–34. Moscow: Novoe literaturnoe obozrenie, 2012.

"Pushkin as a Poet of Blackness." *Pushkin Review* 12–13 (2009–2010): 97–104.

"Jane Austen and Russian Chat." *Ulbandus: The Slavic Review of Columbia University* 11 (2008): 115–25.

"Man in Black: Putin. Power. Image." *Przeglad Rusycystyczny* 4 (2007): 19–32.

Updated and republished in a dual language version: "Chelovek v chernom: Putin. Vlast'. Stil'." *Depesha* 3 (Fall/Winter 2009–2010): 231–43.

"Writing in the Margins: In Praise of Emigration." *Toronto Slavic Quarterly* 15 (Winter 2006). Accessed June 7, 2023. http://sites.utoronto.ca/tsq/15/index15.shtml.

"Andrei Siniavsky." In *Dictionary of Literary Biography*, vol. 302: *Russian Prose Writers after World War II*. Edited by Christine Rydel, 296–316. Detroit: Gale, 2004.

"Televizing Marinina: The Representation of Crime in Post-Soviet Russia." *Die Welt der Slaven* 48 (2003): 313–20.

"'Puteshestvie na Chernuiu rechku' Abrama Tertsa." In *XX vek i russkaia literatura. Alba Regina Philologiae. Sbornik nauchnikh statei*. Edited by Iurii Troitskii, 223–36. Moscow: Russian State Humanities University Press, 2002.

"A Note on Gliere's Ballet *The Bronze Horseman*." In *Depictions: Slavic Studies in the Narrative and Visual Arts in Honor of William Harkins*. Edited by Douglas Greenfield, 61–70. Ann Arbor: Ardis, 2000.

"The Seduction of the Story: Flight and 'Fall' in Tolstaya's 'Heavenly Flame.'" In *Twentieth-Century Russian Literature: Selected Papers from the Fifth World Congress for Central and East European Studies*. Edited by Karen L. Ryan and Barry P. Scherr, 239–56. New York: St. Martin's Press, 2000.

"Andrei Donatovich Sinyavsky (1925–1997)." Introduction to the special section "Forum: The Legacy of Andrei Sinyavsky," which Nepomnyashchy organized. *Slavic and East European Journal* 42, no. 3 (Fall 1998): 367–71.

"Perestroika and the Soviet Creative Unions." In *New Perspectives on Russian and Soviet Art and Culture*. Edited by John O. Norman, 131–51. New York: St. Martin's Press, 1994.

"'Vysokoe' i 'nizkoe' v rossiiskoi i amerikanskoi kul'turakh." *Obshchestvennye nauki i sovremennost'* 5 (1992): 184–87.

"Andrei Sinyavsky's 'Return' to the Soviet Union." *Formations* 6, no. 1 (Spring 1991): 24–44.

"Sinyavsky/Tertz: The Evolution of the Writer in Exile." *Humanities in Society: Soviet and East European Literature in Exile* 7, nos. 3–4 (Summer-Fall 1984): 123–42.

    Russian translation of this article published in *Russkaia literatura XX veka: Issledovaniia amerikanskikh uchenykh*. Edited by Elizabeth Neatrour and Boris Averin, 500–25. St. Petersburg: Petro-RIF, 1993.

"Andrei Sinyavsky's 'You and I': A Modern Day Fantastic Tale." *Ulbandus Review* 2, no. 2 (Fall 1982): 209–30.

"The Search for Russian Identity in Contemporary Soviet Russian Literature." In *Ethnic Russia in the USSR: The Dilemma of Dominance*. Edited by Edward Allworth, 88–97. New York: Pergamon Press, 1980.

"*Our Contemporary* and the Development of the Rural Prose Tradition." *Ulbandus Review* 1, no. 2 (Spring 1978): 58–73.

"The Function and Representation of Time in *The First Circle*." *Modern Fiction Studies*, 23, no. 1 (Spring 1977): 63–72.

Articles for Popular Venues and Personal Reflections

"Revising Nabokov Revising the Detective Novel: Vladimir, Agatha, and the Terms of Engagement." *Harriman Magazine* (Fall 2015): 50–55. Accessed August 21, 2022. http://www.columbia.edu/cu/creative/epub/harriman/2015/fall/harriman_winter_2015.pdf.

"Re-Visioning the Past: Russian Literary Classics in Film." *World Literature Today* (November-December 2011): 55–58.

"Columbia's Russian Institute: The Formative Years." In *Living Legacies at Columbia*. Edited by Wm. Theodore de Bary with Jerry Kisslinger and Tom Mathewson, 621–31. New York: A Columbia University Publication, 2006.

    Republished in *Sixty Years of the Harriman Institute at Columbia University, 1946–2006*, 6–14. New York: Harriman Institute, 2006.

"Remembering Ulbandus Review." *Ulbandus: The Slavic Review of Columbia University* 6 (2002): 6–12.

"Russia behind the (Looking) Glass." *Capital Perspective* 9 (May-June 2002): 68–71.

"Pushkin at 200." *Harriman Forum* 12, nos. 2–3 (Winter 1999/2000): 1–5.

"Famine in Time of Feast: Soviet Literary Publishing under Glasnost." *Harriman Institute Forum* 3, no. 3 (March 1990): 1–8.

Short Translations

Abram Tertz. "Art and Reality." *Formations* 6, no. 1 (Spring 1991): 1–5.

Tatyana Nabatnikova. "In Memoriam." In *Soviet Women Writing: Fifteen Short Stories*, 117–30. New York: Abbeville Press, 1990.

Andrei Sinyavsky. "Would I Move Back?" *Time*, April 10, 1989, 129–130, 132.

Valentin Kataev. "The Sleeper." Sergei Zalygin. "Prose." In *The New Soviet Prose: Sixteen Short Stories*, 111–33 and 363–85. New York: Abbeville Press, 1989.

Abram Tertz. "From Little Tsores." *Humanities in Society: Soviet and East European Literature in Exile* 7, nos. 3–4 (Summer-Fall 1984): 173–74.

A. S. Pushkin. "The Bronze Horseman." In *The Ardis Anthology of Russian Romanticism*. Edited by Christine Rydel, 151–55. Ann Arbor: Ardis, 1984.

Interviews

"An Interview with Andrei Sinyavsky." *Formations* 6, no. 1 (Spring 1991): 6–23.

Journals Issues Edited

Guest Editor. *The Return of Abram Tertz: Siniavskii's Reception in Gorbachev's Russia*. Special issue of *Russian Studies in Literature* 28, no. 1 (Winter 1991–1992).

Contains an editor's introduction by Nepomnyashchy: "Notes on the Context of Siniavskii's Reception in Gorbachev's Russia," 3–11.

Editor. Festschrift for Rufus W. Mathewson, Jr. *Ulbandus Review* 2, no. 1 (Fall 1979).

Editor. Inaugural issue of *Ulbandus Review*. *Ulbandus Review* 1, no. 1 (Fall 1977).

Index

"About Our Nihilism apropos Turgenev's Novel" [O nashem nigilizme po povodu romana Turgeneva] (Katkov), 65–66
Abram Tertz and the Poetics of Crime (Nepomnyashchy, 1995), vii
Acmeist poets, 89, 198
action novels (*ostrosiuzhetnye romany*), 290
Adamov, Arkadii, 285
"Adaptation, or the Cinema as Digest" (Bazin), 132
Adolescent, The [Podrostok] (Dostoevskii), 73
"Adventure of Charles Augustus Milverton, The" (Doyle), 127
"Adventure of the Bruce-Partington Plans, The" (Doyle), 127
"Adventure of the Empty House, The" (Doyle), 127
"Adventure of the Second Stain, The" (Doyle), 127
Adventures of Major Pronin [Prikliucheniia maiora Pronina] (Ovalov), 285
Adventures of Mr. West in the Land of the Bolsheviks, The (silent film, dir. Kuleshov, 1924), 138
Adventures of Sherlock Holmes and Doctor Watson, The (Soviet TV series, 1979–1986), 124, 126–28; context of Soviet imperial hierarchy, 129–30; crime originating from contact with the foreign, 137–38; disengagement from the present, 133; expanded role for Holmes's brother, 137, 139; focus on Watson rather than Holmes, 132–33n19, 136–37, 140; "museumizing" of original tales, 134, 140; nostalgia and, 133, 134, 138, 139; self-conscious cinematic quotations in, 130–32, 134; Soviet censorship and, 135, 136; styled as highbrow artefact, 132–33; *The Twentieth Century Begins* (final installment), 127, 134, 138–39; viewers of, 129–30, 131, 135

Afanas'ev, A. N., 54
Afghanistan: British wars of 19th century in, 135, 136; Soviet war in, 127, 136, 290, 291n28
Aitmatov, Chinghiz, 228
Akhmatova, Anna, 13, 24, 26, 139
Akhsharumov, Nikolai, 282
Aksakov family, 59, 178
Aksakov, Ivan, 61n19, 64n31
Aksakov, Sergei, 54, 64n31, 177, 203
Aldanov, Mark, xii
Alekseev, M. P., 24
Alekseeva, Galina, 78n3
Alexander I, Tsar, 9
Alexander II, Tsar, 55, 56, 59
Alexandrov, Vladimir E., 110n22
Algarotti, Francesco, 20n10
Amelina, T. A., 95, 96
Anemone, Tony, 49
Anna Karenina (Tolstoy), serialized publication of, 68–69, 73
Annenkov, Pavel, 54, 62
Another's Mask [Chuzhaia maska] (Marinina), 298, 304, 307
anti-nihilist novels, 69–70
anti-Semitism, 303
Antonovich, M. A., 65, 66
Arbitman, Roman, 288n21, 289n22
Armstrong, Charlotte, 295
Ass, Pavel, 276–77
Astaf'ev, Viktor, 228
At Daggers Drawn [Na nozhakh] (Leskov, 1870), 70
Augustus II, king of Poland, 50
Aurora Floyd (Braddon, 1863), 90
Austen, Jane, xviii, 77, 88; Anglo-American film adaptations of, 97; "Austen-mania" in the West, 97; everyday (family) life and fictive world of, 78, 87, 93; as hidden presence in Russian literature, 86; mentioned in Russia during her lifetime, 77–78; Nabokov and, 80–81, 89–92; in post-Soviet Russia, 96–98; published

traces in Russia, 87–89; Pushkin's possible reading of, 80, 82; Soviet reception of, 92–96; works translated into French, 82. See also *Pride and Prejudice*
avant-garde, early twentieth-century, 199, 203, 234
Averkiev, D. V., 70n55
Avseenko, V. G., 70n55
Azhgikhina, Nadezhda, xiii

"Bad Weapons" [Durnye oruzhiia] (Herzen), 65n34
ballet: ballerinas and the male gaze, 241–43, *241*; Diaghilev and international cultural politics, 246–54; Nepomnyashchy's interest in, vii, xv, xvii, xviii; Russia defined for outside world by, 240; Russian empire/autocracy and, 244–46; Soviet ballet and the Orient, 254–58. See also orientalism, of Russian ballet
Ballets Russes, 240, 246, 253; admiring gaze of foreign audience and, 247; centennial anniversary of, xv; "conquest" of Western Europe by, 249; exotic appeal to Western audiences, 248; Soviet ballet and, 255, 258. See also *Cleopatra*; *Firebird, The*
Balzac, Honoré de, 146
Banes, Sally, 252
Baring, Maurice, 78, 79
Barnard College, xii, xiv, xv–xvi
Barthes, Roland, 16
Battleship "Potemkin," The [Bronenosets "Potemkin"] (film, dir. Eisenstein, 1925), 200
Bayley, John, 79
Bazin, André, 132
Begemotov, Nestor, 276–77
Belaia, Galina, xiii
Belinskii, Vissarion, 226n14
Belknap, Robert, xi
Bell [Kolokol] (journal), 65n34
Belov, Vasilii, 225, 228
Bel'skii, A. A., 96
Benedict, Barbara, 39n4, 40–41
Benois, Alexandre, 251
Berg, F. N., 73n70
Berkh, Vasilii Nikolaevich, 20n10

Berkovskii, N. Ia., 24n20
Bernfeld, Siegfried, 107
Bethea, David, 27n25
Bettelheim, Bruno, 305
Beyond the Pleasure Principle (Freud), 109
Blackamoor of Peter the Great, The [Arap Petra Velikogo] (Pushkin), curiosity in, 42–44, 50; Gannibal as object of curiosity, 44–45, 49–51; Pushkin's African heritage and, 48–49; sexual anxiety and, 47–48. See also Gannibal, Ibrahim/Abram
"Black Cat" (Chernaia koshka) detective series, 290
Blagoi, Dmitrii, 12
Blok, Aleksandr, 209, 253–54
Bloody Murder (Symons), 281
Bloom, Harold, 202
Boborykin, Petr Dmitrievich, 225, 226, 228, 229
Boguslavskaia, Zoia, xiii
Bolshevism, 104, 155, 177, 200; ballet and, 255, 258; civilizing mission of, 258
Bormann, Martin, 266, 267, 270, 277
Boyd, Brian, 107, 110n22
Braddon, Mary Elizabeth, 90
"Braitenbruch" [A/201] (Soviet spy), 265
Brezhnev, Leonid, 93, 128, 138, 261, 277
Bridget Jones: The Edge of Reason (Fielding, 2001), 97
British Chess Problem Association, 107
British Psycho-Analytic Society, 107
Briusov, Valerii, 7, 8, 20n10, 27n25
Bronevoi, Leonid, 265n7, 266
Brontë sisters, 90
Bronze Horseman, The [Mednyi vsadnik] (Glière ballet, 1949), 257n32
Bronze Horseman, The (Pushkin, 1833), "Legend of Sleepy Hollow" and, 25–26; critical receptions and, 27; Evgenii compared to Ichabod Crane, 22–23; Evgenii's confrontation with the tsar as writer's problem, 31–34; protagonist's clash with the state, 27; Pushkin's reading of Irving and, 17; scene setting with historically important river, 21–22
Bronze Horseman, The (Pushkin, 1833), "The Poet" and: Evgenii as figure of the poet, 5–6, 7; "Ezerskii" as possible early variant of, 7n6; first

line compared to "The Poet," 3n3, 5; madness as poetic inspiration in, 10–12; "ring" structure linking introduction and ending, 12; stanzaic structure of classical ode, 12
Brothers Karamazov, The [Brat'ia Karamazovy] (Dostoevskii, 1879–1880), 73, 282
Bukharin, Nikolai, 283–84
Bulgakov, Mikhail, 224, 228
Bunin, Ivan, xii
Burnt by the Sun [Utomnlennye solntsem] (film, 1994), 266
Bury, John, 80
Bushin, Vladimir, 225–28
Buslaev, F. I., 54, 68n51
Bykov, Dmitry, 228
Byron, Lord, 79, 83

Cambridge Psychoanalytic Group, 106
Captain's Daughter, The [Kapitanskaia dochka] (Pushkin), 87
Carter, Nick (fictional character), 282
Case of the Wolf-Man (Freud), 105n7
Cathedral Folk [Soboriane] (Leskov), 70
Cat's House, The [Koshkin dom] (Marshak), 209
Cat's House, The [Koshkin dom] (Siniavskii, 1998), xviii; genesis of, 205; golden shoelace (*zolotoi shnurok*) thread in, 215–16, 217–18; interplay of autobiography and fiction in, 206, 208, 213, 214, 215, 218; matrioshka-like inserted texts in, 211–13, 216–17; metaphor in, 207, 209, 211, 219; plot, 207–9; "White Epic" chapter, 213–14
censors/censorship, ix, xii, 281; *The Bronze Horseman* and, 11; easing and curtailment of, 287; journalism and, 56, 57, 58, 60–61
Chandler, Raymond, 297
Change of Places [Peremena mest] (Gurskii), 288n21
Chapaev, Vasily Ivanovich, 263, 279
Chase, James Hadley, 288
Chechetko, M. V., 95
Chechnya, Russia's wars in, 303
Chekhov, Anton Pavlovich, 224, 234, 306
Cheney, Lon, Sr., 131
Chernichenko, Iurii, 128

Chernyshevskii, Nikolay, 61n21, 62, 63
chess, psychoanalysis and, 107–8, 110; chess as site of Oedipal rivalry, 112, 114; "retrograde analysis" to originary trauma, 117–20; sexuality linked with chess, 114. See also *Defense, The* (Nabokov, 1964)
Christiana Eberhardina, 50
Christie, Agatha, 127, 286, 288, 295
Chujoy, Anatole, 244
Chukovskii, Kornei, 283, 284, 293
Church Slavonic, xi, 12, 172
Cleopatra (Diaghilev ballet), 250–51, 251, 253
Cohen, David G., 105n7
Coincidence [Stechenie obstoiatel'stv] (Marinina), 295–96, 298, 301, 306n51, 307
Cold War, 240, 265, 270, 272; culturally specific hero figures of, 276; spy fiction of, 287
Columbia University, xi–xii, xv–xvi; Columbia Global Scholars Program Summer Workshop, xvi; Russian Institute Certificate, xiv. See also Harriman Institute
Condee, Nancy, x, 289
Congress of Compatriots (Kongress sootechestvennikov), xiii
Contemporary [Sovremennik] (journal), 61, 62, 63, 64, 66
"Contemporary Russian Detective Fiction" (Sovremennyi rossiiskii detektiv) series, 290
"Conversation between the Bookseller and the Poet" [Razgovor knigoprodavtsa s poetom] (Pushkin), 32
Cornwell, Patricia D., 296
Cossacks, The [Kazaki] (Tolstoy, 1863), 68
Council on Foreign Relations, vii
Coutinho, Charles, 80
Crime and Punishment [Prestuplenie i nakazanie] (Dostoevskii, 1866), 72, 282
"crime novels" (*ugolovnye romany*), 282
Culture and Imperialism (Said), 125
curiosity, 38–41, 48; appearance of word "curiosity" (*liubopytstvo*) in Pushkin's prose, 42–44; self-other boundary and, 40; sexual anxiety and, 47–48; unstable meaning of, 41

Curiosity and Pilgrimage (Zacher), 39
Current Events of the Russian Chronicler [Tekushchie izvestiia russkogo letopistsa] (daily news sheet), 56–57
Curtis, James, 202

Dagger, The [Kortik] (Rybakov, 1948), 285
Daigrepont, Lloyd M., 28
Dead Souls (Gogol), 227
Death and a Little Love [Smert' i nemnogo liubvi] (Marinina), 298, 302, 303, 304, 305
Death for the Sake of Death [Smert' radi smerti] (Marinina), 298, 303
"death of the author," 16–17, 218, 307
Debreczeny, Paul, 43n14, 80
Decembrist revolt (1825), 11
deconstructionism, French, 207
Defense, The (Nabokov, 1964), xviii, 105, 108; chess as site of Oedipal rivalry, 118; Freudian uncanny in, 112, 113, 114, 115; Luzhin's diverted attempts to go home, 115–16; as Nabokov's 1963 Preface to English translation of *The Luzhin Defense* (1929), 101–2; as preemptive attack on psychoanalytic readings, 102, 111n23; repetition patterns in, 110–13, 111n24, 115, 121; as response to Freud's "The Uncanny," 110; "retrograde analysis" of chess problem in, 117–18; "suimate" of Luzhin jumping out a window, 111n23, 116–17, 120–21. See also chess, psychoanalysis and
De La Durantaye, Leland, 104, 105
Delpeux, Albane, 25
Demurova, N. M., 93, 94–95, 96
Derzhavin, Gavrila, 3n2
detective fiction (*detektiv*), xviii, 127, 281–82; children's literature and, 285; "detetctive boom" in early twentieth century, 282–83; disappearance under Stalin's rule, 284–85; Dotsenko–Marinina "best-seller" rivalry, 290–91; feminist, 296–99; "home-produced" (otechestvennye), 286; popularity in the Soviet Union, 287; "positive heroes" of, 287–88; post-Soviet collapse of cult of high culture and, 289; "red Pinkertons," 283–84, 285, 286; return in "thaw" after Stalin's death, 285–86; second surge in Russia during NEP period, 283–84; subdivisions of, 289–90; Western/foreign detective fiction, 285, 286
Deutscher, Isaac, 145–46
Diaghilev, Serge, 240, 254; international cultural politics and, 247–54; "Russian Seasons" show in Paris and, 247
"Diary of a Madman" (Gogol), 14
Discourse and Ideology in Nabokov's Prose (Larmour), 102
Doctor's Plot, 303
Doctor Zhivago [Doktor Zhivago] (Pasternak, 1957), xviii, 96, 144–45, 207–8; on abstraction and debasement of language, 163–66; characters' erroneous assumptions, 152–53; coincidence in, 145, 146, 151–53, 154, 156, 165, 166; comparison with *War and Peace*, 144, 145, 147–48; death and resurrection topoi in, 145, 161, 167, 171–73; imagery patterns in, 157–60; memory in, 147, 172; metaphor of Revolution as surgical procedure, 166–67; mimicry as figure for dissolution of self in totality of being, 169–70; narrative idiosyncrasies of, 146–47; as "poet's novel," 144; religious philosophy and imagery in, 160–62, 164, 170–71; *samobytnost'* (originality) of Zhivago, 163–64; structure in relation to narrative, 148–56, 165–66; vision of history as creative cultural project, 160, 163, 165, 168
Don Juan (Byron), 79
Don Juan (Mozart), 20
Dostoevskii, Fyodor, 138, 218, 231; Katkov's *Russian Messenger* and, 54, 70, 71–73; on legacy of Gogol's "Overcoat," 218, 231, 234
Dotsenko, Viktor, 275, 290–91
Doyle, Arthur Conan, 124, 127, 129, 132, 283, 284. See also Holmes, Sherlock (fictional character)
Druzhinin, Aleksandr, 87–88
Dulles, Allen, 267
Dunskii, Iulii, 128

Dzherzhinskii, Feliks, 234, 264, 278

Eco, Umberto, 276, 277, 308
Education of a Serf Dancer (painting, unknown artist), 241, *241*
Egyptian Nights [Egipetskie nochi] (Pushkin), 44, 45, 250, 256n31
Eisenstein, Sergei, 200–1
Eksmo (*dektektiv* publisher), 290, 292, 293
Ellison, Ralph, 221, 224
Emma (Austen), 78
Enchanted Pilgrim [Ocharovannyi strannik] (Leskov), 71
"Engineer's Thumb, The" (Doyle), 127
English Literature Journal of Moscow, 25
"English Women Novelists" [Anglichanki romanistki] (Tsebrikova, 1871), 88–89
Epoch [Epokha] (journal of Dostoevskii), 72
Era of Mercy [Era miloserdiia] (Vainer brothers, 1975), 286
Erofeev, Venedikt, xiii
Essay on Universal History, the Manners, and Spirit of Nations (Voltaire), 38, 48
Eugene Onegin [Evgenii Onegin] (Pushkin, 1823–1831), 10–11, 214–15, 227, 242–43; parallels with *Pride and Prejudice*, 79–80, 98; contrast of endings, 84–86; estate visits by the women compared, 83–84; film adaptation of *Pride and Prejudice* (2005) and, 97; "happy ending" with two marriages, 83; Nabokov and, 80–81, 92; structural similarities, 81–82
Eurasian studies, xv
European Herald [Vestnik Evropy] (journal), 77
Evdokimova, Svetlana, 46
Everything is Ahead [Vse vperedi] (Belov, 1986), 225
Evsiukova, Svetlana, 97
Evstigneev, Evgenii, 266
"Ezerskii" (Pushkin), 7–9

Family Chronicle [Semeinaia khronika] (Aksakov, 1856), 177, 181, 198; plotless narrative of, 184; "Stepan Mikhailovich's Good Day," 177–79

Family Happiness [Semeinoe schast'e] (Tolstoy, 1859), 62, 68
Family in Decline [Zakhudalyi rod] (Leskov), 70, 71
"Fatal Question, The" [Rokovoi vopros] (Strakhov), 72
Fatherland Notes [Otechestvennye zapiski] (Druzhinin, 1854), 87–88
Fathers and Sons [Ottsy i deti] (Turgenev, 1862), 65
Feat [Podvig] (mass detective series), 287
Fedorov, Nikolai, 161
Festin de pierre (Molière), 20
Fet, Afanasy, 54, 67
Fielding, Helen, 97
Fielding, Henry, 79
film/television adaptations of literary works, 123–24; "fidelity" of, 124, 126; literary classics adapted for American public television, 129
"Final Problem, The" (Doyle), 127, 140
Firebird, The (Diaghilev ballet), 250, 251–53
"*Firebird* and the Idea of Russianness" (Banes), 252
Firth, Colin, 97
Fish, Stanley, 124
"five in four" slogan, 180, 186–87
five-year plan, first (USSR, 1928–1932), 179, 180
Flaubert, Gustave, 146
Forrester, John, 106, 108
Forster, E. M., 145
Forsythe Saga, The [Galsworthy] (BBC TV adaptation), 127
Foucault, Michel, 102
Frank, Viktor, 148
Freedman, Ralph, 157
Freud, Sigmund, viii, xviii, 106–7, 118, 231; anxiety about "aesthetics" in exposition of psychoanalytic theory, 120; control of meaning and, 103; theory of dreams, 106. *See also* psychoanalysis
Freud and Nabokov (Green), 102
"Freud and the Sandman" (Hertz), 120
Frid, Valerii, 128
Friedburg, Maurice, 133
"From the Countryside" [Iz derevni] (Fet), 67
"From the Height of Her Mound" [S vysoty svoego kurgana] (Bushin, 1987), 225–28

"Fur Hat, The" [Shapka] (Voinovich, 1988), 232n21
Futurist poets, 89, 216

Galsworthy, John, 127
Gambrell, Jamey, xiii
Gannibal, Ibrahim/Abram: as cultural mediator, 46; as "double foreigner," 46; "German biography" of, 49; as object of curiosity, 44–45; as observer of curiosity, 45–46, 49–50. See also *Blackamoor of Peter the Great, The*
Garafola, Lynn, xv, 248, 249
Gates, Heny Louis, Jr., 235
Gautier, Théophile, 247
Gavriiliada (Pushkin), 2
Geintse, N. E., 282
Geltser, Ekaterina, 256
gender, 77, 227; ballet performance and, 241–43, 250–54, 258; in detective fiction, 302, 304, 305, 307, 308; Russian reception of Austen and, 78, 86–89
Gendering Bodies/Performing Art: Dance and Literature in Early Twentieth-Century British Culture (Koritz), 241
Genieva, Ekaterina, 93n30, 96
George V, king of the United Kingdom, 248
Georgia, Russian invasion of (2008), ix
Gilbert, Sandra, 305, 306
Gillette, William, 125
glasnost, xii, 96, 127, 138, 216, 226, 285; joke anthologies published during, 263; surge in detective fiction during, 282, 287
Glière, Reinhold, 255–56
Gogol, Nikolai, 14, 87, 218, 227, 234
"Golden Shoelace, The" [Zolotoi shnurok] (Tertz, 1987), 216, 217
Goncharov, Ivan, 54, 78n3
Goodnight [Spokoinoi nochi] (Tertz), 206
Gorbachev, Mikhail, xiv, xv, 235
Gradova, Ekaterina, 266
Grafton, Sue, 296–97
Granin, Daniil, 228
Granovskii, Timofei, 57n8, 59
Green, Geoffrey, 102
Greenblatt, Stephen, 40, 46n19
Gregg, Richard, 27n26
Grin, Aleksandr, 229

Groys, Boris, 199
Gubar, Susan, 305, 306
Gulag Archipelago (Solzhenitsyn, 1962–1973), 96, 183
Gurskii, Lev, 288n21
Gustafson, Richard, xi

Hammett, Dashiell, 297
Harari, Manya, 144n1
Harkins, William, xi
Harriman Institute, vii, viii, xiv, xvii; founded as Russian Institute (1946), xiv; Nepomnyashchy as director, xiv–xv. See also Columbia University
Harriman Magazine, xiv
Haynsworth, Leslie, 125–26
Hayward, Max, 144n1
Helsinki Accords, xi
hermeneutics, 103, 104
Hertz, Neil, 120
Herzen, Aleksandr, xix, 64–65
Himmler, Heinrich, 267, 270
"His Last Bow" (Doyle), 127
History of New England Witchcraft (Mather), 18
History of New York, A (Irving), 24
History of the Russian Ballet from Its Origins to the Present Day [Histoire du ballet russe depuis les origines jusqu'à nos jours] (Lifar, 1954), 246–47
"History of the Village of Goriukhino, The" [Istoriia sela Goriukhina] (Pushkin), 24
Hitler, Adolf, 267–68, 273, 275
Hoffmann, E.T.A., 13, 109, 210
Holmes, Sherlock (fictional character), xviii, 112, 282, 295; bastardized literary offspring of, 283; British imperial ambitions/fears represented by, 125–26, 135–36; "canonic" features of, 125; capitalist system upheld by, 285; junction of market, literature, and empire in British context, 128–29; middle-class readership and, 129; naive belief in powers of reason and science, 140. See also *Adventures of Sherlock Holmes and Doctor Watson, The* (Soviet TV series, 1979–1986)
Hoogenboom, Hilde, vii
Hound of the Baskervilles, The (Doyle), 127, 135

Hutcheon, Linda, 16

"Icy Weather" [Gololeditsa] (Tertz), 207, 209
Idiot, The [Idiot] (Dostoevskii, 1868), 73
"I erected a monument not built by hands..." [Ia pamiatnik sebe vozdvig nerukotvornyi...] (Pushkin, 1836), 202
Inchbald, Elizabeth, 91
"influence" studies, 16
intelligentsia: detective fiction (*detektiv*) and, 283, 284, 287, 306–7, 309; in *Doctor Zhivago*, 163, 164; Solzhenitsyn and, 200, 201; Soviet Sherlock Holmes and, 131, 135; Tolstoy family and, 227
internet, 97, 262, 263, 264, 276
Irving, Washington, 13, 24, 32. *See also* "Legend of Sleepy Hollow, The" (Irving, 1819–1820)
Isaev, Maksim. *See* Shtirlits (Soviet television character)
Iser, Wolfgang, 17
Iskander, Fazil, xiii
Istomina, Avdot'ia, 242–43
Ivanov, Avtonom, 50
Ivan the Fool (Russian folk character), 208
Ivan the Fool: An Essay in Russian Popular Belief [Ivan-durak: Ocherk russkoi narodnoi very] (Siniavskii, 1991), 210–11
Ivan the Terrible [Ivan Grozny], Part Two (film, dir. Eisenstein, 1958 [1946]), 201
Ivasheva, V. S., 96

Jakobson, Roman, 9, 13n16, 21; on metonym in Pasternak's early prose, 150; on myth of the destructive statue in Pushkin's works, 19–20
Jane Austen: A Bio-Bibliographical Index (Genieva, ed.), 96
John Tenner [Dzhon Tenner] (Pushkin), 16, 24n17
Jowitt, Deborah, 245
Joyce, James, 90

Kadare, Ismail, xv
Kamenskaia, Anastasiia (fictional character), 294–96, 302–3, 309; androgyny and, 305–6; male protectors and mentors, 299, 300; political element of crimes and, 302–4; private life of, 299–301; sexual allure as disguise, 294, 299; Western feminist detective fiction counterparts of, 298–99. *See also* Marinina, Aleksandra (Marina Alekseeva)
Karamzin, Nikolay, 9, 33
Kardin, V., 275, 286–87
Karlinsky, Simon, 90, 93
Karsavina, Tamara, 252
Kataev, Valentin, xviii, 177, 182, 199, 203
Katkov, Mikhail, xi, xviii, 62; censors and journalistic ambitions of, 56–58; consolidation of editorial control by, 63–64; as controversial figure, 55; as founder of *Russian Messenger* journal, 54; "honeymoon" of Russian liberalism and, 59; Leskov's break with, 71; opposition to "useful" art, 62–63; Tolstoy and, 68–69; Turgenev and, 65–68. *See also Russian Messenger* [Russkii vestnik] (journal)
Katkova, S. P., 73n70
Katz, Michael R., 57n8
Kenny, Neil, 38–39, 40
Kern, Gary, 200
Kertez, Imre, xv
Kestner, Joseph A., 136
Khrushchev, Nikita, 93, 128
Kitaev, V. A., 61nn19–20
Kliushnikov, V. P., 70n55
Knightley, Keira, 97
knowledge: curiosity and, 41, 42; human and divine, 39; secularization of, 40
Kopelian, Efim, 266
Koritz, Amy, 241, 248
Korsh, E. F., 58, 59n14
Kostunica, Vojislav, xv
Kotzebue, August von, 91
Krandievskaia, Anastasia, 222
Krandievskaia, Nataliia, 222
Krasnolistov, O., 282
Kruze, N. F. von, 60–61
Kschessinska, Mathilde, 245
Kudriavtsev, P. N., 58, 59n14
Kuleshov, Lev, 138
Kuravlev, Leonid, 266
Kutuzov, Mikhail, Field Marshal, 145

Larmour, David, 102
Lastochka (dwarf in Peter's court), 48, 49, 50
Le Carré, John, 287
Lectures on Literature (Nabokov), 90, 92
Ledkovsky (Astman), Marina, vii, xi
"Legend of Sleepy Hollow, The" (Irving, 1819–1820), 13n16, 17–18; critical receptions of, 27; Disney animated version (1949), 18n5; as parable of American literary culture, 29–31; plot summary, 18–19; Pushkin's reading of, 24–26; scene setting with historically important river, 21–22; "supernatural" quality of the horseman, 23; tensions created by emergence of American republic in, 28–30. See also *Bronze Horseman, The* (Pushkin, 1833), "Legend of Sleepy Hollow" and
"Legend of the Arabian Astrologer" (Irving), 20, 24, 26
Leman, Willy, 265
Lenin, Vladimir, 166, 264, 277
Leonov, Leonid, 274
Leonov, Nikolai, 285, 288
Leont'ev, P. M., 58, 65
Leskov, Nikolai, 54, 70–71
Lifar, Serge, 246–47
Life and Opinions of the Tomcat Murr [Lebensansichten des Katers Murr] (Hoffmann, 1819–1821), 210
Lioznova, Tatiana, 265
literary theory, Western, 17
Literaturnaia gazeta (journal), 286
Little Tsores [Kroshka Tsores] (Tertz), 210
Little Zaches [Klein Zaches] (Hoffmann), 210
Liubimov (Siniavskii), 209, 212
Liubimov, N. A., 57n8, 70, 72
Livanov, Vasilii, 126
Livingstone, Angela, 152
Lokid (*dektektiv* publisher), 290, 292
Lolita (Nabokov), 91–92
Lomonosov, Mikhail, 3n2
Lovers' Vows (Kotzebue), 91
Luzhin Defense, The [Zashchita Luzhina] (Nabokov, 1929). See *Defense, The* (Nabokov, 1964)
Lynch, Deirdre, 92

Mafia, Russian, 288, 291, 292, 302, 303
Magnitogorsk, "socialist city" of, 179, 182, 183, 197
Maguire, Robert A., xi, xii
Maiakovskii, Vladimir, 179, 199, 203
Male Games [Muzhskie igry] (Marinina, 1997), 304n47
Mandelstam, Osip, 198
Mansfield Park (Austen), 81, 90, 91
"March of Time" [Marsh vremeni] (Maiakovskii, 1929), 179
Marinina, Aleksandra (Marina Alekseeva), xviii, 290–96, 308–9; "best-seller" rivalry with Dotsenko, 290–91; detective fiction as reworked fairy tales, 295–96; political element in fiction of, 302–4; as "Russian Agatha Christie," 291, 292n31; Western feminist detective fiction and, 296–99; wide spectrum of readers, 308–9
Markevic, Boleslav, 70n55
Marshak, Immanuil, 94
Marshak, Samuil, 94, 209, 215
Maslennikov, Igor' F., 125, 126, 128, 132–33n19, 139
"Masters of European Fiction" (Cornell course taught by Nabokov), 90
Mather, Cotton, 18
Mathewson, Rufus W., Jr., xi
Matlaw, Ralph, 146
Maugham, Somerset, 94
McBain, Ed (Evan Hunter), 295
Meeting Place Cannot Be Changed, The [Mesto vstrechi izmenit' nel'zia] (Soviet TV mini-series, 1966), 127, 286
"M. E. Lobanov's Opinion about the Spirit of Literature" [Mnenie M. E. Lobanova o dukhe slovesnosti] (Pushkin), 43–44
memory, 103, 147, 160, 172, 231; destruction and failure of, 166, 167, 234; language and, 165; life in a Gulag camp and, 193
Mess-Mend: A Yankee in Petrograd [Mess-Mend: Yanki v Petrograde] (Shaginian, 1923), 284, 286
"Metel" [The snowstorm] (Pushkin), 24n20
Meyer, Charles S., 250–51
Meyer, Priscilla, 92

Mickiewicz, Adam, 20n10, 26
Mighty Handful, 255
Military Adventures [Voennye prikliucheniia] (mass detective series), 287
Milton, John, 78
Mitry, Jean, 123
modernism, 103, 203; Freudian discourse and, 120; socialist realism and, 199, 203, 234; Solzhenitsyn's rejection of, 176, 177, 202
Molière, 20
"Monument of Peter the Great" (Mickiewicz), 26
Moscow Gazette (Moskovskie vedomosti), 56, 58, 59, 66
Moskovskii Telegraf (journal), 25
Motyl, Alexander, xvi
Murav'eva, Irina, 228–29n16
Muscovite [Moskvitianin] (journal), 56
MVD (Ministry of Internal Affairs), 287, 292n31, 293
"Myth of Superman, The" (Eco), 276

Nabokov, Vladimir, viii, xviii; on Austen, 80–81, 89–92; as chess problemist, 107; cultural hybridity of, 90; on Gannibal in Peter's court, 49–50
Nabokov, Vladimir, antipathy to Freud, 101–3, 120, 121, 229; art and unrepeatable individuality of author's voice upheld by Nabokov, 103; 121; Freudian discourse in space of Nabokov's prose, 103–4; Nabokov's familiarity with Freud's ideas, 105–6; psychoanalysis compared to totalitarianism, 103, 104. *See also Defense, The* (Nabokov, 1964)
"Nabokov and Freud: The Play of Power" (Shute), 103–4
Napoleon I, 83, 145
Naremore, James, 124
"Nat Pinkerton" (Chukovskii, 1908), 283
Nechaeva, V. S., 72n63
Nekrasov, Nikolay, 61
NEP (New Economic Policy) period, xi, 201, 283
Nepomnyashchy, Catharine Theimer, vii–x, xix; ballet/classical dance as interest of, vii, xv, xvii, xviii; courses taught by, xvi; as Harriman Institute director, xiv–xv; life and career of, x–xvii; translations by, 3n3
Nepomnyashchy, Olga, xvii
Nepomnyashchy, Viacheslav (Slava), x–xi, xii–xiii
New Journal (Novyi zhurnal), xii
Neznanskii, Fridrikh, 288
Nicholas I, Tsar, 32
Nicholas II, Tsar, 245
Nijinsky, Vaslav, 249, 251
Norov, A. S., 56
nostalgia: in *The Adventures of Sherlock Holmes and Doctor Watson*, 133, 134, 138, 139; Shtirlits character and, 264, 270, 271, 277
"Note for the Editor of the *Bell*, A" [Zametka dlia izdatelia "Kolokola"] (Katkov), 65nn34–35
Notes of the Fatherland [Otechestvennye zapiski] (journal), 62, 68
"Notes on the Gogol Period in Russian Literature" [Ocherki gogolevskogo perioda russkoi literatury] (Chernyshevskii), 62
Novellas and Literary Excerpts [Povesti i literaturnye otryvki] (journal), 25

Oblomov (Goncharov, 1859), 78n3
October Revolution (1917), 89, 166, 171, 240
Ogonek (weekly magazine), 262
Olesha, Yury, 224
One Day in the Life of Ivan Denisovich [Odin den' Ivana Denisovicha] (Solzhenitsyn, 1962), xviii, 177, 203; Sergei Aksakov's *Family Chronicle* as intertext for, 177–79; conversations about aesthetics in, 199–201, 202; ethical and metaliterary implications of intertexts, 197–203; Kataev's *Time Forward!* as intertext for, 179–83; plotless narrative of, 184. *See also* time, in the Stalin-era Gulag
On the Eve [Nakanune] (Turgenev, 1860), 62
"On the Tasks of Production Managers" [O zadachakh khoziaistvennikov] (Stalin speech, 1931), 180
orientalism, of Russian ballet, 243, 249–50; in *Cleopatra*, 250–51, 251, 253–54, 253; femme fatale figure, 251;

in *The Firebird*, 252; Orient subdued by Soviet ballet, 254–58
Ostrovskii, A. N., 54
Othello (Shakespeare), 120
Otis, Laura, 125
Our Contemporary [Nash sovremennik] (journal), 225
"Our Foreign Refugees" [Nashi zagranichnye refugies] (Katkov), 65n34
Ovalovl, Lev (Lev Shapovalov), 285
"Overcoat, The" [Shinel'] (Gogol), 231

Padget, Sidney, 125
Padunov, Vladimir, 289
Panov, A. S., 282
Paretsky, 296–97
Pasternak, Boris, xiii, xviii, 96; on causality in the novel, 146–47, 150–51; familiarity with Austen, 89–90n23; poetry of, 144
Pasternak, Evgenii Borisovich, xiii, 90n23
Pavlova, Anna, 244, 254
Pazukhin, A. M., 282
Penrose, Lionel, 106–7
Peter the Great, 3, 34n45, 38; birth of curiosity in Russia and, 41; as collector of human oddities, 49–50; matchmaker for Ibrahim Gannibal, 47
Peter the Great, statue of, 2, 11, 12, 13; Headless Horseman compared with, 21; as metonym of place, 22; Petrine "revolution" and, 23, 27; "supernatural" quality of the horseman, 23. See also *Bronze Horseman, The* (Pushkin, 1833)
Petrovka, 38 (Semenov novel, 1963), 264
Phantom of the Opera (silent film, 1925), 131
"Phantoms" [Prizraki] (Turgenev), 59–60n14
Philosophy of the Common Cause, The [Filosofiia obchchego dela] (Fedorov), 161
Pinkerton, Nat (fictional character), 282
"pinkertons" (detective novels), 89
Pisarev, D. I., 65
Pisemskii, Aleksei, 54, 66, 69
"Pkhents" (Tertz), 206–7, 215
Platonov, Andrei, 224
Platt, Rostislav, 266

Playing on Another's Field [Igra na chuzhom pole] (Marinina), 298, 302, 303
"Plodomasov Dwarfs, The" [Plodomasovskie karliki] (Leskov, 1869), 70
Pobedonostsev, Konstantin, 55
Poe, Edgard Allan, 92
"Poet, The" (Pushkin, 1827), 4–5, 7, 10, 14. See also *Bronze Horseman, The* (Pushkin, 1833), "The Poet" and
"Poet and the Crowd, The" [Poet i tolpa] (Pushkin, 1828), 10
"Poetics of Motivation, The: Time, Narrative, and History in the Works of Pasternak, Sinyavsky, and Solzhenitsyn" (Nepomnyashchy, dissertation), xi, xii
poetry, 79, 156, 198; Acmeist, 89, 198; as "art of the impossible," 14; in *Doctor Zhivago*, 153, 155, 156, 159–60, 164, 167–68, 170, 172; Futurist, 89, 216; madness identified with, 10–11, 14; of Maiakovskii, 179; moment of poetic creation, 13; of Pasternak, 144, 167–68; of Pushkin, 2, 5, 24, 87, 202; Symbolist, 89, 168
Pogodin, Mikhail, 56
Police [Militsiia] (journal), 292
Polikushka (Tolstoy, 1863), 68
Polin'ka Saks (Druzhinin, 1847), 87
Polish Uprising (1863), 67
Politics of Tradition, The: Rerooting Russian Literture after Stalin (Nepomnyashchy, unfinished), viii, ix, xviii
Poltava (Pushkin), 2–3, 12
Possessed, The [Besy] (Dostoevskii, 1871–1872), 70, 73
Postmortem (Cornwell), 296
post-structuralism, 219
Pride and Prejudice (Austen), 78, 80–81, 91; *Bridget Jones Diary* as update of, 97; "comedic" ending of, 85; English-language Russian edition (1961), 93; first Russian translation (1967), 90, 93, 94, 96. See also *Eugene Onegin* [Evgenii Onegin] (Pushkin, 1823–1831), parallels with *Pride and Prejudice*
Prime Suspect (British television series), 296
Prince Regent, British (George IV), 95

production novels, Soviet, 179
Provincial Sketches [Gubernskie ocherki] (Saltykov-Shchedrin), 63
psychoanalysis: literature domesticated by, 120; *Nachträglichkeit* (reading back from symptoms to originary trauma), 118; repetition compulsion, 110, 120; totalitarianism of meaning and, 103, 104; unresolved childhood trauma, 109. *See also* chess, psychoanalysis and
"Psycho-Analysis and Chess" (Penrose, 1925), 107–8
Pugacheva, Alla, 262
Pumpianskii, L. V., 12–13
Pushkin, Aleksandr, viii, 19, 38, 62, 78; America in imagination of, 34–35; autobiographical parallels with Evgenii character, 9, 31; ballet and, 242–43, 250; Boldino estate of, 25–26, 31; dachshund named after, xi; dispute over legacy of, 227–28; indebtedness to Irving's works, 24; language and form of classical ode used by, 2–3, 12; possible familiarity with Austen's works, 80, 82; as progenitor of Russian national literary tradition, 235; true literary heirs of, 225–26; as vampire, 209. *See also Blackamoor of Peter the Great, The; Bronze Horseman, The; Eugene Onegin*
Putin, Vladimir, ix, 261, 277–78
Putsykovich, V. F., 73n69

"Queen of Spades, The" (Pushkin), 14

Rabinovich (Russian/Soviet joke figure), 263
Racine, Jean, 78
Radcliffe, Ann, 90
Radway, Janice A., 301n44
Rasputin, Valentin, 228
Rathbone, Basil, 125
realism, nineteenth-century: Austen and, 79, 96; *Doctor Zhivago* and, 144, 145; Solzhenitsyn and, 203; Soviet cultural establishment and, 133; Stalinist appropriation of, 235. *See also* socialist realism
"Reconfiguring the Sexes" (Garafola), 249

Red Poppy, The [Krasnyi mak] (Soviet ballet, 1927), 255–58
"Relentless Cult of Novelty and How It Wrecked the Century, The" (Solzhenitsyn, 1993), 202–3
Revolution (1905), 152, 200, 246, 282
Revolution (1917). *See* October Revolution (1917)
Reyfman, Irina, vii
Ringe, Donald, 28
"Rip Van Winkle" (Irving), 18, 29n31
Rivers, W.H.R., 106
Road to Calvary, The [Khozhdenie po mukam] (A. N. Tolstoi, 1920–1942), 222
Romanticism: Romantic balled, 2; Hoffmann's Romantic grotesque, 13; animation of statues or portraits as motif, 21n11
Rotkirkh, Aleksei Karlovich, 49n22
Rozanova, Maria, 205, 208, 217
Ruban, Vasilii Grigor'evich, 20n10
Rubinstein, Ida, 250–51, *251*
Rubinstein as Cleopatra (Bakst), *251*
Rudia, Alina, 97
Rurik, 98
Russian Chronicler [Russkii letopisets] (journal), 56, 57
Russian Classics in Soviet Jackets (Friedburg), 133
Russian Federation, ix
Russian Forest, The (Leonov novel), 274
Russian Messenger [Russkii vestnik] (journal), 54, 55; "Contemporary Chronicle," 60, 64; Dostoevskii and, 54, 71–73; history of, 56, 73; Leskov and, 54, 70–71; liberal defectors from *Contemporary*, 61–62; movement to the right, 67; "Peasant Question," 60; popularity of, 63; publication approved by the tsar, 58; as rallying point for Russian liberals, 59; Tolstoy and, 54, 65–68; Turgenev and, 54, 65–68
Rybakov, Anatolii, xiii, 285
Rzhevskii, Lieutenant (Russian/Soviet joke figure), 263

Sahsenem (Azerbaijani opera), 255
Said, Edward, 125, 129n14

Saint Petersburg, xv, xvi, 12–14, 61; flood (1824), 5, 9, 10, 11, 12; Pushkin as "curiosity" in, 48
Saltykov-Shchedrin, M. E., 54, 63
Sanson [Samson], Charles-Henri, 43
"Sandman, The" (Hoffmann), 109, 118, 120
Saussure, Ferdinand de, 218
"Scandal in Bohemia, A" (Doyle), 127
Schellenberg, Walter, 265
Scherr, Barry, 151
Scholl, Tim, 246, 248
Scott, Walter, 87
"Scythians, The" [Skify] (Blok, 1918), 253–54
"Sealed Angel, The" [Zapechatlennyi angel] (Leskov), 70, 71
Semenov, Iulian, 264, 265, 266, 270, 285, 287
Sense and Sensibility (Austen), 78
Seventeen Moments in Spring [Semnadtsat' mgnovenii vesny] (Soviet TV series, 1973), 127, 261–62; cast of actors, 265–66; documentary traces in, 265, 269–70; identity and ideological allegiance ambiguities in, 272–74; plot, 266–69; popularity of, 262–63; self-exposure as artifice, 266, 267. See also Shtirlits (Soviet television character)
sexuality: ballet and, 241–43, 244, 249, 250, 251; Kamenskaia (detective fiction character) and, 294, 299–301; in Nabokov's *The Defense*, 112, 113–14, 119
Shaginian, Marietta, 284, 286
Shakespeare, William, 94, 120, 165, 166
Shchekochikhin, Iurii, xiii, xiv
Sheldon, Sidney, 295
Shkliarevskii, A. A., 282
Shklovskii, Viktor, 179–80
"Short Excerpts, News, and Comments" [Kratikie vypiski, izvestiia i zamechaniia] (1816), 77–78
Shteinman, Alla, 291n28
Shtirlits, Max Otto von [Maksim Isaev] (Soviet television character): analogy with James Bond, 276; analogy with Putin, 261, 277–78; duplicity of, 275; fictional biography of, 264–65; jokes involving, 263, 267–68, 270, 271–73; parodic novels about, 276–77; proposed monument to, 278–79; in *samizdat* parodies, 264. See also *Seventeen Moments in Spring* [Semnadtsat' mgnovenii vesny] (Soviet TV series, 1973)
Shtirlits, or How Hedgehogs Muliply [Shtirlits, ili Kak razmnozhaiutsia ezhiki] (Ass and Begemotov, 1986), 276–77
Shtirlits, or Second Youth [Shtirlits, ili vtoraia molodost'] (Ass), 277
Shute, Jenefer, 103, 104
Siberia, x, 156n14
"signifying chain," rupture of, 235
Silence of the Lambs, The (film), 296, 297
Silver Age of Russian literature, 229
Simenon, Georges, 295
Siniavskii, Andrei, xiv, xviii, 145, 205; socialist realist positive hero, 274; vexed relationship with readers, 212n10, 213. See also Tertz, Abram
Sisters [Sestry] (Tolstaia, 1998), 222
Six-Winged Seraphim [Shestikrylyi Serafim] (Marinina), 292n30
Sketchbook of Geoffrey Crayon, Gent., The (Irving, 1819–1820), 17, 24, 25, 30n36
Slavic studies, viii, ix, xvi
Slavophiles, 56, 64n31
Sleeping Beauty (Tchaikovsky ballet), 246, 248, 253
"Sleep Soundly, Son" [Spi spokoino, synok] (Tolstaia), 230–36
Slezkine, Yuri, 41–42
Smoke [Dym] (Turgenev), 67
"socialist competition," productivity and, 179
socialist realism, xviii, 93, 176, 229, 274; Chekhov claimed as progenitor of, 234; modernist avant-garde associated with, by Solzhenitsyn, 199, 203; Tolstoi (Aleksei) and, 222, 224
Sokolov, A. A., 282
Solomin, Vitalii, 126
Solzhenitsyn, Aleksandr, xi, xviii, 96, 139; efforts to recover Russia's past, 177; modernism rejected by, 176, 177, 202; Western democracy criticized by, 176, 203. See also *One Day in the Life of Ivan Denisovich*

Son of the Fatherland [Syn otechestva] (journal), 56
Soviet Union (USSR), xiv, 182, 270; Catharine T. Nepomnyashchy's visits to, x–xi, xii; collectivization, 196, 199; decline reflected in Soviet Sherlock Holmes adaptations, 124, 127; dissolution of, xiii, 96, 261; "era of stagnation" under Brezhnev, 93; first five-year plan (1928–1932), 179, 180; function of ballet in, 240; ideology and production of culture in, 128–29; Jewish emigration from (1970s and 1980s), 273; priority of literature over film in, 129; reception of Austen in, 92–96
Speak, Memory (Nabokov, 1951; revised and extended, 1966), 104–5n6
"Speckled Band, The" (Doyle), 126, 132
"Spectre Bridegroom, The" (Irving), 24n20
Stakheev, D. I., 73n70
Stalin, Joseph, 178, 180, 200, 202, 213; death of, 285, 286; marriage of politics and highbrow culture under, 284; in *Seventeen Moments in Spring*, 270, 273; "social mandate" for composers, 255
Stalinism, 89, 93, 199, 275; cultural amnesia and, 235; as misappropriation of national cultural tradition, 230; post-Soviet afterlife of, ix. *See also* socialist realism
Stalin Revolution, 197
Stankevich, A. V., 59
"Statue in Pushkin's Poetic Mythology, The" (Jakobson), 13n16, 19
Stendhal, 146
Stone Guest, The [Kamennyi gost'] (Pushkin), 19, 20
Stout, Rex, 295
Strakhov, N. N., 72
Strolls with Pushkin (Tertz, 1993), vii, xiv, 205, 209, 214
Study in Scarlet, A (Doyle), 126, 131, 135–36, 137
Stylist, The [Stilist] (Marinina), 300n43, 301, 302, 306n51, 307–8
Surits, Elizaveta Iakovlevna, 240, 258
Svobodny, Nicole, vii

"Symbolism and Immortality" [Simvolizm i bessmertie] (Pasternak, 1913), 168, 169
Symbolist poets, 89, 168
Symons, Julian, 281, 289

Tabakov, Oleg, 266
"Tale of the Golden Cockerel, The" [Skazka o zolotom petushke] (Pushkin), 19, 20, 24, 26
Tales of Belkin [Povesti Belkina] (Pushkin), 24
Taroshchina, Slava, 228
Taruskin, Richard, 249–50
Tatishchev, Ivan Ivanovich, 58n12, 67n44
Tchernicheva, Liubov, 253
television serials, late Soviet. *See Adventures of Sherlock Holmes and Doctor Watson, The*; *Seventeen Moments in Spring*
Tempest, Richard, 80
Tertz [Terts], Abram, vii, xiv, 205, 206–7, 216, 219. *See also* Siniavskii, Andrei
Theimer, Ernst, x
Theimer, James, x
Theimer, Jo-Anne Wright, x
Three Days in August [Tri dnia v avguste] (Nepomnyashchy and Azhgikhina, 2014), xiii
thriller fiction (*boeviki*), 290, 291
Tikhonov, Viacheslav, 262, 265–66
time, in the Stalin-era Gulag, 183–97; accelerated Soviet productivity and, 180–83; authorities' control over, 187–88, 192; competition among prisoners and, 187, 191; "decree time" in the Soviet Union, 185; food and, 189–90, 192, 195; jettisoning of the past, 198; "no time" (*nekogda*) motif, 185, 191–93, 194; spiritual versus material concerns and, 192–97; "stolen," 187–88, 189; time as commodity, 190. *See also One Day in the Life of Ivan Denisovich* [Odin den' Ivana Denisovicha] (Solzhenitsyn, 1962)
Time [Vremia] (journal of Dostoevskii), 71–72
Time Forward! [Vremia vpered!] (Kataev, 1932), xviii, 177, 179–83, 186, 197, 198, 199

Timofeev, N.P., 282
Tolstaia, Nataliia, 222
Tolstaia, Tatiana, viii, xviii, 221; Bushin's diatribe against, 226–28, 236; chosen literary genealogy of, 224, 235; genetic literary family of, 222–24, 235; on Russian literary tradition, 228–30
Tolstoi, Aleksei K., 54
Tolstoi, Aleksei N., 222, 223, 224
Tolstoy, Lev, xix, 54, 59, 68, 87, 144, 222; causality and, 146; compulsion to document life in art, 212; ignorance of Austen, 78n3; on "infectious" nature of true art, 202
Tome, Sandra, 296, 297–99, 304n47, 306
Topol', Eduard, 288
"To the Senators and Privy Counselors of Journalism" [Senatoram i tainym sovetnikam zhurnalizma] (Herzen), 65n34
"To What Party Do We Belong?" (Katkov), 65n34
Trigos, Ludmilla, vii, xvi
Troubled Sea, The [Vzbalamuchennoe more] (Pisemskii, 1863), 69
Tsebrikova, Mariia Konstantinovna, 88–89
Tsertelev, D. N., 73n70
Tsetlin, Mikhail, xii
Turgenev, A. I., 25n21, 54, 59, 65–68
"Turgenev's Novel and its Critics" [Roman Turgeneva i ego kritiki] (Katkov), 65

Udensiva-Brenner, Masha, xiv
Ukraine, ix, 3
Ulanova, Galina, 255–58
Ulbandus Review, xii, xviii
"Uncanny, The" [Das Unheimlich] (Freud, 1919), 103, 109, 110, 120, 231; Nabokov's possible reading of, 108–9; repetition in two-part structure of, 118
Under the Sky of My Africa: Alexander Pushkin and Blackness (Nepomnyashchy, Svobodny, and Trigos, eds., 2006), vii, xvii–xviii

Vainer, Arkadii and Grigorii, 285, 286, 295
Verne, Jules, 112
Viazemskii, Petr Andreevich, 20n10, 57n8
Viel'gorskii, M. Iu., 20n10

Village of Stepanchikovo [Selo Stepanchikovo] (Dostoevskii, 1857), 71, 72n64
Villetard, Comte Joseph, 25
Vishnevskaia, Iuliia, 208
Vizbor, Iurii, 266
"Vladimir Nabokov and Sigmund Freud, or a Particular Problem" (De La Durantaye), 104
Voice from the Chorus, A [Golos iz khora] (Siniavskii), 214
Voinovich, Vladimir, 232n21
Voltaire, 38, 48
von Hagen, Mark, xvi
Vorontsova, Countess Elizaveta, 82
Vovochka (Russian/Soviet joke figure), 261, 263
Voznesenskii, Andrei, xiii
Vrangel, A. E., 72n64

War and Peace [Voina i mir] (film, 1966–1967), 266
War and Peace [Voina i mir] (Tolstoy, 1869), 68, 90, 144, 145
We (Zamiatin, 1921–1922), 96
Wells, Robert V., 28–29
West, the, 46, 128, 130; Austen–Pushkin comparison and, 79, 86, 94–95, 97; "decadent" civilization of, 181, 197, 198, 253; *Doctor Zhivago* scholarship in, 144; Russia and the Western gaze, 253–54; Russian and Soviet ballet in, 240, 247–50; Russia's sense of inferiority in relation to, 180; Solzhenitsyn's criticism of, 176, 203
Westernizers, 55, 57n8
"What Is an Author?" (Foucault), 102
What is Art [Chto takoe iskusstvo] (Tolstoy), 202
What is Socialist Realism (Siniavskii), 274
Wilson, Edmund, 90, 91
Wolfe, Nero (fictional character), 295
"woman question," 87, 88
"woman's roman noir" (*chernyi zhenskii roman*), 290
women: in ballet performance, 241–43; in British fiction, 77–78, 87–91; Russian detective fiction (*detektiv*) writers, 290–309
Workers' News, The (Rabochaia gazeta), 179
World War I, 106, 254

World War II, x, 93, 262, 265, 270–71

Yastremski, Slava, vii

Zacher, Christian K., 39
Zamiatin, Evgenii, 96
Znamia (journal), 205, 206

www.ingramcontent.com/pod-product-compliance
Lightning Source LLC
Chambersburg PA
CBHW071359300426
44114CB00016B/2120